W9-CHS-455

Hiking
Alabama

A Guide to Alabama's
Greatest Hiking Adventures

Second Edition

Joe Cuhaj

FALCON®

GUILFORD, CONNECTICUT
AN IMPRINT OF THE GLOBE PEQUOT PRESS

Photo credits: All photos are by the author.

ISSN 1545-6080
ISBN 0-7627-1102-7

Manufactured in the United States of America
Second Edition/First Printing

Contents

Central Alabama

Northern Alabama

Acknowledgments

The completion of this book is the culmination of a dream of mine, but it could not have happened without a supporting cast, and to them I am greatly appreciative. First and foremost, thanks goes to my wife, Maggie, for being a part-time hiking partner, knee-mender, and driver; for keeping me on track during this process; and for forgiving me for not mowing the lawn for weeks on end. Thanks also go out to my daughter Kellie for being a part-time photographer, hiking partner, proofreader, and, best of all, comic relief on the trail, especially during "The Great Flood."

A big thank-you is also in order for Pastor Tony LaGear, his family, and all of our friends at the Eastern Shore Christian Center for their thoughts, prayers, and words of encouragement.

Special thanks also go to the many clubs throughout the state that were kind enough to give guidance and suggestions, including the Alabama Trail Association; the Vulcan Trail Association; the Cahaba, Coastal, East Alabama, Mobile, and North Alabama chapters of the Sierra Club; and the dozens of cyber-buddies who made trail suggestions.

The research for this book could not have been completed without the help of a variety of people from around the state and the South, including Frank Lepore from the National Hurricane Center, Barry Gooden with the National Weather Service, and of course, all the staff and rangers at the state parks and national forests, too many to mention here, but thank you for your advice!

Finally, thanks to the members and friends of the "Mahwah Hiking Club," Gary, Tom, Jay, Mark, Kevin, Terri, Debbi, Debbie, and Steve, for being with me when the hiking bug first hit so many years ago.

How to Use This Book

This little guide contains just about everything you'll ever need to choose, plan for, enjoy, and survive a hike in Alabama. To assist in your hiking choices, Alabama has been divided into four regions: the Gulf Coast, Southeast Alabama, Central Alabama, and Northern Alabama.

To aid in quick decision making, we start each hike chapter with a short summary to give you a taste of the hiking adventure to follow. You'll learn about the trail terrain and what surprises the route has to offer. If your interest is piqued, read on; if it isn't, skip to the next hike.

The hike specifications that follow are fairly self-explanatory. Here you'll find the quick, nitty-gritty details of the hike: where the trailhead is located, the nearest town, hike distance, approximate hiking time, difficulty rating, type of trail terrain, what other trail users you may encounter, trail contacts (for updates on trail conditions), trail schedules and use fees, and available maps. **Finding the trailhead** provides dependable directions from a nearby city right down to where you'll want to park. **The Hike** is the meat of the chapter. Detailed and honest, it's the author's carefully researched impression of the trail. While it's impossible to cover everything, you can rest assured that we won't miss what's important. **Miles and Directions** provides mileage cues to identify turns and trail name changes, as well as points of interest. The **Hike Information** section at the end of each hike is a hodgepodge of information. Here we'll tell you where to stay, what to eat, and what else to see while you're hiking in the area.

The **Honorable Mentions** for each section detail hikes that didn't make the cut. In many cases it's not because they aren't great hikes, but they may be overcrowded or environmentally sensitive to heavy traffic. Be sure to read through these. A jewel might be lurking among them.

How to Use These Maps

We don't want anyone to feel restricted to just the routes and trails that are mapped here. We hope you will have an adventurous spirit and use this guide as a platform to explore Alabama and discover new routes for yourself. One of the simplest ways to do this is to just turn the map upside down and hike the trail in reverse. The change in perspective is fantastic, and the hike should feel quite different. It will be like getting two distinctly different hikes on each map.

You may wish to copy the directions for the trail onto a small sheet to help you while hiking. Or just slip the whole book in your pack and take it with you. Enjoy your time in the outdoors—and remember to pack out what you pack in.

Regional Location Map

This map (there is one presented in each Section Intro) helps you find your way to the start of each hike from the nearest sizeable town or city. Coupled with the detailed directions at the beginning of the cue, this map should visually lead you to where you need to be for each hike.

Elevation Profile

This gives you a cross-sectional look at the hike's ups and downs. Elevation is labeled on the left; mileage is indicated at the top. Road and trail names are shown along the route, with towns and points of interest labeled in boldface.

Route Map

This is your primary guide to each hike. It shows all the accessible roads and trails, points of interest, water, towns, landmarks, and geographical features. It also distinguishes trails from roads and paved roads from unpaved roads. The selected route is highlighted, and directional arrows point the way.

Map Legend

Symbol	Description	Symbol	Description	Symbol	Description
5	Interstate Highway	Airfield		Golf Course	
8	U.S. Highway	Airport		Hiking Trail	
3	State Road	Bike Trail		Mine	
CR 23	County Road	No Bikes		Overlook	
T 145	Township Road	Boat Launch		Picnic	
FS 45	Forest Road	Bridge		Parking	
	Paved Road	Bus Stop		Quarry	
	Paved Bike Lane	Campground		Radio Tower	
	Maintained Dirt Road	Campsite		Rock Climbing	
	Unmaintained Jeep Trail	Canoe Access		School	
	Singletrack Trail	Cattle Guard		Shelter	
	Highlighted Route	Cemetery		Spring	
	Ntl Forest/County Boundaries	Church		Swimming	
	State Boundaries	Covered Bridge		Train Station	
	Railroad Tracks	Direction Arrows		Wildlife Refuge	
	Power Lines	Downhill Skiing		Vineyard	
	Special Trail	Fire Tower		Most Difficult	
	Rivers or Streams	Forest HQ		Difficult	
	Water and Lakes	4WD Trail		Moderate	
	Marsh	Gate		Easy	

Introduction

I'll be honest; I'm a Jersey boy, born and raised. So what would possess me to move from the Yankees, egg creams, and traffic jams to the land of Bear Bryant and cheese grits? My wife, for one—a Mobile native and New Jersey transplant. After we married, we decided to try life along the Gulf Coast and headed to the "Heart of Dixie." And was I in for a surprise.

If all you know about an area is based on hearsay and casual history, chances are your understanding is warped, if not blackened. For example, many New Jerseyans see Alabama as being full of lazy hills and backward hillbillies. Conversely, people from Alabama think of New Jersey as a dumping ground for New York City.

A former governor once referred to Alabama as "The State of Surprises." As it turned out, this Northerner's opinion would change quickly.

The first surprise was the state's terrain. Alabama is divided into four distinct regions: the Highland Rim, the Piedmont Plateau, the Black Belt, and the Coastal Plain. To the extreme north is the Highland Rim. Thousands of years ago the entire region was covered with a shallow ocean. As the waters receded and the land began to rise, ancient shell banks and coral reefs dried out and died, forming the limestone bedrock that makes up the mountains of north and northwest Alabama. Over the years the action of the elements on the soft rock created huge crags, cliffs, and caves. Areas such as the Stone Cuts in Monte Sano State Park near Huntsville are the result and provide excellent caving and climbing opportunities. To the west, this same action combined with the flow of dozens of rivers has created the canyons of the Sipsey Wilderness, with spectacular waterfalls and again plenty of caves.

Just as the receding ocean created the Highland Rim, so, too, did it unveil the Piedmont Plateau. As the land thrust upward, forming the southernmost end of the Appalachian mountain chain, it created the highest peaks in the state. It's in this region that you'll find the state's highest point, Cheaha Mountain, which stands just over 2,100 feet above sea level. You'll also encounter the largest canyon east of the Mississippi, Little River Canyon, carved by the Little River, the longest mountain-top river in the country.

The fertile Black Belt, the land from Montgomery to just above the coast, has gently rolling hills and notoriously rich soil, which makes this region prime agricultural territory. Here rivers flow and create sanctuary for birds and wildlife, like at Eufaula National Wildlife Refuge along the Chattahoochee River.

Finally, there is the Coastal Plain. This region has some of the most pristine white beaches to be found along the Gulf of Mexico, in addition to the second largest delta in the country. The Tensaw River Delta encompasses one of the largest protected areas for wildlife in the state, with a multitude of endangered species calling the area home. Such locations as Bon Secour National Wildlife Refuge and the Weeks Bay National Estuarine Research Reserve allow us to visit this wildlife firsthand.

Another surprise is the amount of history that can be found in Alabama. Native American history can be traced back to 7,000 B.C. at Russell Cave National Monument in northeast Alabama. Europeans came to the region in the 1500s—first the Spanish, then the French, and then the British. The United States finally took control in the early 1800s, following such bloody engagements as the Battle of Horseshoe Bend, where General Andrew Jackson took down the last of the Creek Indian defenses.

Time and time again, the Civil War pops up in our travels. The last major battle of the war was fought near Mobile in what is today Blakeley Historic State Park. Tannehill State Historic Park is the site of a major foundry, rebuilt to its original operating condition, where munitions for the Confederacy were forged. The first capital of the Confederacy was Montgomery. And don't think that all of Alabama was behind the succession of the South. Winston County, where the Sipsey Wilderness is located, actually declared itself a free county and aligned itself with the Union.

History continues to be made in the state. As humans reach for the stars, the city of Huntsville is home to NASA's Marshall Space Flight Center, where the *Saturn V* moon rocket was designed and built and the modules for international space station *Freedom* are being constructed.

The biggest and best surprise about Alabama is the people. The state may be known as the "Heart of Dixie," but it is also the heart of Southern hospitality. The people make this state as great as it is.

Every time I travel and hike the state, I can truthfully say that I uncover more and more surprises. New adventures and beautiful scenery are always just a hill or turn away. Hopefully the trails and experiences described in this guide will help you appreciate all that Alabama has to offer and help you discover your own surprises.

Alabama Flora and Fauna

More than two-thirds of Alabama is covered in forest. On the whole these forests are largely Southern yellow, red, white, loblolly, and slash pine forests, though red cedar is also prevalent. Of the deciduous trees, you'll likely encounter hickory, sweet gum, and several varieties of oaks including live oaks. Favorite aromatic and blooming trees in the state include the magnolia and dogwood.

Alabama is blessed with a wide variety of wildflowers along its trails and roadways. Some of the more interesting varieties include bollworms, also known as merry bells. These flowers are part of the lily family and bloom from April to June throughout the state. The plant has very thin and delicate stems topped with hay-yellow bells.

Along the marshes and streams, the cardinal flower blooms into bright scarlet in late summer. In early March the vines of the Carolina jessamine will be found clinging to fences and trees. These vines with yellow flowers can be found throughout the state.

Another common wildflower is the yellow orchid, which blooms in late summer through early fall and can be found along just about any trail. From late July through September the yellow fringed orchid can be found in roadside ditches, bogs, woods, and fields.

Rhododendron and a variety of azaleas line most of the trails through the state, adding bright colors and fragrances to the hikes in springtime.

Alabama has a varied wildlife population. Although the hiker is more apt to find white-tail deer and gray squirrels along the trail, the state hosts many other species of animals. Black bears roam from one end of the state to the other, with the largest concentration found in the Tensaw River Delta of the Gulf Coast. Bobcat (or lynx) are also quite common throughout the state but are rarely seen.

From north to south, wild turkey scurry along the trails of the state. The turkey population was once on a dangerous decline but made an astounding recovery in the middle of the twentieth century. (Farmers used the Eastern wild turkey to develop all current domestic varieties of turkeys.) Armadillos can frequently be seen foraging through the leaves along trails. Although cute, their bite is nasty. I'll confess: ten armadillos chased me down the Skyway Loop Trail in the Talladega National Forest, so don't doubt their ability to get angry.

The American alligator, one of only two species of alligator in the world, can be found in the Southeast and Gulf Coast regions. Alligators feed on fish, frogs, snakes, turtles, birds, and small mammals. Luckily they tend to be wary of humans, but feeding or harassing them in any manner changes the rules. The alligator was declared an endangered species in 1967 due to overhunting, but the species has made a strong comeback and some states have reinstated alligator hunting (Alabama is not one of them).

Several species that are currently considered endangered have found sanctuary within the state, including the beach mouse, the loggerhead seaturtle, and the brown pelican. The American bald eagle has also found a new refuge in Alabama.

Alabama Weather

The range of weather in Alabama is striking—from its subtropical climate in the south to the cold and snowy winters of the north. In general, the weather for hiking Alabama is near perfect. Even in the northern part of the state in the higher elevations, winters are generally short-lived with frequent springlike days scattered throughout January and February.

In the north, average temperatures range from 46 degrees Fahrenheit in January to 80 degrees Fahrenheit in July. Colder temperatures are more frequent in the north, and, yes, significant accumulations of snow can occur, though rarely.

In the southern portion of the state, average temperatures range from 52 degrees in January to 85 degrees in July. Cold snaps of below 30 degrees, even below zero, do occur, but seldom, and they only last a day or two.

Though the weather in Alabama is generally ideal for hiking, there are exceptions. The mix of heat and 100 percent humidity in June through August, can make a deadly combination, with heat indexes that frequently soar well into the hundreds. On these days, outdoor activity of any kind is discouraged by weather services and state officials.

Also during the summer, extremely heavy and severe late-afternoon thunderstorms can pop up without warning. Although they are widely scattered and short in duration, the large amount of rain and dangerous lightning can make outdoor travel a challenge.

Finally, May through November is hurricane season in Alabama. Though a hurricane will only hit a relatively small area with its full fury, the surrounding areas some hundreds of miles from the storm can still feel its effects. In fact, most injuries and deaths resulting from hurricanes come from flash flooding in areas that are not even in the storm's center.

When hiking during hurricane season, especially in September when most of the storms in the Atlantic Ocean make their way into the Gulf of Mexico, check the weather and be alert for any tropical disturbances before heading out. If there are any storms reported, keep tabs on their progress to determine if hiking is a good idea at that time. There is typically plenty of advance warning to react to a storm, so don't let hurricane season discourage you from coming to Alabama to hike!

Alabama Wilderness Restrictions/Regulations

Alabama has twenty-six state parks, five national forests, and a national monument and preserve. With the exception of high-altitude mountain climbing, these protected lands offer every type of hiking experience imaginable, from a short walk with endangered species through preserves to true wilderness hiking. As is the case across the country, the number of people hitting the trail is ever increasing. Fortunately, the state and federal agencies tasked with managing these facilities do an excellent job of maintaining the balance between use and preservation.

Alabama's state parks provide an ideal setting for families looking to get away to the great outdoors, or for those seeking a bit more of an adventure. Generally speaking, camping is not allowed on state park trails. Trailside camping is allowed in some parks and is noted in the trail descriptions in this book. All state parks have primitive camping areas for tents, which usually only run $8.00 a night (this includes those with trailside camping). Most also have what is called "improved campsites" that have their own water spigot and electrical outlets. These usually run $14 a night.

Reservations are not required for primitive campsites at the state parks. Reservations are recommended for improved sites and are accepted up to twelve months in advance. A maximum of eight people are allowed per site. Additional regulations may apply, so be sure to check at the ranger station of each park.

Within the state's national forests, camping is permitted along the trails at no cost. The rangers ask only that you follow the policy of dispersal camping in which campsites are spread far apart and at least 100 feet from the trail. In some areas, others have set up campsites close to the trail. If this is the case, rangers suggest using these sites to minimize any further impact of camping on the location. Some of the national forests have recreational areas set up for camping. Again, these have both primitive and improved campsites ranging in price from $6.00 a day to $17.00 a day, respectively.

Most of the trailheads described in this book at the national forests do not charge for parking. There are some, noted within the trail descriptions, that charge a day-use fee of $3.00.

Since you'll almost always be within a stone's throw of a lake, river, or ocean, you may want to try your hand at fishing. A combination fresh- and saltwater fishing license is available for only $24.50 and is valid for a full year. Dogs are usually welcomed at the state parks, but a leash is required unless otherwise noted. Also keep in mind that hunting is allowed in national forests. Contact the national forest or district forest ranger about the dates for hunting season, which can restrict camping locations and hiking trails. Permits are not required for hiking the national forests; however, they do ask that you register at the trailheads in case of an emergency.

Now that all the loose ends are tied up, it's time to get outside and hit the trails of Alabama!

Getting around Alabama

Area Codes: The area code **256** covers Huntsville and northern Alabama. For Birmingham and central Alabama the area code is **205.** The area code for Mobile and the Gulf Coast is **251.**

Roads: For road conditions, contact the Alabama Department of Transportation. Call **(251) 242–4128** or visit www.dot.state.al.us for current road closings and openings, traffic updates, and road construction plans and timetables.

By Air: Birmingham Airport (BHM) is Alabama's main point of entry www.bhamintlairport.com. Your travel agent can best advise you on the least expensive and/or most direct way to connect from wherever you're departing.

Mobile Regional Airport (MOB) serves greater Mobile and the Gulf Coast (www.mobairport.com). Shared-ride vans and taxis serve Mobile and the surrounding areas.

To book reservations on-line, visit your favorite airline's Web site or search one of the following travel sites for the best price: www.cheaptickets.com, www.expedia.com, www.previewtravel.com, www.priceline.com, travel.yahoo.com, www.travelocity.com, www.trip.co—just to name a few.

By Bus: Greyhound serves all major towns and cities in Alabama. Greyhound also carries connecting Amtrak passengers to off-line cities (see below). Schedules and fares are available on-line at www.greyhound.com or by phone at (800) 231-2222.

By Train: Amtrak has two routes that serve Alabama. The Crescent train runs daily to Anniston, Birmingham, and Tuscaloosa from Atlanta, New Orleans, and New York. A bus transfer in Atlanta connects the Crescent to Mobile and Montgomery. The Sunset Limited train serves Atmore and Mobile three times a week from Orlando, New Orleans, and Los Angeles. On days when the Sunset Limited does not run, Amtrak offers bus service to the New Orleans Amtrak station to connect with the City of New Orleans train to Memphis and Chicago. Amtrak information and reservations are available on-line at www.amtrak.com or by phone at (800) 872-7245.

Visitor Information: For visitor information or a travel brochure, call the Alabama Office of Tourism at **(800) 252-2262 (ALABAMA)** or visit their Web site at www.touralabama.org\index_fl.htm.

Gulf Coast

The Gulf Coast region of Alabama supports not only a wide variety of endangered wildlife but also countless perches from which to view them. The traveling by foot in this region is rarely strenuous. Elevations range from sea level to around 100 feet. It's in this region that the Mobile and Tensaw Rivers converge to form the Tensaw River Delta, and ultimately empty into the Gulf of Mexico. The Tensaw River Delta has the distinction of being the second largest river delta in the country—second only to the Mississippi Delta. The American alligator calls this area home, as do the largest population of black bear in the state and the once-endangered brown pelican.

This region is also home to the white sand beaches of Gulf Shores and Orange Beach. The Pine Beach Trail in Bon Secour National Wildlife Refuge takes hikers directly to the beach. The refuge protects such endangered species as the beach mouse and the loggerhead sea turtle.

History abounds in the region, as well, with the centerpiece being the city of Mobile, the state's second largest city. Mobile is known as the "Mother of Mystics" and is recognized as the birthplace of Mardi Gras in the United States. Hiking along the USS Alabama Historic Trail is a good way to soak in the 300-year history of the city.

The Battle of Mobile Bay was fought here during the Civil War. It was in this battle that Union Admiral David Farragut uttered the immortal words, "Damn the torpedoes, full speed ahead!" Just across the Mobile River in Spanish Fort is Blakeley Historic State Park, site of the Battle of Blakeley, the last major battle of the Civil War.

The weather in the region is subtropical. Late summer heat is accentuated with high humidity that often hits 100 percent, making outdoor activity a bit uncomfortable and sometimes not recommended. The warm air and its location on the Gulf of Mexico mean that sudden and very heavy rainfall can be expected without warning. The storms are short, but the rain is plentiful. In fact, Mobile has held the National Weather Service title of "wettest city in America" a number of times.

Perhaps the worst weather system you'll see in summer is a hurricane. Mobile and Baldwin Counties have been hit by several large and devastating hurricanes in the past, but an eye on the weather forecast will keep you safe. Hurricane season "generally" runs between May and November.

Gulf Coast

Fall and winter along the Gulf Coast are wonderful, to say the least. Most of the time, moderate temperatures, averaging in the low to mid-70s, last well into fall. During this time, the humidity is quite low, making hiking a real pleasure. Temperatures in January average around 52 degrees. Now don't get me wrong; it does get cold in Dixie. Temperatures have dropped to below zero on occasion, but those days are few and usually short lived.

1 Pine Beach Trail

This is one of those surprising trails—a simple walk down a forested nature trail that unfolds to reveal the sand dunes and pristine white beaches of the Gulf of Mexico. As the trail meanders to the sea, you're treated to a close look at the marshes of southern Alabama, where American alligators may be found.

Start: From the southeast end of the Pine Beach parking area at Bon Secour National Wildlife Refuge.

Distance: 4.0 miles out-and-back.

Approximate hiking time: 1½ hours.

Difficulty: Easy, along flat roadways.

Trail surface: Dirt and sand service road; fine beach sand.

Type of hike: Forest of slash pine, dotted with sawgrass and live oak; sea oats and scrub pines along the dunes; marshes and beaches.

Land status: National wildlife refuge.

Nearest town: Gulf Shores.

Schedule: Trails are open year round 7:00 A.M.–sunset. Refuge headquarter hours are Monday through Friday, 7:00 A.M.–4:00 P.M.

Fees/Permits: No fees charged. No camping is allowed.

Maps: USGS maps: Bon Secour Bay Pine Beach Trail Map, Bird List, and Refuge Pamphlet—available at the Bon Secour Wildlife Refuge headquarters.

Trail contacts: Bon Secour National Wildlife Refuge, 12295 AL 180, Gulf Shores, 36542; (251) 540-7720; bonsecour.fws.gov/index_files/slide0001.htm.

Other trail users: Service vehicles on service-road portion of trail.

Canine compatibility: Not dog friendly due to wildlife and the fragile nature of the preserve; if you do take a dog, leash required.

Finding the trailhead: From Mobile take Interstate 10 west to Alabama Highway 59 (Exit 44). Head south on AL 59 toward Gulf Shores. Travel 0.5 mile past the Intracoastal Waterway to the intersection with Alabama Highway 180. Follow AL 180 west 9 miles to the refuge headquarters on the right. To get to the trailhead, continue past the refuge headquarters another mile. The parking area is on the left side of the highway and marked with a large wooden sign that reads PINE BEACH TRAIL. The trailhead is at the southeast end of the parking lot. *DeLorme: Alabama Atlas & Gazetteer:* Page 65, F1.

The Hike

Along a stretch of highway at the extreme southern tip of Alabama, a peninsula stretches westward along the Gulf of Mexico to form the mouth of the Mobile Bay delta. On this spit of land, between outcroppings of beachside condominiums, lies Bon Secour National Wildlife Refuge.

The refuge encompasses more than 6,500 acres of fragile landscape and is home to more than 500 species of animals and birds, providing hikers with endless photo ops. The key to viewing this wide variety of animal life is to take the time to sit quietly on one of the many benches situated just off the trail. Patience will be rewarded every time.

End of the trail at the Gulf of Mexico.

The Pine Beach Trail is the longest in the refuge. Early in the hike, the trail crosses a marshy area as it works its way between Little Lagoon and Gator Lake. This is the best vantage point for viewing alligators. Many visitors leave disappointed because they didn't see an alligator—but they are there. Most of the time, they lie just below the surface of the water, looking like submerged logs. Stay quiet and be patient and you'll see them. Alligators are naturally wary of humans; do not feed them or approach them in any way.

Saltwater fishing is allowed along the banks of Little Lagoon; a saltwater fishing license is required. Across the trail from Little Lagoon is Gator Lake—a forty-acre freshwater lake known for its largemouth bass and catfish. It's open for fishing year-round, with a freshwater fishing license required.

Among the rare animals in the refuge is the Alabama beach mouse. Although you'll probably never see one, you can tell they're here from the numerous burrows and mouse trails near the beaches. Avoid disturbing the burrows.

Another unusual animal that visits the refuge is the loggerhead sea turtle. The loggerhead species has remained virtually the same for more than 200 million years. The loggerhead population has declined due to habitat loss along the coastlines. At Bon

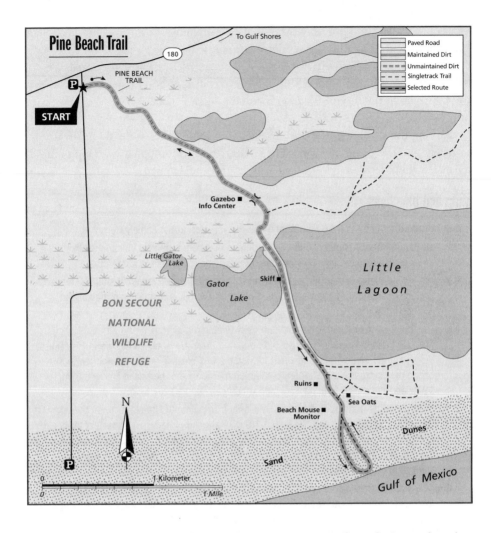

Secour, loggerheads have a safe nesting area. From May through September they make their way to the dunes at night, lay their eggs, and then crawl back into the sea.

Wildlife is not the only striking feature of the trail. The flora in the refuge is just as fascinating. Blueberries and huckleberries grow along the trail, though berry picking isn't allowed in order to preserve the feeding plots for the wildlife. Among other plant life is the hairy wicky (no kidding)—a plant similar to mountain laurel, with white blooms in summer.

Marshy areas support floating bladderworts—aquatic plants with yellow flowers. Trees include live oaks, myrtles, dwarf sand oaks, and several varieties of pine. Along the beach, the tall, golden grasses known as sea oats wave in the sea breeze—but again, no picking!

The trail culminates in a breathtaking view and walk along white beaches on the Gulf of Mexico. You can fish in the surf here (as long as you have a saltwater license).

Swift currents and an undertow mean that swimming is not allowed, but Gulf State Park offers swimming only a few highway miles away.

If you decide to bushwhack off the designated trails, it's best to wear boots for thicker brush areas and waders through the marshes. A good pair of sneakers will work fine along the service road, with either sandals or bare feet on the sandy parts of the trail.

Among the wildlife you'll wish to avoid are mosquitoes and sand gnats. Rather than rely on luck, bring bug spray. The swampy marsh, combined with high humidity, makes this a fertile environment for these formidable pests.

Miles and Directions

0.0   Start from the end of the Pine Beach Trail parking area at the cable gateway.

0.2   As the trail heads southeast, the first of fifteen numbered markers indicate the flora of the area. Be sure to pick up a brochure at refuge headquarters to follow along.

0.3   Here you encounter the toughest gradient—a gradual downhill jaunt of about 10 feet as the trail heads toward sea level. At the bottom of this hill is a small sign marking an abandoned route.

0.4   The trail begins to curve to a more southerly direction and comes to a gazebo. Notices and additional information are posted here, and there are benches to sit and view the marsh and its inhabitants. A few feet further, the trail crosses a 10-foot wooden footbridge over a small canal that feeds the marsh. Evidence of hurricane Frederic from 1979 and the debris from its 150-mph winds can still be seen here.

0.5   The trail heads due south. A brown directional sign points to Little Lagoon on the left, Gator Lake to the right, and the beach 1.0 mile straight ahead. Just a few feet farther and there are excellent views of Little Lagoon. The condominiums of Gulf Shores are in the distance. The trail travels the banks of Little Lagoon. You'll likely see mussels and clams and small schools of fish.

0.6   A sign marks the beginning of the Gator Lake Trail to the right. This 0.8-mile trail is used to portage boats to the lake for fishing. There is also a small skiff here that the refuge allows visitors to use to float around the forty-acre lake. At this point, the trail becomes progressively more sandy, all the way to the Gulf.

1.0   Reach a Y intersection and continue on to the right. A BEACH sign points you in the right direction.

MULLET OVER
The Flora-Bama Lounge in Perdido Key, Florida, on the Gulf of Mexico directly on the Florida-Alabama border, is renowned not only for its annual National Songwriter Festival but also for its mullet. And not just for eating. Each winter, this bar and restaurant hosts the National Mullet Tossing Championships. Participants toss mullet (dead, of course) as far as they can across the border for cash and prizes.

Each year, people flock to the Flora-Bama to compete in the contest. For the past several years, South Alabama native and former NFL quarterback Kenny Stabler has tossed out the first mullet to get the event under way. The event became so popular that at Mobile Mysticks hockey games, instead of throwing octopus like they do in Detroit when a goal is scored, fans began throwing mullet—a practice that has since been banned by the East Coast Hockey League.

1.3 The trail now passes by the ruins of a beach house that was destroyed by Hurricane Frederic. Notice the Alabama beach mouse holes along the sides of the trail in the sand. Also, the Gulf's sea oats begin to line the trail. The waters of the Gulf of Mexico can be seen straight ahead.

1.5 The trail crests a sand dune, and you can see a beautiful panoramic of the Gulf as well as the skyline of Gulf Shores. Continue another 0.5 mile along the dunes and take in the sea breeze and views. In the summer months you can see the tracks of nesting loggerhead sea turtles.

2.0 Turn around and retrace your route back to the trailhead.

4.0 Arrive back at the trailhead.

Hike Information

Local Information
Alabama Gulf Coast Convention and Visitors Bureau, 3150 Gulf Shores Parkway, Gulf Shores 36542; (800) 745-7263; www.gulfshores.com.

Local Events/Attractions
National Shrimp Festival, first weekend of October, 3150 Gulf Shores Parkway, Gulf Shores 36542; (251) 968-6904; www.nationalshrimpfestival.com. This is the biggest shrimp festival in the country, featuring live bands, arts and crafts, and plenty of delicious Gulf shrimp.
Gulf State Park, 20115 AL 135, Gulf Shores 36542; (251) 948-4853 or (800) 544-4853; www.dcnr.state.al.us. (Refer to the Gulf Coast Honorable Mention section for a description.)

Lodging
Acadian Inn, 4633 Wilson Boulevard, Orange Beach 36561; (251) 981-6710.
Romar House Bed and Breakfast, 23500 Perdido Beach Boulevard, Orange Beach 36561; (800) 487-6627; www.bbonline.com/al/romarhouse.

Restaurants
Original Oyster House, 701 Gulf Shore Parkway, Gulf Shores 36542; (251) 948-2445.
Sea-N-Suds, East Beach Boulevard, Gulf Shores 36542; Gulf Shores; (251) 948-7894.

Organizations
Mobile Sierra Club, Mobile 36601; alabama.sierraclub.org/coastal.html.

2 Weeks Bay Nature Trail

This trail provides a short and very easy walk at the Weeks Bay Estuary. The estuary, home to a wide variety of birds and other plant and animal life, offers an interesting, enjoyable experience for all members of the family.

Start: From the Weeks Bay Estuary office.
Distance: 1.3 miles out and back.
Approximate hiking time: 1 hour.
Difficulty: Easy, over level paths.
Trail surface: Dirt path and boardwalks.
Type of hike: Magnolias and cypress trees.
Land status: National estuarine research reserve.
Nearest town: Fairhope.
Schedule: Open 9:00 A.M.–5:00 P.M. Monday through Saturday, 1:00 P.M. Sunday; closed state and federal holidays.
Fees/Permits: No fees charged.
Maps: USGS maps: Magnolia Springs. Brochures are available at the estuary office.
Trail contacts: Weeks Bay National Estuary, P.O. Box 731, Fairhope 36533; (251) 928-9792; inlet.geol.sc.edu/WKB/index.html.
Other trail users: None.
Canine compatibility: Dog friendly; leash required.

Finding the trailhead: From Fairhope take U.S. Highway 98 south 10 miles. Come to a stop sign and turn left (Alabama Highway 42 and US 98 now head to the east). Travel 5 miles. The estuary is clearly marked on the right. If you cross the Weeks Bay Bridge, you've over shot the turn. *DeLorme: Alabama Atlas & Gazetteer:* Page 63 G6.

The Hike

This is not a high-tech, high-altitude, three-day backpacking trip. This short and simple nature path is included here for the purposes of spotlighting an endangered habitat and providing the perfect hike for couples looking to take the kids—and who knows, the children just might learn something in the process.

Weeks Bay National Estuarine Research Reserve is one of twenty-six estuaries administered by the National Oceanic and Atmospheric Administration. An estuary, by definition, is a semienclosed body of water where fresh water from rivers mixes with salt water from the ocean. Because of this merger of diversity, estuaries generally support a wide variety of plant and animal life.

The Weeks Bay reserve, established in 1986, protects land that was once at high risk of development—Baldwin County, in which the reserve is situated, is the fastest growing county in the state of Alabama. The reserve maintains for posterity 3,000 acres along Weeks and Mobile Bays and is fed by the Magnolia and Fish Rivers.

The reserve's nature trail utilizes a combination of vegetation-friendly boardwalks and dirt paths to lead you through the forested swamps, along the banks of salt- and freshwater marshes, and through the tidal flats. Signs along the boardwalks identify animals and plants (the same information is also provided in a brochure available

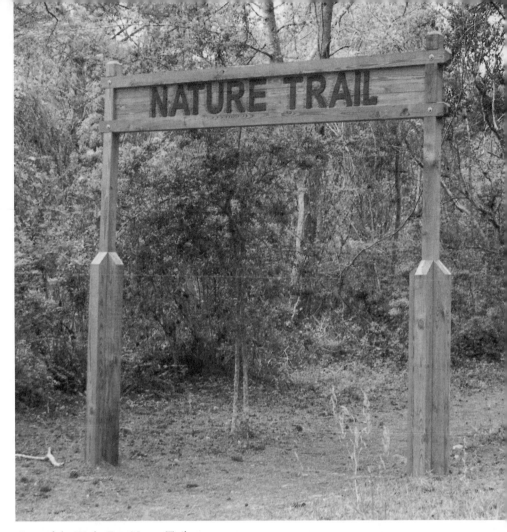

Start of the Weeks Bay Nature Trail.

at the reserve office). Among the animals that live here are blue crabs, red-bellied turtles, and American alligators. More than 350 species of birds are found at Weeks Bay, either permanently or during migration periods. Among them are the black needlerush, the great blue heron, and the once-endangered brown pelican.

The first place to visit is the estuary office, where you'll find displays that describe the estuary and its plants and animals. At the back of the office building, where the trail begins, is a mini-zoo with fish, blue crabs, and an alligator.

While you're in the neighborhood, be sure to head down to the Weeks Bay Pitcher Plant Bog. (Take U.S. Highway 98 over the nearby Weeks Bay Bridge and turn left onto County Road 17.) The curious pitcher plant is worth the visit. This wily carnivore feasts on insects and other tiny creatures—so watch the ankles (just kidding). The Wintermeyer Nature Trail guides visitors easily through the bog—which, contrary to what you might think, is a relatively dry environment.

Another boardwalk takes hikers to the banks of Weeks Bay.

Miles and Directions

0.0   Start from the rear of the estuary office and head south onto the boardwalk. The path turns to the southeast in about 200 feet.

0.1   The boardwalk comes to a Y intersection. Take the right fork and continue to the south.

0.2   Come to the banks of the bay. There are binoculars here for you to use. Turn right and head to the east. The path winds to the northwest and in 300 feet, returns to the previous Y intersection. Turn left and head north back toward the office.

0.3   When you arrive back at the office, follow a sidewalk around to the right side of the building—between the office and conference building—and arrive at the front parking lot. Turn left and head west. In 200 feet, come to a large wooden sign that reads NATURE TRAIL. Take the dirt path into the woods.

0.4   Head to the southwest over this flat, wide path. Downed trees surround the area, but the path is well cleared. In 200 feet, come to a wooden footbridge over a small creek. Cross the bridge to the west. In 100 feet, cross another footbridge to the southwest. Along this section, diamond WB markers lead the way.

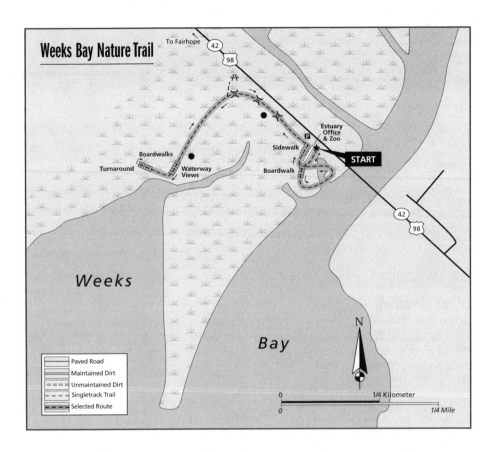

0.5 Cross another bridge to the west. **Option:** To the right, a short side trail leads to a picnic area near US 98. Make a left turn and head southwest. The trail narrows somewhat but is still level and dirt.

0.8 The trail comes to a boardwalk that leads to the banks of the bay with great views of the waterway. Turn right and in 50 feet come off the footbridge and travel on a dirt path to the northwest until you reach another boardwalk that offers another perspective of the bay. Turn around here and follow the trail and boardwalk back to the parking lot.

1.3 Arrive back at the trailhead.

THE JUBILEE CITY

It's a phenomenon that occurs only once or twice a year between June and September, if at all, and only occurs in a few rare places on earth. It's a time after the sun sets when the breeze is still, the water of Mobile Bay is calm, and the residents of the Eastern Shore of Mobile Bay in the city of Daphne wait for the call.

What happens is hundreds of thousands of fish, crabs, and other marine life swim right up to the shores of the bay and end up on the sandy beaches. The cry goes out around town, "JUBILEE!"—that's what this phenomenon is known as. Residents pick up buckets full of fresh seafood for their tables. But just as quickly as it starts, the Jubilee is over.

No one is exactly sure what causes the Jubilee, but it's believed that a seasonal drop in the water's oxygen level draws both prey and predator to the surface looking for food and air.

Hike Information

Local Information

Eastern Shore Chamber of Commerce, 29750 Larry Cawyer Drive, Daphne 36526; (251) 928-6387; www.siteone.com/towns/chamber. **City of Fairhope,** P.O. Box 429, Fairhope 36533; (251) 928-2136; www.cofairhope.com.

Local Events/Attractions

Fairhope Arts and Crafts Festival, Second weekend of March, P.O. Drawer 429, Fairhope 36533; (251) 621-8222. One of the largest such events on the Gulf Coast with lots of music, food, and of course, arts and crafts. **Fairhope Municipal Pier,** P.O. Drawer 429, Fairhope 36533; (251) 928-2136. This 1-quarter-mile-long pier juts into beautiful Mobile Bay. The pier is open for fishing and walks twenty-four hours. The beach next to the pier for swimming is open 9:00 A.M.–5:00 P.M. The city hosts an impressive Fourth of July fireworks show over the bay, with music provided by the Eastern Shore Symphony.

Lodging

The Parker House, 413 North Section Street, Fairhope 36532-2634; (251) 928-8472.

Restaurants

The Yardarm, 1 Fairhope Avenue, Fairhope 36532; (251) 928-0711. Fresh Gulf seafood is the fare at this restaurant located smack dab in the middle of the Fairhope Municipal Pier.

Hike Tours

Weeks Bay National Estuary, P.O. Box 731, Fairhope 36533; (251) 928-9792. Contact the estuary office to set up times for a guided tour of the research facility and the estuary.

Organizations

Weeks Bay Watershed Project, 710 South Mobile Street, Fairhope 36532; (251) 928-9792. **Weeks Bay Reserve Foundation,** 710 South Mobile Street, Fairhope 36532-1102; (251) 990-5004.

Other Resources

Alabama Department of Environmental Management, 1400 Coliseum Boulevard, Montgomery 36101; (334) 271-7710; www.dcnr.state.al.us.

3 USS Alabama Historical Trail

The city of Mobile is justly proud of its history and heritage, from the early Native Americans to the Europeans' first exploration of the region in 1528, through the Civil War, and into the city's present-day rejuvenation. This trail allows you to experience this history firsthand as you stroll by antebellum homes, historical museums, and old cemeteries. The route passes under towering live oaks draped in Spanish moss, making an archway above the road. Azaleas, blooming fiery red each spring, line the streets.

Start: From the Fort Conde Museum.
Distance: 6.5-mile loop.
Approximate hiking time: 3 to 4 hours.
Difficulty: Easy, on sidewalks.
Trail surface: Concrete sidewalks and paved road.
Type of hike: Historical sites and museums; ancient oak trees.
Land status: City streets.
Nearest town: Mobile.
Schedule: Open year-round. One of the best times to take in the trail is the two weeks prior to Ash Wednesday (Mardi Gras).
Fees/Permits: No fee is charged for hiking the trail or visiting the city museums.

Maps: USGS maps: Mobile.
USS Alabama Historical Trail Map and assorted city brochures—available at Fort Conde Welcome Center and Museum, Mobile.
Trail contacts: Fort Conde Visitor Center, 164 Saint Emanuel Street, Mobile 36601; (251) 209-1822. Open seven days a week 8:00 A.M.–5:00 P.M., closed Christmas and Mardi Gras Day (Fat Tuesday).
Other trail users: Cyclists and pedestrians.
Canine compatibility: Dog friendly; leash required. Bring water; dogs not permitted in homes or museums.

Finding the trailhead: From Interstate 65 in Mobile, take U.S. Highway 90 east 15 miles to downtown Mobile. Turn right onto South Royal Street at the Bankhead Tunnel. Travel down the brick roadway 0.3 mile. Fort Conde, the starting location, is on the right with parking on the left. *DeLorme: Alabama Atlas & Gazetteer:* Page 62, D4.

The Hike

It's time to get off the beaten path and hit the pavement with this city excursion created by the Boy Scouts as a badge and medal hike. The path travels the streets of Mobile, passing through centuries of history.

This history begins with the Maubilian, Choctaw, and Alibamu Indians who occupied this region for centuries. The first Europeans to visit and eventually settle the area were the Spanish in 1528, followed by the French in 1699, then the British in 1763. The United States seized control in 1812.

Many of the events in Mobile history may amaze the average person. For example, forget what New Orleans says about Mardi Gras. That city's Mardi Gras may be bigger, but Mobile is the birthplace of this carnival celebration in the United States—beginning in 1830.

Mobile Bay was the site of the naval battle in which Union Admiral David Farragut uttered the famous words, "Damn the torpedoes! Full speed ahead!" It was also here that William A. Alexander built the world's first successful submarine, the *Hunley*. It was eventually used to sink a Federal ship off the coast of South Carolina. Currently, author Clive Cussler is preparing to search Mobile Bay for the precursor to the *Hunley*, the *Pioneer,* which sank during trials with no one onboard.

This trail through time—named for the USS *Alabama* battleship, which is on display nearby—begins at the Fort Conde Welcome Center and Museum. This recreation of the 1711 fort built by the French is only a third the size of the original but is located on the exact site of the old fort. A tour of the museum's pictures and artifacts offers a taste of what's in store on the walk. While at the fort, be sure to catch the musket firings by people dressed in early French marine uniforms and the cannon firings from the ramparts.

From the fort, the trail swings past the original 1865 city hall, which is seeing renewed life as the new city museum. Next door are the J. L. Bedsole IMAX Theater and the Gulf Coast Exploreum. The Exploreum features hands-on science activities, especially attractive to children. Just past the IMAX Theater is a statue honoring Admiral Raphael Semmes, commander of the *Alabama* during the Civil War.

The trail travels down to the Mobile River, which made Mobile a thriving seaport second only to New Orleans. At the riverfront you'll see the modern spire of the Mobile Convention Center, and coming soon is the Gulf Coast Maritime Museum.

Looping back around to the southwest, the trail passes a series of historic buildings, including the Catholic Basilica of the Immaculate Conception (built in 1835) and the Berstein House (built in 1872), which until 2000 housed the city museum. The trail passes Magnolia National Cemetery, named a national cemetery in 1866, which holds the remains of soldiers from the War of 1812 and the Civil War.

You can also visit Church Street Cemetery, established in 1819 for victims of a yellow fever epidemic. Since then, many area notables have been laid to rest here, including Joe Cain, the man who brought Mardi Gras back to the South after the Civil War.

A word of caution about the weather: Bring a raincoat or umbrella if you visit in summer. Heavy afternoon downpours are not uncommon.

Miles and Directions

0.0   Start from the Fort Conde Welcome Center and Museum. Be sure to pick up the trail pamphlet and spend a few minutes browsing the exhibits. Head north on South Royal Street.

More than 1,100 Civil War soldiers rest in Magnolia National Cemetery.

0.1 Pass the former city hall. This building was built in 1856 as a city fish market and later became the city hall/marketplace. In 1999 the city government moved to their new building and renovation is now under way to make this building the new home of the city museum. Next to the city hall is the Gulf Coast Exploreum and the J. L. Bedsole IMAX Theater. Both are fantastic stops if you are traveling with children. Just past the theater is a statue honoring Admiral Raphael Semmes, the commander of the Civil War warship *Alabama.* Turn right onto Government Street (US 90 east).

0.5 The trail heads to the waterfront. It was here that Mobile became a booming port city. Paddleboats and steamers would move cotton to ports all over North America. Today the waterfront is being revitalized. The Cooper Riverside Park allows visitors to sit and take in the ships moving in and out of the harbor. The modern spire of the Mobile Convention Center is here, as well as the *Cotton Blossom,* an authentic Southern riverboat. The trail loops here and then heads southwest back down Government Street.

0.7 The trail passes a marker indicating the boundary of the city limits back in 1711—the year Fort Conde was constructed—and then turns right onto South Joaquim Street. Travel 1 block and then turn left onto Conti Street.

0.9 To the right at the intersection with Claiborne Street sits the Catholic Basilica of the Immaculate Conception. This cathedral was built in 1835 and features beautiful ornate statues and stained glass. Every statue has a story, and the staff is more than happy to tell the tales. The trail now turns left down Franklin Street.

USS Alabama Historical Trail

Mobile River

START

Mobile

Magnolia Cemetery

Woodmen of the World

LEGEND

1. Imax Theater and
   Gulf Coast Exploreum
2. Cooper Riverside Park
3. Catholic Basilica of the
   Immaculate Conception
4. Spanish Plaza
5. Barton Academy
6. Washington Square
7. Twelve Oaks Mansion
8. Oakleigh District
9. Government Street Methodist
   Church
10. A.M.E. Zion Church
11. Boyington Oak Tree
12. Junior Miss HQ
13. Church Street Cemetery
14. Mobile Public Library
15. Phoenix Fire Station Museum
16. Bernstein House
17. William Ketchum House
18. Convention Center
19. Cotton Blossom

Fort Conde

BANKHEAD TUNNEL

S. ROYAL

Bienville Square

S. JOAQUIN ST

JACKSON ST

FRANKLIN

CONTI ST

WASHINGTON ST

SCOTT ST

BAYLOR ST

JEFFERSON ST

BROAD ST

GOVERNMENT

CHURCH

CHARLES ST

PALMETTO ST

OAKLEIGH PL

GEORGE ST

CHATHAM ST

GAYLE ST

RAPIER ST

SELMA

VIRGINIA ST

N

1/4 Kilometer

1/4 Mile

98

45

90

16

10

1.0 At the corner of Franklin and Government Streets is the home of Confederate Major William Ketchum—now the home of the Archbishop of the Mobile Catholic Church. The home has twenty-three rooms and a 60-foot drawing room. Directly across the street is the Bernstein House, former home of the Mobile City Museum. From here, turn right, heading southwest once again back onto Government Street. Just next door to the museum is Spanish Plaza, built in honor of the relationship between Spain and Mobile. The statue of Queen Isabella in the plaza was given to Mobile from the Spanish exhibit at the 1965 World's Fair in New York.

1.2 Barton Academy is on the right. Built in 1836 and now the home of the Mobile County Board of Education, this building served as a hospital during the Civil War.

1.5 Continuing southwest, the trail passes the home of Admiral Raphael Semmes. This home was given to Semmes by the city in honor of his service to the Confederacy during the Civil War.

1.7 Turn left onto Charles Street.

1.9 The trail comes to Washington Square. This small park area was deeded to the city in 1859 for use as a promenade. Decorated with statues and fountains, the park was occupied by the Union Army during the Civil War and relieved of everything but the iron statue of a deer, which still remains. The trail turns right onto Augusta Street for 1 block. Turn right onto Chatham Street and head north for 1 block to Palmetto Street.

2.0 At the intersection of Palmetto and Chatham Streets is Twelve Oaks Mansion, built in 1867. Travel to the southwest on Palmetto Street.

2.1 Take a left turn and head south on George Street. In about 1 block, George Street inter- sects Savannah Street. Make a right turn onto Savannah and continue until it intersects Oakleigh Place.

2.3 Turn south onto Oakleigh Place. Be sure to pay a visit to Oakleigh Mansion. Built in the 1830s, this house is now the home of the Historic Mobile Preservation Society and is a museum of the beautiful historic homes of the city. Admission is $1.00 for adults, 50 cents for students. Travel past Oakleigh 1 block and turn east onto Selma Street.

2.4 Follow Selma Street 2 blocks and turn right onto Chatham Street. In 3 blocks, Chatham turns into Gayle Street. Magnolia Cemetery, established in 1866, is on the right. There is a Confederate cemetery here.

2.8 Continuing down Gayle Street, come to the northwest corner of Magnolia Cemetery on your right. Turn right here down an unnamed street; in approximately 0.1 mile, reach the main entrance gate on your left. Enter the cemetery here to the south and stroll around the cemetery and its history, including the graves of such notables as Apache chief Geronimo's son; Micheal Krafft, founder of Mardi Gras in the United States with his ornate mystic society marker; and the Confederate Rest, containing the graves of more than 1,100 Confederate soldiers and tributes to the crew of the submarine *Hunley,* many of whom were from Mobile. (Visit the city's Web site for a detailed map and history at www.ci.mobile.al.us/html/parks/graveyardmap.html.)

3.3   Leave the cemetery the way you came in, turning right and returning to Gayle Street. Turn left and head north. Travel 3 blocks and Gayle Street again becomes Chatham Street. Continue another 2 blocks and make a left onto Selma Street.

3.7   Take a left turn (westward) onto Selma Street.

4.0   Turn right onto Rapier Street.

4.5   Turn right and head northeast onto Government. **Option:** For a longer trip, turn left (southwest) here onto Government Street (US 90 west). The longer trip is detailed in the literature provided at the fort and passes an original 11-inch cannon used at Fort Morgan during the Battle of Mobile Bay. Also along this route is Murphy High School, the oldest high school in Alabama and the only high school listed on the National Register of Historic Places. This longer trip is 11.0 miles in total length.

5.0   At the corner of Government and Broad Streets, the trail passes the Government Street Methodist Church, built in the 1890s and patterned after Spanish Baroque architecture of the seventeenth century. The building was known as the "Beehive" because of the bustle of activity that occurred there day and night. Visitors are welcome. Special services are held each day at noon. From the church, continue northeast across Broad Street 1 block. Turn southeast onto Jefferson Street. Follow Jefferson 1 block to Church Street. Turn left onto Baylor Street, passing the A.M.E. Zion Church, built in 1860.

5.2   As you head northwest on Baylor, pass the Boyington Oak Tree. On November 16, 1834, John Boyington was hanged on this site for murder. Before the execution, Boyington said, "I am innocent, but what can I do? From my grave shall grow a tree of many branches that will prove my innocence." Years later, an oak tree, the Boyington Oak, began to grow on this site as the real murderer turned himself in. A few short feet past the tree, the trail turns right onto Government Street, heading northeast, and passes the home of Amer-

RAISING CAIN IN MOBILE The term "raising cain" takes on a new meaning in Alabama's southernmost city, Mobile. The city was the scene of the first Mardi Gras celebration in the United States, back in 1830. The annual event was prohibited by Union troops during their occupation of the city following the Civil War.

Mobilian Joe Cain brought the celebration back to life one evening when he and fellow revelers dressed as Indians and paraded through the streets of the city. Following Cain's death, townspeople honored Cain by gathering around his grave during Mardi Gras and partying in an attempt to "raise Cain." The tradition continues to this day.

Joe Cain's grave after the Mardi Gras celebration commemorating him.

ica's Junior Miss. This national competition is held every June in Mobile and awards scholarships to the brightest and most outstanding high school students in the country.

5.5 Turn right and head southeast on Scott Street. After a block, make a left onto Church Street. This is the site of the Church Street Cemetery, established in 1819 for victims of a yellow fever epidemic. The cemetery is divided into several sections including veterans, strangers, Catholics, and Protestants. Many Mobile notables are buried here, including Joe Cain. Just past the cemetery is the Mobile Public Library, housed in a building constructed especially for the facility in 1928. Make a left turn onto the unnamed side street and continue 50 feet to Government Street, where the trail turns right and continues northeast.

5.6 Take a right onto Washington Street and proceed 0.1 mile. Take a left onto Church Street and continue heading northeast. The Church Street East District—where you are—is the second oldest neighborhood in the city, with many of the houses dating back to 1850.

6.2 Turn right onto Claiborne Street and head southeast for about 100 feet, arriving at the Phoenix Fire Station. This 1838 building was the original home of Fire Station Number 6 of the Phoenix Steam Fire Company. Today it is a museum dedicated to to the city's history of fire fighting. The station is open Tuesday through Saturday 10:00 A.M.–5:00 P.M., Sunday 1:00–5:00 P.M. Admission is free. From the fire station, turn left onto Jackson Street and return to Church Street. Make a right here and continue 0.3 mile to return to Fort Conde.

Hike Information

Local Information

City of Mobile Department of Tourism, One South Water Street, Mobile 36601; (800) 252-3862; www.mobile.org.

Mobile Transit Authority, 1224 West I-65 Service Road South, Mobile 36601; (251) 344-6600. All bus routes serve Bienville Square. The Highway 90 bus travels the main route of this trail, Government Street. Buses run down Government Street every 30 minutes. Service runs Monday through Saturday until 6:30 P.M.

Local Events/Attractions

Mardi Gras, two weeks prior to Ash Wednesday, Mobile; (800) 252-3862; www.mobile.org.

First Night Mobile, December 31, One South Water Street, Mobile 36601; (800) 5-MOBILE; www.mobile.org. This celebration is a nonalcoholic family festival celebrating the New Year with fireworks, live bands, and family activities.

Mobile Bay Bears, Mobile; (251) 479-2327. Southern league baseball at its finest, the Bay Bears, named for the Mobile Bears of the 1940s and 1950s, are a Double-A farm team of the San Diego Padres; they play at beautiful Hank Aaron Stadium, named for the Mobile native.

J. L. Bedsole IMAX Theater, 65 Government Street, Mobile 36601; (877) 625-4FUN; www.exploreum.net. The theater is open

Monday through Friday 9:00 A.M.–5:00 P.M.; Saturday 10:00 A.M.–5:00 P.M.; Sunday noon–5:00 P.M. Admission is $7.00 adults, $6.00 for youths and seniors, and $5.50 for children.

Gulf Coast Exploreum, 65 Government Street, Mobile 36601; (877) 625-4FUN; www.exploreum.net. The museum is open in summer Monday through Friday 9:00 A.M.–8:00 P.M.; Saturday 10:00 A.M.–5:00 P.M.; Sunday noon–5:00 P.M. Admission is $7.00 adults, $6.00 for youths and seniors, and $5.50 for children.

Lodging

Adam's Mark Hotel, 64 South Water Street, Mobile 36601; (800) 444-ADAM; www.adamsmark.com/mobile.

Radisson Admiral Semmes Hotel, 251 Government Street, Mobile 36601; (251) 432-8000; www.rdadmsemmes.com.

Restaurants

Wintzell's Oyster House, 605 Dauphin Street, Mobile 36601; (251) 432-4605.

Rousso's, 166 South Royal Street, Mobile 36601; (251) 433-3322.

Other Resources

Mobile Parks & Recreation, Magnolia Cemetery, Mobile; www.ci.mobile.al.us/html/parks/graveyardmap.html.

In Addition

Back to the Future in Mobile

Mobile, Alabama, one of the oldest cities along the Gulf Coast, may be a perfect example of the New South—preserving its past while moving aggressively into the future.

The annual Mardi Gras celebration demonstrates this mix of old and new. Mobile is the birthplace of the Mardi Gras carnival season in the United States. About 1830, Mobile resident Michael Kraft formed a secret society that attracted prominent citizens as members. One night after a bit of drinking, the group began parading in the streets. The revelry drew a lot of attention, some of it from spectators who wanted to join in the fun.

The celebration caught on. Soon other societies were formed and likewise began showing off with parades, music, and dancing. By 1840, the parades included floats depicting special themes, and participants rode the floats in costume. Word of the celebration spread, and New Orleans began its own Mardi Gras festivities after seeing the work of the Mobile societies.

With only a short cessation during and just after the Civil War, Mardi Gras has continued and thrived in Mobile. The original parades were held on New Year's Eve, but after the Civil War they became synonymous with the religious season of Lent and began two weeks prior to Ash Wednesday.

The Mobile celebration has since become known more as a family event. Each night parades fill the streets, and people turn out to catch the beads, candy, and marshmallow pies thrown by parade participants.

While respecting the past, the downtown area has seen an extraordinary revitalization in the past few years. There is the Exploreum, with its hands-on science activities, and the J. L. Bedsole IMAX Theater. A nautical museum is taking shape on the waterfront. On Dauphin Street, nightclubs, comedy venues, and restaurants keep the city electric.

Mobile is a big sports town, and the folks here love their football. Every Friday night during the season, thousands of people flock to high school football games, whether or not they follow the teams playing. Each January the city hosts the Senior Bowl, a game showcasing the best professional football prospects among the nation's graduating seniors. A recent addition to the scene is the Mobile Alabama Bowl, a new event on the NCAA holiday schedule.

Baseball is another city tradition. From the 1930s to the 1950s, the Mobile Bears played here. A legend of the Negro League, Satchel Paige, was born in Mobile, as were other notable professional baseball players such as Tommy Agee and Cleon Jones of the 1969 Miracle Mets, the "Wizard of Oz" Ozzie Smith, and former home run king Hank Aaron. The new Mobile Bay Bears are now playing here as part of Major League Baseball's Southern AA minor league.

4 Cemetery Trail

An interesting trail within Chickasabogue Park, the Cemetery Trail is used by both hikers and cyclists, with hikers heading in one direction, cyclists the other. The directions are reversed each month. The trail is ideally located for family hiking, with plenty to do at the park, and it provides easy trekking for young hikers.

Start: From the parking lot at the northwest side of the sports field at Chickasabogue Park.
Distance: 2.7-mile loop.
Approximate hiking time: 1½ hours.
Difficulty: Easy, on level and well-maintained trail.
Trail surface: Dirt and sand path; gravel in washout-prone areas.
Type of hike: Slash pine forest; many fern-lined creeks.
Land status: County park.
Nearest town: Saraland.
Schedule: Open year-round 7:00 A.M.–dusk. Rangers are on duty 24 hours for campers.
Fees/Permits: $1.00 day-use fee for ages 12–59, 50 cents for children 6–11, free for children 5 and younger and adults 60 and

older. Primitive camping is $5.00 a night, $10.00 for improved sites. Canoe rentals are $5.00 per hour or $20.00 per day.
Maps: USGS maps: Chickasaw. Cycling and hiking map as well as park information—available free at the Chickasabogue Park Information Center, Saraland.
Trail contacts: Chickasabogue Park, 760 Aldock Road, Mobile 36601; (251) 574-2267; www.mobilecounty.org/recreation-chickasabogue.htm.
Other trail users: Cyclists.
Canine compatibility: Dog friendly; leash required. Bring water, as sources are seasonal; dogs are not allowed at the pavilion at the beach along the creek.

Finding the trailhead: From Saraland take the Saraland exit (exit 13) from Interstate 65. Head west on Shelton Beach Road for 0.1 mile to the intersection of Alabama Highway 213 south. Make the left turn onto AL 213 and travel 3 miles to Whistler Street (a sign for Chickasabogue Park will be seen on the right). Take a left onto Whistler Street and follow it 0.7 mile to Aldock Road. Turn left onto Aldock Road and follow it 1 mile. Aldock Road runs straight into the main gate of the park. The park information center is located next to the gate. Trail parking is available by making a right turn from the information center and continuing down Aldock Road for 0.2 mile. A large playing field is on the right. Parking spots run alongside the playing field. This is also where the hike will begin. *DeLorme: Alabama Atlas & Gazetteer:* Page 62, B3.

The Hike

Owned and maintained by the Mobile County Commission, Chickasabogue Park encompasses more than 1,100 acres of forest, wetlands, and creeks. In addition to preserving the natural environment, the commissioners have made it their mission to provide a quality family getaway—and they have succeeded.

Chickasabogue features easy trails over lightly rolling hillsides, just right for children. The trails are mostly sandy and cross several creeks. The wildlife, including

The information center at Chickasabogue Park.

white-tailed deer, gives parents plenty to talk about with their children as they spend an afternoon together.

In addition to superb hiking and cycling trails, the park offers ball fields, a swimming beach along Chickasaw Creek, playgrounds, and picnic areas. The park is also home to an eighteen-hole disc golf course that is sanctioned by the Professional Disc Golf Association. Located in one of the state's bigger counties, the park can get crowded on weekends, so try to arrange your visit during the week if possible.

A little history education is also part of the Chickasabogue experience. At the entrance to the park, next to the information center, is the former Eight Mile A.M.E. Church. This small structure, built in 1879 in the neighboring town of Eight Mile, was moved to the park to serve as a museum. The museum features artifacts of Native American culture from as far back as 1500 B.C. The museum, open to the public without charge, also displays photos of old Mobile.

Explorer Hernando de Soto first visited the area around 1540. Pirates also ventured through the region, using Chickasaw Creek as their primary point of entry. The outlaw Cooper Gang, who roamed the Southeast robbing stagecoaches and businesses, lived here in the late 1800s. This rugged band helped runaway slaves flee the area, only to then sell them to plantations in other states.

Chickasabogue Park provides three walking routes: Cemetery Trail, Indian Loop Trail, and Beach Loop Trail. The Cemetery Trail, used by both hikers and cyclists, incorporates portions of the Indian Loop Trail. The trail is marked with small wooden planks that can be a bit confusing to a first-timer. In one direction they are painted red; in the other direction, yellow—a way to help hikers and cyclists stay in opposite directions and thus see each other coming. Check with the information center to confirm which direction you're meant to travel.

The Cemetery Trail begins at the parking area next to the playing field. As the trail meanders away from the parking area, it runs parallel to I–65 for a short distance before coming to a small cemetery established in the 1800s. Continuing on, the trail circles around and travels to a small nature center. Here you'll find posters and information about the park and its wildlife and plant life.

At this point, the sports field will again be nearby, offering a good opportunity to cut the trip short and head back to the parking area if you're hiking with small children.

From the nature center, the trail moves into the woods and follows a sandy path that crosses several creeks and marshes on wooden footbridges. Ferns are abundant. The trail travels to the banks of Chickasaw Creek before heading back to the parking area.

Miles and Directions

0.0   Start from the grass parking area at the northwest side of the sports field. Head across the field to the southeast. The woods of Chickasabogue can be seen at the opposite side of the field. Just before the woods is a nature study pond. Beautiful water lilies float atop the pond, with small fish schooling under the surface. A small gazebo sits at the end of a pier that protrudes into the pond. No fishing is allowed here! Continue south along the right or east bank of the pond toward the woods.

0.2   A sign marking the Cemetery Trail appears as the trail ducks into the woods heading west. There are very few trail markers along this portion of the route, but early in the hike several trees are marked with white blazes. As the trail sinks a few hundred feet into the woods, a campground appears through the trees on the left.

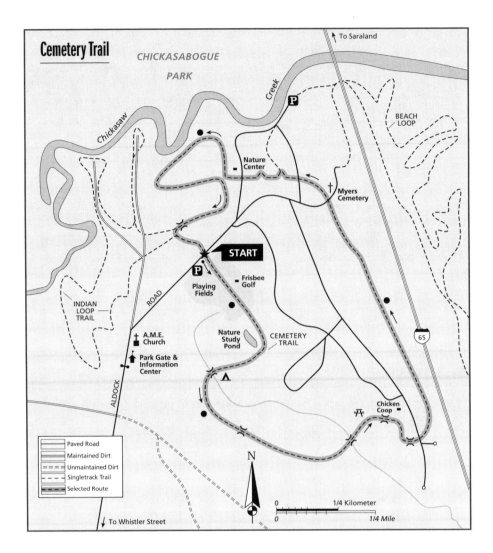

Cemetery Trail

CHICKASABOGUE PARK

To Saraland

BEACH LOOP

Nature Center

Myers Cemetery

START

Frisbee Golf

Playing Fields

INDIAN LOOP TRAIL

A.M.E. Church

Park Gate & Information Center

Nature Study Pond

CEMETERY TRAIL

65

Chicken Coop

ROAD

ALDOCK

Paved Road
Maintained Dirt
Unmaintained Dirt
Singletrack Trail
Selected Route

N

0   1/4 Kilometer

0   1/4 Mile

To Whistler Street

0.4 The trail takes a turn to the south and heads down into a ravine. At the bottom, the trail crosses one of several small streams and creeks over wooden footbridges.

0.6 Cross a larger 50-foot-long footbridge.

0.8 After leveling off at the top of a ridge and traveling about 30 yards, the path takes a turn to the east and then makes a steep descent once again about 100 feet to the bottom of another ravine. At the bottom, a 20-foot footbridge crosses another stream. If the crowds are small, white-tailed deer may be seen foraging and drinking nearby. Off through the trees, a picnic area can be seen to the left. Follow the trail a few more feet and it makes a hook to the south and then to the east, where there is another footbridge. In the distance you can hear the sound of I-65.

1.0 Trail signs become more frequent. Don't be confused about the red and yellow trail signs. Remember, they are both part of the Cemetery Trail. A chicken coop can be seen off to the northeast just off the trail. In about 50 feet, the trail comes to the paved park road. Cut diagonally across the road to the north and continue on the trail.

1.1 Continuing to the north, the trail runs parallel to I-65. A large 130-foot bridge spans a marshy area. Here you'll find marsh marigold growing, as well as cardinal flower, morning glory, and wild geranium, depending on the season.

1.4 Come to a Y intersection. The Cemetery Trail continues to the northwest on the left fork. Take this. (To the right is the Beach Loop Trail.) Separating the two trails is the cemetery for which the Cemetery Trail is named. The small cemetery of ten to fifteen graves dates back to 1870.

1.5 Cross the paved park road and head back into the woods. The trees thin out here.

1.7 Encounter a sign that reads SHORT and points to the northwest. (This is a section of the Beach Loop Trail and leads to the northernmost parking lot in the park.) Continue to the west. The trail scampers up a short hill. After weaving around thick brush, the trail once again intersects the paved park road. To the left is the playing field. Cross straight across the road to the gravel road on the other side. Continue down the gravel road to the north, passing a Cemetery Trail sign on the left. Continue about 50 feet and the Chickasabogue Nature Center will come into view. A series of informative posters display the wildlife and plant life in the area. From here, continue north.

EYES ON THE HURRICANE
The most dreaded words along the Gulf Coast are "The National Hurricane Center in Miami has issued a hurricane warning."

Hurricanes are among the deadliest forces of nature. According to Frank Lepore of the National Hurricane Center, more people die from flash flooding as a storm moves inland than from the storm where it makes landfall. Storm rainfall in the mountains of Alabama can result in flash floods that sweep people away, including hikers.

Although the technology for tracking storms is considerably better than in the past, hurricanes are still difficult to predict. A storm that seems to be heading up the East Coast can, without warning, make a beeline for the Gulf Coast. Hurricane Elena was a puzzler, traveling back and forth just off the Gulf Coast several times over several days, keeping residents guessing until it finally moved inland over the Florida panhandle.

To avoid being surprised by a major storm, hikers can carry a lightweight battery-powered weather radio. Most of these radios monitor the U.S. Emergency Alert System and activate when an emergency weather situation is imminent.

The good news is that most hurricanes do not make landfall. But the best advice is to stay alert. Check the weather often, and in the meantime enjoy the normally balmy weather of the South.

1.8 The trail now makes a left turn around some marshy areas until it reaches the banks of Chickasaw Creek. The slow-moving muddy waters of the creek provide an excellent and relaxing canoe trip after the hike. Canoes are available at the information center.

2.2 The trail returns to the nature center. Turn to the south.

2.5 One final 60-foot-long footbridge crosses a marsh and a small feeder creek of the Chickasaw. Shortly after the crossing, the trail turns to the south. Following the turn, encounter a Y intersection. To the right, the Indian Loop Trail continues to another meeting with the Chickasaw. Take the left fork.

2.6 The Cemetery Trail intersects with the Indian Loop Trail once again at a T intersection. Go left.

2.7 Reach a Y intersection. Either fork will lead back to the parking area.

2.8 The trail ends at Aldock Road, directly across from the playing field and the parking area.

Hike Information

Local Information

Saraland Area Chamber of Commerce and Welcome Center, 939 Highway 43, Saraland 36571; (251) 675-4444; www.saralandcoc.com.

Local Events/Attractions

Wildland Expeditions, Highway 43, Saraland 36571; (251) 460-8206; www.wild-land. com. Take a scenic boat tour of south Alabama's wetlands and salt marshes.

Lodging

Best Western, 1320 Industrial Parkway, Saraland 36571; (251) 679-7953.

Comfort Inn, 1210 Industrial Parkway, Saraland 36571; (251) 675-0020.

Restaurants

Benzi's Pizza, 311 Shelton Beach Road, Saraland 36571; (251) 675-9600.

Kings Seafood, 10 Saraland Boulevard South, Saraland 36571; (251) 679-4703.

Leroy's Real Pit Barbecue, 5675 Highway 43, Saraland 36571; (251) 675-5750.

Something Special Deli, 128 Industrial Parkway, Saraland 36571; (251) 675-3023.

5 CCC Trail

A wake-up call for those who have hiked the flatter trails of the Gulf Coast region, the CCC Trail leaves the sea level hiking behind and starts to take on some hills. Granted these are not massive mountains, but some of the inclines can get you breathing hard. The trail crosses the beautiful stream that flows from the spillway of the dam at Blacksher Lake and then rounds the lake and ducks into a thick forest.

Start: From the southwest end of the main parking area of Claude D. Kelley State Park.
Distance: 1.5-mile lollipop loop.
Approximate hiking time: 1 hour.
Difficulty: Easy to moderate, with a few steep grades; some rocky stretches because of washouts.
Trail surface: Dirt path; some travel on a dirt logging road.
Type of hike: Dense forest, including slash pine, dogwood, sweet gum, hickory, and live oak.
Land status: State park.
Nearest town: Atmore.
Schedule: Open year-round.
Fees/Permits: Admission to the park is $1.00 for visitors 12 and older, 50 cents for children

6-11. Tent camping is $11.00 per day, base rate. Boats are available for use on the lake at $7.50 per day or pedalboats at $4.00 per hour. A freshwater fishing license is required for fishing in the lake.
Maps: USGS maps: Uriah East. Hiking map and park brochure—available at Claude D. Kelley State Park gatehouse or at the park's beach and bathhouse next to the main parking area.
Trail contacts: Claude D. Kelley State Park, 580 H. Kyle, Atmore 36502; (251) 862-2511.
Other trail users: None.
Canine compatibility: Dog friendly along the trails; leash required. Bring water, sources are seasonal; dogs not permitted at the beach area.

Finding the trailhead: From Atmore take Alabama Highway 21 north. Go 11 miles past where it crosses Interstate 65. Turn right onto H. Kyle Road—a sign marking Claude Kelley State Park will be seen on the right. Travel 0.4 mile to the park gatehouse. If the gatehouse is closed, pay at the honor box located on the side of the shack. Continue down H. Kyle Road 0.1 mile to the main parking area on the bank of Blacksher Lake. Hiking brochures can be picked up at the gatehouse or from the bathhouse at the parking lot. *DeLorme: Alabama Atlas & Gazetteer:* Page 57, D6.

The Hike

The folks who drive past Claude D. Kelley State Park and never stop to visit don't know what they're missing. The park, hidden in the woods about 18 miles north of Atmore, features 960 forested acres and 25-acre Blacksher Lake. This man-made lake provides swimming and fishing year-round. The CCC Trail affords wonderful views of the lake, plus a bit more of a hiking challenge than many other Gulf Coast hikes.

The Civilian Conservation Corps (CCC) built the trail, and the park itself, in 1938. You can also thank the CCC for the log pavilion and bathhouse, as well as the

A picturesque scene as the trail meanders next to Blacksher Lake's overflow stream.

log gazebo perched at the ridge, accessed by the Gazebo Trail (see the following chapter).

The area in which the park lies, Monroe County, was immortalized in Harper Lee's *To Kill a Mockingbird,* the best-selling novel about racial tensions in a small town. The story was set in Maycomb, a fictional alias for the nearby town of Monroeville.

This region is home to the Poarch band of Creek Indians. Following the 1814 battle of Horseshoe Bend, which pitted the Creek's Red Stick band against U.S. soldiers and the Lower Creek tribe, the federal government relocated most of the local tribes to Oklahoma. In appreciation for fighting alongside General Andrew Jackson's troops, the Poarch Creeks were allowed to establish a reservation here. Each Thanksgiving the tribe invites the public to its annual Thanksgiving Powwow, featuring native foods, rituals, costumes, and dances. The powwow is held on the Poarch Creek Reservation on Jack Springs Road in Atmore.

The CCC Trail begins by tracing the banks of Blacksher Lake. Early on, you cross the lake's overflow stream. The crossing makes for a scenic spot to rest up or have a bite to eat. At the opposite side of the lake, the trail enters a forest so thick that you

CCC Trail

To Monroeville

CLAUDE D. KELLEY STATE PARK

GAZEBO ROAD

GAZEBO TRAIL

H. KYLE ROAD

CAMPGROUND ROAD

Gatehouse

START

Footbridge

Dam

P

Bathhouse

Little River

5 Yellow Pipes

Fishing Pier

Cabins

Blacksher Lake

21

Dirt Pit

N

Paved Road
Maintained Dirt
Unmaintained Dirt
Singletrack Trail
Selected Route

0   1/4 Kilometer
0   1/4 Mile

To Atmore

can feel the drop in temperature—a blessing during hot and humid summer months. A sign along here says BELL TRAIL, but don't worry: This is still the CCC Trail.

Slash pine, sweet gum, and hickory fill the forest. In fall, live oaks provide a sparkling display of color that reflects from the surface of the lake. In early spring the dogwood blooms are particularly beautiful. While hiking, be sure to watch for the many varieties of woodpeckers that live here, including downy, hairy, red-headed, and pileated.

As the trail heads off into the woods, it follows an old dirt and gravel logging road. The grades are a bit steeper here than on other Gulf Coast hikes covered in this guidebook, but the average hiker shouldn't find too much difficulty. The route has many washouts, so watch your footing.

At the top of a ridge, the trail comes to the very edge of the soft clay banks of a large pit. Be careful here: There's a drop-off of 75 to 100 feet. The path eventually loops back down toward the lake to the east, rejoining the main path back to the parking area.

Miles and Directions

0.0   Start from the southwest end of the main parking area in Claude D. Kelley State Park. Head to the southwest around the banks of Blacksher Lake, passing the dam that forms the lake.

0.1   The trail comes to a 50-foot-long footbridge that spans the spillway stream. A CCC TRAIL sign is here. Cross the bridge heading to the south; once across, turn to the east and head back to the lake. Once you reach the lake, turn right and follow the dirt road along the banks of the lake.

0.2   Pass a T fishing pier that extends out into Blacksher Lake. Continue straight until the dirt road ends in a cul-de-sac. To the right is a series of five yellow pipes. This is where the loop of the trail rejoins the road on the trip back. A BELL TRAIL sign is off to the southeast corner of the cul-de-sac. This is the alternative name for the CCC Trail. Stay left, following the dirt path into the woods to the southeast.

0.3   A short footpath off the main trail leads to the banks of Blacksher Lake for more spectacular views.

0.4   The trail turns to the south and heads away from the lake.

0.5   The trail now starts its climb to the top of the hill, and the slash pines become thicker. A few feet up the hill, the dirt path becomes an abandoned dirt road. Due to washouts, the travel becomes rocky in areas.

0.9   The road reaches the top of the hill at a clay dirt pit that is 75 to 100 feet deep. Be careful of loose footing. A dirt road crosses here from north to south, while the road from the lake continues on to the northwest. Turn right and follow the intersecting road. This road is more gravel than sand and begins the descent back down to the lake.

1.2   Continuing downhill, the trail starts heading more to the east. At this point the downhill walk is on about the same incline as the trip up.

1.3   A jog in the trail is encountered as it starts heading to the north. The trail turns abruptly to the northwest then to the northeast to avoid a 20-foot drop-off that looks as though it was created by a washout. Continue in this direction. The road runs into the five yellow pipes first encountered at the 0.2-mile point of the trip. Turn left here and follow the dirt road along the west bank of Blacksher Lake.

1.4   Turn left at the dam and head west back to the footbridge over the stream. Cross the bridge and head northeast along the banks of the lake toward the main parking area.

1.5   Return to the parking area.

THE STORY OF THE CCC

The Civilian Conservation Corps was formed in 1933 as the United States was suffering through the Great Depression. The goal of this New Deal program was to provide employment and training for young men and to help conserve the nation's natural resources.

In exchange for a salary of $30 a month plus food and lodging, unmarried and unemployed men spread out across the country to work on reforestation and other conservation programs. They built fire-lookout towers, worked on flood control projects, and helped with soil conservation. They contributed to wildlife protection programs, and they helped develop national and state parks—including Claude D. Kelley State Park, site of this CCC Trail.

The Corps ceased operation by order of Congress in 1942, but in less than ten years, this agency provided more than three million jobs and brought countless benefits to all citizens, including hikers and others who love the outdoors.

Hike Information

Local Information

Atmore Chamber of Commerce, 501 Pensacola Avenue, Atmore 36502; (251) 368-3305; www.frontier.net/~atmoreal/.

Local Events/Attractions

William Station Day, third weekend of October, 501 South Pensacola Avenue, Atmore 36502; (251) 368-3305; www.frontiernet.net/~atmoreal/events.htm. "A simpler way of life," that's how the residents of Atmore describe the William Station Day celebration. This is a day to celebrate the town's founding in 1866. Back then the town was a supply stop called William Station. There are plenty of arts and crafts, music, and stories of the trains that once ruled the area and the legends of the Poarch Creek Indians.

Poarch Creek Indian Bingo Palace, Highway 21 south at Poarch Road, Atmore 36502; (800) 826-9121; www.frontiernet.net/~cbingo.

Annual Poarch Creek Indian Thanksgiving Pow-wow, 501 South Pensacola Avenue, Atmore 36502; (251) 368-3305 or www.frontiernet.net/~atmoreal/events.htm. Each year, the public is invited to celebrate Thanksgiving with the Poarch Creek Indians. The event brings tribal members together and features brilliant displays of authentic dress and exhibition dancing by a variety of tribes. In addition, there are arts and crafts, barbecue, fried chicken, and more.

Lodging

Best Western, 6141 Highway 21, Atmore 36502-6317; (800) 528-1234; www.frontiernet.net/~bestwest.

Days Inn of Atmore, 1610 South Main Street, Atmore 36502-3560; (251) 368-9999.

Restaurants

Buster's Restaurant, 1310 East Nashville Avenue, Atmore 36502-2619; (251) 368-4931.

Creek Family Restaurant, 6141 Highway 21, Atmore 36502-6317; (251) 368-4422.

6 Gazebo Trail

The first sign of any elevation gain in the hikes of the Gulf Coast region of Alabama occurs in Claude D. Kelley State Park. Here the Gazebo Trail travels up the shallow inclines of 300-foot ridges past slash pines towering over pine-needle floors. The trail crosses several creeks and streams that feed Blacksher Lake. Along the way, look for small fern forests, as well as eastern wild turkeys, white-tailed deer, and red-tailed hawks.

Start: From the north end of the main parking area at Claude D. Kelley State Park.
Distance: 3.2-mile loop.
Approximate hiking time: 1½ hours.
Difficulty: Easy, on relatively flat trails; moderate during some steep changes in elevation along ridges.
Trail surface: Dirt and sand trails; dirt and gravel road.
Type of hike: Slash pine, sweet gum, and oak trees; ferns and wildflowers.
Land status: State park.
Nearest town: Atmore.
Schedule: Open year-round.
Fees/Permits: Admission to the park is $1.00 for visitors 12 and older, 50 cents for children 6–11. Tent camping is $11 per night, base

rate. Boats are available for use on the lake at $7.50 per day or pedalboats at $4.00 per hour. A freshwater fishing license is required for fishing in the lake.
Maps: USGS maps: Uriah East.
Hiking map and park brochure—available at Claude D. Kelley State Park gatehouse or at the park's beach and bathhouse next to the main parking area.
Trail contacts: Claude D. Kelley State Park, 580 H. Kyle, Atmore 36502; (251) 862-2511.
Other trail users: Equestrians and motorists on park road.
Canine compatibility: Dog friendly along the trails; leash required. Bring water, sources are seasonal; dogs not permitted at the beach area.

Finding the trailhead: From Atmore take Alabama Highway 21 north. Go 11 miles past where it crosses Interstate 65. Turn right onto H. Kyle Road—a sign marking Claude Kelley State Park will be seen on the right. Travel 0.4 mile to the park gatehouse. If the gatehouse is closed, pay at the honor box located on the side of the shack. Continue down H. Kyle Road 0.1 mile to the main parking area on the bank of Blacksher Lake. Hiking brochures can be picked up at the gatehouse or from the bathhouse at the parking lot. *DeLorme: Alabama Atlas & Gazetteer:* Page 57, D6.

The Hike

Tucked away like a little secret off AL 21 is Claude D. Kelley State Park, yet another gift of the Depression era's Civilian Conservation Corps program. The centerpiece of the 960-acre park is Blacksher Lake. A swimming beach and canoe and paddleboat rentals make the lake easily accessible and a great spot for the family. The twenty-five-acre lake is also good for anglers anxious to reel in a few bass, bream, or catfish—but don't forget your freshwater fishing license.

The Gazebo Trail's namesake.

The park is the home of two superb hiking trails: the CCC Trail and the Gazebo Trail (the longer of the two). The CCC Trail, featured in the previous chapter, heads south from the parking area, skirting the lake and forming a lollipop loop. The Gazebo Trail heads north to east of the lot into the rolling ridges above the lake, staying largely on the well-maintained Gazebo Road.

The trail begins at the main parking lot behind the bathhouse next to the lake. You can get park information and a free trail map at the main gate or at the bathhouse. Drinks, snacks, and ice are available for sale.

As you meander down the Gazebo Trail, you'll encounter a variety of plant life. Sweet gums and live oaks provide shade in the hot, humid summer; in fall, they blaze in colors of red, yellow, and gold. Like most of the Gulf Coast region, the trail courses through an abundance of slash pines.

While gazing up at the pines that tower above the trail, be on the lookout for red-tailed hawks flying high overhead. Back down on the trail, in the right season, you'll see a wide variety of wildflowers lining the way: black-eyed Susans, yellow-flowered winter honeysuckle, and the lavender flowers of the morning glory.

Gazebo Trail

CLAUDE D. KELLEY
STATE PARK

Blacksher Lake

START

Gazebo

Culvert

GAZEBO TRAIL

GAZEBO ROAD

CAMPGROUND ROAD

Bathhouse

Cabins

Dam

Fishing Pier

CCC TRAIL

CCC TRAIL

H. KYLE ROAD

Gatehouse

Little River

To Monroeville

To Atmore

21

N

1/4 Kilometer
1/4 Mile

Paved Road
Maintained Dirt
Unmaintained Dirt
Singletrack Trail
Selected Route

The trail crosses several creeks on wooden footbridges. From the bridges you can view the masses of ferns that spring up like miniature forests in the damp surroundings. This is also a place to see white-tailed deer and eastern wild turkeys.

On the way down the trail, you'll notice the boundaries and service roads of Little River State Forest. This forest, maintained by the Alabama Department of Forestry, is used mostly for timber operations.

The Gazebo Trail reaches its farthest point at the top of a ridge, where you'll find a log gazebo with stone fireplace built by the CCC. You can reserve the gazebo for picnics, but reserve it early as it can get a bit crowded here during summer. Picnickers use the Gazebo Road to ferry their supplies and guests to the gazebo, so watch for vehicles. The trail loops around the gazebo and begins to descend the hill at this point.

As the trail heads back to the parking area, the woods thin out a bit. Watch for woodpeckers in the trees, including red-headed and downy species. Also look along the sandy shoulders of the road for the tracks and burrows of armadillos and gopher tortoises.

Miles and Directions

0.0 Start from the north end of the main parking area and head north until you reach the dirt and gravel park road. Follow the road to the northeast.

0.1 The dirt road intersects Campground Road. Looking ahead to the north, there will be a closed pipe gate with a sign that reads GAZEBO ROAD. Turn right and head east on Campground Road.

0.2 Come to a wooden Gazebo Trail sign. Take the trail to the left, which leaves the road and heads into the woods. From here out, the trail is only occasionally marked, but the path itself should be easily discernable. Look out for armadillo tracks in the sand.

0.3 The trail crosses several streams and creeks that feed Blacksher Lake. Cross the first creek using a small footbridge. Ferns are plentiful around these crossings.

0.4 Come to the second creek crossing, this one a 40-foot bridge. After the bridge, expect the most difficult climb of the trip. It begins with a 70-foot scramble uphill to the top of a ridge. At the top, the trail levels off for a bit and then sprints up another 75-foot hillside. At the top of this hill, a third footbridge crosses a marshy area.

Gazebo Road section of the Gazebo Trail.

0.5 Pass a GAZEBO TRAIL sign as the trail becomes a dirt and gravel Park Service road. This road merges with Gazebo Road. Continue east. After about 100 feet, pass a HORSE TRAIL sign on the left and a GAZEBO TRAIL sign on the right. Along this section, you'll see morning glories and black-eyed Susans, along with stone water culverts built by the CCC.

0.7 A dirt road cuts back off to the right—this is where the loop will return at Mile 1.5. To the left is a sign indicating another horse trail. Stay straight.

0.9 Reach the top of the ridge. A GAZEBO TRAIL sign points to the west as the trail begins to round the loop.

1.1 Reach the gazebo. This is a nice stopping point for a bite to eat or to watch wildlife. White-tailed deer are common in the area. The gazebo's stone fireplace is good for cooking. Continue on Gazebo Road as it now swings around to the east and back down the hill.

1.5 The loop is completed and you're back to Gazebo Road (Mile 0.7). Turn to the left and head downhill.

2.5 Come to a Y intersection. To the left is the trail you took earlier. Continue straight on Gazebo Road.

2.7 The trail begins a turn to the southwest.

3.1 Gazebo Road runs into the closed pipe gate encountered at the beginning of the trip. Continue down the dirt road to the southwest. You'll see the main parking area to the south.

3.2 Arrive back at the main parking area.

A FAVORITE OF THE SOUTH: BREAD PUDDING

1½ cups milk

10 slices white bread

2 tablespoons butter

¼ teaspoon salt

½ teaspoon cinnamon

¼ teaspoon cloves

¼ teaspoon nutmeg

2 egg yolks

⅓ cup sugar

¼ cup sherry

¼ cup white raisins or chopped dates

Heat milk but do not boil. Trim crust off the bread. Slice bread into half-inch cubes. Melt butter in the milk, then add the bread. Soak bread 10 minutes. Stir in remaining ingredients. Pour into oiled skillet and cook over a fire for 30 minutes. Turn and cook 30 more minutes. Best served topped with jam or honey.

Hike Information

Local Information
Atmore Chamber of Commerce, 501 South Pensacola Avenue, Atmore 36502; (251) 368-3305.

Local Events/Attractions
William Station Day, third weekend of October, 501 South Pensacola Avenue, Atmore 36502; (251) 368-3305; www.frontiernet.net/~atmoreal/events.htm. "A simpler way of life," that's how the residents of Atmore describe the William Station Day celebration. This is a day to celebrate the town's founding in 1866. Back then the town was a supply stop called William Station. There are plenty of arts and crafts, music, and stories of the trains that once ruled the area and the legends of the Poarch Creek Indians.

Poarch Creek Indian Bingo Palace, Highway 21 south at Poarch Road, Atmore 36502; (800) 826-9121; www.frontiernet.net/~cbingo.

Annual Poarch Creek Indian Thanksgiving Pow-wow, 501 South Pensacola Avenue, Atmore 36502; (251) 368-3305 or www.frontiernet.net/~atmoreal/events.htm. Each year, the public is invited to celebrate Thanksgiving with the Poarch Creek Indians. The event brings tribal members together and features brilliant displays of authentic dress and exhibition dancing by a variety of tribes. In addition, there are arts and crafts, barbecue, fried chicken, and more.

Lodging
Best Western, 6141 Highway 21, Atmore 36502-6317; (800) 528-1234; www.frontiernet.net/~bestwest.

Days Inn of Atmore, 1610 South Main Street, Atmore 36502-3560; (251) 368-9999.

Restaurants
Buster's Restaurant, 1310 East Nashville Avenue, Atmore 36502-2619; (251) 368-4931.

Creek Family Restaurant, 6141 Highway 21, Atmore 36502-6317; (251) 368-4422.

7 Redoubt Trail Loop

Historic Blakeley State Park looks like a postcard of the archetypal South: long flowing Spanish moss hanging from the trees, shady walkways along the riverbank, and let us not forget Civil War history. Only hours after Lee's surrender to Grant in Virginia, the last major battle of the war occurred here in Blakeley State Park. Today the park is a National Civil War Historic Register Site—in fact, it's the largest site of its kind east of the Mississippi River.

Start: From the picnic area off the service road at the east end of the park.
Distance: 6.1-mile loop.
Approximate hiking time: 3 hours.
Difficulty: Easy travel on slightly rolling hills.
Trail surface: Dirt path, some paved and gravel roads, and a boardwalk section.
Type of hike: Magnolia and slash pine forest with riverside and marsh walks.
Land status: State park.
Nearest town: Spanish Fort.
Schedule: Open year-round 9:00 A.M.–5:00 P.M.
Fees/Permits: $2.50 per person for hiking ($1.00 children 6–12). Camping is allowed in designated primitive areas but not on the trails.
Maps: USGS map: Bridgehead.
Park brochure and trail map—available for no charge at the park headquarters, Spanish Fort. You can call the park at (251) 580-0005 to have them mailed to you.
Trail contacts: Historic Blakeley State Park, 34745 State Highway 225, Spanish Fort 36527; (251) 626-0798; www.siteone.com/tourist/blakeley.
Other trail users: Cyclists, motorists, and equestrians.
Canine compatibility: Dog friendly.

Finding the trailhead: From Montgomery take Interstate 65 south to the Stockton exit (Alabama Highway 225 south). The exit is marked with a brown HISTORIC BLAKELEY sign. Follow the winding highway approximately 5 miles. The Blakeley State Park entrance sign is on the right. From Mobile: Take Interstate 10 east to the Spanish Fort exit (AL 225 north). Follow the winding highway approximately 5 miles. The Blakeley State Park entrance sign is on the left. *DeLorme: Alabama Atlas & Gazetteer: Page 62, C5.*

The Hike

The Paleo-Indians first moved into the area around 4,000 years ago—evidenced by the ancient burial mounds that still dot the park. Over the years the land changed hands numerous times—it would fall under the rule of six different flags—until the United States captured the region from Spain in 1813. Soon thereafter, Josiah Blakeley stepped into the picture to buy the land and establish a town in his name.

The town of Blakeley, long since vanished, was chartered in 1814 and became a bustling port city that rose to rival neighboring Mobile. By 1828 a series of yellow fever epidemics, coupled with the greed of land speculators, forced the city of 4,000 into a spiral of decay. By the close of the Civil War, the town was abandoned. Today

One of the many breastworks along the Redoubt Trail.

all that remains of the old port town are the 400-year-old live oaks that once lined the city streets.

But the biggest thing to hit Blakeley came as the town lay in ruin. On April 8, 1865, 55,000 Union and Confederate soldiers converged in the fields surrounding the old town. The Union army intended to seize Fort Blakeley and then attack and capture the city of Mobile from its eastern shore. The fighting was fierce—216 killed, 955 wounded, and 3,054 captured (3,050 of them Confederates). It was a decisive Union victory, but what made the battle significant had little to do with the casualties. On the second day of this two-day campaign, Confederate General Robert E. Lee surrendered to Union General Ulysses S. Grant at Appomattox Courthouse in Central Virginia—thus making the battle at Blakeley the last major battle of the Civil War.

More than a hundred years later, in 1974, the Alabama Historical Commission placed the site on the National Register of Historic Places, and the effort to preserve the battle site began. Trails were built, breastworks were located. In 1993, Congress designated the site a Class A Civil War Site. Three years later it was added to the National Civil War Trail list.

Within Blakeley State Park's 3,800 acres are a total of 15 miles of nature and historic trails. The trails cross one another so that you can form shorter or longer loops

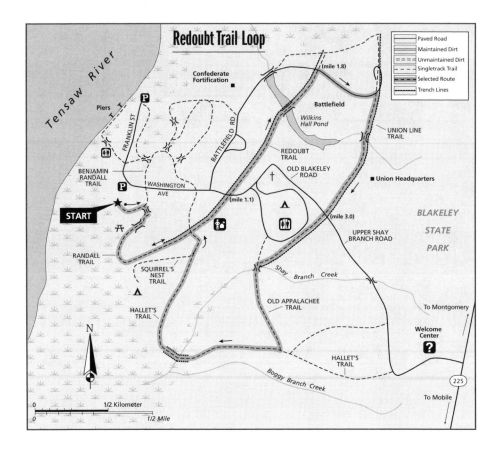

Redoubt Trail Loop

Paved Road
Maintained Dirt
Unmaintained Dirt
Singletrack Trail
Selected Route
Trench Lines

Tensaw River

Confederate
Fortification

(mile 1.8)

Piers

FRANKLIN ST

Battlefield

Wilkins
Hall Pond

UNION LINE
TRAIL

BATTLEFIELD RD

REDOUBT
TRAIL

BENJAMIN
RANDALL
TRAIL

OLD BLAKELEY
ROAD

Union Headquarters

WASHINGTON
AVE

(mile 1.1)

START

(mile 3.0)

BLAKELEY

STATE

UPPER SHAY
BRANCH ROAD

PARK

RANDALL
TRAIL

SQUIRREL'S
NEST
TRAIL

Shay Branch Creek

HALLET'S
TRAIL

OLD APPALACHEE
TRAIL

To Montgomery

N

Welcome
Center

HALLET'S
TRAIL

Boggy Branch Creek

225

To Mobile

0   1/2 Kilometer

0   1/2 Mile

to suit your schedule. All the trails are well marked with signs at the beginning and end of each trail and at intersections.

To access the Redoubt Trail, take the Benjamin Trail from the parking lot for a short hike to a small bridge that crosses a narrow tributary of the Tensaw River. Here the trail connects with the Randall Trail. Hike the Randall Trail for another quarter of a mile through low-lying, swampy areas and over another bridge before circling around to the Redoubt Trail, about half of a mile into the trip.

The Redoubt Trail runs along the top of a small ridgeline. Like all trails in the park, the area is heavily forested with magnolia and slash pine trees. Several dugout areas appear along this ridge. These entrenchments were used by Confederate troops "digging in" for the battle to come.

After about a half mile, the trail intersects the Hallet's Trail. This is a long trail that leads over a number of creeks and swamplands that feed the Tensaw River. Continuing straight on the Redoubt Trail for another 0.6 mile, the trail crosses the Washington Avenue service road.

After a total of 1.5 miles of hiking, the trail dips into a ravine and makes its way over Wilkins Hall Pond. Here brown pelicans and great egrets can be seen, as well as

The Redoubt Trail crosses many marshes.

turtles and an occasional alligator. Slash pines and live oaks surround the pond, with various marsh grasses waving in the breeze. This part of the trail is along a board-walk. In the center of the pond area, you'll find a platform with benches.

After passing over the pond on the boardwalk, the most difficult part of the trail is upon you—a 100-foot scramble up the other side of the ravine. Along this incline there are some wooden stairs, but it's mostly dirt path. Although it is not difficult, those out of shape could feel winded afterward.

After you clear the ravine, the large fortifications of the battlefield come into view. To the right is the actual battlefield, where Union troops raced across to take on the Confederates. This is where the Rebel troops were headquartered. The redoubts, now reinforced with wood, have been restored to their original condition.

Horseback riders enjoying the trails of Blakeley.

From here the trail loops around to the opposite side of the battlefield, where the Union troops were headquartered. Still visible are the entrenchments and cannon pits used by the Union army before their charge on the Confederates. Across the flat, grassy battlefield lie the opposing Confederate fortifications.

At this point, the Redoubt Trail converges with the Old Appalachee Trail and follows it for half a mile before merging once again with the Hallet's Trail. Take a right on Hallet's and walk the remaining 2.1 miles back to the parking area, enjoying the spectacular and calming views of the Tensaw River and the wildlife that live along its banks.

Miles and Directions

0.0 Start at the Washington Avenue parking area on the east side of the park along the Tensaw River. The Benjamin Trail begins at the extreme east side of the lot.

0.1 Cross a small wooden walkway over an inlet of the Tensaw River—now on the Randall Trail.

0.3 Cross another small walkway, back over the same inlet from the river.

0.6 The Randall Trail circles around from the inlet to the east approximately 0.2 miles and then heads back to the west for another 0.2 miles. This is the beginning of the Redoubt Trail.

1.1 The Redoubt Trail runs along a small ridgeline dropping down only slightly in places where it crosses streams and creeks, which are usually dry during the summer months.

The trail crosses Washington Avenue near the Blakeley Cemetery. While walking, be sure to notice the dugout foxholes used by Confederate troops.

1.5 The trail takes its largest dip down to Wilkins Hall Pond. This pond, usually dry in summer, provides excellent wildlife viewing opportunities during spring and winter. The trail across the pond is a boardwalk. A 100-foot climb up the west bank of the ravine is the most difficult part of the hike.

1.8 The trail meanders to the top of the main Confederate Headquarters. Directly in front is the main fortification, reconstructed to the way it actually looked during the Battle of Blakeley. On the right is the large grassy field where the Union army charged the Confederate stronghold. Following the fortifications, the trail intersects Battlefield Road, where you'll turn right.

2.2 Follow Battlefield Road for a quarter mile. Come to the Union Line Trail and turn right.

2.5 Follow the Union Line Trail along the opposite side of the battlefield and cross a small wooden walkway over a creek that feeds Wilkins Hall Pond.

3.0 Cross Old Blakeley Road.

3.5 The Union Line Trail ends at a small wooden bridge that crosses Shay Branch Creek and turns into the Old Appalachee Trail.

4.0 Follow the Old Appalachee Trail through heavily forested areas until it intersects Hallet's Trail. Turn right onto Hallet's Trail.

6.1 Follow Hallet's Trail over a wooden bridge that spans Shay Branch Creek and another inlet of the Tensaw River. The city of Mobile can be seen to the southwest. The trail intersects the Redoubt Trail once again. Take a left onto the Redoubt Trail and retrace the Randall and Benjamin Trails back to the parking area.

Hike Information

Local Information

Eastern Shore Chamber of Commerce, 29750 Larry Cawyer Drive, Daphne 36526; (251) 626–0798; www.siteone.com/towns/chamber.

Local Events/Attractions

Annual Blakeley Reenactment, 34745 State Highway 225, Spanish Fort 36527; (251) 626–0798. Hundreds of descendants of Battle of Blakeley participants gather and reenact the battle. The event occurs around the weekend of the actual battle date of April 9.

Mardi Gras, two weeks before Ash Wednesday, 29750 Larry Dee Cawyer Drive, Spanish Fort 36527; (251) 621–8222. The city of Mobile is the birthplace of Mardi Gras in the United States, and the surrounding area has taken up the Carnival spirit. This is one of the smaller parades, but grows in size every year. Unlike other such celebrations, this one is family oriented.

Lodging

Comfort Suites, 29450 North Main Street, Daphne 36526; (251) 626–1113.

Ramada Inn on the Bay, 1525 Battleship Parkway, Spanish Fort 36527; (251) 626–7200.

Restaurants

Blue Gill Restaurant, 3775 Battleship Parkway, Spanish Fort 36527; (251) 625–1998.

Junkyard Restaurant, 10880 Highway 31, Spanish Fort 36527; (251) 626–0547.

David's Catfish House, Highway 31, Spanish Fort 36527; (251) 626–7903.

8 Mound Island Canoe Trail

This is a combination trip featuring the best of both worlds in south Alabama—an unbelievably beautiful paddle through the bayous of one of the largest river deltas in the country plus a hike to ancient Indian mounds in the absolute middle of nowhere. The hike itself is reminiscent of hiking in South American rain forests.

Start: From Rice Creek Landing.
Distance: 10.6-mile loop float trip/hike, including 1.4-mile out-and-back hike.
Approximate hiking time: 7 hours; can be made into an overnight (see text).
Difficulty: Easy 1-mile hike; difficult paddle to island, special precautions required (refer to text).
Trail surface: Canoe float trip; hiking trail is level dirt path.
Type of hike: Southern bayous with Spanish moss–lined banks. Mound Island features abundant wildlife, saw palmetto, greenfly orchid, and cypress trees.
Land status: Forever Wild and private property.
Nearest town: Bay Minette.
Schedule: Mostly year-round, but during some periods the water levels may be too high or too low (see Hike Description and Other Resources).
Fees/Permits: $2.00 day-use fee at the put-in. Camping on the platform is first come, first served; call for reservations. Visit the state Web site at www.dcnr.state.al.us for more information.
Maps: USGS map: Stiggins Lake. Brochures available from the Alabama Department of Conservation (see Organizations) or on their Web site at www.dcnr.state.al.us.
Trail contacts: Alabama Department of Conservation and Natural Resources, 64 North Union Street, Montgomery 36130; www.dcnr.state.al.us.
Other trail users: Motorboats.
Canine compatibility: If your dog likes to canoe, great; dogs should be leashed on the island because of wild pigs.

Finding the trailhead: At the intersection of Alabama Highways 59 and 31, take AL 59 north 10.1-miles. Bear left onto Hodgson Road. Travel 0.5 mile. Hodgson becomes County Road 21. Take CR 21 north 0.8 mile. Turn left onto Rice Creek Road. Follow the dirt road 1.2 miles to the end and the put-in. *DeLorme: Alabama Atlas & Gazetteer:* Page 56, G-2 and G-1.

The Hike

This trip just might be one of the most adventurous hikes you can take in Alabama—and the most dangerous. It is a combination canoe paddle and hike through the second largest river delta system in the country and one of the largest intact wetland systems left in the United States. But before we get to the good stuff, let's cover the bad stuff.

First of all, the delta has countless side channels and bayous, and although the canoe trail is marked, it's still easy to make a wrong turn and end up heading deeper

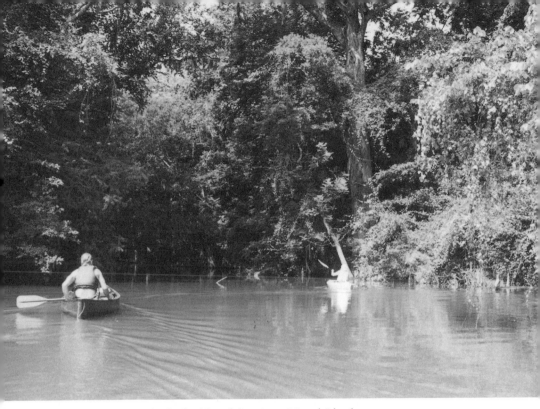

Entering Bottle Creek, the final leg of the trip to Mound Island.

and deeper into the wilds. Someone in your party should have navigation experience and know how to handle a compass and read maps. Or hire a guide such as EcoTours (see Hike Tours at the end of this chapter) to lead the way. And always remember to tell someone where you are going and the route you will be taking before you head out.

Nature can make this trip into more than you bargained. For instance, the paddle can be very strenuous. Tidal flows and high winds on the Tensaw River can make crossings difficult if you are not in shape, and paddling this trip in the summer heat can result in rapid dehydration and heat exhaustion. The water flow in the delta can also be extremely dangerous. Refer to Other Resources at the end of this chapter to find out where you can get water-level information before heading out. Any river stage above 19 feet is extremely hazardous.

There is also danger from the wildlife found here, including alligators. Although they are normally wary of humans, feeding or taunting alligators or disturbing their nesting areas changes the rules. Feral pigs run rampant through these woods and can be quite nasty if confronted. Always keep an eye out for a sturdy tree to shimmy up if necessary.

Mound Island Canoe Trail

Rice Creek
Landing

START

Briar
Lake

.8

1.2

Tensaw
Lake

Richardson
Island

1.8

Fisher
Island

2.8

2.9

Aikin Island

Mound
Island

4.0

4.5

5.0

Indian
Mound

N

Last but not least are the man-made hazards, most notably motorboats. Normally the boats can't make it down the narrow, shallow bayous and sloughs of this trip, but there are some open-water river crossings. Farther down Rice Creek, motorboats tend to barrel around the bends and can't see small canoes. The best advice is to keep close to the bank at all times.

That said, let's take a trip to the Mobile–Tensaw River Delta.

The delta encompasses more than 300,000 acres of swampland, river bottom, and marshes and is host to more than 300 species of birds, 70 percent of all Alabama's reptiles, and 40 different species of mammals. Geographically speaking, the delta is the largest drainage basin in the world, with runoffs from four states feeding the Mobile and Tensaw Rivers, which eventually drain into the Gulf of Mexico.

The Bartram Canoe Trail, created by the state to promote safe and ecologically sound exploration of this vast wilderness, was named for William Bartram, a botanist to the queen of England, who first explored and documented this wonderland in 1778. The most amazing part is that the delta remains virtually unchanged from when Bartram first visited.

The paddling part of this trip takes you through beautiful and pristine Southern bayous, with cypress, tupelo, and sweet gum trees adorned in long, flowing Spanish moss. The air is thick with the aroma of such rare plants as the greenfly orchid and buckthorn.

The hike, a 1.4-mile out-and-back, leads to Mound Island, which Native Americans called home as far back as 1500 B.C. Through the efforts of local colleges, eighteen separate mounds have been discovered here, dating back to the Mississippian period. The largest mound, "Mound A," rises 45 feet aboveground and is believed to have been the home of the tribe's aristocracy.

Signs along the trail on Mound Island describe the mounds and their significance. Remember, however, that this is a National Historic Landmark; removing any artifacts is a federal crime.

Besides the alligators and pigs mentioned before, the wildlife of the delta is astounding. When it comes to birds, great and white herons are frequently spotted, as well as the formerly endangered brown pelican; you may even spot a bald eagle. Mammals that roam the delta include bobcat and the largest concentration of Florida black bear in the state.

And there are plenty of insects, especially mosquitoes, which can swarm with ferocity; be prepared. Another intimidating but far from dangerous bug is the golden orb spider. This spider can grow to 3 to 4 inches in length but is normally not aggressive. The biggest problem you will face from this spider is its web, which spans some of the bayous and is so thick that birds can get entangled in it. If you run into one of these webs, it is extremely tough to remove.

The trip may be made into an overnight excursion, when even more of the delta environment can be experienced. The state has erected floating camping platforms to protect the fragile environment—and canoeist/hiker—that are available on a first-come, first-served basis. Find out more by visiting the state's Web site at www.dcnr.al.us.

Miles and Directions

0.0 Start from Rice Creek Landing heading southwest. The Bartram Canoe Trail, or BCT, is marked with diamond-shaped BCT markers on the banks.

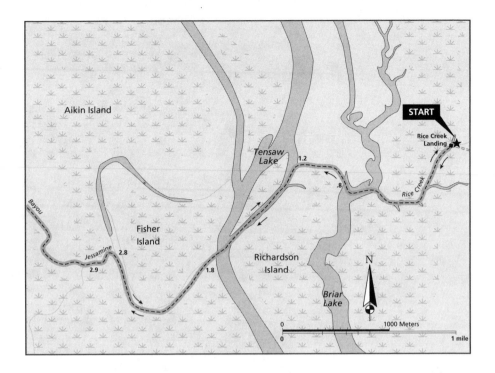

0.8 Paddle 0.1 mile to the west across Briar Lake and into a small bayou. In high water you may notice that this small stream has a Y in the middle of it. Take the left branch.

1.2 Arrive at Tensaw Lake. Paddle across the lake 0.6 mile to the southwest and the opposite bank, where you will reach the southern tip of Larry Island.

1.8 Head into Bayou Jessamine to the southwest. Fisher Island is to your right.

2.8 Although the bayou continues straight, Bayou Jessamine turns to the west. Turn here.

2.9 Pass Little Bayou Jessamine on the left. Continue heading west.

4.0 Come to a T where Bayou Jessamine meets Bottle Creek. Turn left and head southwest.

4.5 As Bottle Creek turns due south, a white sandbar will be on your right. This steep 6-foot bank is Mound Island. Pull your boat up here and *securely* tie it to nearby trees. Alligators have been known to sun in this area. Climb the bank about 30 feet into the woods. The trail will be easily discernable to your left.

5.3 As you approach what is known as "Mound A," the largest mound, signs will tell you the history and significance of the mounds. After exploring, turn around and retrace your steps to the boat and then paddle back the way you came.

10.6 Return to Rice Creek Landing.

Hike Information

Local Information

North Baldwin Chamber of Commerce, 301 McMeans Avenue, Bay Minette 36507; (251) 937-5665; www.northbaldwinchamber.com.

Local Events/Attractions

Stapleton Bluegrass Festival, May and September, 301 McMeans Avenue, Bay Minette 36507; (251) 937-5665. A great weekend of bluegrass music from around the Southeast held twice a year.

Lodging

Windwood Inn of Bay Minette, 610 McMeans Avenue, Bay Minette 36507; (251) 937-8800.

Restaurants

Hurricane Drive-In, 42514 State Highway 225, Bay Minette 36507; (251) 937-1850.
Songwriter's Cafe, 35080 State Highway 59, Bay Minette 36507; (251) 937-4400.

Hike Tours

Tensaw EcoTours, 3809 Battleship Parkway, Spanish Fort 36527; (251) 625-0339. Tour guide: Jeff Evans.

Organizations

Forever Wild, Alabama Department of Conservation/Alabama Division of Wildlife and Freshwater Fisheries, 64 North Union Street, Montgomery 36130; (334) 242-3465; www.dcnr.state.al.us/agfd/forever.html.
Coastal Land Trust, P.O. Box 7414, Mobile 36670; (251) 470-0902.
Alabama Black Bear Alliance, P.O. Box 26, Leroy 36548; www.alawild.org/abba.html.

Other Resources

National Weather Service; South Alabama Marine Forecast Online;
www.srh.noaa.gov/mob/marine.htm.
South Alabama Tidal Information Online;
www.co-ops.nos.noaa.gov/tab2ec4.html#106.

◀ *The banks of the Tensaw River are draped in Spanish moss.*

9 Jeff Friend Trail

A perfect short hike for the entire family through the Bon Secour Wildlife Refuge takes you through pine and magnolia forests, wetlands, and to the beaches of Little Lagoon, where you can swim.

Start: From trailhead on Alabama Highway 180.
Distance: 1-mile loop.
Approximate hiking time: 1 hour.
Difficulty: Easy.
Trail surface: Combination gravel-dirt trail; white sand along lagoon.
Type of hike: Wetlands, marshes, pines, saw palmettos, and the white sand beach of Little Lagoon.
Land status: Bon Secour Wildlife Refuge.
Nearest town: Gulf Shores.
Schedule: Open year-round; however, the entrance gates to the parking area open and close automatically at sunrise and sunset. Refuge headquarter hours are Monday through Friday, 7:00 A.M.–4:00 P.M.

Fees/Permits: There is no fee to hike and swim. Camping and open fires are prohibited.
Maps: USGS maps: Pine Beach. Brochures available free of charge by mail from the Bon Secour Wildlife Refuge office or at refuge headquarters, approximately 0.2 miles past the trail on AL 180; also available at an information board just after the start of the hike. Some brochures are available on-line.
Trail contacts: Bon Secour Wildlife Refuge, 12295 State Highway 180, Gulf Shores 36542; (251) 540-7720; bonsecour.fws.gov.
Other trail users: None.
Canine compatibility: Dogs must be on leash.

Finding the trailhead: Take Alabama Highway 59 south from the Intracoastal Waterway 0.5 mile to the intersection of AL 180 west. This is a right turn and is clearly marked with a large wooden sign identifying area businesses and the wildlife refuge. Follow AL 180 west 5.6 miles. The turn to the trailhead comes up quickly on the left side of the highway, so be watching for it. Drive down the gravel road 0.1 mile to the large parking area. *DeLorme: Alabama Atlas & Gazetteer:* Page 63, F2.

The Hike

If you are looking for a nice trip to the outdoors with the family—nothing too strenuous but with beauty, wildlife, and a little activity for the kids—then the Jeff Friend Trail is perfect. This short, 1-mile loop trail is located in the Bon Secour Wildlife Refuge, just north of the Gulf of Mexico. The refuge comprises 6,700 acres of coastal lands and was established by Congress on June 9, 1980.

The name Bon Secour is very appropriate. It is a French word meaning "safe harbor," and the refuge is the home to more than 370 different species of birds and

There's no mistaking this trailhead.

Jeff
Friend
Wildlife
Trail

Jeff Friend Trail

180

Gazebo
Info Center ■

START

Childress
Point

N

Gulf of Mexico

Paved Road
Maintained Dirt
Unmaintained Dirt
Singletrack Trail
Selected Route

an unbelievably diverse population of other wildlife, including such rare and endangered species as the gopher tortoise, and several types of snakes, including the eastern diamondback rattlesnake and the eastern indigo snake.

A favorite time to hike this trail is in September and October, when fall wildflowers such as red basil bloom into vibrant color and fragrance. Another favorite time for locals is mid-October, when hundreds of Monarch butterflies flock to the area during their yearly migration.

The trail—a combination of a white sand path and packed dirt—takes hikers through thick forests of pines and fragrant magnolias. The path is bordered by row upon row of saw palmetto. The last half of the trail is through a beautiful wetland and swamp. Signs here remind us that this is the natural habitat of the American alligator, and, as we have noted before, while they are naturally wary of humans, don't push your luck.

The main attraction for most visitors is the beach of Little Lagoon. This is a huge saltwater lagoon rimmed with white sand beaches. Swimming is allowed here, so bring a picnic lunch and enjoy. Open fires and camping are not permitted and there are no lifeguards here.

The Jeff Friend Trail arrives at the banks of Little Lagoon.

Note: The parking lot for the Jeff Friend Trail has gates that open automatically at sunrise and close at sunset. Be sure not to get locked in.

Miles and Directions

0.0   Start from the trailhead to your right from the parking area (west). In 100 feet come to a T intersection. An information board describing the refuge, its inhabitants, and brochures will be found here. Turn left and head east. The trail is easily discernable and is marked with brown metal markers with the "hiker" symbol printed on it in white. You will be travel-ing through a thick covering of pines and magnolias and surrounded by countless saw palmettos and a variety of wildflowers.

0.2   As you near the lagoon, the trees thin out and the trail becomes white sand. Through the low shrubs you will see the lagoon to your left.

0.3   Arrive at the beach along Little Lagoon, a saltwater bay. The swimming is excellent here, and it's a wonderful place for a picnic—just remember to pack everything out and *no campfires!*

0.4   Come to a Y. The left fork takes you back to the beach; take the right fork.

0.5   As you reenter the woods, come to a 40-foot-long footbridge across a wetland. Signs remind us that alligators call this area home.

0.6   Come to a T intersection. To the left, a dirt road is marked with a sign that reads NO ENTRY TO THE GENERAL PUBLIC. Turn to the right.

0.7 A dirt road can be seen fairly close to the trail to the north (left). Shortly you will see a sign pointing to your right (east) that reads TRAILHEAD/PARKING. Do not go straight; make this right turn.

0.8 Return to the information board; make a left turn here. In 100 feet you will be back at the trailhead.

Hike Information

Local Information

Gulf Shores Area Chamber of Commerce, 3150 Gulf Shores Parkway, Gulf Shores 36547; (251) 968-6904; www.alagulfcoastchamber.com.

Local Events/Attractions

Frank Brown Songwriter's Festival, second week of November, 3150 Gulf Shores Parkway, Gulf Shores 36547; (251) 968-6904; www.gulf-shores-alabama.net/songwriter-festival.html. This ten-day annual event features hundreds of songwriters performing their songs, some of which became the nation's biggest hits and some new ones as well.

Alabama Gulf Coast Zoo, 1204 Gulf Shores Parkway, Gulf Shores 36542; (251) 968-5731; www.alabamagulfcoastzoo.com.

Lodging

Island Oasis Motel, P.O. Box 4552, Gulf Shores 36547; (251) 968-6561.

Restaurants

A Wok on the Beach, 120 East First Avenue, Gulf Shores 36542; (251) 948-5333.

Gulf Bay Seafood Grill, Corner of Canal and Gulf, Orange Beach 36561; (251) 974-5090.

Other Resources

Alabama Coastal Birding Trail, Alabama Gulf Coast Convention and Visitors Bureau, P.O. Drawer 457, Gulf Shores 36547; (251) 968-7511. This trail was created by the coordinated efforts of volunteers, businesses, and the U.S. Fish and Wildlife Service. Throughout south Alabama, signs along the highways indicate locations for prime bird-watching opportunities (there are fifty sites total). Brochures listing the rare birds and where they can be found are available from the above source.

Honorable Mentions

Gulf Coast

There are plenty of great hikes throughout the Gulf Coast region of Alabama that didn't make the A-list. Although many are shorter in length, fantastic scenery and interesting wildlife are still in store. Pay a visit and let us know what you think. Maybe the hike should be upgraded, or maybe you know of a little-known hike that would make a good honorable mention. Let us know.

A Black Willow Trail–Meaher State Park

Meaher State Park is interesting in that the park itself occupies only 1,347 acres. But in this small park, a wide variety of flora and fauna can be found, as well as beautiful views of Mobile Bay.

Meaher is known as the "Gateway to the Mobile–Tensaw River Delta," the second largest river delta in the country, second only to the Mississippi. Within the delta are American alligators, wood ducks, blue crabs, brown pelicans, osprey, great egrets, and the largest black bear population in the state. As for plant life, pitcher plants and cypress and Tupelo gum trees are in abundance.

The Black Willow Trail is a boardwalk trail that's only 0.5 mile in length, but the views are superb as it hops several islands in the bay. Begin the trip from the west

The boardwalk stretches out into Mobile Bay at Meaher State Park.

end of the parking area, and travel down a gravel road 100 feet to a small gate. The gate can be opened for wheelchair access. Continue 0.1 mile to the start of the boardwalk. From here the boardwalk travels out into the bay and across several small islands. Be sure to check out the plants and birds, but also look over the railing to see the different varieties of fish and shellfish. The trail loops around and returns to the parking area.

The park is open 7:00 A.M.–4:00 P.M. Admission is $1.00 per person, 50 cents for children twelve and younger and senior citizens. There's a large picnic area on the shores of the bay, as well as a fishing pier. Camping is allowed near the picnic areas. Dogs are welcomed, but keep an eye on them. A recent visitor nearly lost his dog to an alligator while playing fetch in the bay.

To get to the park from Mobile, go east on U.S. Highway 90 for 9 miles. The park's chain link gate and a brown MEAHER STATE PARK sign mark the entrance and the ranger station. Turn right onto the paved park road. Travel 0.4 mile past the gate to the picnic area on the right, where there's ample parking. For more information contact the park at (251) 626–5529. *DeLorme: Alabama Atlas & Gazetteer:* Page 62, D5.

B Nature Trails of Gulf State Park

Two and a half miles of sugar white beaches, a 500-acre freshwater lake, bicycling trails, and 4.25 miles of nature trails are in store for visitors to Gulf State Park. Located on the Gulf of Mexico, Gulf State Park is one of Alabama's resort parks, featuring lodging in rustic cabins or at the Beachfront Resort Inn. The park is ideal for families.

All the nature trails within the park loop around the area from the headquarters and are generally 0.3 mile in length. Along the Hurricane Ridge Trail, hikers see the effects of 1979's Hurricane Frederic, plus live oak trees, palmettos, and sawgrass. Muscadine grapes, commonly used for wine in this region, also grow here and provide food for birds, gray fox, and black bears.

The Bear Creek Trail is wheelchair accessible. Along its course you'll see aquatic plants such as water lilies, arrowhead, and pickerelweed. The Bobcat Branch Trail intersects Bear Creek Trail and provides glimpses of marsh rabbits. The longest trail in the park is the 1.5-mile Middle Lake Trail. This trail travels alongside 500-acre freshwater Middle Lake, one of three natural springwater lakes in the park, and takes hikers to the park's Nature Center. The trail crosses a small canal that connects Middle Lake with Lake Shelby. Here small alligators are often seen floating just beneath the surface of the water—remember not to feed them.

The Alligator Marsh Trail and the Holly Trail highlight smaller wildlife found in the park, such as frogs, turtles, lizards, and rabbits.

To get to the park from Gulf Shores, go east on Alabama Highway 180 from Alabama Highway 58 for 0.5 mile. The park headquarters is on the left and is open Monday through Friday 8:00 A.M.–5:00 P.M., 8:00 A.M.–4:00 P.M. weekends and holidays. For park information contact park headquarters at (251) 948–7275. For information about resort lodging, call (800) 544–4853. *DeLorme: Alabama Atlas & Gazetteer:* Page 64, F3.

Ⓒ Beach Loop Trail–Chickasabogue Park

Mobile County owned and operated, Chickasabogue Park is renowned for its mountain bike trails, but it's also known for being a family park with plenty of activities for all ages. In addition to Cemetery Trail (see Hike 4), you'll also want to check out the Beach Loop Trail. Though it's primarily a mountain bike route, the Beach Loop Trail is just as inviting to hikers. The hike begins at a creekside pavilion, where swimming is allowed. Of interest along this 3.0-mile trail is "Woodsky's Wallow," a marsh where turtles, frogs, and lizards can be found throughout the day. The trail also travels for approximately 0.3 mile along the banks of Chickasaw Creek.

The trail intersects a few other smaller trails, such as the Sand Pit Trail, which could make the trip up to 5 miles long. The only real drawback of this trail is its close proximity to Interstate 65 for the majority of the trip. For more information, contact Chickasabogue Park at (251) 574–2267. (See Hike 4 for park directions and additional information.) *DeLorme: Alabama Atlas & Gazetteer:* Page 62, B3.

A water lily–covered pond along the Beach Loop Trail of Chickasabogue Park.

D Roland Cooper State Park

Along the banks of the Alabama River just south of Selma is the 22,000-acre Dannelly Reservoir. Formed by a dam created by the U.S. Army Corps of Engineers, the reservoir has been a popular recreation area for many years. On the banks of the reservoir is Roland Cooper State Park.

The park consists of 236 acres of pine forests and offers vacation cottages, swimming, fishing, boating, camping, and of course hiking. Hikers can take in breathtaking views of the reservoir along the park's 1.5 miles of nature trails.

Each August, a nine-hole golf course here is the site of an annual golf tournament to benefit the American Cancer Society. To get to the park, travel south from Selma on Alabama Highway 41 for 20 miles. To find out more, call (251) 682–4838. *DeLorme: Alabama Atlas & Gazetteer:* Page 50, A3.

Southeast Alabama

The Southeast region of Alabama borders the states of Georgia and Florida. Geographically speaking, this region does not differ greatly from the Gulf Coast region. The hills are a bit higher, at times around 300 feet above sea level, but overall the region is flat coastal plain.

Two distinct features make this region stand out. The first is the Chattahoochee River, which forms the eastern border between Alabama and Georgia. The river begins in northern Georgia at the convergence of several small streams in the Blue Ridge Mountains and gathers steam before flowing into the Gulf of Mexico.

Hikers will encounter the Chattahoochee twice in this guide: first at the Eufaula Wildlife Refuge. Here the U.S. Fish and Wildlife Service has established an 11,184-acre wetland by building levees along the banks of the river. Bird-watchers are in for a real treat here, with more than three-hundred species of birds to be found. In addition, the refuge is home to forty species of animal life. The second stop along the Chattahoochee is at Chattahoochee State Park, located directly on the southeast corner of Alabama at the Alabama/Georgia/Florida state lines.

The second highlight of the Southeast region is the Conecuh National Forest, renowned for its crystal blue spring lakes and its cypress ponds. It is also known for the 20-mile-long Conecuh Trail, an easy weekend hike along ponds and lakes and through dogwood, holly, longleaf pine, magnolia, and cypress forests.

As with the Gulf Coast region, the weather in the Southeast is subtropical, and late summer heat and humidity can make outdoor activities impossible at times. If you're hiking the region during this time, carry plenty of water and of course insect repellent. Much of the hiking in this region is around swamps and marshes, and mosquitoes can be a nuisance. Also like the Gulf Coast region, close proximity to the Gulf of Mexico means that the warm, moist Gulf air can produce brief but very heavy rainfall unexpectedly.

Although this area is not known for getting the full force of hurricanes, its location near the Gulf still requires hikers to keep an eye on the weather during hurricane season (May through November). A hurricane pushing on shore from the Gulf can mean dangerous tornadoes and flooding to these inland areas.

In spring the temperature moderates from the mid 60s to low 70s. The hot, humid summer gives way to great hiking weather in fall and winter. It does get a bit colder in this region than in the Gulf Coast, with temperatures averaging in the 40s in January. Cold snaps of below 30 degrees are more frequent here than in the Gulf Coast region.

10 Open Pond Trail

The Open Pond Trail, at the southern end of Conecuh National Forest, travels around three ponds—Open, Buck's, and Ditch Ponds. The travel is easy, and the scenery is beautiful. The trail begins along the grassy banks of Open Pond, where cypress trees line the banks and an occasional alligator may be seen. As the trail turns into a sandy footpath, it heads into the woods and around Buck's Pond. Finally it follows a dirt Forest Service road as it rounds Ditch Pond, where herons and egrets abound.

Start: From the parking lot at Open Pond Recreation Area.

Distance: 2.1-mile loop.

Approximate hiking time: 1½ hours.

Difficulty: Easy, over low, gentle hillsides.

Trail surface: Dirt roads and sand-covered paths; grassy banks along Open Pond.

Type of hike: Forests of longleaf and slash pine, magnolia, and dogwood; cypress ponds.

Land status: National forest.

Nearest town: Andalusia.

Schedule: Open year-round. The ranger station is open 7:00 A.M.–4:30 P.M. Monday through Friday. Camping is allowed in primitive areas and along some sections of the Conecuh Trail. Camping is restricted during hunting season. Check with the forest rangers before making plans.

Fees/Permits: $2.00 per person day-use, $1.00 for children. Camping at primitive sites is $6.00 per day, $12.00 at improved sites with electricity and water. State freshwater fishing license is required to fish in the ponds and lakes of the forest. A state hunting license is required for hunting.

Maps: USGS map: Wing.

Trail maps—available at the Conecuh National Forest Ranger Station, Andalusia, or by mail for $5.00; call (334) 832-4470. Two brochures, *Carnivorous Plants of Conecuh National Forest* and *Camping in Conecuh National Forest,* are available at no cost.

Trail contacts: Conecuh National Forest, Route 5, Box 157, Andalusia 36420; (334) 222-2555.

National Forestry Supervisor, 2946 Chestnut Street, Montgomery 36101; (334) 832-4470; www.southernregion.fs.fed.us/alabama/conecuh/default.htm.

Other trail users: Motorists and cyclists.

Canine compatibility: Dog friendly—over easy trails; permit and leash required.

Finding the trailhead: From Andalusia take U.S. Highway 29 south for 9.7 miles. Turn left and head south on Alabama Highway 137 for 5 miles. Make a left onto County Road 24 east and travel 0.5 mile. Make a right on Forest Service Road 336A (County Road 28) south. The road comes to a fee station at a Y intersection. Be sure to pay and place the receipt on your dash. Take the left fork. Travel 0.1 mile and turn right. The parking area is the dead end of this road, about 50 feet ahead. *DeLorme: Alabama Atlas & Gazetteer:* Page 58, F5.

The Hike

Conecuh National Forest, established in 1935, lies on the Alabama-Florida border and comprises just under 83,000 acres. Within its boundaries, the forest provides

A beautiful fall sky reflects off Open Pond.

areas for hunting, timber for local lumber companies, oil and gas wells, and grazing land for cattle. Hikers are treated to easy hiking over small, rolling hillsides and through forested land.

As the Open Pond Trail passes the three separate cypress ponds, you'll encounter a big variety of plant and animal life. Dogwood, holly, longleaf pine, magnolia, and cypress line the trail. Animals that may be seen include white-tailed deer, red foxes, bobcats, river otters, and eastern wild turkeys.

Keep an eye out while traveling around the ponds for a wake in the water, like an invisible boat moving across the surface. Look just below the surface, and you may see an American alligator.

In common with many of the hiking areas of the Gulf Coast and Southeast Alabama, Conecuh National Forest offers bird-watchers a wealth of subjects to feast their eyes upon. Wood ducks are the most prominent birds along the trail. Large herons and egrets soar above the ponds, while blue kingfishers, doves, wrens, and goldfinches often dart out of the brush.

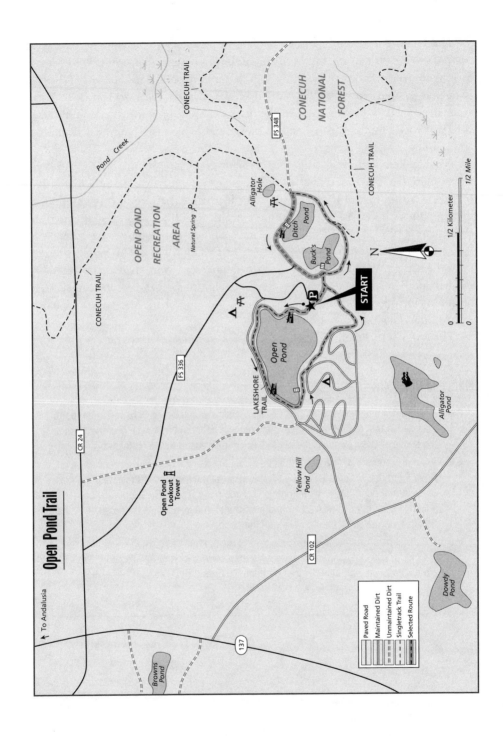

Open Pond Trail

The Open Pond Trail begins by circling its namesake pond, running parallel to a paved service road. At the southern end of the pond, the trail becomes sandy before turning into a dirt footpath as it moves away from the pond. This portion of the trail is carefully designated by white plastic diamond markers every 20 feet or so. Turns are marked by dark black arrows on the markers, pointing in the direction of travel. The trail passes by the Open Pond Campground, which can be crowded summer and hunting season.

Heading away from the campground, the dirt path circles a marsh of Open Pond to the southeast. The trail crosses a footbridge over the marsh and a runoff area. The trail then crosses several feeder creeks until it reaches the second cypress pond on the trip, Buck's Pond. A T-shaped fishing pier juts into Buck's Pond, and many fishermen come here to launch their boats and spend an afternoon on the water.

The trail moves off to the northeast to reach Ditch Pond. This pond is farther from the campground and visited by fewer humans, so your chances are greater to see wildlife. The pond is home to gray and blue herons and white egrets. Their neighbors include swallows, doves, blackbirds, and kingfishers. Also watch for hawks and woodpeckers.

The trail circles Ditch Pond and heads back to Buck's Pond, where it then turns and travels back to the parking area.

Miles and Directions

0.0   Start from the northwest end of the parking lot. A cement sidewalk heads to the northwest for 50 feet toward the bathhouse. Continue past the bathhouse over the grass to the banks of Open Pond. At the pond, turn right and head to the northeast.

0.2   The trail starts a turn to the north as it passes the fee station at the entrance to the Open Pond Recreation Area to the right. At this point the trail is still following the grassy banks of the pond but is running parallel to the paved Forest Service road. About 20 feet ahead, a boat ramp is passed. In another 20 feet, a parking area will be straight ahead. Turn to the west along the north side of the pond.

0.3   The travel begins to curve around the lake to the southwest. Along these banks, keep an eye out for alligators under the surface. Remember not to feed the alligators. Though they are naturally wary of humans, feeding them changes the rules.

0.5 Pass another parking area on the right.

0.6 Come to a T intersection. This is a connector to the Conecuh Trail, marked with white diamond markers like the Conecuh is. Turn left, heading south. Camping areas are to the right.

1.0 A T intersection is reached. A spur of the Conecuh Trail heads off to the right to the north. Go left, continuing south. After crossing a short footbridge, come to a sign reading BUCK'S POND and DITCH POND. Head into the woods to the north.

1.2 Come to an intersection. This is where the Open Pond loop closes. Continue to the north 50 feet to the fishing pier at Buck's Pond. The trail turns to the south and heads around the west bank of the pond. The path is once again grass.

1.4 This is a sharp turn to the north. A Conecuh Trail marker points the direction.

1.5 Reach Ditch Pond on the left side of the trail. Shortly the trail turns to the south; a Conecuh Trail marker with one large arrow points the direction of the turn.

1.6 A side trail intersects the Conecuh Trail to the east. Of the two wooden signs, follow the one to the east that reads BLUE LAKE RECREATION AREA 3 MILES. From here on out, there will be no trail markers. The trail circles around Ditch Pond and comes to a T intersection with a dirt service road. Turn to the left and head west. This sandy road splits into two lanes, as it heads around some thick brush. Take the left lane, which follows the edge of the pond.

1.7 The road passes a picnic area, a dirt boat ramp, and a fishing pier.

1.9 The road forks. Stay right. (**FYI:** The right fork is the dead end of FS 336A.)

2.0 The road reaches the intersection passed earlier (Mile 1.2). Turn right and head to the northwest.

2.1 Come to six wooden poles with yellow paint topping them. This is the end of the trail.

QUICK AND TOO EASY CHICKEN AMANDINE

4 cups water

16 ounces canned chicken

4 cups instant rice

½ teaspoon onion salt

½ teaspoon celery salt

2 teaspoons chopped dried onion

1 package sliced almonds (2¾ ounces)

⅔ cup raisins

Place chicken and water in pot and bring to boil. Add remaining ingredients and return to a boil. Remove from heat. Let stand in pot for 10 minutes. Fluff with fork and serve. Makes three servings.

Hike Information

Local Information

Andalusia Chamber of Commerce, 1208 West Bypass, Andalusia 36420; (334) 222-2030; www.alaweb.com/~chamber/city.html.

Local Events/Attractions

World Domino Championship, Annually mid-July, 1208 West Bypass, Andalusia 36420; (334) 222-5830.

Three Notch Museum, Central Street, Andalusia 36420; (334) 222-2030; www.alaweb.com/~chamber/3notch.html. This superb museum is located in the 1899 Central of Georgia Railroad depot and features photographs, railroad memorabilia, authentic log cabins, and a one-room country store. Admission is free.

Lodging

Days Inn, 1604 Highway 84 East Bypass, Andalusia 36420-3414; (334) 427-0050.

Scottish Inn, Highway 84 East Bypass, Andalusia 36420; (334) 222-7511.

Mama's House, 18284 Andalusia Highway, Andalusia 36028-2619; (334) 496-2154; www.mamashouse.net.

Restaurants

Golden Corral, 1110 North Bypass, Andalusia 36420; (334) 222-7749.

Organizations

Covington County/South Alabama Birding Association, 1040 Fort Dale Road, Greenville 36037; (800) 382-2696; www.alaweb.com/~kenwood/saba/index.html. This organization provides a tour of the birding areas, bogs, and creeks of Conecuh National Forest in late March.

11 Five Runs Loop Trail

A beautiful section of trail takes hikers to Five Runs Creek, a nice swift-flowing creek that flows through the forest into the Yellow River, and Blue Springs Recreation Area. Here the trail comes to Blue Springs, a beautiful, large aqua-blue natural spring pond.

Start: From the parking lot at Open Pond Recreation Area.
Distance: 5.4-mile loop.
Approximate hiking time: 2 hours.
Difficulty: Easy; moderate in one short stretch due to steepness.
Trail surface: Clay, sand, and dirt roads.
Type of hike: Forest of longleaf and slash pine, magnolia, and dogwood; marsh and ponds.
Land status: National forest.
Nearest town: Andalusia.
Schedule: Open year-round. The ranger station is open 7:00 A.M.–4:30 P.M. Monday through Friday. Camping is allowed in primitive areas and along some sections of the Conecuh Trail. Camping is restricted during hunting season. Check with the forest rangers before making plans.
Fees/Permits: $2.00 per person day use, $1.00 for children. Camping at primitive sites is $6.00 per day, $12.00 at improved sites

with electricity and water. A state freshwater fishing license is required to fish in the ponds and lakes of the forest. A state hunting license is required for hunting.
Maps: USGS map: Wing.
Trail maps—available at the Conecuh National Forest Ranger Station, Andalusia, or through their office by mail for $5.00; call (334) 832-4470. Two brochures, *Carnivorous Plants of Conecuh National Forest* and *Camping in Conecuh National Forest,* are available at no cost.
Trail contacts: Conecuh National Forest, Route 5, Box 157, Andalusia 36420; (334) 222-2555.
National Forestry Supervisor, 2946 Chestnut Street, Montgomery 36101; (334) 832-4470; www.southernregion.fs.fed.us/alabama/ conecuh/default.htm.
Other trail users: Equestrians and motorists.
Canine compatibility: Dog friendly—over easy trails; permit and leash required.

Finding the trailhead: From Andalusia take U.S. Highway 29 south for 9.7 miles. Turn left and head south on Alabama Highway 137 for 5 miles. Make a left onto County Road 24 east and travel 0.5 mile. Make a right on Forest Service Road 336A (County Road 28) south. The road comes to a fee station at a Y intersection. Be sure to pay and place the receipt on your dash. Take the left fork. Travel 0.1 mile and turn right. The parking area is the dead end of this road, about 50 feet ahead. *DeLorme: Alabama Atlas & Gazetteer:* Page 58, F5.

The Hike

Many endangered species call the Conecuh National Forest home, including the flattened musk turtle and the red-cockaded woodpecker. This woodpecker was placed on the Endangered Species List in the 1970s due to timber cutting that resulted in rapid disappearance of the bird's habitat. The good news is that cooperation among timber companies, government agencies, and private organizations

Five Runs Trail arrives at its namesake.

seems to be resulting in survival of both the red-cockaded woodpecker and the lumber industry.

This species differs from other woodpeckers in that it is only about 6 inches long, does not sport a red head, and resides in live trees instead of dead or dying ones. These woodpeckers prefer to burrow into live pines, taking advantage of the tree sap, which serves as a deterrent to predators and protection from fire.

The woodpecker got its name during the Civil War. The Confederate army distinguished the rank of its officers with a red feather, known as a cockade, on the side of their hats. The male woodpecker of the species has a small red cockade on the side of its head.

While you're in the Conecuh Forest you can expect to see all sorts of wildlife, such as white-tailed deer, bobwhite quail, and wild turkeys, as well as a variety of waterfowl, including wood ducks, pied-billed grebes, and belted kingfishers.

From the parking lot at Open Pond Recreation Area, the Five Runs Loop Trail travels along the banks of Buck's Pond, Ditch Pond, and Five Runs Creek. The creek, with an average width of 10 feet, is a feeder stream for the Yellow River that eventually joins the Blackwater River, which then flows to the Gulf of Mexico. One

Five Runs Loop Trail

To Andalusia

Browns Pond

Dowdy Pond

Open Pond Lookout Tower

OPEN POND RECREATION AREA

Open Pond

Alligator Pond

Natural Spring

Pond Creek

CONECUH TRAIL

Alligator Hole 4.8

Ditch Pond

Buck's Pond

START

5.1

.6

1.0

3.8

3.4

1.8

FS 348A

CONECUH TRAIL

FS 337

Five Runs Creek

Blue Springs

CONECUH NATIONAL FOREST

N

1 Mile

1 Kilometer

CR 24

137

137

CR 102

FS 336

Paved Road
Maintained Dirt
Unmaintained Dirt
Singletrack Trail
Selected Route

of the best times to visit this area is during spring, when pitcher plants, orchids, and other wildflowers bloom along the banks of the creek and neighboring bogs.

As you make the return loop and start to head away from Five Runs Creek, you will come to Blue Springs—a beautiful 100-foot-wide natural spring pond, aqua blue in color but clear so that you can see the rock formations below the surface. The sandy banks makes it an inviting stop to take a refreshing dip on hot summer days.

One especially interesting pond near the trail is called Alligator Hole. This small pond is out of sight, about 50 feet from the trail, at a point only 0.3 mile from the start of the hike. Alligators are sometimes sighted here. Heed the posted warnings. It is a federal crime punishable by jail time and $5,000 for an individual or $10,000 for a group, to injure or molest an alligator. I'm sure you're thinking the same thing—who in their right mind would molest an alligator. Just DON'T tangle with them!

The only drawback to hiking the Five Runs Loop, and the Conecuh for that matter, is that all trails within the forest use the same white diamond blazes. Several times on this loop trail you will come to intersections where you will see a white diamond blaze in any direction you look. Review the Miles and Directions section carefully for tips on not repeatedly looping back around to the start of the trail or the other side of Open Pond.

Less than half a mile after leaving the trailhead, the loop passes through a wide marsh. The marsh is well worth the time for a visit, especially in spring, to look for some of the amphibians, reptiles, and marsh plants that live here. On the return trip from Five Runs Creek, the trail ascends somewhat steeply for about 0.2 of a mile.

Miles and Directions

0.0 Start from the parking lot by heading to the west on the paved road. In 100 feet, turn to the right (south) and notice the sign reading HIKER'S TRAIL. Follow the footpath to the south into the woods. This is a portion of the Conecuh Trail, identifiable by a white diamond metal marker. For the most part, the trail is wide, sandy, and pine-needle covered.

0.2 Come to an intersection. To the left you will see Buck's Pond and a sign for the pond. Turn left. Go 50 feet to the banks of the pond. At the pond turn right (south), following the blazes. (Ditch Pond will be seen ahead to the left beyond Buck's Pond.)

0.5   Pass Ditch Pond to your left.

0.6   Come to two signs. One points back the way you came and says OPEN POND ½ MILE. The other says BLUE LAKE RECREATION AREA and points to the left and BLUE SPRINGS RECREATION AREA 2½ MILES and points straight ahead (south); go straight.

0.7   The trail briefly narrows and becomes dense with brush that forms tunnels. Several signs will be seen here that read SAFETY ZONE—NO HUNTING.

1.0   Travel straight across a dirt Forest Service road (a HIKER TRAIL sign on the other side indicates reentry into the woods).

1.2   Cross a 10-foot-long wooden bridge over a stream and swamp. Plenty of white-tailed deer will be seen here.

1.5   Come to the top of a ridge. The trees and brush open up here, with scrub pines lining the trail.

1.8   Cross a dirt forest road.

2.3   Cross another dirt forest road.

2.4   Ford a small stream (Pond Creek); in about 50 feet come to the banks of Five Runs Creek. Make a left turn here to the north.

2.5   Cross a small bridge over a runoff stream that feeds the creek. There's a very nice view of the creek here. Shortly, come to two bridges over a wide runoff feeder to the creek. Take either bridge to cross.

2.6   Arrive at Blue Springs. There is a rope swing hanging from a tree. You will be looking at the spring from atop a 15-foot-tall wooden bulkhead. Turn left at the spring and come to a Y. Take the left fork, continuing to follow the white blazes.

2.9   Travel through a wide field used as a parking area. The trail briefly follows a dirt road here before heading back into the woods.

3.4   Cross a dirt forest road.

3.8   Cross another dirt forest road.

4.1   Cross a 30-foot-long wooden bridge over a swamp.

4.3   Come to a sign, WILDLIFE PLOT, that points to a wide field to the right. In 100 yards, pass a closed Forest Service road to the left.

4.5   Cross a small bridge over a runoff area.

4.7   Come to a T intersection. Blazes go either direction. There are two signs here. The first points to the right (north) and reads BLUE POND RECREATION AREA 1¾ MILES; the other points to the left (south) and reads OPEN POND RECREATION AREA ¾ MILE. Turn left.

4.8   Cross a footbridge over a creek and swamp. Alligator Hole is to your right.

4.9   Come to a dirt Forest Service road. Turn right and follow the road for 50 feet. At Ditch Pond, a smaller dirt road Y's to the left. Take this road and travel around the banks of the pond.

5.1   A paved road dead-ends into the trail from the right at the north end of the pond. Continue straight (southwest) on the trail.

5.3   Continue on the trail until you come to a T intersection. Buck's Pond is to the left. Turn right, heading west. Shortly you'll come to five metal pipes spaced a few feet apart. This is the west end of the parking lot and the end of the trip.

Hike Information

Local Information

Andalusia Chamber of Commerce, 1208 West Bypass, Andalusia 36420; (334) 222–2030; www.alaweb.com/~chamber/city.html.

Local Events/Attractions

World Domino Championship, Annually mid-July, 1208 West Bypass, Andalusia 36420; (334) 222–5830.

Three Notch Museum, Central Street, Andalusia 36420; (334) 222–2030; www.alaweb.com/~chamber/3notch.html. This superb museum is located in the 1899 Central of Georgia Railroad depot and features photographs, railroad memorabilia, authentic log cabins, and a one-room country store. Admission is free.

Lodging

Days Inn, 1604 Highway 84 East Bypass, Andalusia 36420-3414; (334) 427–0050.

Scottish Inn, Highway 84 East Bypass, Andalusia 36420; (334) 222–7511.

Mama's House, 18284 Andalusia Highway, Andalusia 36028-2619; (334) 496–2154; www.mamashouse.net.

Restaurants

Golden Corral, 1110 North Bypass, Andalusia 36420; (334) 222–7749.

Organizations

Covington County/South Alabama Birding Association, 1040 Fort Dale Road, Greenville 36037; (800) 382–2696; www.alaweb.com/ ~kenwood/saba/index.html. This organization provides a tour of the birding areas, bogs, and creeks of Conecuh National Forest in late March.

◀ *Blue Springs.*

12 North Loop Trail

This trail is actually the northern loop of the Conecuh Trail (see Hike 13). The loop provides 12 miles of easy walking that can be completed in one day. The path winds in and out of open forests and sections of dense, shady tree cover. You're likely to see plenty of wildlife. Eastern wild turkeys dart from the brush, and hawks sail overhead. Along the loop, away from campgrounds, there's a better chance of seeing an alligator—assuming you want to.

Start: From the trailhead on Alabama Highway 137.
Distance: 12-mile loop.
Approximate hiking time: 6 to 7 hours.
Difficulty: Easy, over flat to gently rolling hills.
Trail surface: Sandy and grass-covered paths.
Type of hike: Forest of magnolia, dogwood, holly, and longleaf pine; cypress ponds.
Land status: National forest.
Nearest town: Andalusia.
Schedule: Open year-round. During hunting season, hunter orange must be worn and camping is restricted to Open Pond Recreational Area. The ranger station is open 7:00 A.M.–4:30 P.M. Monday through Friday.
Fees/Permits: Camping is allowed along the trail following National Forest Service guidelines. Camping is restricted to the Open Pond Recreational Area during hunting season. Camping at either Blue Pond or Open Pond Recreation Area is $6.00 per day at primitive sites, $12.00 at improved sites with electricity and water. State freshwater fishing license is required to fish in the ponds and lakes of the forest.
Maps: USGS map: Carolina.
Trail maps—available at the Conecuh National Forest Ranger Station, Andalusia, or through their office by mail for $5.00; call (334) 832-4470. Two brochures, *Carnivorous Plants of Conecuh National Forest* and *Camping in Conecuh National Forest,* are available at no cost.
Trail contacts: Conecuh National Forest, Route 5, Box 157, Andalusia 36420; (334) 222-2555.
National Forestry Supervisor, 2946 Chestnut Street, Montgomery 36101; (334) 832-4470; www.southernregion.fs.fed.us/alabama/conecuh/default.htm.
Other trail users: Motorists along a portion of dirt road; cyclists along the path.
Canine compatibility: Dog friendly—over easy trails; permit and leash required.

Finding the trailhead: From Andalusia take U.S. Highway 29 south for 9.7 miles. Turn left and head south on Alabama Highway 137 for 4 miles. The parking area and trailhead will be on the left. *DeLorme: Alabama Atlas & Gazetteer:* Page 58, E5.

The Hike

The Conecuh National Forest provides some interesting hiking along the Conecuh Trail, which runs for about 20 miles. The bulk of the Conecuh consists of this one segment, the North Loop Trail.

The trail at the trailhead is wide and open.

There is plenty to take in along this loop. Over its 12-mile length, you will be treated to large cypress ponds and marshes, wide-open spaces, thick forest, sandy trails, and opportunities to see wildlife.

A state highway, AL 137, cuts the loop cleanly in half, seeming to create two distinctly different experiences. To the west, towering longleaf pines and grassland are home to woodpeckers and wild turkeys. The eastern side features a thick dogwood and magnolia forest with two large cypress ponds, blue herons, and, yes, alligators.

Several species of frogs can be seen, and heard, along the North Loop Trail. These include the dusky gopher frog and the pine barren tree frog. The dusky gopher frog came close to being named the official state amphibian but lost out to the red hill salamander.

Because the trail is far removed from campgrounds and picnic areas, you may see foxes and will definitely see white-tailed deer. There is also a good chance of hearing a loud splashing sound as you pass the ponds. That's the sound of alligators retreating to safety.

North Loop Trail

A variety of plant life grows along the banks of the ponds, including the carnivorous pitcher plant, with its long tubular stem and covered cup at the tip. Water lilies blanket the surface of Gum and Nellie Ponds, blooming with large white flowers in spring. Black-eyed Susans, honeysuckle, and blackberry bushes are also plentiful along the route.

Along the eastern half of the trail, the path crosses through several wooden cattle gates, used to keep cattle on designated grazing lands. Some farm fences are attached to the gates with plastic insulators, normally used for electrified fences. For safety, it's best to assume that all such fences are electrified.

Conecuh is the only national forest in the state to allow livestock grazing on the grasses of the forest—for a fee. Through this area, you'll see several areas that have been intentionally burned in recent years. The prescribed burns help increase the supply of grass for the cattle as well as reduce the chances of range wildfires.

Although the trail can readily be hiked in a day, some folks chose to camp out. The Forest Service permits camping but asks that tents be pitched far from the trail. Be careful with fire. The best bet is to use a backpacking stove.

During hunting season, camping in Conecuh National Forest requires written permission of the Forest Service (except at Open Pond Recreation Area). Contact the Conecuh ranger office for dates of hunting seasons. If you hike the forest during hunting season, wear hunter orange.

Miles and Directions

0.0 Start from the AL 137 trailhead by crossing the highway to the west. Here the first of many HIKER TRAIL signs will be seen. These signs are posted on the opposite side of all road crossings to show where the trail crosses. Here the trail heads up a series of four wooden steps that go over a barbed-wire fence surrounding the forest. A sign here reads TRAIL POND 2½ MILES, MOSSY POND 3 MILES. After crossing the stairs, the trail turns to the southwest. This first section is very open, with towering longleaf pines and open, grassy terrain. Trail markers are white plastic diamonds and can be seen up to a half mile away through this area.

0.5 Cross a bridge.

0.9 Cross a dirt road.

1.4 Cross a bridge.

The trail passes some thick pasture land.

1.5 Turn to the south.

1.7 Cross a dirt road.

2.3 Cross a bridge.

2.4 Come to a small marsh and pond on the left. This is Trail Pond. Many blue herons call the ponds along this trail home.

2.5 The trail forks with a dirt road. Take the right fork and continue northwest.

2.7 Cross a dirt road and follow the trail west.

2.8 Cross another dirt road and head west.

2.9 A dirt road merges with the trail from the northeast. Continue to the west; in 50 feet a sign reads ROAD CLOSED MARCH 10–OCTOBER 18. Mossy Pond is on the right.

3.4 Pass a pond on the left and in 300 feet cross dirt Forest Service Road 330D.

3.8 Cross a dirt road.

4.0 Cross a dirt road.

4.1 From here to the crossing of AL 137—3.1 miles away—is a controlled-burn area.

4.3 Come to a trail marker with three arrows pointing to the right. Continue east.

4.5 Come to a trail marker with three arrows pointing to the left. Go left and pass a bench on the right. A lush field is on the right behind a barbed-wire fence.

4.6 Climb the steepest hill on the trip, which isn't that steep. In 100 feet, cross a dirt road.

4.9 Pass a bench on the left and come to a fork. Go right.

5.2 Go right at the trail marker.

5.6 Go right at the trail marker.

6.7	Come to a T intersection with a dirt road. Turn right and follow the road 100 feet to AL 137. After crossing the highway, another short set of stairs crosses over a barbed-wire fence.
7.0	Gum Pond is to the right.
7.1	Come to a T intersection with a dirt road. Turn right. In 100 feet, the trail comes to the edge of the pond. The road turns to the right and dead-ends in 50 feet. Turn left and continue to the northeast along the edge of the pond.
7.2	Pass through a cattle gate. The farm fence is attached to the gate with plastic insulators that make it look as though it might be electrified.
7.3	Cross a dirt road.
8.3	Cross a dirt road. In 50 feet, pass through a cattle gate.
8.4	Pass the banks of Nellie Pond.
8.6	Pass through another cattle gate and cross a dirt road. A sign here reads NELLIE POND and points back in the direction you just traveled and BLUE POND RECREATIONAL AREA 3 MILES.
9.1	Cross a bridge. After crossing, travel 75 feet and cross another bridge over a large marsh.
10.1	Climb a short set of wooden stairs over a barbed-wire fence and cross a dirt road. A sign here reads CONECUH TRAIL.
10.9	Cross a dirt road. (**FYI:** By turning left and heading down the road 30 feet, the Conecuh Trail continues to the south.) A sign on the other side reads HIGHWAY 137 1 MILE, BLUE POND RECREATIONAL AREA ½ MILE. Remember, the Conecuh, North Loop, and connectors all use the white diamond markers. Continue into the woods to the southwest.
11.4	Cross a dirt road.
12.0	Arrive at the trailhead.

Hike Information

Local Information

Andalusia Chamber of Commerce, 1208 West Bypass, Andalusia 36420; (334) 222-2030; www.alaweb.com/~chamber/city.html.

Local Events/Attractions

World Domino Championship, Annually mid-July, 1208 West Bypass, Andalusia 36420; (334) 222-5830.

Three Notch Museum, Central Street, Andalusia 36420; (334) 222-2030; www.alaweb.com/~chamber/3notch.html. This superb museum is located in the 1899 Central of Georgia Railroad depot and features photographs, railroad memorabilia, authentic log cabins, and a one-room country store. Admission is free.

Lodging

Days Inn, 1604 Highway 84 East Bypass, Andalusia 36420-3414; (334) 427-0050.

Scottish Inn, Highway 84 East Bypass, Andalusia 36420; (334) 222-7511.

Mama's House, 18284 Andalusia Highway, Andalusia 36028-2619; (334) 496-2154; www.mamashouse.net.

Restaurants

Golden Corral, 1110 North Bypass, Andalusia 36420; (334) 222-7749.

Organizations

Covington County/South Alabama Birding Association, 1040 Fort Dale Road, Greenville 36037; (800) 382-2696; www.alaweb.com/~kenwood/saba/index.html. This organization provides a tour of the birding areas, bogs, and creeks of Conecuh National Forest in late March.

13 Conecuh Trail

The Conecuh Trail provides the best opportunity for an overnight hike in the Southeast and Gulf Coast regions of Alabama. The trail is just over 20 miles long and travels point-to-point, but connector trails allow for loop trips. The trail passes cypress ponds, and wildlife abounds.

Start: From the trailhead on Alabama Highway 137.
Distance: 19.2-mile point-to-point.
Approximate hiking time: 10–12 hours.
Difficulty: Easy, over Forest Service roads and gentle footpaths.
Trail surface: Sandy and grass-covered paths.
Type of hike: Forests of hickory, dogwood, magnolia, and longleaf pine; cypress ponds.
Land status: National forest.
Nearest town: Andalusia.
Schedule: Open year-round. During hunting season, hunter orange is required to be worn and camping is restricted to Open Pond Recreational Area. The ranger station is open 7:00 A.M.–4:30 P.M. Monday through Friday.
Fees/Permits: Camping is allowed along the trail following National Forest Service guidelines. Camping is restricted to the Open Pond Recreational Area during hunting season. Camping at either Blue Pond or Open Pond Recreation Area is $6.00 per day at primitive

sites, $12.00 at improved sites with electricity and water. A state freshwater fishing license is required to fish in the ponds and lakes of the forest.
Maps: USGS maps: Wing, Carolina. Trail maps—available at the Conecuh National Forest Ranger Station, Andalusia, or through their office by mail for $5.00; call (334) 832-4470. Two brochures, *Carnivorous Plants of Conecuh National Forest* and *Camping in Conecuh National Forest,* are available at no cost.
Trail contacts: Conecuh National Forest, Route 5, Box 157, Andalusia 36420; (334) 222-2555.
National Forestry Supervisor, 2946 Chestnut Street, Montgomery 36101; (334) 832-4470; www.southernregion.fs.fed.us/alabama/conecuh/default.htm.
Other trail users: Cyclists on North Loop.
Canine compatibility: Dog friendly—over easy trails; permit and leash required.

Finding the trailhead: From Andalusia take U.S. Highway 29 south for 9.7 miles. Turn left and head south on AL 137 for 4 miles. The parking area and trailhead will be on the left. *DeLorme: Alabama Atlas & Gazetteer:* Page 58, E5.

Shuttle point

Take US 29 south for 9.7 miles. Turn left and head south on AL 137 for 5 miles. Make a left onto County Road 24 east and travel 0.5 mile. Make a right on Forest Service Road 336A (County Road 28) south. The road comes to a fee station at a Y intersection. Be sure to pay and place the receipt on your dash. Take the left fork. Travel 0.1 mile and turn right. The Open Pond parking area is the dead end of this road, about 50 feet ahead. *DeLorme: Alabama Atlas & Gazetteer:* Page 58, F5.

Conecuh wildflowers will be found everywhere along the trail from early spring to early fall.

The Hike

The North and Central regions of Alabama may have the most challenging hikes in the state, but the Southeast and Gulf Coast weigh in with wild and scenic landscapes. And the wildlife is especially diverse here. The Conecuh Trail, which winds through the Conecuh National Forest, provides an opportunity to take it all in over an easy trail.

Among the wildlife along the Conecuh Trail are white-tailed deer, red foxes, bobcats, and river otters. Eastern wild turkeys are plentiful, often popping out of the brush without warning. And, of course, everyone who comes here wants to see an alligator. Well, the American alligator calls the ponds of Conecuh National Forest home. On the North Loop portion of the trail, listen for the loud splashes of alligators getting out of your way. (Although alligators are naturally wary of humans, don't take chances: Stay a safe distance away.)

The vegetation is as varied as the wildlife. Dogwood, holly, longleaf pine, magnolia, and cypress trees line the trail and ponds. Wildflowers such as black-eyed Susans brighten the landscape. At the ponds, look for the carnivorous pitcher plant. Many of the ponds are covered to overcrowding with water lilies.

The bulk of the Conecuh Trail uses the North Loop Trail (see Hike 12). This 14–mile loop takes you far from campgrounds and recreation areas, past remote cypress ponds and marshes over predominantly sandy trails. Here is the best chance to see wild turkeys, herons, and alligators.

The next part of the Conecuh Trail passes Blue and Open Ponds. Blue Pond is popular for fishing, canoeing, and picnicking and provides a swimming beach. You'll find campsites near Open Pond.

The Conecuh Trail's lower portion, about 5 miles long, is a smaller version of the Five Runs Loop Trail (see Hike 11). The Five Runs Trail uses Forest Service roads, while the Conecuh takes to the woods. This portion travels past three other ponds: Alligator, Ditch, and Buck's.

The trail also hits the banks of Five Runs Creek, a feeder stream for the Yellow River. A good time to hike here is during spring, when wildflowers, pitcher plants, and orchids bloom on the banks of the creek and neighboring bogs. The Conecuh Trail then swings around to end at the bathhouse at Open Pond.

The trail is well blazed with white diamond markers on trees, spaced about 50 feet apart. Keep in mind that some connecting trails that help create loops also use an identical marker, such as the path just to the east of Open Pond (see Hike 10).

Although a fast traveler could easily hike the Conecuh in a single day, the hike is best enjoyed as an overnight trip. You can camp along the way, as long as you keep tents well off the trail itself. Use a backpacking stove to help prevent fires. Camping along any trail in Conecuh National Forest during hunting season requires written permission of the Forest Service (except at Open Pond Recreation Area). The Conecuh ranger office can supply the applicable dates. Plan to wear hunter orange if you hike during hunting season.

Miles and Directions

0.0 Start from the AL 137 trailhead by crossing the highway to the west. Here, the first of many HIKER TRAIL signs will be seen. These signs are posted on the opposite side of all road crossings to show where the trail crosses. Here the trail heads up a series of four wooden steps that go over a barbed-wire fence surrounding the forest. A sign here reads TRAIL POND 2½ MILES, MOSSY POND 3 MILES. After crossing the stairs, the trail turns to the southwest. This first section is very open, with towering longleaf pines and open, grassy terrain. Trail markers are white plastic diamonds and can be seen up to a half mile away through this area.

0.6 Cross a bridge.

1.1 Cross a dirt road.

1.6 Cross a bridge.

1.7 Turn to the south.

2.0 Cross a dirt road.

2.7 Cross a bridge.

2.8 Come to a small marsh and pond on the left. This is Trail Pond. Many blue herons call the ponds along this trail home.

2.9 The trail forks with a dirt road. Take the right fork and continue northwest.

3.1 Cross a dirt road and follow the trail west.

3.2 Cross another dirt road and head west.

3.3 A dirt road merges with the trail from the northeast. Continue to the west; in 50 feet a sign reads ROAD CLOSED MARCH 10–OCTOBER 18. Mossy Pond is on the right.

3.9 Pass a pond on the left and in 300 feet cross dirt Forest Service Road 330D.

4.4 Cross a dirt road.

4.6 Cross a dirt road.

4.7 From here to the crossing of AL 137—3.1 miles away—is a controlled-burn area.

5.0 Come to a trail marker with three arrows pointing to the right. Continue east.

5.2 Come to a trail marker with three arrows pointing to the left. Go left and pass a bench on the right. A lush field is on the right behind a barbed-wire fence.

5.3 Climb the steepest hill on the trip, which isn't that steep. In 100 feet, cross a dirt road.

5.7 Pass a bench on the left and come to a fork. Go right.

6.1 Go right at the trail marker.

6.5 Go right at the trail marker.

7.8 Come to a T intersection with a dirt road. Turn right and follow the road 100 feet to AL 137. After crossing the highway, another short set of stairs crosses over a barbed-wire fence.

8.0 Gum Pond is to the right.

8.1 Come to a T intersection with a dirt road. Turn right. In 100 feet, the trail comes to the edge of the pond. The road turns to the right and dead-ends in 50 feet. Turn left and continue to the northeast along the edge of the pond.

8.4 Pass through a cattle gate. The farm fence is attached to the gate with plastic insulators that make it look as though it might be electrified.

8.5 Cross a dirt road.

8.8 Pass through another cattle gate.

9.0 Cross a bridge.

9.4 Cross a bridge.

9.6 Cross a dirt road. In 50 feet, pass through a cattle gate.

9.7 Pass the banks of Nellie Pond.

9.9 Watch the pond for alligators.

10.0 Pass through another cattle gate and cross a dirt road. A sign here reads NELLIE POND and BLUE POND RECREATIONAL AREA 3 MILES.

10.6 Cross a bridge. After crossing, travel 75 feet and cross another bridge over a large marsh.

11.1 Cross a bridge.

11.8 Climb over a short set of wooden stairs over a barbed-wire fence and cross a dirt road. A sign here reads CONECUH TRAIL.

12.7 Come to a dirt road. (**FYI:** By crossing the road to the southwest, the trail completes the North Loop in 1.3 miles.) Turn left here and head down the road 30 feet. A sign reads CONECUH TRAIL where the trail turns right and heads back into the woods. Don't be confused here! The Conecuh Trail, North Loop Trail, and connectors all use the white diamond markers.

13.0 The trail merges with a dirt road for 50 feet and reenters the woods to the southeast. In 200 feet, the brush and trees thicken as you reach a marshy area. Cross a creek.

13.2 Cross another creek.

13.3 Cross a dirt road and head up a short hillside.

13.5 The trail arrives at the Blue Pond Recreation Area picnic area. In 200 feet, cross Blue Pond Road.

13.6 Cross a creek.

14.0 The trail bottoms out and crosses a creek.

14.2 Cross CR 24.

14.9 Come to a fork in the trail and go left. (**FYI:** The right fork is a connector that forms a loop around Open Pond.)

15.6 Cross a dirt road.

15.7 The trail merges with a dirt road for about 50 feet and then separates.

15.8 Cross a dirt road.

16.2 Cross a dirt road. In 100 feet, the path meets the banks of Five Runs Creek. The trail follows the creek for the next 0.6 mile.

17.3 Cross a dirt road. In 50 feet, cross a creek.

17.6 Cross another creek.

18.2 Reach a T intersection and turn left toward Buck Pond. (**FYI:** The right fork is part of the Open Pond Loop Trail.)

18.9 Come to a fork and go right. (**FYI:** The left fork is used for the Open Pond Loop.) In 200 feet, cross a wooden bridge over a creek that feeds Buck Pond. After crossing, make a right turn and head to the north.

19.2 Arrive at the eastern Open Pond parking area and your shuttle car.

Hike Information

Local Information
Andalusia Chamber of Commerce, 1208 West Bypass, Andalusia 36420; (334) 222-2030; www.alaweb.com/~chamber/city.html.

Local Events/Attractions
World Domino Championship, Annually mid-July, 1208 West Bypass, Andalusia 36420; (334) 222-5830.

Three Notch Museum, Central Street, Andalusia 36420; (334) 222-2030; www.alaweb.com/~chamber/3notch.html. This superb museum is located in the 1899 Central of Georgia Railroad depot and features photographs, railroad memorabilia, authentic log cabins, and a one-room country store. Admission is free.

Lodging
Days Inn, 1604 Highway 84 East Bypass, Andalusia 36420-3414; (334) 427-0050.

Scottish Inn, Highway 84 East Bypass, Andalusia 36420; (334) 222-7511.

Mama's House, 18284 Andalusia Highway, Andalusia 36028-2619; (334) 496-2154; www.mamashouse.net.

Restaurants
Golden Corral, 1110 North Bypass, Andalusia 36420; (334) 222-7749.

Organizations
Covington County/South Alabama Birding Association, 1040 Fort Dale Road, Greenville 36037; (800) 382-2696; www.alaweb.com/~kenwood/saba/index.html. This organization provides a tour of the birding areas, bogs, and creeks of Conecuh National Forest in late March.

14 Chattahoochee Trail

The Chattahoochee Trail provides an enjoyable stroll through the woodlands of the southeastern corner of Alabama. This hike actually combines several trails, providing close-up looks at a variety of plant and animal life. This is excellent flatland hiking for families with small children.

Start: From the northwest end of the parking lot at Chattahoochee State Park ranger station.
Distance: 1.5-mile loop.
Approximate hiking time: 1 hour.
Difficulty: Easy, along flat roads.
Trail surface: Clay and sand roads.
Type of hike: Forest of dogwood, muscadine, oak, and loblolly and slash pine.
Land status: State park.
Nearest town: Dothan.
Schedule: Year-round.
Fees/Permits: $1.00 entrance fee for adults, 50 cents for senior citizens and children 12 and younger. $2.00 fishing freshwater license; $6.50 camping at primitive sites.
Maps: USGS map: Saffold.
Park brochure—available free of charge at one of the honor boxes.
Trail contacts: Chattahoochee State Park, 250 Chattahoochee State Park Road, Gordon 36343; (334) 522-3607.
Other trail users: Equestrians and motorists.
Canine compatibility: Dog friendly—over a level route. Bring water, because it is available only at the lake; leash not required.

Finding the trailhead: From Dothan take U.S. Highway 84 south for 14 miles to Alabama Highway 95. Turn right and travel 9 miles to the Chattahoochee State Park entrance on the left. Turn left between two stonewalls and travel down the dirt road (Upper Road) for 0.3 mile. Come to a fork in the road. Take the right fork (Chattahoochee State Park Road). The ranger station is located just to the right. An honor box for the entrance fee is here. Park and begin the hike here. *DeLorme: Alabama Atlas & Gazetteer:* Page 61, G10.

The Hike

The 600-acre Chattahoochee State Park is one of the smaller parks in the state, though it still provides an excellent hiking experience along trails lined with dogwood, muscadine, and oak. The park is situated close to the Chattahoochee River, which forms the mutual boundaries of Alabama, Georgia, and Florida.

The Civilian Conservation Corps built the facilities at Chattahoochee in the late 1930s. Throughout the park are remnants of CCC occupation, including a chimney where the main dining room was located, bunkhouses, and a star-shaped flagpole. Creeks in the park flow into the Chattahoochee River and eventually into the Gulf of Mexico. The CCC built a stone dam to form a pond on one of these creeks.

The routes that combine to make up the Chattahoochee Trail include the Dogwood Trail (with a dogwood tree marking the start of the path), the CCC Trail

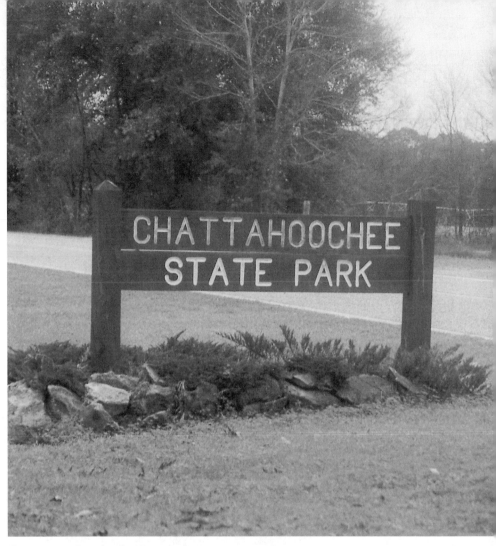

Entrance to Chattahoochee State Park.

(where many camp remains can be found), and the K. O. Smith Trail, named for a former ranger of the park. The Buck Fever, Tortoise, and Scout Trails round out the circuit. Individually, each trail is very short, but they can be combined in many ways to provide hiking variety.

Some of the trails use a fire lane that forms the boundary around the park. Areas outside the lane are privately owned, so visitors should not travel outside the boundary, especially during hunting season. (Hunting is not allowed within the park.)

Many of the trails pass through lightly forested grassy areas. These are excellent places for viewing white-tailed deer and eastern wild turkeys. Other park inhabitants include opossums, foxes, and coyotes. Of particular interest is the gopher tortoise, which is one of only four species of tortoise in the United States. The gopher tortoise is known for burrowing in the sand. Hikers can examine the burrows—and perhaps a tortoise—firsthand along the Tortoise Trail.

The Scout Trail portion of the Chattahoochee Trail takes you to the twenty-five-acre spring-fed pond built by the CCC. There is excellent bass fishing here (a freshwater license and park permit are required). You can also rent a boat. A short walk to the center of the dam provides excellent views of the pond to one side and the marsh and its wildlife on the other.

While in the area, consider visiting the nearby town of Dothan and its revitalized historic district, which includes the Wiregrass Museum of Art, the Dothan Area Botanical Gardens, and the Basketcase Dinner Theater.

Miles and Directions

0.0 Start at the parking lot at the ranger station and head to the northwest about 50 feet, crossing the dirt Upper Road. Come to a wooden sign that reads DOGWOOD TRAIL and the tree that gives the trail its name. Turn left onto the trail and head into the woods. At this point the trail is an abandoned dirt road. Come to a fork—this is the intersection of the CCC and Dogwood Trails. Take the right fork onto the CCC Trail. The CCC Trail is marked with orange ribbons tied to trees. Two ribbons together indicate a turn in the trail, just like painted blazes. The trail meanders through ruins of the old CCC camp.

0.1 The trail runs into a T intersection with Upper Road. Turn to the left on the dirt road. Head up the road .05 mile and turn left on the K. O. Smith Trail.

0.3 Come to a split in the trail that reconnects.

0.4 Come to a T intersection with the Buck Fever Trail and turn right. Small birds such as finches and cardinals dart back and forth along this stretch of the trail through the thickets.

0.5 The trail, still a dirt road, continues south but travels through a marshy area. On damp days this could make travel rather muddy. Scrub and slash pines become more prevalent.

0.6 Reach a T intersection with the Tortoise Trail and turn right. Look carefully for the tracks and burrows of the gopher tortoise along this section. In .05 mile, reach a picnic area at the CCC pond. Continue straight to the banks of the pond. A dirt road is here. Turn left and head down the road.

0.7 Come to a T intersection with another dirt road. Turn left. Travel over the stone dam built by the CCC to form the pond to the north. Head to the sluice at the middle of the dam for excellent views of the pond and the marsh to the north. Turn around here and head back across the dam, retracing the previous path.

0.8 A few feet after you step off the dam, the dirt road veers off to the left. Turn left here. In .05 mile, pass the Tortoise Trail on the right.

1.0 Come to a fork. The main dirt road continues to the northeast and a smaller, unused dirt road (the Scout Trail) heads off into the woods to the north. Take the Scout Trail to the left. Fifty feet into the woods, pass the first of three side roads on your right that lead back to Chattahoochee State Park Road. By the third side road, the main Scout Trail is hard to discern. There are no markings. The trail narrows to a small footpath, and the thick leaves make the trail look more like a deer trail.

The other side of the dam, where a marsh is home to many species of wildlife.

1.4 Encounter another SCOUT TRAIL sign. Reach a T intersection with the clay Chattahoochee State Park Road. Turn right.

1.5 Reach the parking lot at the ranger station.

Hike Information

Local Information

Dothan Area Chamber of Commerce, P.O. Box 638, Dothan 36302-1156; (888) 449-0212; www.dothanalcvb.com.

Local Events/Attractions

National Peanut Festival, early November, 5622 U.S. Highway 231 South, Dothan 36301-7899; (334) 793-4323; www.nationalpeanutfestival.com. Dothan is known as the "Peanut Capital of the World." Each November, the town celebrates with this festival featuring rides, music, plenty of food, and, of course, peanuts.

Landmark Park and Planetarium, Dothan; (334) 794-3452; www.landmarkpark.com. A unique mixture of an 1890s farmstead, wildlife studies, and planetarium in a hundred-acre park.

Army Aviation Museum, Fort Rucker; (334) 598-2508; www.armyavnmuseum.org. View more than 160 military aircraft, including the largest collection of military helicopters in the world. The museum takes visitors from the Wright Brothers' first flight through today's modern military machines. Open Monday through Saturday 9:00 A.M.–4:00 P.M., Sunday noon–4:00 P.M. Admission is free.

Restaurants

Opus Nostrum Dinner Theater, 115 West Church Street, Dothan 36345-1737; (334) 774-8713; www.opusnostrum.com.

15 Wildlife Drive

Wildlife Drive can be driven, but the best viewing is clearly on foot. The waterfowl and wildlife of the area are simply more approachable by foot. The scenery is varied, from areas of hardwood and pine to grasslands and cropland to marshes and the banks of the Chattahoochee River. More than three hundred species of birds and forty species of mammals have been spotted here.

Start: From the parking lot at the Eufaula National Wildlife Refuge ranger station.
Distance: 7-mile loop.
Approximate hiking time: 3½–4 hours.
Difficulty: Easy, due to flat walking.
Trail surface: Gravel road.
Type of hike: Forests of longleaf and slash pine, hickory, and live oak; aquatic plants; farmlands.
Land status: National wildlife refuge.
Nearest town: Eufaula.
Schedule: Open year-round. The trail is shortened to 5 miles in fall and winter to protect wintering birds as they prepare to return to the north. Portions of the trail are closed in fall for hunting. Check with the refuge office for exact dates.

Fees/Permits: No fees for permits required to drive or walk Wildlife Drive.
Maps: USGS maps: Georgetown, Twin Springs. Drive map and interpretive brochure—Available free of charge at the Eufaula National Wildlife Refuge office.
Trail contacts: Eufaula National Wildlife Refuge, 509 Old Highway 165, Eufaula 36027-8105; (334) 687-4065; eufaula.fws.gov. Office is open Monday through Friday 7:00 A.M.–4:30 P.M.
Other trail users: Motorists and cyclists.
Canine compatibility: Not dog friendly due to the wildlife in the refuge; if you do take a dog, a leash is required.

Finding the trailhead: From Eufaula take U.S. Highway 431 north for 7.1 miles. Turn right onto Alabama Highway 285. Travel 1.9 miles and take a right onto Refuge Road. Travel 0.1 mile to a fork in the road. A sign that lists permitted activities separates the forks. Take the right fork and travel 0.2 mile to the ranger station and parking lot. *DeLorme: Alabama Atlas & Gazetteer:* Page 54, B5.

The Hike

The 11,184-acre Eufaula National Wildlife Refuge is situated along the banks of the Chattahoochee River, which forms the border between Alabama and Georgia. Maintained by the U.S. Fish and Wildlife Service, Eufaula Wildlife Refuge is a multifaceted preserve. The refuge oversees 2,200 acres of hardwood and pine forest and 1,100 acres of cultivated land. Farmers produce a variety of crops, such as corn and short-grass hay, within the refuge, providing both income for the farmers and food for wildlife.

Canada geese down for the winter.

Eufaula Wildlife Refuge also has water, and lots of it: more than 4,000 acres of open water along the Chattahoochee River and its feeder creeks, plus more than 3,000 acres of marshland. Wildlife Drive takes you past all of this.

Although Wildlife Drive is touted as the driving tour of the refuge, the best way to experience the multitude of animal and bird life is on foot. The beauty of this hike is to walk quietly through the refuge and come upon a marsh or pond where ducks or Canada geese are going about their daily business or a family of white-tailed deer is foraging for food. Patience and quietness are rewarded with surprising and beautiful encounters.

Short gravel footpaths take you from Wildlife Drive to the two observation platforms within the refuge. Walking along the flat road is easy, and the most difficult part of the trip may be just the distance covered. Most of the areas you'll pass are wetlands, and in summer that could mean mosquitoes—so bring repellent.

The route described here is the summer route. Between November 15 and March 1, portions of the route are closed to protect wintering birds and to allow them to rest before heading north in the spring. During this period Wildlife Drive is shortened to about 5 miles.

From the ranger station, the road heads southeast to the Summer Route road. This road leaves Wildlife Drive and loops around the Upland Impoundment Area and what is called the Goose Pen. These areas are used to grow corn during spring and summer and then are flooded in the fall to provide additional resting areas for wintering waterfowl.

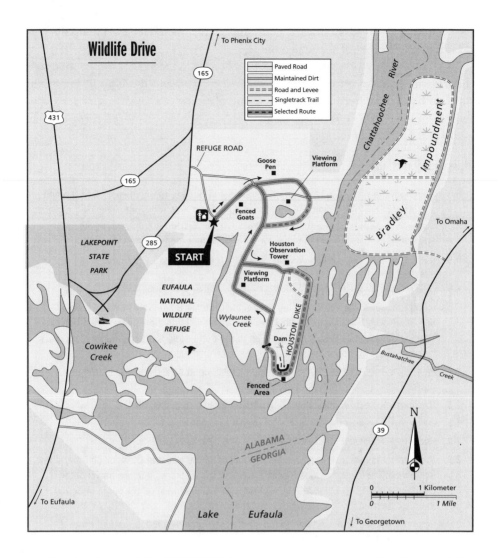

Shortly after rejoining Wildlife Drive, the route turns east and heads toward the Chattahoochee River. Before it gets there, however, you'll reach the Houston Observation Tower. This tower provides views of the Chattahoochee River and surrounding wetlands.

After the tower, the road travels on top of the Houston Dike along the banks of the Chattahoochee. Be on the lookout for white-tailed deer foraging along the river. To the west of the river is the Houston Impoundment Area, a wetland created by the man-made dike. The wetland harbors wood storks, sand cranes, and other shorebirds.

The road circles the Houston Impoundment Area and begins to head back north on the return trip. This section features longleaf pine, slash pine, hickory, and live oak to the west of the road. Bobcats, coyotes, and white-tailed deer are among the animals that call this part of the refuge home.

A second observation deck, the Upland Waterfowl Viewing Platform, rounds out the trip and provides a panoramic view of Goose Pen and the Upland Impoundment wetlands that were circled earlier. The platform is a favorite spot for early-morning bird-watchers. A set of binoculars is mounted at the platform and are available to use free of charge.

Miles and Directions

0.0 Start from the parking lot at the ranger station and head to the northeast. Shortly reach a T intersection. Take a right. Pass a fenced equipment area with goats keeping the grass in shape. Alongside the road are short-grass hay fields, used not only as hay for cattle and horses but also to provide food for the wildlife that roam the refuge.

0.4 Come to a sign that reads WILDLIFE DRIVE. The road makes a right and heads to the southeast.

0.7 Reach a fork. Turn left. (**FYI:** To the right and southwest is the Winter Route, open year-round to visitors. The left fork to the east is the Summer Route. This route is closed between November 15 and March 1 to allow wintering birds the chance to rest before heading back north.) Pass the Goose Pen to the north—this is a large marshy area that's home to many migrating birds.

1.4 Pass another pond area. Flocks of Canada geese, wood ducks, and cranes call this pond home.

1.5 The road intersects Wildlife Drive. Turn left and head to the southeast.

1.7 Come to a fork. Take the left fork and head to the southeast.

2.2 Come to a gravel side road and turn onto it, heading northeast.

2.3 The road turns into a short gravel path and leads to the Houston Observation Tower a few feet ahead. The tower provides excellent views of a marsh area and the banks of the Chattahoochee River. After viewing, turn back to the southwest on the same path and road just traveled.

2.9 Return to Wildlife Drive and turn to the southeast. Come to a fork a few feet down the road and go left.

One of many bird observation decks along Wildlife Drive—this one overlooking the Chattahoochee River.

JUST THE FACTS ... ABOUT ALABAMA

Nickname: Heart of Dixie

Motto: Audemus Jura Nostra Defendere (We Dare Maintain Our Rights)

Entered the Union: December 14, 1819, as the twenty-second state

Capital: Montgomery

Population: 4,464,356

Area: 51,705 square miles, including 938 square miles of water surface

Highest elevation: Cheaha Mountain (2,407 feet)

Lowest elevation: Sea level along the Gulf of Mexico

Temperature-extreme averages:

Birmingham—January 46°F; July 80°F

Mobile—January 52.5°F; July 81.3°F

Annual rainfall averages:

Birmingham—51.86 inches

Mobile—62.23 inches

3.1 The road makes a turn to the south and heads along the banks of the Chattahoochee River along a levee called the Houston Dike. White-tailed deer love this area, and it is not uncommon to see several walking along the banks.

3.4 Pass a dirt road on the right—this is the Winter Route loop.

4.4 Cross a small dam. On the north side is a pond that is part of the Houston Impoundment Area. On the south side is the Chattahoochee River.

4.8 Pass through a gate that marks where the Winter Route ends.

5.3 Come to a fork in the road. Go left. (**FYI:** The right fork heads back to the Houston Observation Tower, this is the Winter Route for Wildlife Drive.)

5.7 Pass a side road. (This is the road taken back at Mile 2.2 that leads to the Houston Observation Tower.)

6.2 Pass the exit road from the Summer Route that was exited at Mile 1.7, and continue to the northeast.

6.6 Pass a side road on the right. (**FYI:** This is a short 0.2-mile out-and-back that travels to the Upland Waterfowl Viewing Platform. This platform—complete with FREE binoculars—overlooks the Upland Impoundment Area.)

6.7 Pass the entrance road of the Summer Route that was taken at Mile 0.7.

7.0 Come to a fork and go left, back to the ranger station parking lot.

Hike Information

Local Information

Eufaula-Barbour County Chamber of Commerce, 102 North Orange Avenue, Eufaula 36027-1620; (800) 524-7529; www.eufaula-barbourchamber.com.

Local Events/Attractions

Annual Eufaula Pilgrimage, first weekend of April, 340 North Eufaula Avenue, Eufaula 36027; (888) EUFAULA; www.eufaulapilgrimage.com. This annual event coincides with the blooming of the azaleas and dogwoods each spring and features tours of historic homes and churches, period costumes from when "Cotton was King," arts and crafts, and an antiques show.

Blue Springs State Park, 2595 Highway 10, Clio 36017-3501; (334) 397-4875. The big attraction at Blue Springs is a crystal-clear springwater swimming hole. There are also picnic areas, playgrounds, tennis courts, and campgrounds.

Tom Mann's Fish World, 1955 North Eufaula Avenue, Eufaula 36027-4609; (334) 687-3655. This attraction features what is billed as the world's largest freshwater aquarium. In addition, a large number of Native American artifacts are on display.

Lodging

Bluff City Inn, 114 North Eufaula Avenue, Eufaula 36027-1550; (334) 687-8203.

Lakepoint State Park Resort, Highway 431 North, Eufaula 36027; (800) 544-5253.

Restaurants

Phil's Bar-B-Que of Eufaula, 430 South Randolph Avenue, Eufaula 36027-2426; (334) 687-3337.

Willy T's Chicken Fingers, 101 State Docks Road, Eufaula 36027; (334) 616-0075.

Other Resources

U.S. Fish and Wildlife Service; www.fws.gov.

Honorable Mentions

Southeast Alabama

Cypress ponds and crystal blue springwater lakes await the hiker in these little-known hikes through Southeast Alabama that didn't make our top list. As with other honorable mention hikes in this book, these treks are typically shorter, but there is plenty of fantastic scenery and interesting wildlife to be seen. Pay a visit and let us know what you think. Maybe a particular hike should be upgraded, or maybe you know of some hidden trip that would make a great honorable mention.

E Frank Jackson State Park

The 2,050-acre Frank Jackson State Park is located in Opp, Alabama, 30 miles north of the Conecuh National Forest and only 10 miles east of Andalusia. In the center of the park is a 1,000-acre stream-fed lake. While there is the standard fare of fishing and swimming here, several very nice nature trails provide excellent hiking, with one located on a small island in the center of the lake.

A foggy morning along the Eufaula Wildlife Refuge Nature Trail.

To get to the park, go east on U.S. Highway 84 from Andalusia for 10 miles to Opp. Once in Opp, head north on U.S. Highway 331 for about 4 miles. The park is on the right. For more information call the park at (334) 493–6988. *DeLorme: Alabama Atlas & Gazetteer:* Page 59, C8.

F Eufaula Wildlife Refuge Nature Trail

As noted in the Wildlife Drive chapter (see Hike 15), the Eufaula Wildlife Refuge along the banks of the Chattahoochee River is a wonderful spot to view the widest variety of wildlife anywhere in the region. In addition to the hike described earlier, you may want to take in the Nature Trail, an out-and-back totaling about 1.5 miles.

This hike begins at the southwest end of the parking lot at the ranger station and is clearly marked with a wooden sign. The path is a dirt road for its entire length. To the left are open fields used to produce hay for livestock. To the right, slash and loblolly pines tower above the trail, with magnolias and oaks intermingled.

Along the trail, many varieties of birds will be seen darting through the trees. In the fields, be sure to watch for white osprey looking for dinner as they follow the tractors cutting the hay.

For more information contact (334) 687–4065. (See Hike 15 for park directions and additional information.) *DeLorme: Alabama Atlas & Gazetteer:* Page 54, B5.

Central Alabama

Central Alabama encompasses the area from just south of Birmingham to Montgomery, the state's capital. The southern boundary of this region, just below Montgomery, is known as the fertile Black Belt, the state's most lucrative cotton-producing area. Geologically, Central Alabama forms the Piedmont Plateau, an area where the Appalachian Mountain Range terminates. The Central region provides the most challenging and most scenic treks you'll find in the state. It's in this region that you'll find the state's highest mountain, Cheaha Mountain, which stands 2,407 feet above sea level.

At Oak Mountain State Park just south of Birmingham, hikers are treated to beautiful panoramas from atop Double Oak Mountain. In Cheaha State Park, the views are more spectacular from atop the tower at the summit of Cheaha. The park is surrounded by the enormous Talladega National Forest, where you'll find the famous Chinnabee Silent Trail. This wonderful trail takes hikers past cascading Cheaha Falls and provides breathtaking views from atop narrow footbridges that traverse gorges leading to the falls. There are several other trails here with equal beauty and challenge, such as the Odum Scout Trail, Skyway Loop, and Nubbin Creek Trail.

One of the more famous trails in the state, the Pinhoti Trail, travels the mountain ridges from the Talladega National Forest through Cheaha State Park for more than 100 miles. The trail recently gained national attention when the White House placed it on the National Millennium Legacy Trail list, giving the trail full protection by the federal government and also funding for its maintenance. In addition, through the efforts of such clubs as the Alabama Appalachian Trail Club and the Alabama Trails Association, the Pinhoti is currently being touted as a new extension to the Appalachian Trail, linking with the AT at Springer Mountain, Georgia.

For history buffs, to the east of Montgomery is Horseshoe Bend National Park. One of only two national park areas in the state, Horseshoe Bend provides a historic hike through this famous battlefield, setting for the decisive 1814 battle between General Andrew Jackson and the local Native Americans. Jackson's victory resulted in the United States' annexation of thousands of acres of land and the tragic displacement of the region's indigenous peoples.

Central Alabama

16 Bartram National Recreational Trail

The Bartram National Recreational Trail in Tuskegee National Forest takes you on an easy jaunt through some nicely varied terrain. You'll stroll over gentle hills for the first half. Then, after crossing Alabama Highway 186, the route makes its way through a dense magnolia forest over marshes as it travels toward Choctafaula Creek.

Start: From the western trailhead on Alabama Highway 29.
Distance: 15-mile out-and-back.
Approximate hiking time: 7–9 hours.
Difficulty: Moderate, due solely to length. Easy hike over gently rolling hills and marshes.
Trail surface: Sand path to the west; dirt path and boardwalks to the east through the marshes.
Type of hike: Longleaf pines, oaks, and dogwoods through the western section; magnolia forest to the east through the bottomlands.
Land status: National forest.
Nearest town: Tuskegee.
Schedule: Open year-round.
Fees/Permits: No fee to hike the trail. Camping is allowed along the trail using the "dispersal method" and by following standard National Forest Service regulations. Camping is allowed only by permit and in designated areas during hunting season (contact the ranger office for dates).
Maps: USGS maps: Tuskegee; Little Texas. Brochures available free of charge at the ranger office. Maps are available at the ranger station for $5.00.
Trail contacts: Tuskegee National Forest, 125 National Forest Road 949, Tuskegee 36083; (334) 727-2652. The ranger office is open Monday through Friday, 7:30 A.M.–5:00 P.M.
Other trail users: Cyclists.
Canine compatibility: Dog friendly—over easy trail, but bring water; leash recommended.

Finding the trailhead: From Tuskegee head north on Interstate 85 to exit 42. Head south on AL 186 for 3 miles to its intersection with U.S. Highway 29 and turn left. Travel 1 mile and turn left onto a short gravel road. Head down the road only 100 feet to the parking area, information sign, and trailhead. *DeLorme: Alabama Atlas & Gazetteer:* Page 46, C5.

The Hike

The Bartram National Recreational Trail was named for William Bartram, son of famed naturalist John Bartram. Born in Philadelphia in 1739, William spent a great deal of his life under the wing of his famous father. Dubbed Botanist Royal by George III, William's father was far and away the most respected botanist in the colonies. In 1765 father and son embarked on an expedition for the king to locate the source of the St. John's River, leading them through Georgia and Florida. Though this would be the elder Bartram's last expedition, it was only the start for William. In 1773 William set out to explore and document the upcountry South, before Europeans would later transform the landscape and disturb the indigenous

A unique tree along the Bartram National Recreational Trail.

cultures. The record of this trip, *Travels through North and South Carolina, Georgia, East and West Florida* (1791), is an American classic and became a tremendous inspiration to such naturalists as Henry David Thoreau and John Muir.

This trail runs along a portion of the route historians believe Bartram traveled. Using land features and historic sites from his journal, historians reconstructed Bartram's path. The western trailhead is believed to be the site of a Native American settlement described in his travel log. Benches along the way share quotes from his observations. The full trail is 8.5 miles long, but a portion of it has been closed indefinitely because of a bridge washout at Choctafaula Creek at the 7.5-mile marker.

The Bartram National Recreational Trail serves up interesting contrasts for a hiker. For its first half, from the western trailhead to the picnic area at the 3.5-mile mark, the trail travels up and down gently rolling hillsides over a sandy footpath. The forest is tall longleaf pine atop low ridges. Through the ravines, the path is lined with oaks, dogwoods, and muscadine.

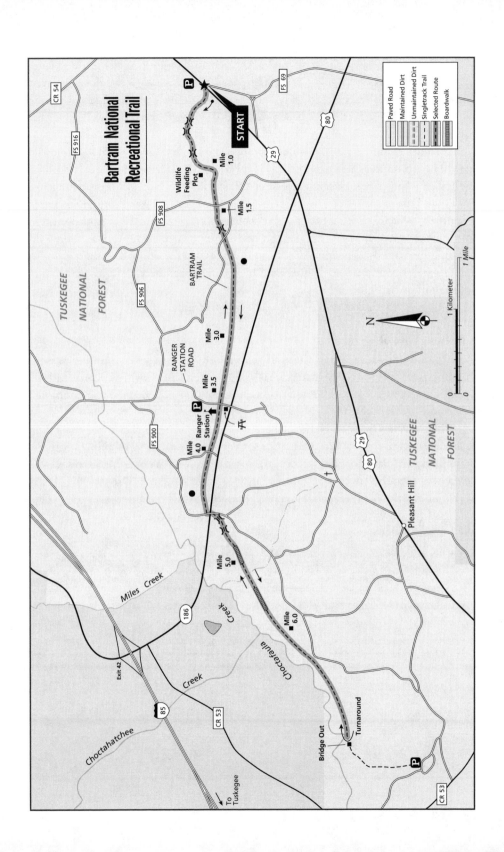

Bartram National Recreational Trail

START

Mile 1.0
Mile 1.5
Mile 3.0
Mile 3.5
Mile 4.0
Mile 5.0
Mile 6.0

Wildlife Feeding Plot

BARTRAM TRAIL

RANGER STATION ROAD

Ranger Station

Turnaround

Bridge Out

TUSKEGEE NATIONAL FOREST

TUSKEGEE NATIONAL FOREST

Pleasant Hill

Miles Creek

Choctafaula Creek

Choctafaula Creek

Choctahatchee Creek

To Tuskegee

Exit 42

CR 54
FS 916
FS 908
FS 906
FS 900
FS 69

CR 53
CR 53

186
85
80
80
29
29

N

1 Kilometer
1 Mile

0
0

| Paved Road |
| Maintained Dirt |
| Unmaintained Dirt |
| Singletrack Trail |
| Selected Route |
| Boardwalk |

After the picnic area, the trail crosses AL 186 and begins to travel through large marshes and near Choctafaula Creek. Many varieties of wildflowers adorn the way, filling the air with fragrance during spring and summer. The area becomes thick with magnolia trees as the trail heads west and southwest over boardwalks and dirt paths.

Expect mosquitoes during some periods of spring, especially in and around the marshes. Also, spring rains can put this section of trail deep in mud. Be aware that the trail is popular with mountain bikers. Of all the trails visited in researching this book, the Bartram was the busiest by far. The trail is fairly open through the western half, so it's easy to see a cyclist approaching. But keep a careful eye out for them in the eastern half through the dense woods. And as nice as the trail is, there's no avoiding the sounds of nearby AL 186 and Wire Road on this half of the route.

The trail is well marked. White paint blazes are spaced between 50 and 100 feet apart. At the road crossings, markers on both sides of the road indicate the trail. Markers show the mileage along the trail every half mile.

Just about any member of the family can hike the Bartram Trail out and back in one day, but camping is allowed if you want to make it an overnight trip. Camping is permitted anywhere along the trail within the forest. During hunting season, camping is restricted to designated areas and requires a permit. If you plan to hike in fall or winter, contact the ranger office for hunting information and additional guidelines.

While in the Tuskegee National Forest, you may want to check out the Tsinia Wildlife Viewing Area, a 125-acre area set aside for the viewing of animals in their natural habitat. Patience and silence are often rewarded with sightings of white-tailed deer, turkeys, hawks, raccoons, or any of a variety of birds. The viewing area is at the intersection of Interstate 80 and Alabama Highway 83.

Miles and Directions

0.0 Start from the western trailhead/parking area off US 29. In 50 feet, come to the first bench. White blazes mark the trail. (**FYI:** Throughout the hike you will see short strips of rubber mat across the trail. These are used to prevent erosion.)

0.1 Come to fork and go right.

Boardwalks cross swampland near the south end of the Bartram National Recreational Trail.

0.3 Cross a footbridge and come to a fork. Take the left fork. In 50 feet, turn to the southwest where the two trails rejoin.

0.6 Come to a fork and go right.

1.3 Come to a dirt road and cross it diagonally—you will see the BARTRAM NATIONAL RECREATION TRAIL sign on the other side.

1.4 Note the firebreaks alongside the trail.

2.1 Come to a fork and go left. The right stem leads to a campsite.

2.3 Come to the road at its "elbow" and head straight across.

2.8 Muscadine can be seen in the trees.

3.7 Come to a T intersection with Ranger Station Road. (**FYI:** If you turn right, the ranger station is 0.5 mile down the road.) Turn left onto the road and travel 50 feet. On the right is a gravel road heading back into the woods. Next to the road is a Bicentennial historic marker telling about William Bartram. Turn right here and head into the woods on this gravel road.

MONTGOMERY: CRADLE OF THE CONFEDERACY

The city of Montgomery holds a very special place in the history of the South. Montgomery was founded in 1817 and quickly became a major cotton market and river port. The capital of Alabama was moved from Tuscaloosa to Montgomery in 1847.

Montgomery earned its distinction as Cradle of the Confederacy in 1861 when seven Southern states seceded from the Union. Jefferson Davis was named President of the Confederate States of America, with Montgomery as its capital. The city held this honor for only six months before the decision was made to move the capital to Richmond, Virginia.

4.4 Come to Forest Service Road 900. Turn left onto the road and walk about 50 feet to AL 186. Cross the highway to the FS 900 sign. Walk up the dirt road another 50 feet and you'll see the white blazes heading into the woods on your right. Reenter the woods.

4.6 Watch for snakes sunning themselves on the boardwalk.

6.3 Come to a dirt road. Turn left and follow the road 100 feet—the white blaze can be seen on the right where you'll reenter the woods.

7.5 Come to the edge of Choctafaula Creek—the bridge that used to cross the creek is now in it. Orange ribbons are tied across the path indicating that this is the end of the road. Turn around and retrace your steps back to the trailhead.

15.0 Arrive back at your vehicle.

Hike Information

Local Information

Tuskegee Area Chamber of Commerce, 121 South Main Street, Tuskegee 36083; (334) 727-6619.

Local Events/Attractions

George Washington Carver Museum, 1200 West Montgomery Road, Tuskegee 36083; (334) 727-3200.

The Oaks, 316 West Glenn Avenue, Tuskegee 36083; (334) 887-8128. Built in 1899 by the students and staff of Tuskegee University, this was the family home of Booker T. Washington.

17 Horseshoe Bend Trail

This easy trek takes you along gravel paths across forested hillsides. The trail uses interpretive exhibits to trace the Battle of Horseshoe Bend, which ended the Creek Indian War in 1814 and started General Andrew Jackson on the road to fame and ultimately the White House.

Start: From the picnic area 0.1 mile from the headquarters of Horseshoe Bend National Military Park.

Distance: 2.8-mile loop.

Approximate hiking time: 2 hours.

Difficulty: Easy, over gently rolling hills.

Trail surface: Gravel.

Type of hike: Rolling, grassy hills; trees including white oak, hickory, chestnut, and dogwood.

Land status: National military park.

Nearest town: Alexander City.

Schedule: Open year-round.

Fees/Permits: No fee required. A donation to support maintenance is requested.

Maps: USGS map: Buttston.

Map and brochures—Available for free at the visitor center.

Trail contacts: Horseshoe Bend National Military Park, 11288 Horseshoe Bend Road, Davidson 36256; (256) 234-7111; www.nps.gov/hobe/index.htm. Open daily 8:00 A.M.–5:00 P.M.; closed December 25.

Other trail users: None.

Canine compatibility: Dog friendly—over easy trail; bring water; leash required.

Finding the trailhead: From Alexander City take Alabama Highway 22 north for 13 miles to Alabama Highway 49. Turn right (south) onto AL 49 and travel 1 mile. The park entrance is on the left, marked with a National Park Service sign. *DeLorme: Alabama Atlas & Gazetteer:* Page 39, D8.

The Hike

Horseshoe Bend National Military Park, just east of Alexander City, is a serene place, far enough out of the way that you'll rarely have to contend with crowds. Operated by the National Park Service, the park is located at a meander, or horseshoe, in the Tallapoosa River. The spit of land within this horseshoe provided the setting for the battle that ended the Creek Indian War (1813–1814).

From the start, as soon as Europeans arrived in the area, they bartered heavily with the Creek Indians, and this trade forged a bond between the two groups. At the end of the American Revolution, this friendship continued as the Creeks and the Americans signed an agreement guaranteeing the Creeks land.

Throughout the years leading up to the war, many of the tribes in the South trusted U.S. Indian Agent Benjamin Hawkins and his programs for social improvement, especially in agriculture. By 1810, the Creek Nation had fractured into two principal camps. The Red Sticks faction was fiercely nationalistic and feared the

A monument commemorating the Battle of Horseshoe Bend and a cannon used in the assault.

expansion of white settlements. In 1813 a group of Red Sticks were told erroneously that war had broken out between the United States and the Creek Nation. The Red Sticks attacked and killed several frontier families.

A Creek tribal council captured and executed those involved in the murders. Red Stick chief Menawa vowed revenge on those connected with the executions and pledged to remove whites from the region. And with that, the Creek War began.

Andrew Jackson was in charge of U.S. forces. Despite outnumbering the Creeks in every battle, his troops could not bring a decisive end to the war. The situation

Horseshoe Bend Trail

Jackson's Reserve Line

To Alexander City

PARK ROAD

START

HORSESHOE BEND NATIONAL MILITARY PARK

Visitor Center

49

Jackson's Line

	Paved Road
	Maintained Dirt
	Unmaintained Dirt
	Singletrack Trail
	Selected Route

NATURE TRAIL

1. The Island

2. Battleground Monument

Creek Battle Line

THE ISLAND

Bean's Line

49

River

5. Newyaucau Village Exhibit

Newyaucau Village Site

Coffee's Line

4. Village Overlook

3. Cherokee Crossing

Tohopeka Village Site

Tallapoosa

N

0   1/4 Kilometer
0   1/4 Mile

became worse in July 1813, when a group of Creeks ambushed a Red Stick ammunition train. The Red Sticks then massacred 250 settlers in Fort Mims, just outside present-day Bay Minette, Alabama.

The war raged for two years, until at last it came to this location—which was called *cholocco litabixee* ("horses flat foot" or "hoof") by the Creeks, Horseshoe Bend by the United States. On the winning side of the battle were 2,000 men from a Tennessee militia and 600 allied Cherokee and Creek Indians. By the end of the battle, 1,000 Red Sticks lay dead.

The end of the war brought a treaty that turned over twenty-one million acres of land to the United States and relocated most of the Creeks to Oklahoma. Those Creeks who fought alongside Jackson were allowed to stay and establish a Poarch Creek Reservation. Formed in 1836, just north of Atmore, today the reservation is home to more than 2,000 Creeks Indians.

The path at Horseshoe Bend Park passes most of the exhibits that describe the battle. At each exhibit, signs describe what to look for. There are benches for rest, and a roof over each exhibit for shade.

Pick up a free brochure from the visitor center before starting out. The brochure describes the exhibits and the battle in more detail. A ten-minute slide show at the visitor center gives an overview of the battle and the park. Admission to the park is free, but a donation is requested to help maintain the facility.

Miles and Directions

0.0 Start from the picnic area located 0.1 mile from the visitor center. Look for the "hiker" emblem and head into the woods here. The trail is basically a gravel path throughout the entire trip. There are no markers except where the trail crosses roads. The hiker emblem will show you where the path reenters the woods.

0.1 The trail tops out and comes to a T intersection in the woods. (This is where the loop later rejoins itself.) Turn right. In 200 feet, reach another T intersection. Turn right and engage a rather steep climb. **Option:** By turning to the left, you can take a short out-and-back walk to an overlook where Andrew Jackson set his battle line.

0.2 From the overlook, look to your right at the series of white poles across the field. These indicate where the huge Upper Creek barricade once stood. Head down the asphalt sidewalk to the parking area in 200 feet, then turn left and head another 100 feet to reenter the woods on the gravel trail.

0.4 Cross Jackson's main line, where the Tennessee Militia/39th U.S. Infantry began the assault.

A view of the Tallapoosa River.

0.5 Come to a fork and go right.

0.6 Reach Exhibit 1, known as the "Island." The view of the Tallapoosa is expansive here, up to 600 feet across. (**FYI:** Straight ahead is a small fifteen-acre island on which Lt. Jesse Bean's Tennessee Militia encamped, preventing the Red Sticks from retreating to this position. To the right is the AL 49 bridge.) Turn around and retrace the trail back to the fork.

0.7 Return to the fork and turn right.

0.9 Reach Exhibit 2. Head down the sidewalk 100 feet to the parking area. Turn left and in 100 feet cross the park road and reenter the woods on a gravel path.

1.4 Cross the park road.

1.5 Topping out on a hill, the trail arrives at the Tohopeka (a Creek word meaning "fort") Village Overlook. Below is where the Red Sticks retreated to a grassy field directly in the curve of the "horseshoe" in hopes of the river protecting them from attack; however, Jackson's tribal allies swarmed across the river to attack this position by a surprise assault.

1.6 Reach Exhibit 4. This was the site of an Upper Creek refugee camp for tribal families to relocate after battles elsewhere in the region.

1.7 Cross the park road.

1.9 Reach Exhibit 5. Across the river stood the Newyaucau Village. The Georgia militia burned the village and forced its inhabitants to join the other fleeing refuges at Tohopeka.

2.7 This is where the loop reconnects with the first section of trail. Turn right.

2.8 Arrive at the picnic area.

Hike Information

Local Information

Alexander City/Lake Martin Chamber of Commerce, 120 Tallapoosa Street, Alexander City 35010; (256) 234–3461; www.alexandercity.org.

Local Events/Attractions

Reenactment of the Battle of Horseshoe Bend, last weekend of March, Horseshoe Bend National Military Park, Davidson; (256) 234–7111.

Lodging

Mistletoe Bough Bed and Breakfast, Anniston; (256) 329–3717; www.bbonline.com/al/mistletoe.

Victoria Inn, 1604 Quintard Avenue, Anniston 36201.

18 Tannehill Historic Trail

The ironworks at Tannehill produced many iron implements used by the Confederate army during the Civil War. The ironworks, which were restored to working condition in 1976, are today the centerpiece of Tannehill Ironworks Historical State Park. The Tannehill Historical Trail travels around the buildings of the ironworks and its furnace. Heading into the woods, the trail encounters the rolling blue–green waters of Roupes Creek and the ruins of the homes of slaves who worked at the ironworks.

Start: From the visitor center parking lot at Tannehill Ironworks Historical State Park.
Distance: 4.2-mile loop.
Approximate hiking time: 2–3 hours.
Difficulty: Easy, over wide paths and roads.
Trail surface: Packed clay and dirt.
Type of hike: Live oak and hickory forest.
Land status: State historical park.
Nearest town: Bessemer.
Schedule: Park and trails open year-round 7:00 A.M.–sunset.
Fees/Permits: $3.00 day-use fee for adults, $2.00 seniors, and $1.00 children six–eleven. Primitive camping is $10.00 per night for up to four people ($3.00 more for each additional person); improved campsites with water and electricity are $16.00 per night.
Maps: USGS maps: McCalla; Halfmile Shoals. Brochures and trail maps available free of charge from the park office.
Trail contacts: Tannehill Ironworks Historical State Park, 12632 Confederate Parkway, McCalla 35111; (205) 477-5711; www.tannehill.org.
Other trail users: Cyclists.
Canine compatibility: Dog friendly, with easy walking; ample water available; leash required.

Finding the trailhead: From Birmingham take Interstate 465 south for 13 miles to exit 1 (Bessemer/McCalla). Turn left onto Eastern Valley Road and travel 7.3 miles. A sign on the left side of the road indicates the turn to Tannehill Park Road. Turn left onto this road and travel 0.5 mile to the park gate. After paying the fee, continue straight for about 100 feet to the visitor center parking lot. *DeLorme: Alabama Atlas & Gazetteer:* Page 30, H3.

The Hike

At one time, Birmingham and its environs rivaled the steel-production machine of Pittsburgh and helped keep the Confederate army supplied with weapons. In 1830 Daniel Hillman came to Alabama from Pennsylvania and built a forge along Roupes Creek. Two years after setting up the operation and well before he had a chance to see the fortune that would be produced by the forge, Hillman died. Local farmer Ninian Tannehill purchased the forge.

Three tall furnaces were constructed on the site with the use of slave laborers who cut the sandstone bricks by hand. By 1862 the ironworks was in full swing,

The Alabama Iron and Steel Museum showcases the Tannehill area's past.

producing pig iron for the Confederacy. On March 31, 1865, the Eighth Iowa Cavalry of the U.S. Army shelled and set fire to the foundry. A few miles up the road, Union troops torched the slave quarters.

A businessman bought the ironworks after the Civil War and tried to rebuild it, but times were bad and the facility was eventually abandoned and soon overgrown.

This brings us to the 1970s, when the state of Alabama and several colleges resurrected the site. Archaeological digs uncovered the old blower house and the main furnace. The furnace was rebuilt and fired up once again. It is now listed on the National Register of Historic Places.

The park encompasses more than 1,500 acres of forest just south of Bessemer. Forty historic structures of the period (1830 to 1870) have been brought in and restored for the public to view. Local craftspeople display the making of quilts, furniture, and pottery at the site between March and November.

Tannehill Historic Trail

Legend	
	Paved Road
	Maintained Dirt
	Unmaintained Dirt
	Singletrack Trail
	Selected Route

Mill Creek

Mill Pond

Miniature Railroad Station

Pioneer Farm

Robert Pavilion

Mill Creek

Furnace Master's Restaurant

Bubbling Springs

Slave Quarters Ruins

OLD BUCKSVILLE STAGE ROAD

Roupes

Gatehouse

START

Visitor Center

SLAVE QUARTERS TRAIL

Amphitheater

Iron & Steel Museum

Furnace Area

Snead House

TANNEHILL IRONWORKS

HISTORICAL

Slave Cemetery

FURNACE TRAIL

STATE PARK

IRON ROAD

Roupes

Creek

N

0   .5 Kilometer
0   .5 Mile

The Tannehill Historic Trail takes you through the major sites of the park. The trail itself is actually a combination of four separate routes: the Furnace Trail, Slave Quarters Trail, Old Bucksville Stage Road, and Iron Road. Along its route, the trail passes through thick oak and dogwood forests and along several creeks, including Roupes Creek, which helped power the furnace.

Beginning at the visitor center, the path first leads to the Alabama Iron and Steel Museum, which exhibits many of the artifacts discovered through the years at the site. The trail also passes Plank Road, which features cabins from the mid to late 1800s.

Farther up the trail is the main attraction, the Tannehill furnace. A long wooden walkway leads to the top, and you are invited to stroll around the furnace as well as the blower house next to it.

As the trail moves into the woods away from the campgrounds, it joins the Slave Quarters Trail. You'll pass the foundations of several of the slave cabins burned by the Union troops during their raid. The trail soon turns onto the Old Bucksville Stage Road, which was the main highway into the area during the mid 1800s.

At the end of the road, a short side trail leads to the slave cemetery. Of the simple, flat rock tombstones that mark the area, only one, that of Josh Stroup, is engraved.

The hike is easy, over well-maintained roads of dirt and clay. After a good rain, however, some of the route can be deep in mud. A $3.00 entry fee covers admission to the craft houses, museum, and furnace. Artifacts are protected by the state of Alabama and cannot be removed. In other words, don't take home a brick from the furnace.

Miles and Directions

0.0 Start from the visitor center parking lot. Head to the southwest over the paved park road. In 100 feet it becomes gravel. Continue to the southwest toward the Iron and Steel Museum at the top of a small hill. Travel down the right side of the museum to the north along the gravel road. Behind the museum, turn left and head west down a series of cement stairs.

0.1 Cross a wide cement dam with a creek flowing over it to the north. It's shallow but requires getting a little wet. Come to a fork and go left—this dirt road is the Furnace Trail.

0.2 Pass a set of cement stairs that lead to Plank Road and the craft cabins next to the trail to the left. Continue to the southeast; the wide white water of Roupes Creek will first be seen to the left.

0.3 Arrive at the furnace and blower house. Continue 300 feet to the southeast until the Snead House is reached (originally built in 1840).

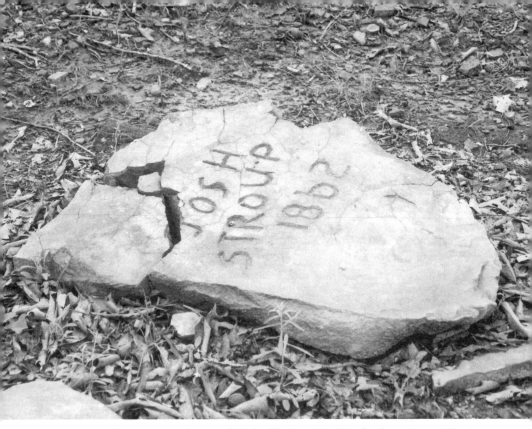

Just prior to the intersection of Iron and Bucksville Stage Roads is the slave cemetery. This is the only engraved tombstone.

0.4 Cross Folsom Bridge, named for former governor "Big Jim" Folsom. The trail turns into gravel Iron Hill Road. (This is where the loop rejoins itself for the return trip.) In just a few feet, the trail forks. Go straight—this is the Slave Quarters Trail. The short trail to the left leads to the creek.

0.5 Pass a small amphitheater to the right used for nature and historical lectures.

0.6 The trail travels between two ridges.

0.8 Come to the SLAVE CABIN SITES CIRCA 1860 sign. Keep an eye out through the next 0.4 mile for the foundations of the cabins.

1.0 A sign on a tree here says, C.S. ARMY QUARTERS FURNACE HELP. Continue for 100 feet and pass a bench on the left and an old road to the right that leads to a second amphitheater.

1.2 The dirt Old Bucksville Stage Road merges from the east (the right). Turn right onto this road.

2.0 Come to a fork and go right. This dirt road is a side trail that leads to the slave cemetery. A sign points the way.

2.2 Reach the cemetery. When you're done, turn around and retrace your route back to the fork.

2.4 Turn right onto Old Bucksville Stage Road.

2.5 Come to a fork and go right, onto Iron Road.

2.6 Come to a fork and go right.

2.9 The red pebbles that line the trail are iron slag.

3.0 **Side trip:** The short 250-foot trail to the left leads to Roupes Creek, a nice place to sit and take in the stream.

3.4 Roupes Creek lies straight ahead.

3.5 Come to a fork and go right. (**FYI:** The left fork is a short grassy trail leading to the creek.) In 200 feet you'll need to rock-hop across a 5-foot-wide creek.

3.6 Roupes Creek and the furnace area are in view to the left.

3.8 Come to a T intersection with the gravel road from the start of the trip. Turn left onto the road. In 100 feet turn to the right and cross the Folsom Bridge once again. Continue straight to the Snead House. Follow the dirt road between the furnace and blower house.

4.0 Pass the cement steps that lead to Plank Road. In 100 feet cross the cement dam again. After crossing, head up the stairs again behind the museum (a cotton gin is on the left). Travel 200 feet; on the other side of the museum, turn to the right and head down the gravel road.

4.2 The gravel road turns to asphalt and returns you to the visitor center.

Hike Information

Local Information

Bessemer Area Chamber of Commerce, 321 Eighteenth Street North, Bessemer 35020-4952; (888) 4-BESSEMER; www.bessemerchamber.com.

Local Events/Attractions

Bessemer Hall of History, 1905 Alabama Avenue, Bessemer 35020-5009; (205) 426-1633. A truly unique museum featuring photos and artifacts from the 1800s, artifacts from the 28th Alabama Infantry from the Civil War, even Adolph Hitler's typewriter. Open Tuesday through Saturday 9:00 A.M.–4:00 P.M. **Annual Civil War Reenactment,** last weekend of May, Tannehill Historic State Park, 12632

Confederate Parkway, McCalla 35111; (205) 477-5711. Each year Union and Confederate troops gather to reenact the battle for the ironworks and to demonstrate life during the 1860s.

Lodging

Sleep Inn, 1259 Greenmor Drive, Bessemer 35023; (205) 424-0000.

Restaurants

Bob Sykes Barbecue, 1724 Ninth Avenue North, Bessemer 35020-3418; (205) 426-1400.

Johnny Ray's Barbecue, 2910 Morgan Road, Bessemer 35022; (205) 424-6639.

19 Blue Trail (South Rim Trail)

Although not the most difficult trail at Oak Mountain State Park, the Blue Trail does have some long, constant climbs for the first 2 miles of the trip up the side of Double Oak Mountain. Once on top, with the help of a little bushwhacking, you will be rewarded with superb views of surrounding mountains and the valley below.

Start: From the North Trailhead at Oak Mountain State Park.
Distance: 6.7-mile point-to-point.
Approximate hiking time: 3–4 hours.
Difficulty: Difficult to easy, with steep, rocky inclines at the start but more level walking the rest of the way.
Trail surface: Dirt path.
Type of hike: Stands of longleaf pines.
Land status: State park.
Nearest town: Birmingham.
Schedule: Open year-round.
Fees/Permits: A day-use permit costs $2.00 per person. Camping is base rate, $13.00 per night.

Maps: USGS maps: Cahaba Heights; Chelsea; Helena.
Brochures and trail maps available at the park office. Maps are 50 cents.
Trail contacts: Oak Mountain State Park, P.O. Box 278, Pelham 35124; (205) 620–2520; (800) ALA–PARK; www.bham.net/oakmtn.
Other trail users: None.
Canine compatibility: Dog friendly. Bring water (sources can be intermittent); leash not required.

Finding the trailhead: From Birmingham take Interstate 65 south for 14 miles to Cahaba Valley Road (exit 246). Take a right onto Cahaba Valley Road (Alabama Highway 119) and travel 2 miles to County Road 33 and turn left. Go 2.5 miles to the park gate. Pay the entrance and camping fees and get general information brochures. Trail maps are available at the park office. Travel 6.5 miles straight ahead, the well-marked parking area will be on the left. This lot offers access to the North Trailhead. *DeLorme: Alabama Atlas & Gazetteer:* Page 31, G6.

Shuttle point
From Birmingham take I–65 south for 14 miles to Cahaba Valley Road (exit 246). Take a right onto Cahaba Valley Road (AL 119) and travel 2 miles to CR 33 and turn left. Go 2.5 miles to the park gate. Travel 2.5 miles and turn right onto Terrace Drive. Travel around the lake and up the winding road 2 miles to the Peavine Falls parking area (the South Trailhead). Be careful driving up the last mile of this dirt road. It winds, and there are steep drop-offs. *DeLorme: Alabama Atlas & Gazetteer:* Page 31, G6.

The Hike

Alabama is blessed with some beautiful country—and the foresight to protect it. While each Alabama state park has something special, none offers more variety than Oak Mountain State Park. Located just fifteen minutes south of Birmingham, Oak

A view of the Pelham Valley far below.

Mountain's offerings run the gamut from a championship eighteen-hole golf course to world-class mountain bike trails to vacation cottages. There is a horse stable where trail rides can be organized and even a demonstration farm. The park is the home of the Alabama Wildlife Rehabilitation Center, which offers shelter and a place of recuperation for injured or orphaned animals.

Oak Mountain's 9,940 acres comprise pine forests and hardwood valleys and mountain ridges that top out at 1,200 feet. This park offers a combination of challenging treks, spectacular views from the top of Double Oak Mountain, and the beauty of Peavine Falls.

Because the park provides such variety and is so close to the state's largest city, it gets a bit crowded in summer—and even more so in the fall when the leaves turn. But the crowding hasn't reached the point where the park has lost any of its appeal to hikers.

The Blue Trail is one of the more popular trails in the park's network because of the views it affords. The trail is 6.7 miles long, from the North Trailhead to the South Trailhead (which is also the Peavine Falls trailhead), but by traveling on connector routes, you can fashion a number of loop trips. The South Trailhead provides access to other trails that would make excellent return routes to the North Trailhead.

Oak Mountain is one of the few state parks to allow overnight camping along trails, and the Blue Trail is the most popular for overnighting. Many backpackers head up to the rocky ridge of Double Oak Mountain—so named because of the

Blue Trail (South Rim Trail)

1 Blue - South Rim Trail
2 Red - Double Oak Trail
3 Orange - Horse Trail
4 White - Shackleford Pt Tr
5 Yellow - Foothills Trail
6 Green - Peavine Trail

CAHABA VALLEY ROAD

CAMPSITE RD

START

JOHN FINDLAY DRIVE

Old Lake

Maggie's Glen

The Turnstile

OAK MOUNTAIN STATE PARK

Brook

Dry

Shackleford Point

SHACKLEFORD GAP

JOHN FINDLAY DRIVE

Double Oak Lake

Park Gate

Wildlife Rehab Center

To 65

TERRACE DRIVE

Peavine Branch

DOUBLE OAK MOUNTAIN

BLUFFS

Lake Gizella

Simmsville

PELHAM VALLEY

N

Lake Warren

SHUTTLE

Peavine Falls

South Trailhead

Paved Road
Maintained Dirt
Unmaintained Dirt
Singletrack Trail
Selected Route

0   1 Kilometer
0   1 Mile

dual mountains running parallel to each other—and spend the night overlooking the valley below. Campers must register at the park office before heading out.

The trail is one of the best maintained in the park, due to efforts of the Vulcan Trail Association. The trail is wide and regularly cleared of fallen trees and overgrowth. Berms and washout-prevention steps are replaced frequently. The trail is marked with blue paint blazes about every 50 yards. At the trailhead, a canister invites hikers to make a contribution to help with trail maintenance.

Since the trail is just slightly lower in elevation than the top of the ridge it follows, you may be wondering what is hiding on the other side of the rock formations to your left. By bushwhacking just a few dozen yards to the outcrops, you can see into the Pelham Valley below. Many hikers prefer to continue bushwhacking along the ridge, which for the most part runs parallel to the Blue Trail. Just remember to tread lightly and leave only footsteps.

The hike culminates in a visit to Peavine Falls. The falls can be heard from a mile away, long before the trail swings around the top of the 65-foot falls and gorge. A short bushwhack to the edge of the gorge provides a spectacular view of the falls, but be very careful; the rocks are slick and the drop is precipitous. Although camping is allowed along the trail, it's prohibited above and below the falls.

Miles and Directions

0.0 Start from the North Trailhead. (**FYI:** Make plans to arrive early; the parking lot tends to fill up rapidly since many of the hiking and biking trails begin here.) Cross John Findley Drive to the southeast and come to a red cattle gate. There is plenty of information here on the trail and other activities. Head through the gate down the gravel road. In a few feet, reach a wooden sign that reads BLUE TRAIL, with an arrow pointing to the left, and YELLOW TRAIL, with an arrow pointing to the right. Turn left and head to the east, slightly uphill.

1.4 Pass the first of two connectors to the Red Trail. (The connector is marked by a red blaze above the Blue Trail blaze.)

1.6 To your right (northwest) is Shackleford Point (1,260 feet), highest point in the park.

1.9 Pass through "the Turnstile," two large boulders on either side of the trail.

2.1 **Side trip:** To the right approximately 50 feet away from the trail is a row of rock outcroppings. A short trip provides some nice views of the second mountain forming Double Oak Mountain. This is a popular spot for backpackers to pitch camp for the night as is evidenced by numerous fire rings.

2.5 Pass the second Red-Blue Connector.

3.2 **Side trip:** You can catch some spectacular views of the Pelham Valley by bushwhacking to the rock outcroppings. Many backpackers choose to hike the rocks, which run parallel to the trail for the next 0.9 mile, instead of the trail. Many hikers also use this area to pitch camp for the night.

3.5 The Blue Trail intersects the Orange Trail Connector.

4.7 Pass the White-Blue Connector just past the creek.

5.2 Pass a short side trail to the right. (**FYI:** It leads down to Peavine Branch and a nice level area, good for camping.) Shortly thereafter the trail forks. Go right. Through the trees to the left is Peavine Falls Gorge.

5.3 Come to a NO CAMPING sign. A few feet more and a short footpath will split left. Follow this approximately 50 feet to the edge of the gorge, where you'll find spectacular views of the gorge and 65-foot Peavine Falls. (**Note:** Be VERY cautious here; the rocks are slick and the drop precipitous.) Along the edge of the gorge is a clay footpath. Turn right and in 40 feet reconnect with the Blue Trail. Continue west on the trail. After crossing Peavine Branch, the White Trail (Shackleford Point Trail) joins the Blue Trail for the remainder of the trip.

6.7 Arrive at the South Trailhead and your shuttle. (**FYI:** At the gravel parking area you'll find maps, trail information, a pavilion with picnic tables, and a phone.)

Hike Information

Local Information

Birmingham Chamber of Commerce, 2027 First Avenue North, Birmingham 35203-4109; (205) 324-2100; www.birminghamchamber.com.

Greater Birmingham Convention and Visitor Bureau, 2200 Ninth Avenue North, Birmingham 35203-1100; (800) 458-8085; www.bcvb.org.

North Shelby Chamber of Commerce, P.O. Box 324, Pelham 35124; (205) 663-4542.

Local Events/Attractions

Alabama Jazz Hall of Fame, 1631 Fourth Avenue North, Birmingham 35203-1903; (205) 254-2731. Jazz legends with ties to Alabama, such as Lionel Hampton and Erskine Hawkins, are enshrined here. The Hall of Fame is opened Tuesday through Saturday 10:00 A.M.–5:00 P.M. and Sunday 1:00–5:00 P.M. Admission is free.

Alabama Sports Hall of Fame, 2150 Richard Arrington Jr., Birmingham 35203-1102; (205) 323-6665; www.alasports.org. Through the years, Alabama has provided the sports world with outstanding athletes, and they are all enshrined here at the Sports Hall of Fame. Artifacts from such notables as Paul "Bear" Bryant, Hank Aaron, Joe Louis, Joe Namath, Satchel Paige, and many more will be found here. The Hall of Fame is open Monday through Saturday 9:00 A.M.–5:00 P.M., Sunday 1:00–5:00 P.M.

Birmingham Barons Baseball, 6000 Stadium Trace Parkway, Birmingham 35244-4508; (205) 988-3200; www.barons.com/main.shtml.

Birmingham Zoo, 2630 Cahaba Road, Birmingham 35223-1106; (205) 879-0408. This is the premier zoo in the state, with more than 900 species of rare and exotic animals in natural outdoor settings. Call ahead for their schedule and admission prices.

Smith-Harrison Museum, 50 Lester Street, Columbiana 35051; (205) 669-4545. This museum has the second largest collection of George and Martha Washington artifacts as well as Robert E. Lee artifacts. The museum is open Monday through Friday 9:00 A.M.–5:00 P.M., with free admission.

Lodging

Mountain Brook Inn, 2800 Highway 280, Mountain Brook 35223; (800) 523-7771.

Oak Mountain State Park, P.O. Box 278, Pelham 35124; (800) ALA-PARK.

Ranchouse Inn, 2125 Seventh Avenue South, Birmingham 35233-3105; (205) 322-0691.

Restaurants

The Original Whistle Stop Cafe (Irondale Café), 1900 First Avenue North, Birmingham 35205; (205) 956-5258. Setting for the novel and movie *Fried Green Tomatoes.*

Cafe Trentuno, Pelham; (205) 664-7887.

Hike Tours

Vulcan Trail Association, Birmingham; (205) 328-6198. The Vulcan Trail Association features a "Second Sunday Walk," when else but the second Sunday of each month at Oak Mountain. The trails they feature are a different theme each month and rated easy. Hikes begin at 1:00 P.M. from the park office.

Organizations

Sierra Club Cahaba, 1330 Twenty-first Way South, Suite 110, Birmingham 35205; (205) 795-2043; www.sierraclub.org/chapters/al/cahaba.html.

Vulcan Trail Association, Birmingham; (205) 328-6198.

Other Resources

Alabama Trails Association, P.O. Box 371162, Birmingham 35237; www.alabamatrailsasso.org.

Bama Environmental News, Birmingham; (205) 226-7739; www.bamanews.com.

Wild Alabama, 11312 Alabama Highway 33, Moulton 35650; (256) 974-7678; www.wildalabama.com.

20 White Trail (Shackleford Point Trail)

A bit more overgrown than other trails at Oak Mountain, the White Trail begins at the park's South Trailhead and passes Peavine Falls. The trail continues along gently flowing Peavine Branch before gradually heading up to the highest perch in the park, Shackleford Point. Here the trail turns rocky as it follows the ridgeline, with views of mountains to either side. The trek includes a visit to Maggie's Glen, a favorite spot for relaxing along the banks of the creek.

Start: From the South Trailhead (Peavine Falls trailhead) at Oak Mountain State Park.
Distance: 6.3-miles point-to-point.
Approximate hiking time: 3–4 hours.
Difficulty: Easy travel along Peavine Branch and a ridge; moderate climbs up a rocky slope.
Trail surface: Dirt; some rocky areas.
Type of hike: Forests of longleaf pine, hickory, white oak, and silver maple; boulder-strewn vistas.
Land status: State park.
Nearest town: Birmingham.
Schedule: Open year-round.
Fees/Permits: A day-use permit costs $2.00 per person. Camping is $13.00 per night, base rate for tent sites with water, $14.00 with water and electricity.
Maps: USGS maps: Cahaba Heights; Chelsea; Helena.
Brochures and trail maps—Available at the park office. Maps are 50 cents.
Trail contacts: Oak Mountain State Park, P.O. Box 278, Pelham 35124; (205) 620-2520; (800) ALA-PARK; www.bham.net/oakmtn.
Other trail users: None.
Canine compatibility: Dog friendly, though could be tough on older or out-of-shape dogs on steeper portions; bring water; leash not required.

Finding the trailhead: From Birmingham take Interstate 65 south for 14 miles to Cahaba Valley Road (exit 246). Take a right onto Cahaba Valley Road (Alabama Highway 119) and travel two miles to County Road 33 and turn left. Go 2.5 miles to the park gate. Travel 2.5 miles and turn right onto Terrace Drive. Travel around the lake and up the winding road 2 miles to the Peavine Falls parking area (the South Trailhead). Be careful driving up the last mile of this dirt road. It winds, and there are steep drop-offs. *DeLorme: Alabama Atlas & Gazetteer:* Page 31, G6.

Shuttle point

From Birmingham take I–65 south for 14 miles to Cahaba Valley Road (exit 246). Take a right onto Cahaba Valley Road (AL 119) and travel 2 miles to CR 33 and turn left. Go 2.5 miles to the park gate. Pay the entrance and camping fees and get general information brochures. Trail maps are available at the park office. Travel 6.5 miles straight ahead; the well-marked parking area will be on the left. This lot offers access to the North Trailhead. *DeLorme: Alabama Atlas & Gazetteer:* Page 31, G6.

Peavine Falls.

Legend:
1. Blue - South Rim Trail
2. Red - Double Oak Trail
3. Orange - Horse Trail
4. White - Shackleford Pt Tr
5. Yellow - Foothills Trail
6. Green - Peavine Trail

White Trail

CAHABA VALLEY ROAD

JOHN FINDLAY DRIVE

CAMPSITE RD

North Trailhead

SHUTTLE

The Turnstile

Old Lake

Maggie's Glen

OAK MOUNTAIN STATE PARK

Brook

Dry

Shackleford Point

SHACKLEFORD GAP

Stone Culvert

JOHN FINDLAY DRIVE

Double Oak Lake

Wildlife Rehab Center

Park Gate

Peavine Branch

Lake Gizella

Simmsville

BLUFFS

DOUBLE OAK MOUNTAIN

To 65

TERRACE DRIVE

Lake Warren

PELHAM VALLEY

START

South Trailhead

Peavine Falls

N

0   1 Kilometer
0   1 Mile

Paved Road
Maintained Dirt
Unmaintained Dirt
Singletrack Trail
Selected Route

The Hike

In Oak Mountain State Park, most trails lead to Peavine Falls. The White Trail, also known as the Shackleford Point Trail, is no exception. The trail begins at the South Trailhead and travels north to the park's aptly named North Trailhead. Several trails interconnect through this area, making a variety of loop hikes possible. One of the more popular hikes is to begin at the North Trailhead, hike south on the Blue Trail (see Hike 19) to the South Trailhead, and then take the White Trail back to the North Trailhead. This combination makes for a nice overnight backpacking trip. Camping is permitted along the trails, but be sure to register at the park office before heading out. Camping is not allowed just below or above Peavine Falls.

The White Trail follows the northern summit of Oak Mountain, which is not really a single mountain but two mountains that run parallel to each other, and together are known as Double Oak Mountain. The Blue Trail follows the ridges of the southern summit.

From its beginning at the South Trailhead, the White Trail is narrow as it winds through heavy brush. As it sets out along the banks of Peavine Branch, it runs rocky through white oaks, hickories, maples, and dogwoods. After passing Peavine Falls, the route opens up and enters some fine stands of longleaf pine.

In spring you're likely to hear the sounds of yellow-billed cuckoos and pine warblers. In summer, thrushes and wrens dart through the brush, and throughout the year, broad-wing and red-shouldered hawks soar overhead. You also may see wild turkeys.

As the trail moves up the ridgeline, the trail becomes more and more rocky. On top of the mountain, the trail follows just below the rocky outcroppings of the ridge, which block many views. A short bushwhack to the ridge reveals outstanding views of Pelham Valley.

The trail eventually makes its way to the top of some bluffs and outcroppings just before heading back down the mountain. Along this section are some excellent spots to just sit down, kick back, watch the hawks overhead, and take in the views from a rock ledge. Along its route, the White Trail reaches the highest spot in the park, Shackleford Point, at an elevation of 1,260 feet.

A couple of miles before the White Trail nears its end at the North Trailhead, it passes through Maggie's Glen, a flat area situated in a hollow. The glen is grassy, with a wide stream running through it. Spring is a favorite time to visit, when white beeches and dogwoods bloom.

A word of praise has to go out to the men and women of the Vulcan Trail Association. Not only do they provide outdoor training programs to the public but they also help with trail maintenance. At each trailhead is a metal container for contributions to help with their efforts.

Miles and Directions

0.0 Start from the north end of the South Trailhead at Peavine Falls. At first the trail is a combination of the Blue (South Rim) and White Trails.

0.2 Come to a fork and go straight (the left fork). **Side trip:** The Blue Trail splits right. It's just a short out-and-back down this trail to the headwaters of Peavine Falls and Peavine Gorge. The next 0.1 mile is a combination of the White and Green (Peavine) Trails.

0.3 The Green Trail splits and heads back to the park office. Continue straight.

A stream crossing along the White Trail.

0.4 Pass a popular campsite for backpackers along the Blue Trail, right next to the stream.

1.0 Pass the White-Blue Connector Trail.

1.2 A short bushwhack to the rocks on the left and a hike along them will afford excellent views of the mountains to the northeast.

1.9 Pass the wide dirt Red Trail, used by mountain bikes. At the top of the hill, pass the Yellow-White Connector Trail, which splits left.

2.6 Come to a T intersection (with several directional signs) and turn left.

3.3 To the right is the parallel mountain that makes up the pair of Double Oak Mountain and where the Blue South Rim Trail can be found.

3.9 The White and Yellow Trails converge and head northeast.

4.4 Reach Maggie's Glen. (**FYI:** This is a very nice, flat glen with a wide stream running through it. It is a scenic and popular site among hikers.) Cross a small footbridge and the Yellow and White Trails split. Continue on the White Trail.

6.3 Arrive at the gate of the North Trailhead.

Hike Information

Local Information

Birmingham Chamber of Commerce, 2027 First Avenue North, Birmingham 35203-4109; (205) 324-2100; www.birminghamchamber. com.

Greater Birmingham Convention and Visitor Bureau, 2200 Ninth Avenue North, Birmingham 35203-1100; (800) 458-8085; www.bcvb.org.

North Shelby Chamber of Commerce, P.O. Box 324, Pelham 35124; (205) 663-4542.

Local Events/Attractions

Alabama Jazz Hall of Fame, 1631 Fourth Avenue North, Birmingham 35203-1903; (205) 254-2731. Jazz legends with ties to Alabama, such as Lionel Hampton and Erskine Hawkins, are enshrined here. The Hall of Fame is opened Tuesday through Saturday 10:00 A.M.–5:00 P.M. and Sunday 1:00–5:00 P.M. Admission is free.

Alabama Sports Hall of Fame, 2150 Richard Arrington Jr., Birmingham 35203-1102; (205) 323-6665; www.alasports.org. Through the years, Alabama has provided the sports world with outstanding athletes, and they are all enshrined here at the Sports Hall of Fame. Artifacts from such notables as Paul "Bear" Bryant, Hank Aaron, Joe Louis, Joe Namath, Satchel Paige, and many more will be found here. The Hall of Fame is open Monday through Saturday 9:00 A.M.–5:00 P.M., Sunday 1:00–5:00 P.M.

Birmingham Barons Baseball, 6000 Stadium Trace Parkway, Birmingham 35244-4508; (205) 988-3200; www.barons.com/ main.shtml.

Birmingham Zoo, 2630 Cahaba Road, Birmingham 35223-1106; (205) 879-0408. This is the premier zoo in the state, with more than 900 species of rare and exotic animals in natural outdoor settings. Call ahead for their schedule and admission prices.

Smith-Harrison Museum, 50 Lester Street, Columbiana 35051; (205) 669-4545. This museum has the second largest collection of George and Martha Washington artifacts as well as Robert E. Lee artifacts. The museum is open Monday through Friday 9:00 A.M.–5:00 P.M., with free admission.

Lodging

Mountain Brook Inn, 2800 Highway 280, Mountain Brook 35223; (800) 523-7771.

Oak Mountain State Park, P.O. Box 278, Pelham 35124; (800) ALA-PARK.

Ranchouse Inn, 2125 Seventh Avenue South, Birmingham 35233-3105; (205) 322-0691.

Restaurants

The Original Whistle Stop Cafe (Irondale Café), 1900 First Avenue North, Birmingham 35205; (205) 956-5258. Setting for the novel and movie *Fried Green Tomatoes.*

Cafe Trentuno, Pelham; (205) 664-7887.

Organizations

Sierra Club Cahaba, 1330 Twenty-first Way South, Suite 110, Birmingham 35205; (205) 795-2043; www.sierraclub.org/chapters/al/ cahaba.html.

Vulcan Trail Association, Birmingham; (205) 328-6198.

Other Resources

Alabama Trails Association, P.O. Box 371162, Birmingham 35237; www.alabamatrailsasso. org.

Bama Environmental News, Birmingham; (205) 226-7739; www.bamanews.com.

Wild Alabama, 11312 Alabama Highway 33, Moulton 35650; (256) 974-7678; www.wildalabama.com.

21 Yellow Trail (Foothills Trail)

The Yellow Trail travels the lower foothills of Oak Mountain State Park through concentrated tree growth that provides a welcoming canopy of shade during hot weather. On the ridges above, longleaf pines tower over the trail. During the hike, watch for large turtles in some of the creeks you'll cross. One of the most popular stopping points along the route is Maggie's Glen.

Start: From the North Trailhead at Oak Mountain State Park.
Distance: 8.2-mile point-to-point.
Approximate hiking time: 5-6 hours.
Difficulty: Moderate to difficult due to travel up steep ridges; easy to moderate for the last half of the trip.
Trail surface: Dirt path.
Type of hike: Thick forest of magnolia, hickory, black walnut, and oak; stands of longleaf pines; many stream crossings.
Land status: State park.
Nearest town: Birmingham.
Schedule: Open year-round.

Fees/Permits: A day-use permit costs $2.00 per person. Camping is $13.00 per night base rate.
Maps: USGS maps: Cahaba Heights; Chelsea; Helena.
Brochures—General park information available free at the main gate. Trail maps are available for 50 cents at the park office.
Trail contacts: Oak Mountain State Park, P.O. Box 278, Pelham 35124; (205) 620-2520; (800) ALA-PARK; www.bham.net/oakmtn.
Other trail users: None.
Canine compatibility: Dog friendly, but can be tough on the initial steep parts; water available through most of the hike; leash not required.

Finding the trailhead: From Birmingham take Interstate 65 south for 14 miles to Cahaba Valley Road (exit 246). Take a right onto Cahaba Valley Road (Alabama Highway 119) and travel 2 miles to County Road 33 and turn left. Go 2.5 miles to the park gate. Pay the entrance and camping fees and get general information brochures. Trail maps are available at the park office. Travel 6.5 miles straight ahead; the well-marked parking area will be on the left. This lot offers access to the North Trailhead. *DeLorme: Alabama Atlas & Gazetteer:* Page 31, G6.

Shuttle point

From Birmingham take I-65 south for 14 miles to Cahaba Valley Road (exit 246). Take a right onto Cahaba Valley Road (AL 119) and travel 2 miles to CR 33 and turn left. Go 2.5 miles to the park gate. Continue on 2 miles and make a right turn onto Terrace Drive. Head southwest 1 mile on Terrace Drive, passing the park office. The parking area will be on the right. *DeLorme: Alabama Atlas & Gazetteer:* Page 31, G6.

The Hike

Quiet solitude. That's what's in store for you along the Yellow Trail at Oak Mountain State Park. This trail, in the middle of one of the most popular state parks in Alabama, sees little traffic except near its two ends.

The Yellow Trail, also known as the Foothills Trail, travels up and down the northern ridges of Double Oak Mountain. Unlike the higher White and Blue Trails,

The Yellow Trail crosses several streams as it meanders northwest.

the Yellow Trail reaches a maximum elevation at only 820 feet. The trail commences from the North Trailhead, where several other routes are accessed, including the Red Bike Trail. The parking area isn't that large here, so arrive early to get a parking spot.

To judge by park maps, the trail looks as though it should be fairly easy, but the first half of this trip has some difficulty. The trail weaves its way steeply up the foothills of Double Oak Mountain, reaching the 820-foot high point in less than a mile. From there it's a steep descent into Maggie's Glen. Then things level out and the walking becomes easier.

The trail passes through a dense forest of magnolia, oak, hickory, and black walnut. The forest blocks views of the surrounding mountains, but the shade is welcome on hot, humid days. At the points where the Yellow Trail crosses one of the fast-flowing creeks over a wooden footbridge, look in pools at the creek to see if you can spot large turtles.

Of the two areas along the trail that get a fair amount of foot traffic, Maggie's Glen is the first you come to, about a mile from the North Trailhead. Many people come in spring to this grassy area with its lovely stream in order to view the white beeches and dogwoods in bloom. The second popular area is about a mile from the southern end of the trail, where it crosses the Wildlife and Treetop Trails. These short interpretive trails make their way down the hillside from the Alabama Wildlife Rehabilitation Center.

You'll cross several other routes on your hike down the Yellow Trail—including the Orange (Horseshoe), Red, and Green Trails—plus encounter a connector path to the White Trail. These trails can be combined into several loop hikes and some

Map Legend:
1. Blue - South Rim Trail
2. Red - Double Oak Trail
3. Orange - Horse Trail
4. White - Shackleford Pt Tr
5. Yellow - Foothills Trail
6. Green - Peavine Trail

CAHABA VALLEY ROAD

CAMPSITE RD

North Trailhead

START

JOHN FINDLAY DRIVE

OAK MOUNTAIN STATE PARK

Old Lake

Maggie's Glen

The Turnstile

Shackleford Point ▲

SHACKLEFORD GAP

Brook

Dry

JOHN FINDLAY DRIVE

Double Oak Lake

Peavine Branch

BLUFFS

DOUBLE OAK MOUNTAIN

Lake Gizella

Simmsville

SHUTTLE

Park Gate

Wildlife Rehab Center

To 65

TERRACE DRIVE

Lake Warren

PELHAM VALLEY

Peavine Falls

South Trailhead

Legend:
- Paved Road
- Maintained Dirt
- Unmaintained Dirt
- Singletrack Trail
- Selected Route

0   1 Kilometer
0   1 Mile

---

excellent overnight trips. Be forewarned that if you plan to use the White-Yellow Connector Trail at the 4.5-mile mark, the climb to the White Tail consists of difficult travel straight up the side and over the bluffs of Double Oak Mountain.

Once again we need to mention the work of the Vulcan Trail Association, which helps maintain the trails at Oak Mountain. The Yellow Trail is kept in good shape. Downed trees are cleared away quickly, and trail markers are clear and frequent. The association sponsors excursions in the park on the second Sunday of each month. The public is invited to join these guided hikes, which usually start just after lunch.

Miles and Directions

0.0   Start from the North Trailhead. (**FYI:** Make plans to arrive early; the parking lot tends to fill up rapidly since many of the hiking and biking trails begin here.) Cross John Findley Drive to the southeast and come to a red cattle gate. There is plenty of information here on the trail and other activities. Head through the gate down the gravel road. In a few feet, reach a wooden sign that reads BLUE TRAIL with an arrow pointing to the left, and YELLOW TRAIL, with an arrow pointing to the right. Turn right and head west on the gravel road leading into the woods.

1.1   Arrive at Maggie's Glen. (**FYI:** This is a very nice, flat glen with a wide stream running through it. It is a scenic and popular site among hikers.) Cross a small footbridge; the Yellow and White Trails merge for the next 0.1 mile.

1.2 Come to a fork. Take the right fork. (The White Trail forks left.)

2.0 This is a finger of Old Lake, a small lake created by a narrow dam located at Mile 2.5.

2.5 Pass Picnic Area Number Two. This quiet, secluded area with picnic tables makes for a nice place to take a break.

3.0 Cross a footbridge.

3.1 Cross a footbridge and then the Red Trail.

4.2 Cross the Red Trail a second time. To the left, the ridge of Double Oak Mountain can be seen.

4.4 Cross a footbridge. In 100 feet come to a dirt road. A sign here reads MAIN ROAD. Turn left (to the east) on the road and travel 50 feet. Cross a short bridge; in another 50 feet, a sign will point to the YELLOW TRAIL. Turn right here and return to the woods. (**FYI:** Just past this sign, about 30 feet farther on the road, is another sign pointing the way to the Yellow-White Connector Trail.)

4.5 Cross a footbridge.

6.0 The Orange (Horseshoe) Trail merges briefly with the Yellow Trail as they head to the southwest.

6.1 Come to a fork and go right. (The Orange Trail branches left.)

6.7 Cross the Orange Trail again.

6.8 Cross the Orange Trail again. In 100 feet cross a park road—two yellow lines are painted on the road to show the direction. Reenter the woods after crossing a 3-foot-wide cement culvert.

6.9 Cross the Orange Trail again.

7.0 Come to a fork where the Wildlife Center Trail merges with the Yellow Trail. Go right.

7.1 Come to a sign that reads YELLOW TRAIL (points back the way you came), WILDLIFE CENTER (points left), and TREETOP TRAIL (points right). Continue straight. In 100 feet come to a signed intersection. The sign reads WILDLIFE TRAIL (points to the south) and YELLOW TRAIL (points to the west). Turn south. In just a few feet cross the Orange Trail again.

7.3 Cross the Green Trail. In 100 feet the Orange Trail merges with the Yellow Trail for the next 0.4 mile.

7.7 A line of rocks across the trail indicates that both the Yellow and Horseshoe Trails are turning. There is a path that does continue straight, but make sure to make this turn.

7.8 Come to a tree with an Orange (Horseshoe) Trail marker on it. Follow the Yellow Trail as it leaves the Orange Trail and heads into a ravine.

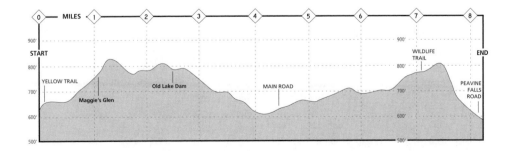

8.2 Come to an intersection with a dirt road. A YELLOW TRAIL sign is here. This is Peavine Falls Road. Turn right onto the road. In 100 feet come to a cattle gate used to shut down the road at night. The road becomes asphalt and is now Terrace Drive. Continue another 100 feet and arrive at the South Trailhead parking lot.

Hike Information

Local Information

Birmingham Chamber of Commerce, 2027 First Avenue North, Birmingham 35203-4109; (205) 324-2100; www.birmingham chamber.com.

Greater Birmingham Convention and Visitor Bureau, 2200 Ninth Avenue North, Birmingham 35203-1100; (800) 458-8085; www.bcvb.org.

North Shelby Chamber of Commerce, P.O. Box 324, Pelham 35124; (205) 663-4542.

Local Events/Attractions

Alabama Jazz Hall of Fame, 1631 Fourth Avenue North, Birmingham 35203-1903; (205) 254-2731. Jazz legends with ties to Alabama, such as Lionel Hampton and Erskine Hawkins, are enshrined here. The Hall of Fame is opened Tuesday through Saturday 10:00 A.M.–5:00 P.M. and Sunday 1:00–5:00 P.M. Admission is free.

Alabama Sports Hall of Fame, 2150 Richard Arrington Jr., Birmingham 35203-1102; (205) 323-6665; www.alasports.org. Through the years, Alabama has provided the sports world with outstanding athletes, and they are all enshrined here at the Sports Hall of Fame. Artifacts from such notables as Paul "Bear" Bryant, Hank Aaron, Joe Louis, Joe Namath, Satchel Paige, and many more will be found here. The Hall of Fame is open Monday through Saturday 9:00 A.M.–5:00 P.M., Sunday 1:00–5:00 P.M.

Birmingham Barons Baseball, 6000 Stadium Trace Parkway, Birmingham 35244-4508; (205) 988-3200; www.barons.com/main.shtml.

Birmingham Zoo, 2630 Cahaba Road, Birmingham 35223-1106; (205) 879-0408. This is the premier zoo in the state, with more than 900 species of rare and exotic animals in natural outdoor settings. Call ahead for their schedule and admission prices.

Smith-Harrison Museum, 50 Lester Street, Columbiana 35051; (205) 669-4545. This museum has the second largest collection of George and Martha Washington artifacts as well as Robert E. Lee artifacts. The museum is open Monday through Friday 9:00 A.M.–5:00 P.M., with free admission.

Lodging

Mountain Brook Inn, 2800 Highway 280, Mountain Brook 35223; (800) 523-7771.

Oak Mountain State Park, P.O. Box 278, Pelham 35124; (800) ALA-PARK.

Ranchouse Inn, 2125 Seventh Avenue South, Birmingham 35233-3105; (205) 322-0691.

Restaurants

The Original Whistle Stop Cafe (Irondale Café), 1900 First Avenue North, Birmingham 35205; (205) 956-5258. Setting for the novel and movie *Fried Green Tomatoes.*

Cafe Trentuno, Pelham; (205) 664-7887.

Organizations

Sierra Club Cahaba, 1330 Twenty-first Way South, Suite 110, Birmingham 35205; (205) 795-2043; www.sierraclub.org/chapters/al/cahaba.html.

Vulcan Trail Association, Birmingham; (205) 328-6198.

Other Resources

Alabama Trails Association, P.O. Box 371162, Birmingham 35237; www.alabamatrailsasso.org.

Bama Environmental News, Birmingham; (205) 226-7739; www.bamanews.com.

Wild Alabama, 11312 Alabama Highway 33, Moulton 35650; (256) 974-7678; www.wildalabama.com.

22 Green Trail (Peavine Falls Trail)

The Green Trail is the most direct route to the most popular attraction at Oak Mountain State Park, Peavine Falls. The trail travels steeply up and down ridges through a forest lush with vegetation in spring and summer, giving a comfortable enclosed feeling. Although the climbs are steep, the trail may be crowded on weekends because of the popularity of the falls.

Start: From the South Trailhead (Peavine Falls trailhead) at Oak Mountain State Park.
Distance: 4.6-mile out-and-back.
Approximate hiking time: 3–4 hours.
Difficulty: Moderate to difficult due to steep grades.
Trail surface: Dirt path.
Type of hike: Stands of longleaf pine, white oak, and silver maple.
Land status: State park.
Nearest town: Birmingham.
Schedule: Open year-round.
Fees/Permits: A day-use permit costs $2.00 per person. Camping is $13.00 per night, base rate.

Maps: USGS maps: Cahaba Heights; Chelsea; Helena.
Brochures—General park information available free at the main gate. Trail maps are available for 50 cents at the park office.
Trail contacts: Oak Mountain State Park, P.O. Box 278, Pelham 35124; (205) 620-2520; (800) ALA–PARK; www.bham.net/oakmtn.
Other trail users: None.
Canine compatibility: Dog friendly, but bring water (there are no sources until Peavine Branch at the end); leash recommended due to large number of people.

Finding the trailhead: From Birmingham take Interstate 65 south for 14 miles to Cahaba Valley Road (exit 246). Take a right onto Cahaba Valley Road (Alabama Highway 119) and travel 2 miles to County Road 33 and turn left. Go 2.5 miles to the park gate. Pay the entrance and camping fees and get general information brochures. Trail maps are available at the park office. Continue on 2 miles and make a right turn onto Terrace Drive. Head southwest 1 mile on Terrace Drive. The park office and parking area will be on the right. *DeLorme: Alabama Atlas & Gazetteer:* Page 31, G6.

The Hike

Hundreds of people flock to Peavine Falls each weekend—and anytime during the summer when school is out—to view this 65-foot beauty that cascades down a sheer rock wall into a clear pool. Many visitors take the Green Trail down to the falls because it starts right at the park office and is the most direct route.

The Peavine Falls trailhead is close to some of Oak Mountain's main attractions, including the Alabama Wildlife Rehabilitation Center and the Oak Mountain demonstration farm. Far more than just a petting zoo, the demonstration farm exhibits life on a farm and the care of livestock. Next door to the farm are the Oak

A view looking down into Peavine Falls.

Mountain Stables, with horseback rides available up the mountain or along the Orange (Horseshoe) Trail.

Eighty-five-acre Oak Lake is right next to the park office. Canoes and paddleboats are available for rent, and a swimming beach lies at one end. There is even a bicycle motocross facility just down from the park office. If you like to hit the links, you can take advantage of the eighteen-hole golf course here. Being in the heart of all this activity, it's no wonder the Green Trail sees so much traffic.

Although the path is a well-maintained dirt route, the climbs up and down the ridges are steep. The trail starts into the woods and then turns sharply uphill, next to the Wildlife Rehabilitation Center. After topping out on the first ridge, it's a steep walk down to the bottom—then back up steeply again to the ridgeline of Double Oak Mountain. The trail finally descends to meet the White Trail and then levels out, making its way to the falls.

As with many of the trails at Oak Mountain State Park, the Green Trail crosses several other trails, including the White, Red, and Orange (Horseshoe) Trails. This makes it easy to create several different loop hikes and some interesting overnight pack trips.

Views along the trail are not as open as those from high atop the twin ridges of Double Oak Mountain on the White and Blue Trails. The thick cover of trees

THE ALABAMA WILDLIFE REHABILITATION CENTER

The largest environmental organization in the state, the Alabama Wildlife Rehabilitation Center (AWRC) is located in the heart of Oak Mountain State Park. Established in 1977, the center was founded by Anne Miller and a staff of six volunteers.

The AWRC provides both long- and short-term care for orphaned and injured animals. A wide variety of animals are brought to the center for care and treatment. Whenever possible, the animals are put into the Release Preparation Facility to get them ready to return to the wild.

At Oak Mountain, the AWRC facility is located 0.5 mile south of the park office on AWRC Drive. Inside, there are a variety of educational exhibits to demonstrate the role of the center. Don't be surprised to see a few squirrels running in and out of the rafters as you walk through.

The highlight of the facility is the viewing area. Behind a screen, visitors can view the animals as their handlers help them recuperate.

Next to the facility is the Treetop Nature Trail. This wide, wheelchair-accessible, elevated boardwalk takes hikers through the valley. Here you can see red-shouldered and red-tailed hawks, horned owls, and turkey vultures. These and many more such animals live in very spacious cages along the trail and receive the best of care. Admission to the facility and the trail is free.

---

on the Green Trail is the scenic highlight on the way to the falls. When you're not concentrating on getting up a hillside, take a look around at the live oaks, silver maples, and dogwoods. At the top of the ridges, the aroma of longleaf pines stands out.

The hike culminates in Peavine Falls, formed by Peavine Branch, a slow meandering flow of water that runs between the two ridges of Double Oak Mountain. Both the Green and White Trails follow the creek for a portion of their length.

Overnight camping is permitted along the trails in the park but not in the areas just above and below the falls. Rappelling and climbing are not allowed on the rock walls of the gorge formed by the stream.

Canada geese greet campers at Oak Mountain.

Miles and Directions

0.0 Start from the park office. Turn right onto Terrace Drive and head to the west 50 feet. The trailhead, with a GREEN TRAIL sign, will be on your left, directly across from the tennis courts. Turn left and head into the woods to the south.

0.6 Cross the Orange (Horseshoe) Trail.

0.7 Cross the Yellow Trail.

1.2 The Green Trail merges with the Red Trail for the next 0.1 mile.

1.3 The Red Trail leaves the Green. Stay on the Green Trail.

2.2 The Green Trail merges with the White Trail for the next 0.1 mile along the banks of Peavine Branch.

2.3 The White Trail leaves the Green. In reality, the Green Trail has officially ended. This short, remaining length of trail is actually the Blue Trail. Continue to the east following blue blazes about 50 feet to the head of Peavine Falls. From here the trail overlooks the gorge for the next 0.1 mile. (**Note:** Be VERY cautious here. The rocks are slick and the drop precarious. The edge of the gorge is a clay footpath.) Turn around here for the return trip over the same path described above.

4.6 Arrive back at your vehicle.

Hike Information

Local Information

Birmingham Chamber of Commerce, 2027 First Avenue North, Birmingham 35203-4109; (205) 323-2100; www.birminghamchamber.com.

Greater Birmingham Convention and Visitor Bureau, 2200 Ninth Avenue North, Birmingham 35203-1100; (800) 458-8085; www.bcvb.org.

North Shelby Chamber of Commerce, P.O. Box 324, Pelham 35124; (205) 663-4542.

Local Events/Attractions

Alabama Jazz Hall of Fame, 1631 Fourth Avenue North, Birmingham 35203-1903; (205) 254-2731. Jazz legends with ties to Alabama, such as Lionel Hampton and Erskine Hawkins, are enshrined here. The Hall of Fame is opened Tuesday through Saturday 10:00 A.M.–5:00 P.M. and Sunday 1:00–5:00 P.M. Admission is free.

Alabama Sports Hall of Fame, 2150 Richard Arrington Jr., Birmingham 35203-1102; (205) 323-6665; www.alasports.org. Through the years, Alabama has provided the sports world with outstanding athletes, and they are all enshrined here at the Sports Hall of Fame. Artifacts from such notables as Paul "Bear" Bryant, Hank Aaron, Joe Louis, Joe Namath, Satchel Paige, and many more will be found here. The Hall of Fame is open Monday through Saturday 9:00 A.M.–5:00 P.M., Sunday 1:00–5:00 P.M.

Birmingham Barons Baseball, 6000 Stadium Trace Parkway, Birmingham 35244-4508; (205) 988-3200; www.barons.com/main.shtml.

Birmingham Zoo, 2630 Cahaba Road, Birmingham 35223-1106; (205) 879-0408. This is the premier zoo in the state, with more than 900 species of rare and exotic animals in natural outdoor settings. Call ahead for their schedule and admission prices.

Smith-Harrison Museum, 50 Lester Street, Columbiana 35051; (205) 669-4545. This museum has the second largest collection of George and Martha Washington artifacts as well as Robert E. Lee artifacts. The museum is open Monday through Friday 9:00 A.M.–5:00 P.M., with free admission.

Lodging

Mountain Brook Inn, 2800 Highway 280, Mountain Brook 35223; (800) 523-7771.

Oak Mountain State Park, P.O. Box 278, Pelham 35124; (800) ALA-PARK.

Ranchouse Inn, 2125 Seventh Avenue South, Birmingham 35233-3105; (205) 322-0691.

Restaurants

The Original Whistle Stop Cafe (Irondale Cafe), 1900 First Avenue North, Birmingham 35205; (205) 956-5258. Setting for the novel and movie *Fried Green Tomatoes.*

Cafe Trentuno, Pelham; (205) 664-7887.

Organizations

Sierra Club Cahaba, 1330 Twenty-first Way South, Suite 110, Birmingham 35205; (205) 795-2043; www.sierraclub.org/chapters/al/cahaba.html.

Vulcan Trail Association, Birmingham; (205) 328-6198.

Other Resources

Alabama Trails Association, P.O. Box 371162, Birmingham 35237; www.alabamatrailsasso.org.

Bama Environmental News, Birmingham; (205) 226-7739; www.bamanews.com.

Wild Alabama, 11312 Alabama Highway 33, Moulton 35650; (256) 974-7678; www.wildalabama.com.

23 Flagg Mountain Trail

This is a wonderful little hike to the top of Flagg Mountain, the last mountain in the Appalachian Range over 1,000 feet. As you near the top, the views of the surrounding mountains and valleys are spectacular. The highlight of the trip is Flagg Mountain Tower, with views of several counties and, on a clear day, Cheaha Mountain on the horizon. Please refer to the text about accessing the tower and surrounding cabins.

Start: From dirt road at foot of the mountain off County Road 16.
Distance: 6.4-mile out-and-back.
Approximate hiking time: 3 hours.
Difficulty: Moderate.
Trail surface: Hard-packed clay, gravel, and rock Forest Service road.
Type of hike: Slash, scrub, and loblolly pine forest; excellent views of the valley and surrounding mountains.
Land status: State forest.
Nearest town: Weogufka.
Schedule: Open year-round, but the trail is surrounded by property leased by the Golden Branch Hunting Club. Check hunting dates before heading out.
Fees/Permits: There is no fee to hike or use the cabins at the summit. Permission is required for access to the fire tower and to use the cabins (refer to text).
Maps: USGS map: Flagg Mountain.
Trail contacts: Coosa County Conservation Corporation, Pete Rodgers, Weogufka; (256) 245-2689.
Other trail users: Motor vehicles, ATVs.
Canine compatibility: Dog friendly, but use a leash. Bring water; there's none on the way up.

Finding the trailhead: From Montgomery take Interstate 65 north to exit 200. Turn right onto County Road 59 north and go 2.3 miles. Turn left onto U.S. Highway 31 north and continue 1.3 miles. Turn right and head east on Alabama Highway 22 for 13.4 miles until you come to Kelly's Crossroads (there is a small country store at the intersection of AL 22 and County Road 29). Make a left onto CR 29 north and travel 9 miles. Turn left onto County Road 16. Continue on CR 16 0.6 mile (you will cross Weogufka Creek over a single-lane bridge). A dirt road will be on the right, with a sign reading CCC CAMP ROAD. Park on the shoulder here. This is the trailhead. *DeLorme: Alabama Atlas & Gazetteer:* Page 38, E2-D2.

The Hike

As noted in earlier chapters, the Civilian Conservation Corps (CCC) was a dedicated and hardworking group of men looking for work during the Depression who were given the opportunity by the federal government. These men created hundreds of federal and state facilities, most notably state and national parks.

Flagg Mountain Tower, one of only two in the state (the other being Bunker Tower atop Cheaha Mountain), was to be the centerpiece of a new state park high atop the mountain. The tower, completed in the mid–1930s, is a towering tribute to

the craftsmanship of the CCC. The tower and several log cabins were completed; however, for unknown reasons the park was not completed. The state moved in and made the forest surrounding the mountain into a state forest, with the tower serving as a fire tower.

Years of neglect, the elements, and vandals took their toll on the tower and other facilities. The wood timbers that served as a skeleton for the stone tower were rotting away and the tower was in danger of collapsing.

Enter Joe and Pete Rodgers, Stan Messer, and several other volunteers from the area. They watched the deterioration of this historic site to the point where they couldn't stand it any longer and decided to do something about it. After long negotiations with the State Forest Service, the group, called the Coosa County Conservation Corporation (CCCC), was granted a lease. For $1.00 a year, they could lease the property, including the tower and cabins.

JUST WHAT IS DIXIE? Just before the Civil War, the state of Louisiana issued a note of currency worth $10 called a dix—French for "ten." Eventually the South became known as "Dixie." Montgomery, Alabama, was the first capital of the Confederacy, and Alabama is officially known as the Heart of Dixie.

For the past five years, the CCCC has done remarkable work in restoring the tower to a state where it is actually usable again. The cabins are beautiful restorations, with ornate stone fireplaces, and the group has run electricity, water, and sewers into the site. The group is always in need of help in the form of volunteers and money to continue the restoration. If you'd like to help, contact the CCCC at the address and phone number listed in "Trail contacts."

The CCCC's efforts have not gone unnoticed. The Alabama Hiking Trail Society is currently marking a new trail up the mountain. This trail will serve as another link in the effort to complete the Eastern Continental Trail from Canada to the Everglades. (See the "In Addition" about the trail elsewhere in this book.)

The hike described here travels up the old CCC Camp Road to the summit. It is a moderately difficult hike with no real surprises along the way. Wildlife is plentiful, with wild turkey, doves, hawks, redheaded woodpeckers, and white-tailed deer being commonly seen.

The real pleasure of this trip is the last 0.75 mile as the views of the surrounding mountains begin to open up until, by the time you reach the top, you are engulfed in a beautiful 360-degree panoramic view of the surrounding mountains and valleys.

◀ *A view of the Flagg Mountain fire tower from the cabins.*

Flagg Mountain Trail

Log Cabins

2.7

2.2

N

1.5

START

CR 16

Weogufka Creek

	Paved Road
	Maintained Dirt
===	Unmaintained Dirt
- - -	Singletrack Trail
▬▬	Selected Route
▥▥	Boardwalk

A view from the top of the Flagg Mountain fire tower.

Because of insurance requirements, access to the property is by permission of the CCCC only. If you would like to climb to the top of the tower, you will also need permission and a member to unlock it for you.

The cabins are available to small groups and individual hikers; contact the CCCC at the number under "Trail contacts" at the beginning of this chapter.

Miles and Directions

0.0 Start from the CCC Camp Road at the foot of the mountain directly off CR 16.

1.4 You will start to see some views of the surrounding mountains to the right through the trees.

1.5 Come to a Y in the road. The right fork is marked for the hunting club; take the left fork.

1.7 You will begin seeing excellent views of the surrounding mountains and valley to the left.

2.2 Come to a Y in the road. You will see a metal gate about 50 feet down the right fork. Take the right fork, passing through the gate (with permission; refer to hike description). The views are outstanding to the right.

2.5 Come to an intersection. The road continues straight ahead and loops around to the tower. To the left is a road that leads directly to the tower. Turn right here and head down a rather steep trail to visit the cabins.

2.7 Arrive at the log cabins. After visiting, turn around and retrace your steps to the intersection at Mile 2.5.

2.9 Cross the dirt road and head to the fire tower.

3.2 Arrive at the fire tower, with spectacular views, even at ground level, then retrace your steps back to the trailhead.

6.4 Arrive at the trailhead.

Hike Information

Local Information

Chilton County Chamber of Commerce, 500 Fifth Avenue North, Clanton 35046; (800) 553-0419; chilton.al.us/.

Local Events/Attractions

Verbena Trade Days, 500 Fifth Avenue North, Clanton 35046; (205) 280-0600. First Saturday of October.

Lodging

Sunrise USA, 946 Lake Mitchell Road, Clanton 35045; (205) 280-0306.

Restaurants

Cow Pasture Cafe, 1910 County Road 43, Clanton 35046; (205) 755-4231.

Jeanette's Place, 404 Seventh Street North, Clanton 35046; (205) 280-3133.

Organizations

Alabama Hiking Trails Society, Andalusia; (334) 427-4445; www.alabamatrail.org.

◀ *Constructed by the CCC in the 1930s, this is one of only two remaining such towers left in the state.*

24 Chinnabee Silent Trail

The Chinnabee Silent Trail, meandering up a hillside toward Lake Chinnabee, showcases the beauty of Talladega National Forest. Along the way, the wonders of the forest are revealed again and again. Just when you think it can't get any better, it does. In the gorge leading to the lake, the trail clings to rock walls on an elevated wooden platform and provides views of several waterfalls.

Start: From the trailhead 3 miles south of the Cheaha State Park office.
Distance: 7.4-mile out-and-back.
Approximate hiking time: 4–6 hours.
Difficulty: Easy, over dirt footpaths and some rock; normally moderate sections made easier by steps.
Trail surface: Dirt path; some travel over rock.
Type of hike: Mixture of white oak and long-leaf pine; plants including rhododendron, flame azalea, and dogwood; waterfalls.
Land status: National forest.
Nearest town: Anniston.
Schedule: Trail open year-round. Lake Chinnabee Recreation Area is closed November 15–April 15 due to freeze potential.
Fees/Permits: No fee to hike the trail. Camping is allowed anywhere in the forest by using the "dispersal" method and following national forest guidelines. Camping at both the Lake Chinnabee Recreation Area and Cheaha State Park is $8.00 per night (half price for Golden Age Passport holders).
Maps: USGS map: Cheaha Mountain. Brochures—Cheaha and the national forest brochures are available free of charge at the Cheaha State Park camp store.
Park maps—Pinhoti Trail Map Section 7 is available for $5.20 at the Cheaha State Park camp store or by mail through the Talladega National Forest ranger office. This map also includes the Chinnabee Silent, Odum Scout, Cave Creek, Nubbin, and Skyway Loop Trails.
Trail contacts: Talladega National Forest, 1001 North Street, Talladega 35160; (256) 362-2909; www.r8web.com/alabama—The office is open Monday through Friday, 7:00 A.M.–5:00 P.M.
Other trail users: None.
Canine compatibility: Dog friendly, except for dogs that don't like to climb stairs; ample water available; leash not required.

Finding the trailhead: From Anniston take Interstate 20 east for 5 miles to exit 191. Merge into U.S. Highway 431 south. Travel 3.5 miles and turn right onto Alabama Highway 281. Head south on AL 281 for 16 miles and pass the Cheaha State Park headquarters and lodge on the right. Continue south 4.5 miles. The paved parking area will be on your left. If you pass the Turnipseed Hunting Camp, you've gone too far. *DeLorme: Alabama Atlas & Gazetteer:* Page 32, F5.

The Hike

Everyone who visits Cheaha State Park, Cheaha Mountain, and Talladega National Forest seems to return with endless stories about how gorgeous it all is: the overlooks, the waterfalls, the mountain landscapes. Sometimes it seems they exaggerate a bit, but seeing is believing. The area of Cheaha Mountain—at 2,407 feet elevation, the highest in the state—is truly a sight to behold, with massive rock outcroppings,

One of the many waterfalls along the trail.

raging streams, and impressive waterfalls. The Chinnabee Silent Trail is rightfully one of the most popular hiking routes in Alabama.

The trail is named for Creek Indian chief Chinnabee, an ally of Andrew Jackson during the Creek Indian Wars. The designation of "Silent Trail" comes from the trail's builders. Between 1973 and 1976, Boy Scout Troop 29 from the Alabama Institute for the Deaf and Blind, created the trail with the help of the USDA Forest Service.

The Chinnabee Silent Trail is actually 6 miles long, if you start at the Lake Chinnabee Recreation Area and hike all the way to the Pinhoti Trail at Caney Head on the summit of Talladega Mountain. But the most enjoyable way to hike the trail is to start from the trailhead 3 miles south of the Cheaha State Park office, on AL 281, and then travel north to the Lake Chinnabee Recreation Area. The trip is less

Chinnabee Silent Trail

Lake Chinnabee

LAKE CHINNABEE ROAD

Dam

Information Board

Turnaround

TALLADEGA NATIONAL FOREST

SKYWAY LOOP TRAIL

DEVIL'S DEN

Cheaha Creek

Rocky Section

Creek

Cheaha Falls Shelter

Cheaha Falls

CHINNABEE SILENT TRAIL

Cheaha

SKYWAY MOTORWAY

FS 600

Creek

281

To Anniston

START

N

0   1/2 Kilometer   1/2 Mile

Paved Road
Maintained Dirt
Unmaintained Dirt
Singletrack Trail
Selected Route

BEFORE DRINKING THAT WATER ...

Alabama is blessed with beautiful mountain streams and lakes. But although that clear water may look inviting to drink, even here it's wise to be cautious in order to avoid illness from pollution or disease organisms. Before drinking water along the trail, use one of these three purification methods:

· Boil the water for three to five minutes before using.
· Filter the water with a purifying water bottle or pump.
· Put iodine or chlorine tablets into the water.

If you aren't able to use one of these methods, try to locate a source of water where it first comes out of the ground, because the ground can act as a natural purifier.

difficult in this direction, and it's 2 miles shorter. The real plus, however, is the scenery that unfolds at every turn.

Starting low and slow from the trailhead, the route winds its way around hillsides until the rushing of water can be heard. You'll soon reach Cheaha Falls—a series of falls with a nice pool at the bottom. A side trail leads in 0.1 mile to the pool. The Chinnabee Silent Trail crosses Cheaha Creek at the head of the upper fall. A wooden footbridge once crossed here, but Hurricane Opal took care of that in 1995.

Topping the hill from the falls, a fine view unfolds to the left of the surrounding mountains. Here you'll find the spacious Cheaha Falls Shelter, a first-come, first-served facility for overnight backpackers. Farther along the trail—depending on the season— wildflowers such as spring beauty and downy rattlesnake plantain line the way.

The trail soon ascends to meet Cheaha Creek again, in the canyon section known as the Devil's Den. Through the canyon, the creek churns white over the rocks. The trail moves progressively higher up the cliffs, eventually crossing the face of the cliffs at one point on an elevated wooden walkway clinging to the rock wall.

The trail ends at the Lake Chinnabee Recreation Area. The Lakeshore Trail begins here and loops for 2 miles around the lake. This also serves as a trailhead for the Skyway Loop Trail (see Hike 25). A combination of the Chinnabee Silent Trail, Skyway Loop Trail, and Pinhoti Trail creates a 17-mile loop that provides an excellent weekend backpack trip.

View from the Cheaha Falls Shelter.

All in all, the Chinnabee Silent Trail, with its wildness and beauty, makes for one of the most enjoyable hikes in the state.

Miles and Directions

0.0 Start from the east end of the parking area on AL 281 south. Cross the highway to the north. A sign indicating a hiking trail will be across the highway where the trail enters the woods. The trail is marked with blue blazes.

0.1 At the bottom of the ravine, the trail comes to a small creek. The path looks as though it continues straight, but it doesn't. Turn to the left here and cross the creek to the northeast. The trail now starts going up the other side of the ravine.

0.5 Cross a dirt road (a hiker sign will be seen on the other side where it reenters the woods).

1.0 Come to a fork and go right. **Side trip:** It's worth the effort to take the left fork a short 0.1 mile to the base of Cheaha Falls.

1.2 Reach the Cheaha Falls Shelter.

2.5 This area was cut in 1998 to prevent the spread of the Southern pine beetle through the forest.

3.0 Below to the left is a popular area for camping, along the banks of the stream. In 200 feet the trail basically levels out high above the stream. The views of the falls and the canyon are spectacular in this area, known as Devil's Den.

3.2 At the top of the climb, a 75-foot elevated wooden bridge clings to the rock cliff as it takes the trail to the west.

3.4 Come to a sign that reads CHINNABEE SILENT TRAIL . . . DEVIL'S DEN—0.5 MILE, CHEAHA FALLS SHELTER—3 MILES, TURNIPSEED 4 MILES, PINHOTI 6 MILES. Continue straight. In 50 feet come to another sign that marks the turnoff for the Skyway Loop Trail. Continue straight.

3.5 A stone marker identifies the trail as being built by Boy Scout Troop 29. In 10 feet another sign marks the turn for the Lakeshore Loop Trail. Continue straight.

3.7 Come to the southeast end of the Lake Chinnabee Recreational Area parking lot and turn around. Retrace your tracks back to the trailhead.

7.4 Arrive back at your vehicle.

Hike Information

Local Information

Anniston/Calhoun County Convention and Visitors Bureau, 722 West Fourteenth Street, Anniston 36201-4411; (800) 489-1087; www.calhounchamber.org.

Greater Talladega Chamber of Commerce, 210 East Street South, Talladega 35160; (256) 362-8186; www.talladega.com/business/chamber.htm.

Local Events/Attractions

Church of Saint Michael & All Angels, Anniston; (256) 237-4011; www.brasenhill.com/stmikesaa/index.html. This church was built in 1888 by the founding families of the town of Anniston. The church features impressive examples of Norman architecture with Tiffany glass, a 95-foot bell tower and a 12-foot white Carrara marble altar.

Anniston Museum of Natural History, Anniston; (256) 237-6766; www.annistonmuseum.org. A museum for the ages, literally, with displays of dinosaurs and fossils, 400 species of birds, authentic Egyptian mummies, and more. Open Tuesday through Friday 9:00 A.M.–5:00 P.M., Saturday 10:00 A.M.–5:00 P.M., Sunday 1:00–5:00 P.M.

Berman Museum, Anniston; (256) 237-6261. The Berman Museum has a very rare collection of art and historic artifacts that run the gamut from bronze sculptures by Remington and Fraser's *The End of the Trail* to rare weapons from around the world, including a sword with 1,295 diamonds embedded in it.

Lodging

Cheaha State Park Lodge, Delta; (800) 846-2654. This hotel is situated atop the state's highest mountain. Half the rooms have panoramic views of the surrounding countryside, as does the swimming pool.

McClellan Inn, Anniston; (256) 820-3144.

Restaurants

Cheaha State Park Restaurant, 2141 Bunker Loop, Delta 36258-8709; (256) 488-5115. From catfish to steaks, the Cheaha Restaurant, located next to the state park's hotel, has wonderful food and a rustic feel. A huge fireplace and a gigantic window overlooking the valley from the highest point in the state make this a unique dining experience.

Backyard Burgers, Anniston; (256) 236-4544.

Organizations

Alabama Trails Association, P.O. Box 371162, Birmingham 35237; www.alabamatrailsasso.org.

Sierra Club East Alabama Chapter, Auburn; (334) 821-9817.

Appalachian Trail Club of Alabama, P.O. Box 381842, Birmingham 35238; (205) 991-0534; sport.al.com/sport/atca.

Other Resources

Bama Environmental News, Birmingham; (205) 226-7739; www.bamanews.com.

25 Skyway Loop Trail

This hike can be a pretty good overnight trip culminating in a visit to Lake Chinnabee Recreation Area, where you can swim in the pools formed by the falls of Chinnabee Creek. The hike includes views of the surrounding mountains as you travel the ridgelines.

Start: From Adams Gap trailhead.
Distance: 15.0-mile out-and-back.
Approximate hiking time: 8–9 hours.
Difficulty: Moderate, over rocky ridges; difficult on steep slopes.
Trail surface: Dirt and rock footpath.
Type of hike: Oaks and longleaf pines; rhododendrons, azaleas, and dogwoods.
Land status: National forest.
Nearest town: Anniston.
Schedule: Open year-round.
Fees/Permits: No fee to hike the trail. Camping is allowed anywhere in the forest by using the "dispersal" method and following national forest guidelines.
Maps: USGS map: Cheaha Mountain. Brochures—Available free of charge at the

Cheaha State Park camp store.
Park maps—Pinhoti Trail Map Section 7 is available for $5.20 at the Cheaha State Park camp store or by mail through the Talladega National Forest ranger office. This map also includes the Chinnabee Silent, Odum Scout, Cave Creek, Nubbin, and Skyway Loop Trails.
Trail contacts: Talladega National Forest, 1001 North Street, Talladega 35160; (256) 326-2909; www.r8web.com/alabama—The office is open Monday through Friday, 7:00 A.M.–5:00 P.M.
Other trail users: None.
Canine compatibility: Dog friendly; ample water available; no leash required.

Finding the trailhead: From Anniston take Interstate 20 east for 5 miles to exit 191. Merge into U.S. Highway 431 south. Travel 3.5 miles and turn right onto Alabama Highway 281. Head south on AL 281 for 16 miles and pass the Cheaha State Park headquarters and lodge on the right. Continue south 4.5 miles. The road dead-ends at Adams Gap and the trailhead. *DeLorme: Alabama Atlas & Gazetteer:* Page 32, F5.

The Hike

The Skyway Trail is a long, winding path around the ridges of Talladega National Forest just to the west of the state's highest peak, Cheaha Mountain. Aptly named, the Skyway Trail travels up and down moderate climbs along the ridges as it makes its way to Lake Chinnabee Recreation Area.

The trail beginning at Adams Gap follows the Pinhoti Trail for the first 0.2 mile. After the trail branches off, watch for families of armadillos rooting through the brush and leaves. Armadillos are determined to stand up to anything they feel endangers them. After walking around a group of armadillos, you may find they are chasing you down the trail. Make a loud noise and they should scatter.

Chinnabee Creek.

Also along the trail, you may see large numbers of white-tailed deer and wild turkeys (after all, *Pinhoti* means *turkey* home). The trail makes its way through stands of white oaks and Southern longleaf pines. The path is also lined with rhododendrons, flame azaleas, and dogwoods that bloom and brighten the way in springtime.

Winding along, the trail crosses several creeks. Two of the largest are Barbaree Creek, near the midpoint of the hike, and Hubbard Creek, near the end. About 2

Skyway Loop Trail

Benches

■ Marsh

Lake Chinnabee

Dam

P

LAKESHORE LOOP TRAIL

CHINNABEE SILENT TRAIL

Chinnabee Creek

Hubbard Creek

TALLADEGA

NATIONAL

FOREST

Barbaree Creek

Mtn. Views

■ Outcropping

To Anniston

281

PINHOTI TRAIL

SKYWAY LOOP TRAIL

N

P

ADAMS GAP TRAIL

START

	Paved Road
	Maintained Dirt
	Unmaintained Dirt
	Singletrack Trail
	Selected Route

0 — 1 Kilometer

0 — 1 Mile

miles into the hike, the trail passes through a previously burned area that is very open and affords good views of the neighboring mountains.

The trail eventually begins a steep descent to Chinnabee Creek. The return trip also takes this path, making for a steep uphill climb. Just after the Chinnabee Creek crossing, you have the option of taking a side excursion on the Chinnabee Silent Trail for a half-mile walk to a swimming hole. Here the creek cascades down a rock wall and forms a deep blue-green pool, just the place for a swim in the cold mountain water. There are several nice primitive campsites next to the creek. No fee or permit is required. Camping is also allowed anywhere along the trail except in the Lake Chinnabee Recreation Area.

From Chinnabee Creek, the Skyway Trail leads to Lake Chinnabee and then uses the Lakeshore Loop Trail for the next 2 miles to swing around the lake and head back on your original trail for the return to Adams Gap. Lake Chinnabee offers excellent bass fishing—a state freshwater fishing license is required.

If you are looking for a good overnight hiking experience on a loop route, try connecting the Skyway, Chinnabee Silent, and Pinhoti Trails together (leaving out the Lakeshore Loop). This forms a 17-mile circuit beginning at Adams Gap.

If you plan to hike the Skyway Trail by starting at the Lake Chinnabee Recreation Area and walking to Adams Gap, remember that the recreation area is closed to vehicles between November 15 and April 15. However, the trail is still accessible by parking at the end of the recreation area road and hiking 2 miles down the road to the trailhead at Lake Chinnabee. Deer hunting season generally runs from October 15 to January 31, so wear hunter orange if you're out hiking then. The Talladega National Forest office has exact dates.

Miles and Directions

0.0   Start from the Adams Gap trailhead. A Pinhoti National Recreational Trail sign marks the entrance. The trail has diamond-shaped Pinhoti (turkey) markers on the trees. (**FYI:** Beware of the armadillos—especially if you have a dog with you.)

0.2   Come to a fork and go right. (The left fork is the Pinhoti Trail.) Blue triangle blazes soon mark the Skyway Loop Trail.

0.6 Cross an off-road trail to the west. (The marker is hard to see on the other side of the road.)

1.0 Pass a campsite on the left.

2.0 Cross a dirt road.

2.9 Cross an off-road path.

3.0 Cross a dirt road (a hiker sign on the other side shows the path reentering the woods).

3.9 Come to the banks of Hubbard Creek—a very nice, wide creek. In about 20 feet cross the creek using stepping-stones.

4.0 Come to a fork and go right. (The left fork takes you to a campsite.)

4.5 Cross a dirt road.

4.7 Cross a dirt road.

5.3 Cross the Chinnabee Creek and come to a T intersection with the Chinnabee Silent Trail. Turn left here on this wide dirt footpath. Shortly come to a sign that reads LAKESHORE LOOP 2 MILES and points to the left. Turn left here, crossing the creek over the rocks. On the other side, the trail turns to the right and travels to the northwest. The trail is rocky here, and the white blazes of the loop begin.

6.2 The trail narrows as it passes the information board on the opposite side of the stream. Here the trail is a 3-foot-wide dirt path. In 200 feet the path starts heading up and down a series of shallow runoffs and in general begins a slow rise above the lake. To the right is a steep drop-off to the banks of the lake. Wildflowers line the trail.

6.3 Creosote-coated poles line the right side of the trail to prevent erosion. In 200 feet the trail heads down to the banks of the lake. The water is very clear. The trees become mainly oaks, and the trail is now a dirt path. In 100 feet the trail crosses a rocky runoff area. It also begins to meander to the north-northwest.

6.5 Turning to the west, pass a bench to the right along the side of the lake. The trail is lined with thick pines and carpeted with a thick bed of pine needles. Ahead to the right, a dam can be seen.

6.6 Continuing west, the trail travels uphill 200 feet and tops out next to the dam to the right. At the top, the path turns southwest.

6.7 Come to a sign that reads LAKESHORE TRAIL and points to the right. Turn to the right, crossing the runoff from the dam over rocks. The trail actually makes a hairpin turn here and heads back toward the dam 100 feet, then turns left to the north and crosses the runoff from the dam (make sure those boots are waterproofed). On the other side, the trail turns right and heads back uphill toward the dam to the northeast. Within 200 feet the trail tops next to the dam, where it again travels over a series of shallow runoffs. The trail is about 100 feet above the lake, with a steep drop-off to the right.

6.8 Turning to the north, travel 100 feet and turn to the west. The trail will make a sharp turn within the next 200 feet to the southeast as it heads down through the pines. A nice view of the lake will be seen here. The trail here is a clay path about 3 feet wide.

6.9 The trail turns to the east. Across the lake, the park road will be seen. To the right is the dam. Travel 200 feet and turn to the northeast, heading down to the edge of the lake.

7.0 Pass benches to the right on the edge of the lake. There is a nice view of the surrounding mountains here as the trail turns to the northeast. Travel 200 feet; the trail turns to the north. To the right, a marsh begins to form. There are grass islands and birdhouses here to the right. Wildflowers line the trail and banks of the marsh.

7.1 Encounter a small jog to the north and back to the northwest around some brush.

7.2 Cross a 20-foot boardwalk over a stream to the north. After crossing, turn to the southeast. The trail is very wide, surrounded by pines, and starts heading down the opposite side of the marsh. Watch for lizards darting around the brush. In 200 feet start climbing up and down a series of runoffs.

7.4 At the top of a hill, turn to the southwest. The dam can be seen to the right across the lake. The pines thin out here, and the trail just traveled can be seen on the other side of the lake.

7.5 Turn to the southeast.

7.6 Heading now to the east, reach a small marsh. In 100 feet cross a 10-foot bridge over a creek. On the other side is a sign that reads HIKING TRAIL. The trail is now a pebble-lined path. In 50 feet cross a shorter 6-foot bridge over another creek to the southeast. After crossing, turn to the southwest and in 50 feet come to the paved park road. Pass a sign that reads LAKESHORE TRAIL—2-MILE LOOP. Turn right onto the paved road to the southwest. In 200 feet the road turns to the south. A mowed grass bank runs between the road and the lake. In 100 feet pass a 5 MPH speed limit sign to the left. In another 50 feet pass a sign that reads DAY USE FEE STATION and a cement boat ramp. Continue to the south on the road.

7.7 Pass a split-rail fence to the right.

7.8 Come to a Y in the road. A sign in the center of the Y reads TALLADEGA NATIONAL FOREST/LAKE CHINNABEE RECREATIONAL AREA. Take the right fork onto the paved road.

7.9 Come to an information board detailing various hikes within the forest. In 100 yards come to a sign that reads LAKESHORE LOOP 2 MILES and points to the right. Continue straight; a sign that reads SKYWAY LOOP and points to the right shows the direction back to the trail. Retrace your steps back to the Adams Gap trailhead.

15.0 Arrive back at the trailhead.

Hike Information

Local Information

Anniston/Calhoun County Convention and Visitors Bureau, 722 West Fourteenth Street, Anniston 36201-4411; (800) 489-1087; www.calhounchamber.org.

Greater Talladega Chamber of Commerce, 210 East Street South, Talladega 35160; (256) 362-8186; www.talladega.com/business/chamber.htm.

Local Events/Attractions

Church of Saint Michael & All Angels, Anniston; (256) 237-4011; www.brasenhill.com/stmikesaa/index.html. This church was built in 1888 by the founding families of the town of Anniston. The church features impressive examples of Norman architecture with Tiffany glass, a 95-foot bell tower and a 12-foot white Carrara marble altar.

Anniston Museum of Natural History, Anniston; (256) 237-6766; www.annistonmuseum.org. A museum for the ages, literally, with displays of dinosaurs and fossils, 400 species of birds, authentic Egyptian mummies, and more. Open Tuesday through Friday 9:00 A.M.–5:00 P.M., Saturday 10:00 A.M.–5:00 P.M., Sunday 1:00–5:00 P.M.

Berman Museum, Anniston; (256) 237-6261. The Berman Museum has a very rare collection of art and historic artifacts that run the gamut from bronze sculptures by Remington and Fraser's *The End of the Trail* to rare weapons from around the world, including a sword with 1,295 diamonds embedded in it.

Lodging

Cheaha State Park Lodge, Delta; (800) 846-2654. This hotel is situated atop the state's highest mountain. Half the rooms have panoramic views of the surrounding countryside, as does the swimming pool.

McClellan Inn, Anniston; (256) 820-3144.

Restaurants

Cheaha State Park Restaurant, 2141 Bunker Loop, Delta 36258-8709; (256) 488-5115. From catfish to steaks, the Cheaha Restaurant, located next to the state park's hotel, has wonderful food and a rustic feel. A huge fireplace and a gigantic window overlooking the valley from the highest point in the state make this a unique dining experience.

Backyard Burgers, Anniston; (256) 236-4544.

Organizations

Alabama Trails Association, P.O. Box 371162, Birmingham 35237; www.alabamatrailsasso.org.

Sierra Club East Alabama Chapter, Auburn; (334) 821-9817.

Appalachian Trail Club of Alabama, P.O. Box 381842, Birmingham 35238; (205) 991-0534; sport.al.com/sport/atca.

Other Resources

Bama Environmental News, Birmingham; (205) 226-7739; www.bamanews.com.

26 Rock Garden Trail

The Rock Garden Trail, the most challenging hike in this book, begins easy enough from Cheaha Lake but then becomes more strenuous as it climbs sharply up and over boulders and bluffs to a point near the summit of Cheaha Mountain.

Start: From the Cheaha Lake picnic area.
Distance: 1.6-mile out-and-back.
Approximate hiking time: 2–3 hours.
Difficulty: Difficult, over the towering overlook called the Rock Garden.
Trail surface: Dirt path, becoming a rocky path, then some scrambling up rocks.
Type of hike: Thick hardwood forest; boulders and bluffs.
Land status: State park.
Nearest town: Anniston.
Schedule: Open year-round.
Fees/Permits: A $1.00 day-use fee is charged for parking.
Maps: USGS map: Cheaha Mountain. Brochures—Available free of charge at the Cheaha State Park camp store.

Park maps—Pinhoti Trail Map Section 7 is available for $5.20 at the Cheaha State Park camp store or by mail through the Talladega National Forest ranger office. This map also includes the Chinnabee Silent, Odum Scout, Cave Creek, Nubbin, and Skyway Loop Trails.
Trail contacts: Cheaha State Park, 8 Bunker Loop, Delta 36258-8709; (256) 488-5111. Talladega National Forest, 1001 North Street, Talladega 35160; (256) 463-2273; www.r8web.com/alabama—The office is open Monday through Friday, 7:30 A.M.–5:00 P.M.
Other trail users: None.
Canine compatibility: Not dog friendly due to steep, difficult climb; if you do take a dog, leash not required.

Finding the trailhead: From Anniston take Interstate 20 east for 5 miles to exit 191. Merge onto U.S. Highway 431 south. Travel 3.5 miles and turn right onto Alabama Highway 281 south. Head south on Alabama Highway 281 for 19 miles, passing the Cheaha State Park headquarters and lodge. Turn right onto the Lake Road and travel 3 miles to Cheaha Lake. Turn right and head 0.1 mile to a fork. Take the right fork and travel an additional 0.1 mile. Park at the bathhouse. *DeLorme: Alabama Atlas & Gazetteer:* Page 32, E5.

The Hike

This book covers the spectrum of hiking difficulty. The easy, casual walk along the Weeks Bay Nature Trail in the Gulf Coast region is included to give every member of the family an enjoyable and educational hike. At the opposite end of that spectrum, the Rock Garden Trail described here is included for hikers who like difficulty and steep climbing.

Although this trail in Cheaha State Park is only 1.6 miles, round-trip, there's a huge elevation gain on the way up. Beginning at the Cheaha Lake picnic area at an elevation of 1,264 feet, the trail heads straight up Cheaha Mountain to an elevation of about 2,100 feet. That's not far below the 2,407-foot summit of Cheaha, the highest mountain in Alabama.

The starting point—Cheaha Lake—far below.

Not many trails give you a view of the end of the trail from the very start, but this one does. Standing at the trailhead, look up to the north and you'll see the end of the trail at the top of the outcropping known as the Rock Garden, just to the left of the Cheaha Lodge Restaurant.

The Rock Garden Trail begins up a gradual grade, following the banks of a creek up a ravine. But after 0.3 mile, that's where the joyride ends. From there the trail gets progressively steeper and rockier as it maneuvers around large boulders and outcroppings and courses through a dense forest of white oaks, dappled with rhododendrons, flame azaleas, and dogwoods. At a little over half a mile from the trailhead, the path begins peeking out of the trees at the surrounding views—and they are spectacular.

From this point on, the trail rounds the outcroppings with ever-expanding views of the mountains and valley. Don't be surprised to see rock climbers beginning their ascent of the cliffs or rappelling down. Take a glance skyward and you may even spot a climber high in the air, sliding slowly across on a rope strung from one tall outcropping to another several hundred feet away. Climbers call it "the best view in the house."

The trail finally pops out at the top of two large, flat outcroppings atop the Rock Garden. Here you can relax, take in the view, and watch the activity around the cliffs—and look at your original trailhead far below. Way down at the bottom is Cheaha Lake, waiting for your return.

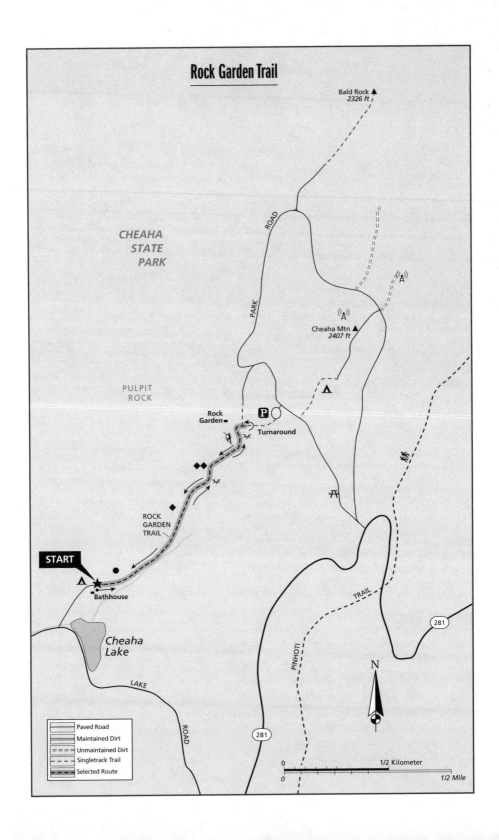

Rock Garden Trail

Bald Rock ▲
2326 ft

CHEAHA
STATE
PARK

ROAD

PARK

Cheaha Mtn ▲
2407 ft

PULPIT
ROCK

Rock
Garden ▬

P ◯
Turnaround

ROCK
GARDEN
TRAIL

START

Bathhouse

Cheaha
Lake

LAKE

ROAD

PINHOTI

TRAIL

281

281

N

	Paved Road
	Maintained Dirt
	Unmaintained Dirt
	Singletrack Trail
	Selected Route

0 ─────────── 1/2 Kilometer

0 ─────────── 1/2 Mile

The best view in the house.

From the Rock Garden, it's only about 0.1 mile to the parking area for visitors who choose to drive to the summit of Cheaha Mountain instead of hiking. Many visitors take the easy approach to hiking the Rock Garden Trail, making a one-way trip out of it by starting from the parking area at the summit and then hiking down to Cheaha Lake (where they can be met by a shuttle car).

When you're done with the hike, you can cool down and relax at Cheaha Lake. Swimming is good in the cold mountain lake, and there are diving boards and lifeguards, plus picnic tables, a picnic pavilion, and a bathhouse. There is a $1.00 day-use fee for parking at the lake or the summit.

Miles and Directions

0.0　Start from the bathhouse at Cheaha Lake. Travel around the paved road until you see a reflective blue trail marker. Head off into the woods on the dirt footpath.

0.5　The hardest part of the trip is upon you.

0.8　The trail levels off considerably and comes to a huge rock outcropping overlooking the valley below. Off to the right is Cheaha Lake, where you started. Another 100 feet up the path is a dirt road and the northern trailhead—where you'd park if you drove up. Turn around here and head back down.

1.6　Arrive back at the trailhead.

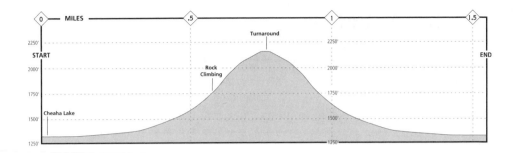

Hike Information

Local Information

Anniston/Calhoun County Convention and Visitors Bureau, 722 West Fourteenth Street, Anniston 36201-4411; (800) 489-1087; www.calhounchamber.org.

Greater Talladega Chamber of Commerce, 210 East Street South, Talladega 35160; (256) 362-9075; www.talladega.com/business/chamber.htm.

Local Events/Attractions

Talladega SuperSpeedway, 3366 Speedway Boulevard, Talladega 35160; (256) 761-4702; www.talladegasuperspeedway.com. NASCAR's most competitive and fastest track. You can make arrangements for a drive around this famous track with an embankment of almost four stories; bus tours available.

International Motor Sports Hall of Fame, 3198 Speedway Boulevard, Talladega 35160; (256) 362-5002; www.motorsportshalloffame.com. Five buildings with cars and memorabilia from 1902 to present. Tributes to sports writers, ARCA champions, and more. Open daily 9:00 A.M.–5:00 P.M. Closed Thanksgiving Day, Christmas Day, and Easter morning.

Lodging

Anniston Efficiency Motel, 107 East G Street, Anniston 36201-6634; (256) 238-0060.

Victoria Inn, 1604 Quintard Avenue, Anniston 36201; (256) 236-0503.

Restaurants

Old Hickory, 405 Fort Lashley Avenue, Talladega 35160; (256) 362-0677.

Cafe 202, 1401 West Twenty-second Street, Anniston 36201-2603; (256) 236-2229.

Cheaha State Park Restaurant, 2141 Bunker Loop, Delta 36258-8709; (256) 488-5115. From catfish to steaks, the Cheaha Restaurant, located next to the state park's hotel, has wonderful food and a rustic feel. A huge fireplace and a gigantic window overlooking the valley from the highest point in the state make this a unique dining experience.

Backyard Burgers, Anniston; (256) 236-4544.

Organizations

Alabama Trails Association, P.O. Box 371162, Birmingham 35237; www.alabamatrailsasso.org.

Sierra Club East Alabama Chapter, Auburn; (334) 821-9817.

Appalachian Trail Club of Alabama, P.O. Box 381842, Birmingham 35238; (205) 991-0534; sport.al.com/sport/atca.

Other Resources

Bama Environmental News, Birmingham; (205) 226-7739; www.bamanews.com.

27 Nubbin Creek Trail

Although the full Nubbin Creek Trail is 4 miles long, the first 2 miles are the most enjoyable and are described here. The trail meanders gradually up the side of Talladega Mountain, passing three waterfalls and ending with panoramic views. The trail is lined with a variety of wildflowers in spring.

Start: From the Nubbin Creek trailhead.
Distance: 3.8-mile out-and-back.
Approximate hiking time: 2–3 hours.
Difficulty: Moderate, due to narrow trail and brush.
Trail surface: Dirt and clay; rock-covered near falls.
Type of hike: White oak and chestnut forest; longleaf pine forest; rhododendron and mountain laurel; waterfalls.
Land status: National forest.
Nearest town: Anniston.
Schedule: Open year-round.
Fees/Permits: No fee to hike the trail. Camping is allowed anywhere in the forest by using the "dispersal" method and following national forest guidelines.

Maps: USGS map: Cheaha Mountain. Brochures—Available free of charge at the Cheaha State Park camp store. Park maps—Pinhoti Trail Map Section 7 is available for $5.20 at the Cheaha State Park camp store or by mail through the Talladega National Forest ranger office. This map also includes the Chinnabee Silent, Odum Scout, Cave Creek, Nubbin, and Skyway Loop Trails.
Trail contacts: Talladega National Forest, 1001 North Street, Talladega 35160; (256) 362-2909; www.wr8web.com/alabama—The office is open Monday through Friday, 7:30 A.M.–5:00 P.M.
Other trail users: None.
Canine compatibility: Dog friendly, though could be tough on older or out-of-shape dogs; ample water available; no leash required.

Finding the trailhead: From Anniston take Interstate 20 east for 5 miles to exit 191. Merge onto U.S. Highway 431 south. Travel 3.5 miles and turn right onto Alabama Highway 281 south. Head south for 7 miles and turn left onto Alabama Highway 49 south. Head south 6.3 miles until the road forks. Take the right fork (Nubbin Creek Road). A sign will be seen that says NUBBIN CREEK TRAILHEAD 3 MILES. In 0.8 mile the paved road turns into a clay road. Continue an additional 2.2 miles to the Nubbin Creek Trailhead to the right. *DeLorme: Alabama Atlas & Gazetteer:* Page 32, F5.

The Hike

Waterfalls abound in the Talladega National Forest, and the Nubbin Creek Trail highlights several of them. The main attractions of the trail fall within its first 2 miles. The final 2 miles, which aren't covered in this description, are overgrown with vegetation and lack sufficient trail markers. The full 4.0-mile trail ends at its intersection with the Cave Creek Trail (see Hike 28). A round-trip hike to this point could make a good overnight trip, with some nice campsites along the ridgetops.

One of many stream crossings along the Nubbin Creek Trail.

Even on the first 2 miles, the Nubbin Creek Trail is dense with rhododendron bushes, covering sections of the route. It's entirely passable, but on a rainy day a poncho won't be enough to keep your pants dry. A couple sections of the trail are especially narrow where feeder creeks have washed away parts of the trail, leaving sharp drop-offs. On a day of heavy rain, these spots can be dangerous.

With that said, on to the good stuff. Overall, the trail is not difficult. There are some moderate climbs up and around rocky waterfalls. The most picturesque time

Nubbin Creek Trail

NUBBIN CREEK
TRAIL

Turnaround

TALLADEGA

NATIONAL FOREST

To
Anniston

NUBBIN CREEK
ROAD

Mill

Shoals

N

Creek

Cave

Creek

0   1/2 Kilometer
0   1/2 Mile

	Paved Road
	Maintained Dirt
	Unmaintained Dirt
	Singletrack Trail
	Selected Route

START

to hike the trail is in early to mid-spring, when rains fill the creeks and the water-falls run full.

From its beginning at the Nubbin Creek trailhead, the route is narrow, with longleaf pines, white oak, and brush giving the path an enclosed feeling. Details on trail conditions and national forest rules are posted on an information board near the start of the trail. There is also a register here. It's a good idea to fill out the registra-tion card before starting any trip into the wilderness, because you never know when you might want searchers to be able to find you in an emergency.

The trail winds gradually uphill, and you begin to hear Mill Shoals Creek. The first of two short side trails toward the creek comes in from the right. This first side trail goes about 100 yards to the banks of the fast-flowing creek. But the real scenery is on the second side trail, which takes off about 50 feet farther along the trail. This short path takes you to the edge of a bluff that rises more than 100 feet above the

'BAMA TRIVIA

- Alabama is the namesake of a Native American tribe, the Alibamu.
- Isabella de Soto, wife of explorer Hernando de Soto, planted the first fig tree in the United States, on Dauphin Island, Alabama.
- The number of acres of forestland in Alabama ranks third in the nation.
- 350,000 endangered American gray bats call a waterside cave at Joe Wheeler State Park near Florence, AL, home. Visitors can see them swarm en mass after sunset between April and October.

creek, which tumbles here over a series of falls. This is definitely the highlight view of the trip.

Back on the Nubbin Creek Trail, you'll hike through an area where white bloodroot and toothwort dot the trail sides in spring. In places where the trees thin out and the surrounding mountains and ridges come into view, look for white dogwoods on the hillsides.

At the 1.4-mile mark—about the time you can spot the next waterfall ahead on the right—the trail makes its way along the side of a ravine and becomes little more than a ledge, less than a foot wide. You'll need to pay close attention to your footing. At one point a feeder creek to the stream far below cuts across the trail. The trail is washed out, and it'll take some careful maneuvering to get safely around this spot.

Shortly after the washout, you'll reach a 70-foot waterfall. The trail crosses the creek at the base of the falls. From here the trail makes its way into a boulder field for good open views. This is the end point of the hike described here.

Miles and Directions

0.0 Start from the Nubbin Creek trailhead. A hiker sign marks the entrance into the pines. White blazes line the trail.

0.3 Pass a short, unmarked trail to the right. In 100 feet pass a second side trail. **Side trip:** This second trail is approximately 100 feet long and rather steep but leads to a beautiful bluff high above the rushing stream and waterfall.

1.4 The trail narrows to a 6-inch rock ledge with a steep drop to the right as it crosses a creek. In 50 feet the trail comes to the base of the falls. Carefully cross the moss-covered rocks of the stream.

1.5 The path runs just below the highest elevation of the trip, 1,600 feet.

1.8 The trail markers are all but nonexistent through this section.

1.9 The brush thins out as the trail comes to a boulder field. To the right the views of the surrounding mountains open up. Turn around here and retrace your route back to the Nubbin Creek Trailhead. **Option:** You can continue on to the intersection of Cave Creek Trail. The hike from this point on is extremely difficult, not marked, and very overgrown.

Hike Information

Local Information

Anniston/Calhoun County Convention and Visitors Bureau, 722 West Fourteenth Street, Anniston 36201-4411; (800) 489-1087; www.calhounchamber.org.

Greater Talladega Chamber of Commerce, 210 East Street South, Talladega 35160; (256) 362-8186; www.talladega.com/business/chamber.htm.

Local Events/Attractions

Church of Saint Michael & All Angels, Anniston; (256) 237-4011; www.brasenhill.com/stmikesaa/index.html. This church was built in 1888 by the founding families of the town of Anniston. The church features impressive examples of Norman architecture with Tiffany glass, a 95-foot bell tower and a 12-foot white Carrara marble altar.

Anniston Museum of Natural History, Anniston; (256) 237-6766; www.annistonmuseum.org. A museum for the ages, literally, with displays of dinosaurs and fossils, 400 species of birds, authentic Egyptian mummies, and more. Open Tuesday through Friday 9:00 A.M.–5:00 P.M., Saturday 10:00 A.M.–5:00 P.M., Sunday 1:00–5:00 P.M.

Berman Museum, Anniston; (256) 237-6261. The Berman Museum has a very rare collection of art and historic artifacts that run the gamut from bronze sculptures by Remington and Fraser's *The End of the Trail* to rare weapons from around the world, including a sword with 1,295 diamonds embedded in it.

Lodging

Cheaha State Park Lodge, Delta; (800) 846-2654. This hotel is situated atop the state's highest mountain. Half the rooms have panoramic views of the surrounding countryside, as does the swimming pool.

McClellan Inn, Anniston; (256) 820-3144.

Restaurants

Cheaha State Park Restaurant, 2141 Bunker Loop, Delta 36258-8709; (256) 488-5115. From catfish to steaks, the Cheaha Restaurant, located next to the state park's hotel, has wonderful food and a rustic feel. A huge fireplace and a gigantic window overlooking the valley from the highest point in the state make this a unique dining experience.

Backyard Burgers, Anniston; (256) 236-4544.

Organizations

Alabama Trails Association, P.O. Box 371162, Birmingham 35237; www.alabamatrailsasso.org.

Sierra Club East Alabama Chapter, Auburn; (334) 821-9817.

Appalachian Trail Club of Alabama, P.O. Box 381842, Birmingham 35238; (205) 991-0534; sport.al.com/sport/atca.

Other Resources

Bama Environmental News, Birmingham; (205) 226-7739; www.bamanews.com.

28 Cave Creek Trail

Cave Creek Trail travels the side of Hernandez Peak for a trip that takes you through tunnels of rhododendron bushes. You'll also enjoy excellent views of the surrounding mountains. The hiking becomes difficult from the Nubbin Creek Trail junction on Little Caney Head to the end of the trail at the Pinhoti connector on Parker High Point because the trail has become overgrown with thorn bushes and shrubs.

Start: From the north parking area on Alabama Highway 281 (Cheaha trailhead).
Distance: 13.8-mile out-and-back.
Approximate hiking time: 6–7 hours.
Difficulty: Easy along the side of Hernandez Peak; moderate climbs over Little Caney Head and Parker High Point; difficult beyond the Nubbin Creek Trail junction due to brush.
Trail surface: Dirt path and rock.
Type of hike: Rhododendrons and wildflowers, along with longleaf pines, white oaks, and dogwoods.
Land status: State park and national forest.
Nearest town: Anniston.
Schedule: Open year-round.
Fees/Permits: No fee to hike the trail. Camping is allowed anywhere in the forest by using the "dispersal" method and following national forest guidelines. Primitive camping at Cheaha State Park is $8.00 per night.

Maps: USGS map: Cheaha Mountain. Brochures—Available free of charge at the Cheaha State Park camp store.
Park maps—Pinhoti Trail Map Section 7 is available for $5.20 at the Cheaha State Park camp store or by mail through the Talladega National Forest ranger office. This map also includes the Chinnabee Silent, Odum Scout, Cave Creek, Nubbin, and Skyway Loop Trails.
Trail contacts: Cheaha State Park, 8 Bunker Loop, Delta 36258-8709; (256) 362-2909. Talladega National Forest, 1001 North Street, Talladega 35160; (256) 463-2273; www.r8web. com/alabama—The office is open Monday through Friday, 7:30 A.M.–5:00 P.M.
Other trail users: None.
Canine compatibility: Dog friendly. Bring water, which is scarce after the creeks at the trail beginning; no leash required.

Finding the trailhead: From Anniston take Interstate 20 east for 5 miles to exit 191. Merge onto U.S. Highway 431 south. Travel 3.5 miles and turn right onto Alabama Highway 281 South. Go 13 miles on AL 281; the Cheaha trailhead will be plainly marked on the left. *DeLorme: Alabama Atlas & Gazetteer:* Page 32, F5.

The Hike

Cave Creek Trail gets its name from a creek at the start of the hike that flows through large rocks to make small "caves." The trail is lined with rhododendron, dogwoods, and white oaks. From spring through fall, wildflowers color the mountaintops like a rainbow. Among the wildlife you're likely to see are white-tailed deer, wild turkeys, wild pigs, and foxes. Hawks are often seen soaring around the bluffs.

Once you leave the trailhead, the path is nice and level, though rocky in many places, as it heads south along the side of Hernandez Peak. The trail narrows in several

Rhododendrons form a tunnel along the Cave Creek Trail.

spots, with a steep drop to one side into a hollow. Be careful here, especially over rocky areas.

All along this part of the route, through Cheaha State Park, the trail is lined with rhododendron bushes. The best time to walk this path is in late spring or early summer, when the bushes are in full bloom. They are so thick that they form flowering tunnels. Soon the trail leaves the state park and enters Talladega National Forest. The trail jogs to the west and at this elbow provides a spectacular view of surrounding mountains.

From here the trail follows the side of a ridge and then starts making its way up to just below the top of 2,000-foot-high Little Caney Head. At this point, 4.7 miles

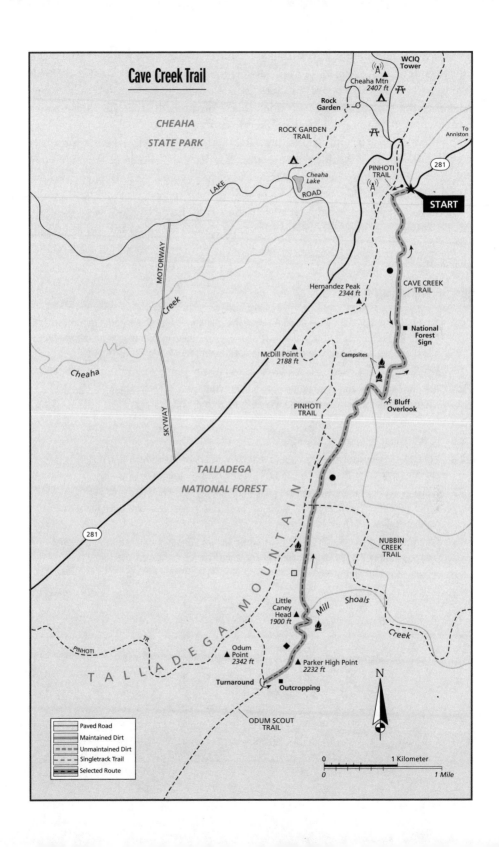

Cave Creek Trail

WCIQ Tower

Cheaha Mtn
2407 ft

CHEAHA
STATE PARK

Rock Garden

ROCK GARDEN TRAIL

To Anniston

281

Cheaha Lake

LAKE ROAD

PINHOTI TRAIL

START

MOTORWAY

Creek

Cheaha

Hernandez Peak
2344 ft

CAVE CREEK TRAIL

National Forest Sign

McDill Point
2188 ft

Campsites

PINHOTI TRAIL

Bluff Overlook

SKYWAY

TALLADEGA

NATIONAL FOREST

281

NUBBIN CREEK TRAIL

T A L L A D E G A   M O U N T A I N

Little Caney Head
1900 ft

Mill

Shoals

Creek

PINHOTI TR

Odum Point
2342 ft

Parker High Point
2232 ft

Turnaround

Outcropping

ODUM SCOUT TRAIL

N

Paved Road
Maintained Dirt
Unmaintained Dirt
Singletrack Trail
Selected Route

| 0 | | | | | 1 Kilometer |
| 0 | | | | | 1 Mile |

into the hike, the Nubbin Creek Trail splits off to the east—and this is where the difficult stuff begins. The park service information will tell you that the Cave Creek Trail is marked with tree blazes, but don't expect to see them. From this point on to the end of the trail, the brush is so thick that it obscures the trail. It's almost easier to bushwhack than to try and follow the official route.

The trail reaches its end atop Parker High Point (2,232 feet), where it intersects the Odum Scout Trail. At this Y intersection, you have the choice of retracing your outbound route back to the Cheaha trailhead or following a loop route back to the trailhead. To make the loop, take the right fork at the Y intersection and head up the Odum Scout Trail until it intersects the Pinhoti Trail. Turn right and walk the Pinhoti Trail along the ridge of Talladega Mountain. You'll climb over the top of McDill Point (2,188 feet) and Hernandez Peak (2,344 feet) before dropping back to the Cheaha trailhead.

Miles and Directions

0.0   Start from the Cheaha trailhead off AL 281. The trail leaves the parking area to the west behind a PINHOTI NATIONAL RECREATIONAL TRAIL sign. The trail forks in 200 feet at an information board and registration box. Take the left fork. (The right fork leads to the Pinhoti Trail.)

1.7   Pass the CHEAHA WILDERNESS/TALLADEGA NATIONAL FOREST sign.

2.1   The trail forks. Go right, around the outcropping. (The left fork heads steeply up an outcropping to the south.) Shortly, the two trails rejoin. Continue through a campsite.

2.3   Pass a campsite on the right.

2.5   Pass another campsite on the right.

2.8   The trail turns rocky and is high above a creek with a steep drop-off into a hollow to the left. It's very narrow here, so be careful of your footing as you go around.

3.8   Come to a fork where a sign reads PINHOTI and points to the north and STATE PARK and points to the northeast. Another sign here reads NUBBIN CREEK ROAD and points to the southwest. Take the left fork.

4.7   Come to the intersection of the Nubbin Creek Trail and another connector to the Pinhoti (two signs mark the crossing). Continue straight. (**FYI:** Box turtles can be found here.)

5.0   Pass a campsite on the right.

5.7   Pass a campsite on the left.

6.3 Come to a fork and go left, continuing uphill.

6.8 The trail is hard to see through the brush as it heads to the west.

6.9 Pass a campsite on the right. The trail is rocky again as it comes to a fork, where a sign marks the intersection with the Odum Scout Trail. Turn around and retrace your route back to the Cheaha trailhead. **Option:** To make a loop, turn right onto the Odum Trail and take it to its intersection with the Pinhoti Trail, where you'll turn right and follow the Pinhoti back to the Cheaha trailhead.

13.8 Arrive back at the trailhead.

Hike Information

Local Information

Anniston/Calhoun County Convention and Visitors Bureau, 722 West Fourteenth Street, Anniston 36201-4411; (800) 489-1087; www.calhounchamber.org.
Greater Talladega Chamber of Commerce, 210 East Street South, Talladega 35160; (256) 362-8186; www.talladega.com/business/chamber.htm.

Local Events/Attractions

Church of Saint Michael & All Angels, Anniston; (256) 237-4011; www.brasenhill.com/stmikesaa/index.html. This church was built in 1888 by the founding families of the town of Anniston. The church features impressive examples of Norman architecture with Tiffany glass, a 95-foot bell tower and a 12-foot white Carrara marble altar.
Anniston Museum of Natural History, Anniston; (256) 237-6766; www.annistonmuseum.org. A museum for the ages, literally, with displays of dinosaurs and fossils, 400 species of birds, authentic Egyptian mummies, and more. Open Tuesday through Friday 9:00 A.M.–5:00 P.M., Saturday 10:00 A.M.–5:00 P.M., Sunday 1:00–5:00 P.M.
Berman Museum, Anniston; (256) 237-6261. The Berman Museum has a very rare collection of art and historic artifacts that run the gamut from bronze sculptures by Remington and Fraser's *The End of the Trail* to rare weapons from around the world, including a sword with 1,295 diamonds embedded in it.

Lodging

Cheaha State Park Lodge, Delta; (800) 846-2654. This hotel is situated atop the state's highest mountain. Half the rooms have panoramic views of the surrounding countryside, as does the swimming pool.
McClellan Inn, Anniston; (256) 820-3144.

Restaurants

Cheaha State Park Restaurant, 2141 Bunker Loop, Delta 36258-8709; (256) 488-5115. From catfish to steaks, the Cheaha Restaurant, located next to the state park's hotel, has wonderful food and a rustic feel. A huge fireplace and a gigantic window overlooking the valley from the highest point in the state make this a unique dining experience.
Backyard Burgers, Anniston; (256) 236-4544.

Organizations

Alabama Trails Association, P.O. Box 371162, Birmingham 35237; www.alabamatrailsasso. org.
Sierra Club East Alabama Chapter, Auburn; (334) 821-9817.
Appalachian Trail Club of Alabama, P.O. Box 381842, Birmingham 35238; (205) 991-0534; sport.al.com/sport/atca.

Other Resources

Bama Environmental News, Birmingham; (205) 226-7739; www.bamanews.com.

In Addition

The Appalachian Trail and Beyond

The Pinhoti Trail System, located within Talladega National Forest and Cheaha State Park, offers the ultimate backpacking excursion in Alabama. The system connects more than 100 miles of Alabama wilderness and leads through the tallest mountains in the state.

The Pinhoti area received its name from the Native Americans who once inhabited the region. Loosely translated, it means turkey home—appropriate because the eastern wild turkey calls these mountains home.

The Pinhoti Trail System takes off from a trailhead on Alabama Highway 77, north of Ashland, and ends at a spot on U.S. Highway 278 just north of Piedmont. Along the hundred-mile hiking route, you'll find comfortable trail shelters and spectacular landscapes. A wide variety of wildflowers bloom from spring through summer, followed later in the year by the beautiful reds and golds of autumn leaves. With 100 miles to cover, a through-hike of the Pinhoti System can be quite a challenge. The weather can change without warning, and some creeks run only intermittently in summer.

The Pinhoti System combines several trails in the national forest, such as the Odum Scout Trail, as it makes its way through the southern portion of the Appalachian Mountains. Using a variety of trails, you can devise weekend loop hikes for yourself. In October 1999 the Pinhoti Trail was named a federal Millennium Legacy Trail, making it eligible for federal funding to help maintain and protect it.

The Appalachian Trail stretches from Mt. Katahdin in Maine to Springer Mountain in Georgia. The idea of the trail was to create a skyway footpath over the entire Appalachian Range. In reality, the Appalachians end in Alabama; the last mountain of the range over 1,000 feet is Flagg Mountain, near Weogufka.

As we mentioned in the last edition of this book, a hardworking group of volunteers—the Alabama Trails Association, along with several local clubs such as the Appalachian Trail Conference, the Georgia-Pinhoti Club, and the National Forest Service—are constructing a link between the Appalachian Trail and the Pinhoti Trail, which would link the AT into Alabama.

But the story doesn't end there. The Alabama Hiking Trail Society is taking the AT one step farther and is playing a key role in creating the Eastern Continental Trail. Their goal is to connect the Pinhoti through to Flagg Mountain, then down through the Conecuh Trail and connect to the Florida Trail System, which runs to the Everglades. Many hikers are already experiencing the coastal trail, including AHTS member "Nimblewill Nomad," who hiked from the Florida Keys to Cape Gaspé, Quebec, using these trails.

TENN

ALA   GA

Chattanooga

TENN   N.C.

CHATTAHOOCHEE
NATIONAL FOREST

BENTON
MACKAYE
TRAIL

APPALACHIAN TRAIL

Springer Mtn

CHATTAHOOCHEE
NTL FOREST

AT EXTENSION
(Proposed)

Rome

New Section

CHIEF LADIGA
RAIL-TRAIL

SILVER COMET
RAIL-TRAIL

SILVER COMET
RAIL-TRAIL
(proposed)

Smyrna   Atlanta

Amtrak

Anniston

Amtrak

Cheaha Mtn

FOREST

NTL

PINHOTI TRAIL

TALLADEGA   PARK

ALA   GA

N

Proposed Trail
Paved Trail
Appalachian Trail
Pinhoti Trail

0   30 Kilometers

0   30 Miles

Volunteers are desperately needed. The process of acquiring and clearing trail is slow and, as with most of us, each member is a volunteer with day jobs. But the dream of completing an Eastern Continental Trail is one worth reaching for and spurs them on.

Information on the progress of the Pinhoti Connection can be found on the ATA Web site at www.alabamatrailasso.org. For information on the Eastern Continental Trail (ECT) and other activities of the AHTS, visit their Web site at www.alabamatrail.org.

The impetus now is to complete the Appalachian Trail connection to Alabama. The Alabama Trails Association is looking for volunteer trail builders. You can write to the association at P.O. Box 371162, Birmingham, AL 35237; send e-mail to wild_flower@mindspring.com; or www.alabamatrails.com. You may also find out more through the Alabama Hiking Trail Society at (334) 427–4445.

Information on securing maps of the Pinhoti Trail is available by calling the Talladega Ranger Station at (205) 362–2909.

29 Odum Scout Trail

The scenery and serenity of the Odum Scout Trail makes this one great hike. Right from the start, High Falls adds to the splendor of the scene—and to the difficulty of the hike, as the route ascends stairs to reach the top of the falls. The path then follows the ridgeline of Cheaha Mountain, with wildflowers displaying all imaginable colors and two bluffs providing spectacular views.

Start: From the High Falls trailhead off County Road 31.

Distance: 9.8-mile out-and-back.

Approximate hiking time: 4–5 hours.

Difficulty: Difficult start, following stairs up rock walls; then easy over the ridge of Cheaha Mountain.

Trail surface: Rock and dirt footpaths.

Type of hike: High bluffs; wildflowers.

Land status: National forest.

Nearest town: Anniston.

Schedule: Open year-round.

Fees/Permits: No fee to hike the trail. Camping is allowed anywhere in the forest by using the "dispersal" method and following national forest guidelines.

Maps: USGS maps: Cheaha Mountain; Lineville West.

Brochures—Available free of charge at the Cheaha State Park camp store.

Park maps—Pinhoti Trail Map Section 7 is available for $5.20 at the Cheaha State Park camp store or by mail through the Talladega National Forest ranger office. This map also includes the Chinnabee Silent, Odum Scout, Cave Creek, Nubbin, and Skyway Loop Trails.

Trail contacts: Talladega National Forest, 1001 North Street, Talladega 35160; (256) 362-2909; www.r8web.com/alabama. The office is open Monday through Friday, 7:30 A.M.–5:00 P.M.

Other trail users: None.

Canine compatibility: Dog friendly, except for the first 0.5 mile, which is steep and includes stairs. Bring water; no leash required.

Finding the trailhead: From Anniston take Interstate 20 east for 5 miles to exit 191. Merge onto U.S. Highway 431 south. Turn right in 3.5 miles onto Alabama Highway 281 south. Go 7 miles and turn left onto Alabama Highway 49 south. Go 10 miles (passing the turn for the Nubbin Creek trailhead on the right at Mile 6.3) and turn right onto CR 31. Travel 1.2 miles; a sign on the right marks the turn for the High Falls trailhead. Turn right here onto the gravel road and travel 0.3 mile to the trailhead. *DeLorme: Alabama Atlas & Gazetteer:* Page 32, F5.

The Hike

Many people believe the Odum Scout Trail is Alabama's most scenic mountain trail. If after hiking it you don't agree, you'll have to at least acknowledge that it comes pretty darn close. Situated in the Talladega National Forest, the trail was built by the Cheaha District of the Choccolocco Council of the Boy Scouts, in cooperation with the USDA Forest Service. Its objective: "to encourage interest in camping and hiking in the great out-of-doors."

Lower Cascade of High Falls.

The trail, which begins at the High Falls trailhead, travels the backbone of Cheaha Mountain until it reaches the Pinhoti Trail at Odum Point. Right from the start, nature takes hold of you with breathtaking beauty. Just 0.1 mile into the hike, the trail reaches High Falls—a three-tiered cascade that leaps from ledge to ledge right next to the trail. The trail heads straight up rock walls to the top of the falls, using steel and wood stairs to make the climb possible. (If you bring the dog, you may end up carrying the animal.)

Farther on, the trail comes to the edge of a bluff on Cedar Mountain, with a panoramic view of the surrounding mountains. Atop the bluff is a flat area that has

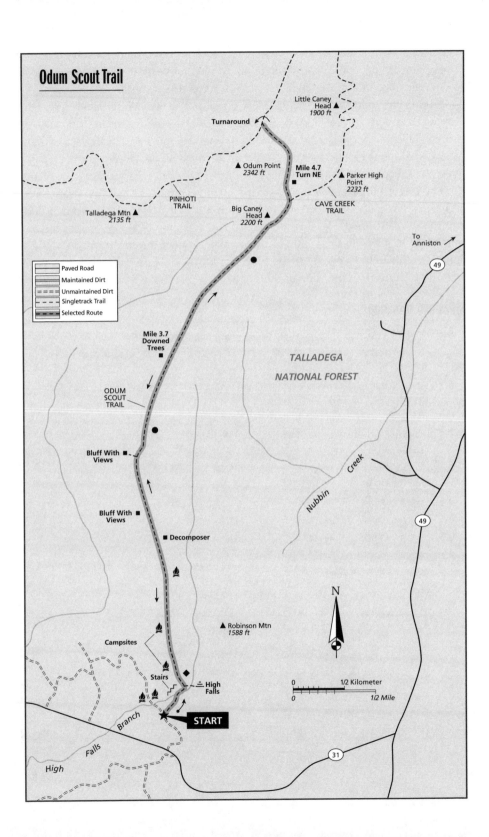

Odum Scout Trail

Little Caney
Head ▲
1900 ft

Turnaround

▲ Odum Point
2342 ft

**Mile 4.7
Turn NE**
■

▲ Parker High
Point
2232 ft

PINHOTI
TRAIL

**CAVE CREEK
TRAIL**

Talladega Mtn ▲
2135 ft

Big Caney
Head ▲
2200 ft

To
Anniston ↗

49

| Paved Road |
| Maintained Dirt |
| Unmaintained Dirt |
| Singletrack Trail |
| Selected Route |

TALLADEGA

NATIONAL FOREST

**Mile 3.7
Downed
Trees**
■

ODUM
SCOUT
TRAIL

**Bluff With
Views** ■

Creek

Nubbin

49

**Bluff With
Views** ■

■ **Decomposer**

N

▲ Robinson Mtn
1588 ft

Campsites

Stairs

⛰ High
Falls

| 0 | 1/2 Kilometer |
| 0 | 1/2 Mile |

Branch

★ **START**

Falls

High

31

been used as a campsite, but it's a windy place. It's better to drop down a bit from the outcropping if you plan to spend the night. As the trail heads up Big Caney Head, it reaches the edge of a second bluff, again with a broad view of the mountains.

Among the animals you might cross on your trip are white-tailed deer, wild turkeys, wild pigs, and foxes. Azaleas, dogwoods, and wildflowers line the path—so many wildflowers, in fact, that from spring through fall much of the area is a rainbow of colors. Along the ridge, travel is fairly easy as you walk up and down small grades. With the exception of the beginning part of the trail, water is scarce, so pack plenty.

The trail is only roughly marked, with faded yellow blazes visible on some trees and rocks. The path is well worn, but brush overgrowing the trail can make it difficult to follow. At places like this, look ahead and you should be able to spot the trail as it continues beyond the brush. In other areas, the trail travels over rocks and disappears completely. Generally if you continue in the same direction of travel, you'll find the path on the other side of the rocks.

Miles and Directions

0.0 Start from the High Falls trailhead. Faded yellow blazes mark the trail. Immediately come to a fork and go right. (The left fork leads to a series of campsites next to High Falls Branch.)

0.1 Pass the trail registration and information board. In 50 feet the trail crosses High Falls Creek.

0.2 The second cascade of High Falls is straight ahead. Turn left at the falls and in 50 feet come to a set of wooden and steel stairs. At the top of the stairs, the upper cascade is straight ahead.

0.3 Climb two sets of stairs and come to a T intersection. Take the left fork. (The right fork leads to the head of the falls.)

0.4 Pass a camp on the left.

0.5 Pass a campsite on the right.

0.7 Pass a campsite on the left. Through the trees to the right is Robinson Mountain.

2.1 Pass a campsite on the right. Thick brush obscures the trail, but you can see it again about 30 feet ahead.

Rock pile at the trailhead.

2.4 Pass a decomposer on the right.

2.8 A 50-foot trail breaks left. Continue straight.

3.5 A short side trail to the left leads to another beautiful view. Continue straight. The trail is difficult to follow over the rocks here, and there are no trail markers; just keep heading northeast.

3.7 Come to a field of rocks. The trail looks as though it could go either north or northeast. Go northeast over the flat rocks (not up the boulders to the left). A faded yellow blaze can be seen on one of the rocks as you walk over it. The path will reappear on the other side.

4.5 Come to a fork with two wooden signs. The right sign reads NUBBIN CREEK TRAIL/CAVE CREEK TRAIL 2.0 MILES, NUBBIN CREEK ROAD 4.0 MILES. The left sign reads ODUM TRAIL. HIGH FALLS 3.0 MILES. Take the left fork.

4.9 Come to a T intersection with the Pinhoti Trail (a wooden sign indicates the intersection). Turn around and retrace your tracks back to the High Falls trailhead.

9.8 Arrive at the trailhead.

Hike Information

Local Information

Anniston/Calhoun County Convention and Visitors Bureau, 722 West Fourteenth Street, Anniston 36201-4411; (800) 489-1087; www.calhounchamber.org.

Greater Talladega Chamber of Commerce, 210 East Street South, Talladega 35160; (256) 362-8186; www.talladega.com/business/chamber.htm.

Local Events/Attractions

Church of Saint Michael & All Angels, Anniston; (256) 237-4011; www.brasenhill.com/stmikesaa/index.html. This church was built in 1888 by the founding families of the town of Anniston. The church features impressive examples of Norman architecture with Tiffany glass, a 95-foot bell tower and a 12-foot white Carrara marble altar.

Anniston Museum of Natural History, Anniston; (256) 237-6766; www.annistonmuseum.org. A museum for the ages, literally, with displays of dinosaurs and fossils, 400 species of birds, authentic Egyptian mummies, and more. Open Tuesday through Friday 9:00 A.M.–5:00 P.M., Saturday 10:00 A.M.–5:00 P.M., Sunday 1:00–5:00 P.M.

Berman Museum, Anniston; (256) 237-6261. The Berman Museum has a very rare collection of art and historic artifacts that run the gamut from bronze sculptures by Remington and Fraser's *The End of the Trail* to rare weapons from around the world, including a sword with 1,295 diamonds embedded in it.

Lodging

Cheaha State Park Lodge, Delta; (800) 846-2654. This hotel is situated atop the state's highest mountain. Half the rooms have panoramic views of the surrounding countryside, as does the swimming pool.

McClellan Inn, Anniston; (256) 820-3144.

Restaurants

Cheaha State Park Restaurant, 2141 Bunker Loop, Delta 36258-8709; (256) 488-5115. From catfish to steaks, the Cheaha Restaurant, located next to the state park's hotel, has wonderful food and a rustic feel. A huge fireplace and a gigantic window overlooking the valley from the highest point in the state make this a unique dining experience.

Backyard Burgers, Anniston; (256) 236-4544.

Organizations

Alabama Trails Association, P.O. Box 371162, Birmingham 35237; www.alabamatrailsasso.org.

Sierra Club East Alabama Chapter, Auburn; (334) 821-9817.

Appalachian Trail Club of Alabama, P.O. Box 381842, Birmingham 35238; (205) 991-0534; sport.al.com/sport/atca.

Other Resources

Bama Environmental News, Birmingham; (205) 226-7739; www.bamanews.com.

Honorable Mentions

Central Alabama

As we've seen, Central Alabama offers the hiker much in the way of scenery and challenging treks. The following trails didn't make our A-list but are well worth mention. Most of these trails are within striking distance of other trails listed in the Central region section of this book, so stop in, pay a visit, and let us know what you think. Maybe one should be upgraded, or maybe you know of some hidden gem that would make a good honorable mention.

G Talladega National Forest–Oakmulgee Unit

The Talladega National Forest is broken into two distinct areas. The first is home to the state's highest mountain, Cheaha. The second is the Oakmulgee Unit, located between Montgomery and Birmingham.

 The highlight of the Oakmulgee Unit is the Payne Lake Recreation Area. Here a variety of activities from swimming to boating to fishing will be found, along with a hiking trail that skirts the banks of the lake. The terrain is not exceptionally difficult, and there are ample opportunities to view the wildlife of the region.

 As with all national forests in the state, camping is permitted along the trail. Camping at the recreational area with water costs $12 per day. Otherwise, a day-use fee of $3.00 is charged. Hunting is allowed in national forests, so camping and hiking are restricted during hunting season. Contact the ranger office Monday through Friday 7:30 A.M.–5:00 P.M. at (205) 926–9765, or visit www.southernregion.fs.fed. us/alabama/oakmulgee/default.htm for dates.

 To get to the forest, go west from Montgomery on U.S. Highway 82 to Alabama Highway 5. Turn left on AL 5 and head south for 6 miles. Turn right onto Alabama Highway 25. The recreational area will be reached in 15 miles. *DeLorme: Alabama Atlas & Gazetteer:* Page 36, E1.

H Red Trail–Oak Mountain State Park

Oak Mountain State Park is well known for its mountain bike trails, and the Red Trail is among its best routes. Totaling 17 miles, this trail follows old dirt roadbeds for the first half of the trip and then a nice footpath around the hillsides for the remainder. Mountain bikers use the trail as a training course, and many contests are held here each year.

 As with many of the other trails in the park, the Red Trail takes the hiker to Peavine Falls and can be accessed either from the Peavine Falls parking lot or the northern parking area near the country store.

The hike is easy to moderate in difficulty. The main drawback is the frequency of bicycles careening down the hillsides. The views are not as spectacular as other trails in the park, but it does travel alongside some streams that make it a pleasant trip. (See Hike 19 for park directions and additional information.) Call (205) 620–2520 or (800) ALA–PARK for more information, or visit www.bham.net/oakmtn. *DeLorme: Alabama Atlas & Gazetteer:* Page 31, G6.

Treetop Trail–Oak Mountain State Park

Just over half a mile in length, the Treetop Trail at Oak Mountain is an elevated walkway through the Oak Mountain forest. What makes the trail interesting is that it's maintained by the Alabama Wildlife Rehabilitation Center. The center provides homes for more than 300 species of wildlife that are found injured throughout the state. Here, the animals are protected and cared for until they are well enough to make it on their own in the wild.

The trail travels through the section of the park where the animals recuperate. All manner of wildlife, from cougars to alligators to eagles, can be seen. AWRC personnel are more than happy to talk with hikers about the wildlife and the rehabilitation program. The trail itself begins at the park ranger office and runs parallel to

Peavine Falls in Oak Mountain State Park.

the Green Trail. (See Hike 20 for park directions and additional information.) Call (205) 620–2520 or (800) ALA–PARK for more information, or visit www.bham.net/oakmtn. *DeLorme: Alabama Atlas & Gazetteer:* Page 31, G6.

⏿ Bald Rock Trail–Cheaha State Park

Located on the very top of the highest mountain in the state, the Bald Rock Trail gives you what you would expect from the highest point, spectacular views! This trail is a 1.0-mile loop that is perfect for families with small children and persons with disabilities.

The CCC built this tower atop Cheaha Mountain, the state's highest peak.

The trail begins at the north end of the parking lot, next to the closed Mt. Cheaha Lodge, which is a fine example of CCC craftsmanship. The trail takes two paths here, one to the left and one to the right of a boardwalk that runs down the center of the loop. Either path leads to the same location.

The trail is easy traveling, mostly a dirt footpath with some exposed rock. Half a mile into the trip the trail turns west and comes out right on top of Bald Rock. The view is spectacular and expansive to say the least.

The boardwalk running down the center of the loop is elevated approximately 4 feet off the ground. It's quite wide, at least 6 feet, with 4-foot-high handrails, and it leads directly to the rock. This makes the trip easily accessible for those with physical disabilities.

The trail opens at 7:00 A.M. and closes at sunset. There is a $1.00 day-use fee to the park. (See Hike 26 for park directions and additional information.) Call (800) ALA–PARK for more information. *DeLorme: Alabama Atlas & Gazetteer:* Page 32, E5.

K Rickwood Cavern State Park

One of the truly magnificent state park experiences in Alabama is Rickwood Cavern State Park, member of the National Caves Association. The cave is maintained by the state and is the state's only operational caving park.

Wildflowers adorn a rocky outcropping atop Cheaha Mountain.

Park rangers guide you along the trail through the "Miracle Mile," a solid mile (2-mile round-trip) of passages, huge carved rooms, and limestone formations. The cave was formed more than 260 million years ago during the Mississippian geologic period. Early fossils of marine life can be seen, as well as colorful flowstones and an exhibit of 2,000-year-old artifacts found in the cave.

The park is located about 20 miles north of Birmingham. Take exit 284 off of Interstate 65. The park is open 10:00 A.M.–5:00 P.M. daily on a seasonal schedule, so it's best to call in advance at (205) 647–9692 before heading out. Admission to the cave is $8.00 for adults twelve and older and $4.00 for children six to eleven. Admission to the park is $1.00 for ages six and older. The fee for camping is $14.00 per night for up to four people. *DeLorme: Alabama Atlas & Gazetteer:* Page 24, H5.

Northern Alabama

Northern Alabama stretches from the Tennessee–Alabama border to the state's largest city, Birmingham. This region is known geologically as the Cumberland Plateau. This mountainous region has seen its sandstone heights carved and weathered by the elements and the many waterways that flow through it to create spectacular gorges, cascading waterfalls, and ancient caverns.

Hikers in the region will find plenty of challenge and beauty. Little River Canyon atop Lookout Mountain is one such stop. Carved for thousands of years, the canyon resonates with the thunder of the river, culminating in a spectacular 60-foot waterfall. The views from the canyon rim are something to behold. This is a popular location for white-water rafters and rock climbers.

The Eberhart Point Trail provides more views of the canyon, but mainly it takes you directly to the raging river for a little rock-hopping and views of the canyon from the bottom. DeSoto State Park is also located here, with a multitude of trails and sites. In addition to the many panoramic views, several falls are encountered, including Lost Falls, Azalea Cascade, and the rapids of the west fork of Little River.

The Russell Cave Trail combines history, hiking, and cave exploration all in one. The trail travels up the side of Montague Mountain and culminates at Russell Cave. More than 8,000 years of Native American history can be found here.

History will probably remember this region most for the Huntsville Space and Rocket Center. This site, along with the nearby Redstone Arsenal, played a key role in sending Americans to the moon. It was here that Werner Von Braun and NASA engineers developed the *Saturn V* rocket that would put Apollo astronauts on the moon. Today the center is used by NASA to test the components of the international space station *Freedom* before delivery to Cape Canaveral for deployment in space by the space shuttle. This is also home to one of the nation's Space Camps for both children and adults. The museum and guided tours are a must-see when in the area.

Northern Alabama

30 Bee Branch Trail

The Bee Branch Trail in the Sipsey Wilderness makes for a great overnight trip. The terrain is easy to moderate over dirt and rock trails through a canyon and past several small waterfalls, culminating in Bee Branch Falls and caves. There is an excellent campsite at the end of the trail, just south of the falls.

Start: From the Trail 201/202 Trailhead on County Road 60.
Distance: 11.4-mile point-to-point.
Approximate hiking time: 6–7 hours.
Difficulty: Easy, except for moderate through a canyon area.
Trail surface: Dirt path; rocky through canyon.
Type of hike: Magnolia, holly, hemlock, and oak trees; trillium and pink lady's slippers wildflowers.
Land status: Wilderness area.
Nearest town: Double Springs.
Schedule: Open year-round.
Fees/Permits: There is a $3.00 day-use parking fee at the trailheads. Walk-ins are free.

Maps: USGS map: Bee Branch.
Brochures—Available at the ranger office or by writing the ranger office.
Trail contacts: USDA Forest Service William B. Bankhead District, 14396 Court Street, Moulton 35650; (205) 489-5111; www.southernregion.fs.fed.us/alabama/bankhead/default.htm; open Monday through Friday 7:30 A.M.–4:00 P.M.
Other trail users: None.
Canine compatibility: Dog friendly—fairly easy walking, with ample water available; no leash required.

Finding the trailhead: From Cullman go west on U.S. Highway 278 for 44 miles to Alabama Highway 33 in Double Springs. Turn right and head 12 miles north on AL 33 to County Road 6. Turn left onto CR 6 and travel 8.6 miles. (CR 6 becomes CR 60 when you enter the Sipsey River Recreational Area.) The trailhead is on the right and is well marked. *DeLorme: Alabama Atlas & Gazetteer:* Page 23, B9.

The Hike

The Appalachian Plateau of northwest Alabama bears a close resemblance to the Great Smoky Mountains, with deep canyons and old-growth forest. For thousands of years, the Creek, Cherokee, and Chickasaw Indians hunted and lived here. They used caves along the riverbanks for shelter and hunted a wide variety of game.

Weather and the many rivers and creeks carved out the sandstone canyons, some with walls 300 feet high. Although much of the old-growth oak forest in northwest Alabama is gone, the Sipsey Wilderness preserves much of its original forest.

The wilderness area lies within the William B. Bankhead National Forest, which covers 180,000 acres in two counties, Winston and Lawrence. The forest was set aside as a protected area in 1918 as the Alabama National Forest. In 1942 Congress

An outcropping on the trail.

changed the name to William B. Bankhead National Forest to honor William Bankhead, who served in Congress from 1917 to 1940 and was Speaker of the House for the last six years.

In 1975 Congress again looked at the forest and decided that the area in its northwest corner met the criteria to be named an official wilderness area, and with that the Sipsey Wilderness was born. The wilderness's original 12,726 acres was increased in 1988 to just under 26,000 acres.

This route, despite its popularity, is not an officially numbered trail. The path incorporates Trail 202 (Johnson Cemetery Trail) and Trail 209 (Sipsey Fork Trail) before it branches off and heads up Bee Branch Creek. The Bee Branch Trail is unmarked, and, if you are hiking up Trail 209, it's easy to make a wrong turn and hike the Beach Branch Trail by accident.

The trail starts level, using the gravel road and then the dirt footpath of Trail 202, passing Johnson Cemetery, established in the mid to late 1800s. Before reaching Trail 209, the trail comes to the canyon with its high walls, multiple caves and overhangs, and an impressive waterfall.

Soon the path meets the Sipsey River, requiring you to ford the river to reach Trail 209. The Sipsey is a clear, cold mountain stream. The current here is not that

Bee Branch Trail

SIPSEY
WILDERNESS

TRAIL
206

TRAIL
205

Kings Cove

SIPSEY FORK
TRAIL

TRAIL
209

TRAIL
201

JOHNSON
CEMETERY
TRAIL

TRAIL
202

† Johnson
Cemetery

SIPSEY
WILDERNESS

Falls &
Caves

Turnaround

BEE BRANCH TRAIL

BUNYAN
HILL
ROAD

TRAIL
204

Bee Branch

WILLIAM BANKHEAD
NATIONAL FOREST

(mile 3.9)

Sipsey

TRAIL
209

River

START

CR 60

CRANAL ROAD

CR 6

To
Cullman

N

0   1 Kilometer
0   1 Mile

Legend
Paved Road
Maintained Dirt
Unmaintained Dirt
Singletrack Trail
Selected Route

fast, and the river's depth is 3 feet at most, depending on rainfall. The bottom is sandy.

Immediately on the other side, Trail 209 heads west, following the river, with nice views of the crystal-clear water, large boulders, and the canyon. In about 2 miles the trail comes to what seems like a dead end and makes a right turn. This is where most hikers discover the Bee Branch Trail by accident. To follow Trail 209, you would continue straight across the creek. For the Bee Branch, turn to the right.

If you feel comfortable with map and compass, feel free to head off the trail to explore. Through the trees you'll hear the rush of many waterfalls and realize why the Sipsey Wilderness is called Land of a Thousand Waterfalls. Remember, this is a wilderness area. It's best to register at the trailhead before heading out, in case of emergency, and also to let someone know where you are going and when you expect to be back. Carry plenty of water, matches, some food, a flashlight, and a map and compass.

It's possible to make the entire trip in one day, but most hikers prefer to do it as an overnight, taking advantage of the campsite just south of the waterfalls and caves at the end of the trail.

Miles and Directions

0.0   Start from the Trail 201/202 trailhead off CR 60. Head into the woods behind the information sign—a wooden sign next to the trail reads 201/202.

0.1   Come to a T intersection with a gravel road that runs northeast-southwest. Turn right.

0.2   Come to a fork and go right. (Trail 201 breaks left.)

0.8   **Side trip:** A short 50-foot side trail heads off to the right to Johnson Cemetery.

2.0   A short spur trail (about 10 feet long) leads to the edge of a bluff.

2.3   Come to a large 100-foot waterfall flowing down a cliff.

2.4   Pass a campsite to the right.

2.5   Ford the Sipsey River straight across. (**FYI:** During normal rain, the river runs up to 3 feet deep here, but during unusually heavy rainfall, it may be deeper and may not be passable.) After the crossing, a sign points to the direction of Trail 209 (Sipsey Fork). Turn left and follow this. Pass a campsite on the left.

3.3 Come to a fork and continue straight.

3.5 Pass a camp on the left.

3.6 The trail splits around a large uprooted tree and rejoins at the other side at a creek.

3.9 Come to a wooden post that points to Trail 204. Go straight. Pass another campsite. Just after, the trail splits again around some brush and rejoins at the other end.

4.1 Pass another camp on the right.

4.3 Pass a campsite on the left

4.4 Come to a fork and go right. (The left fork heads to the river.)

4.5 Come to a fork and go right on the Bee Branch Trail. (The left fork looks like a dead end that drops down a short 8-foot slope to a creek. This is actually the continuation of Trail 209.)

4.8 Pass a campsite.

5.3 Pass a camp on the left. In 200 feet come to a fork and go right.

5.4 Come to a T intersection and turn right.

5.6 Come to a fork and go right. Just below, to the left near the creek, is a large campsite, perfect for splitting the trip.

5.7 Reach the end of the trail at a box canyon, with two huge waterfalls and several caves in the rock walls. Turn around and retrace your tracks back to the trailhead.

11.4 Arrive at the Trail 201/202 trailhead.

Hike Information

Local Information

North Alabama Tourism Association, 25062 North Street, Mooreseville 35649; (800) 648-5381; www.northalabama.org.

Lawrence County Chamber of Commerce, 14220 Court Street, Moulton 35650; (205) 974-1658; www.naiap.com.

Winston County Chamber of Commerce, 1200 Twenty-first Street, Hayleyville 35565; (205) 489-5447.

Cullman Area Chamber of Commerce, 211 Second Avenue Northeast, Cullman 35056; (800) 313-5114; www.cullmanchamber.org.

Local Events/Attractions

Ave Maria Grotto, 1600 Saint Bernard Avenue Southeast, Cullman 35055-3057; (256) 734-4110; www.avemariagrotto.com. In 1934 Brother Joseph began building this site. Covering three acres, the grotto consists of more than 125 miniature, hand-carved and con-

structed reproductions of famous churches, shrines, and buildings.

Looney's Tavern and Amphitheater, 22400 Highway 278, Double Springs 35553; (800) LOONEYS; www.looneystavern.com. This site features the famous *Incident at Looney's Tavern* play and other major musical productions throughout the year. You'll also find miniature golf, a restaurant, and riverboat rides.

Semiannual Bluegrass Superjam, each April and November, 211 Second Avenue Northeast, Cullman 35056; (256) 739-4959. Featuring Grand Ole Opry–style music and pure family entertainment.

Indian Festival, second weekend of June, 211 Second Avenue Northeast, Cullman 35056; (256) 737-9163; www.geocities.com/echota_Cherokee_powwow. This festival features Native American arts and crafts, food, dancing, and more.

Lodging

Moulton Motel, Moulton; (256) 974-0636.

Restaurants

Classical Fruit and Barbeque, 8831 Alabama Highway 157, Moulton 35650; (256) 974-8813.

Cardinal Drive-In, 15240 Court Street, Moulton 35650; (256) 974-9065.

John's Barbeque, 15165 Court Street, Moulton 35650; (256) 974-7721.

Nesmith's Hamburgers, 14396 Court Street, Moulton 35650; (256) 974-9806.

Little Kuntry Kitchen, 14258 Court Street, Moulton 35650; (256) 974-3380.

Organizations

Alabama Trails Association, P.O. Box 371162, Birmingham 35237; www.alabamatrailsasso.org.

Sierra Club North Alabama Chapter, Huntsville; www.alabama.sierraclub.org/na.html.

Other Resources

Alabama Environmental Council, 2431 Second Avenue North, Birmingham 35203-3809; (205) 322-3126; www.aecoline.ws/.

Alabama Wilderness Alliance, P.O. Box 223, Moulton 35650; (334) 265-6529.

Bama Environmental News, Montgomery; (205) 226-7739; www.bamanews.com.

Hikeweb: Sipsey Wilderness; www.montesano.com/hikeweb/sipsey.htm.

Wild Alabama, 11312 Alabama Highway 33, Moulton 35650; (256) 974-6166; www.wildalabama.com.

Wildflowers of Alabama; www.duc.auburn.edu/~deancar/index.html.

Wild Law, Montgomery; (334) 396-4729; www.wildlaw.org.

31 Trail 200 (Borden Creek Trail)

This is a great hike for kids and adults alike through the Sipsey Wilderness. Sandstone cliffs tower along the trail, forming a canyon as the route travels along the Sipsey River. The hike gives you a chance to do a little spelunking through a 100-foot cave next to a waterfall.

Start: From the trailhead on Forest Service Road 224.
Distance: 4.8-mile out-and-back.
Approximate hiking time: 4–6 hours.
Difficulty: Easy, over flat footpaths and easy climbs.
Trail surface: Dirt path.
Type of hike: Hemlock, beech, mountain laurel, and holly forests.
Land status: Wilderness area.
Nearest town: Double Springs.
Schedule: Open year-round.
Fees/Permits: There is a $3.00 day-use parking fee at the trailheads. Walk-ins are free.

Maps: USGS map: Bee Branch.
Brochures—Available at the ranger office or by writing the ranger office.
Trail contacts: USDA Forest Service William B. Bankhead District, 14396 Court Street, Moulton 35650; (205) 489-5111; www.southernregion.fs.fed.us/alabama/bankhead/default.htm; open Monday through Friday 7:30 A.M.–4:00 P.M.
Other trail users: None.
Canine compatibility: Dog friendly, with ample water available; no leash required.

Finding the trailhead: From Cullman take U.S. Highway 278 west for 44 miles to Alabama Highway 33 in Double Springs. Turn right and head 12 miles north on AL 33 to County Road 6. Take a left onto CR 6. The road splits. Take the right-hand FS 224 fork and travel 2.5 miles. Pass a sign that reads WARNING – ROAD CLOSED, but continue past the sign 0.5 mile. The trailhead is at the end of the road. *DeLorme: Alabama Atlas & Gazetteer:* Page 23, B10.

The Hike

Most people don't think of Alabama as a wilderness retreat, but it is. As a matter of fact, the state has three designated wilderness areas. Cheaha Wilderness, with its 7,490 acres, lies in northeast Alabama near Cheaha State Park. The Dugger Mountain Wilderness, near Anniston, has 9,200 acres. And the largest tract is the Sipsey Wilderness, with 26,000 acres—the third largest wilderness area in the United States east of the Mississippi.

The Federal Wilderness Act of 1964 identifies four characteristics for a "wilderness area." First, it's a place where the "earth and its community of life are uncontrolled by man." Second, a wilderness "generally appears to have been affected by the forces of nature, with the imprint of man's work substantially unnoticeable." Third, a wilderness is an area where "man is a visitor who does not remain." Finally, a wilderness provides "outstanding opportunities for solitude or a primitive and unconfined type of recreation."

The Sipsey Wilderness exemplifies these characteristics, with the possible exception of "outstanding opportunities for solitude." Sit at one of the trailheads any weekend and you'll understand. The parking areas are routinely full—so often now that the Forest Service discourages large groups from visiting. But don't let this discourage you. The wilderness is that popular for a reason. Simply call ahead to see when you can hit a slack time, or try to aim for a weekday visit.

Trail 200, better known as the Borden Creek Trail, highlights the best of what makes the Sipsey a true wilderness. Of all of the area's trails, Borden Creek draws together the wilderness's most attractive elements and does so along a trail that's easy enough for the whole family to enjoy.

From the start, the cold, clear waters of Borden Creek flow alongside the path as it winds its way to meet the Sipsey River. Sandstone cliffs rise above both sides of the trail, some 300 feet high. As you hike, you can hear the sound of feeder creeks continuing the work of erosion, cascading down the walls of the canyon.

Less than half a mile into the hike, you'll reach a 50-foot waterfall. Next to the waterfall is a cave, about 100 feet long, which the trail travels right through. At first the cave is large enough to walk in comfortably, but toward the end it narrows to the point where you may have to crawl. But the passage isn't difficult, and it adds to the adventure.

As you travel, keep an eye out for other waterfalls flowing down the canyon walls. At the bottom of the cliffs are shallow caves that invite exploration.

Although trails in the wilderness are not marked—except for signs that mark the trailheads and the occasional intersection—keeping on this trail is easy. Unlike Trail 209 (Sipsey Fork Trail), which has several unmarked branch trails that sometimes lure hikers in the wrong direction, this path is well worn, and the only side trails are short ones leading to campsites.

Miles and Directions

0.0 Start from the trailhead behind the information sign. In about 200 feet pass a campsite to the right next to the river. Continue and cross a feeder creek of the river and another campsite.

0.1 Come to a fork and go left. (**FYI:** The trail passes several of these with one fork leading to a campsite. This one is along the right fork.)

0.2 Pass another campsite.

0.4 Come to a 50-foot waterfall. To the right is a cave, which you'll travel through. The cave is about 100 feet long and gets narrow, and darker, as it goes. By the end, you'll be crawling through it, but it's nothing impassable.

1.1 Come to a fork and go right. (The left fork goes to a campsite.)

1.3 Pass a campsite on the right.

1.4 Pass another campsite on the right.

Trail 200 (Borden Creek Trail)

Legend:
- Paved Road
- Maintained Dirt
- Unmaintained Dirt
- Singletrack Trail
- Selected Route

SIPSEY WILDERNESS

WILLIAM BANKHEAD

NATIONAL FOREST

BUNYAN HILL ROAD

Creek

START

FS 224

To 33

Fall

Creek

CULLMAN MOTORWAY (Abandoned)

Borden

Falls
Cave

TRAIL 200

Sipsey

TRAIL 209

River

TRAIL 209

BORDEN CREEK TRAIL

To 33

CRANAL ROAD

SIPSEY WILDERNESS

CR 6

Dedication Marker

Turnaround

Sipsey

River

N

SIPSEY RIVER RECREATION AREA

0   1 Kilometer

0   1 Mile

1.7 Pass another campsite on the right.

1.9 Pass a campsite on the left.

2.1 Come to a fork and go right. (The left fork is a short trail to the cliffs.)

2.2 The trail is washed out here along the riverbank, but it's passable. Be careful.

2.3 Come to a fork and go right.

2.4 An engraved stone to the left dedicates the creation of the wilderness in May 1975. Arrive at the Sipsey River Recreation Area. Turn around here and retrace your tracks back to the trailhead.

4.8 Arrive back at the trailhead.

Hike Information

Local Information

North Alabama Tourism Association, 25062 North Street, Mooreseville 35649; (800) 648-5381; www.northalabama.org.

Lawrence County Chamber of Commerce, 14220 Court Street, Moulton 35650; (205) 974-1658; www.naiap.com.

Winston County Chamber of Commerce, 1200 Twenty-first Street, Hayleyville 35565; (205) 489-5447.

Cullman Area Chamber of Commerce, 211 Second Avenue Northeast, Cullman 35056; (800) 313-5114; www.cullmanchamber.org.

Local Events/Attractions

Ave Maria Grotto, 1600 Saint Bernard Avenue Southeast, Cullman 35055-3057; (256) 734-4110; www.avemariagrotto.com. In 1934 Brother Joseph began building this site. Covering three acres, the grotto consists of more than 125 miniature, hand-carved and con-structed reproductions of famous churches, shrines, and buildings.

Looney's Tavern and Amphitheater, 22400 Highway 278, Double Springs 35553; (800) LOONEYS; www.looneystavern.com. This site features the famous *Incident at Looney's Tavern* play and other major musical productions throughout the year. You'll also find miniature golf, a restaurant, and riverboat rides.

Semiannual Bluegrass Superjam, each April and November, 211 Second Avenue Northeast, Cullman 35056; (256) 739-4959. Featuring Grand Ole Opry–style music and pure family entertainment.

Indian Festival, second weekend of June, 211 Second Avenue Northeast, Cullman 35056; (256) 737-9163; www.geocities.com/echota_ Cherokee_powwow. This festival features Native American arts and crafts, food, dancing, and more.

Borden Creek.

Lodging

Moulton Motel, Moulton; (256) 974-0636.

Restaurants

Classical Fruit and Barbeque, 8831 Alabama Highway 157, Moulton 35650; (256) 974-8813.

Cardinal Drive-In, 15240 Court Street, Moulton 35650; (256) 974-9065.

John's Barbeque, 15165 Court Street, Moulton 35650; (256) 974-7721.

Nesmith's Hamburgers, 14396 Court Street, Moulton 35650; (256) 974-9806.

Little Kuntry Kitchen, 14258 Court Street, Moulton 35650; (256) 974-3380.

Organizations

Alabama Trails Association, P.O. Box 371162, Birmingham 35237; www.alabamatrailsasso.org.

Sierra Club North Alabama Chapter, Huntsville; www.alabama.sierraclub.org/na.html.

Other Resources

Alabama Environmental Council, 2431 Second Avenue North, Birmingham 35203-3809;

(205) 322–3126; www.aecoline.ws/.

Alabama Wilderness Alliance, P.O. Box 223, Moulton 35650; (334) 265–6529.

Bama Environmental News, Montgomery; (205) 226–7739; www.bamanews.com.

Hikeweb: Sipsey Wilderness; www.montesano.com/hikeweb/sipsey.htm.

Wild Alabama, 11312 Alabama Highway 33, Moulton 35650; (256) 974–6166; www.wildalabama.com.

Wildflowers of Alabama; www.duc.auburn.edu/~deancar/index.html.

Wild Law, Montgomery; (334) 396–4729; www.wildlaw.org.

32 Trail 201 (Magnolia Trail)

Trail 201 takes hikers to the Sipsey River at the end of Trail 209 (Sipsey Fork Trail). The hike is level for most of the trip, over dirt footpaths. The trail then descends to follow a small feeder creek down the canyon wall to the Sipsey. The end of the trail is a great place to relax along the river.

Start: From the Trail 201/202 trailhead on County Road 60.
Distance: 5.0-mile out-and-back.
Approximate hiking time: 5–7 hours.
Difficulty: Easy along dirt footpaths, with a moderate climb down and then up the canyon wall.
Trail surface: Mostly dirt; rocky at the canyon.
Type of hike: Old-growth oak forest, along with magnolia, holly, hemlock, and southern yellow pine; wildflowers such as yellow lady's slipper and trillium.
Land status: Wilderness area.
Nearest town: Double Springs.
Schedule: Open year-round.

Fees/Permits: There is a $3.00 day-use parking fee at the trailheads. Walk-ins are free.
Maps: USGS map: Bee Branch.
Brochures—Available at the ranger office or by writing the ranger office.
Trail contacts: USDA Forest Service William B. Bankhead District, 14396 Court Street, Moulton 35650; (205) 489-5111; www.southernregion.fs.fed.us/alabama/bankhead/default.htm; open Monday through Friday 7:30 A.M.–4:00 P.M.
Other trail users: None.
Canine compatibility: Dog friendly—along easy path, though the descent to the river is a bit steep. Bring water; no leash required.

Finding the trailhead: From Cullman go west on U.S. Highway 278 for 44 miles to Alabama Highway 33 in Double Springs. Turn right and head 12 miles north on AL 33 to County Road 6. Turn left onto CR 6 and travel 8.6 miles. (CR 6 becomes CR 60 when you enter the Sipsey River Recreational Area.) The trailhead is on the right and is well marked. *DeLorme: Alabama Atlas & Gazetteer:* Page 23, B9.

The Hike

The Sipsey Wilderness is the only area of old-growth oak forest remaining in Alabama. Along the trail you'll find magnificent specimens of magnolia, holly, hemlock, and oak. This is also prime wildflower region. Don't be surprised to see a lot of photographers along the trail, capturing images of yellow lady's slippers, shooting stars, yellow and white trilliums, and other flowers.

There's a good chance you'll spot white-tailed deer, wild turkeys, or foxes. Coyotes have made a comeback in the region, but seeing them is a little unlikely. Birdwatchers love the Sipsey Wilderness, where it's not unusual to see such specimens as Acadian flycatchers, eastern phoebes, and belted kingfishers.

This route is one of the few in the wilderness that doesn't come to a waterfall, but what it lacks in cascading water it more than makes up for with its view of the

Trailhead displays in the Sipsey Wilderness have information on trail conditions and safety precautions.

Sipsey River and surrounding canyon. The route may have a bit of moderate difficulty, but not to the point where hikers of all ages cannot enjoy the trip.

The first three-quarters of the trail, along Trail 201, is a level dirt path. It then intersects Trail 209 and descends steeply down the canyon to the river. The brush gets thick in some areas, narrowing the trail. The thorny leaves of holly and blackberry vines may leave you with a few scrapes. The real concern is poison ivy, which also lines the path.

Bushwhacking and off-trailing is encouraged if you are experienced and feel comfortable with orienteering (using map and compass), but be cautious. The area is dotted with high bluffs and waterfalls that can suddenly appear as you come out of dense brush.

The wide, open Magnolia Trail (Trail 201).

Whether off-trailing or not, remember to practice Zero Impact hiking. Take only pictures; leave only footprints. Carry ample water, even for short hikes. Don't forget that even those lovely waters of the Sipsey and its feeder creeks should be boiled for at least two minutes, purified, or filtered before drinking. To help prevent fires, use a camp stove instead of a wood fire. If you do use an established fire ring, be sure the coals are completely out before you leave. Hunting is allowed in the wilderness generally between November 15 and March 15. Contact the Forest Service to verify the dates.

If you're looking for a good full-day loop, or even a good overnight, use Trail 201 in conjunction with Trails 209 and 202. There are numerous campsites along the banks of the Sipsey.

Trail 201 (Magnolia Trail)

	Paved Road
	Maintained Dirt
	Unmaintained Dirt
	Singletrack Trail
	Selected Route

SIPSEY WILDERNESS

TRAIL 206

BEE BRANCH TRAIL

TRAIL 205

TRAIL 204

Kings Cove

Bee Branch

Turnaround

SIPSEY FORK TRAIL

TRAIL 209

TRAIL 209

Sipsey

River

TRAIL 201

WILLIAM BANKHEAD

NATIONAL FOREST

JOHNSON CEMETERY TRAIL

TRAIL 202

† Johnson Cemetery

SIPSEY

WILDERNESS

wilderness boundary

START

N

CR 60

CRANAL ROAD

To Cullman

| 0 | | | | 1 Kilometer |
| 0 | | | | 1 Mile |

Miles and Directions

0.0 Start from the Trail 201/202 trailhead off CR 60. Head into the woods behind the information sign—a wooden sign next to the trail reads 201/202.

0.1 Come to a T intersection with a gravel road that runs northeast-southwest. Turn right.

0.2 Come to a fork and go left. (Trail 202 breaks right.)

2.0 The gravel trail comes to an intersection. Turn right onto Trail 209 (the Sipsey Fork Trail). Trail 201 continues to the left.

2.5 Come to a fork. Go left and head steeply down the canyon wall, following a stream to the bottom, where the trail ends at the Sipsey River. (The right fork is a short trail that leads to the edge of the canyon with a nice view of the river.) A wooden sign at the bottom indicates the intersection of the two trails. Turn around and retrace your tracks to the trailhead.

5.0 Arrive back at the Trail 201/202 trailhead.

Hike Information

Local Information

North Alabama Tourism Association, 25062 North Street, Mooreseville 35649; (800) 648-5381; www.northalabama.org.

Lawrence County Chamber of Commerce, 14220 Court Street, Moulton 35650; (205) 974-1658; www.naiap.com.

Winston County Chamber of Commerce, 1200 Twenty-first Street, Hayleyville 35565; (205) 489-5447.

Cullman Area Chamber of Commerce, 211 Second Avenue Northeast, Cullman 35056; (800) 313-5114; www.cullmanchamber.org.

Local Events/Attractions

Ave Maria Grotto, 1600 Saint Bernard Avenue Southeast, Cullman 35055-3057; (256) 734-4110; www.avemariagrotto.com. In 1934 Brother Joseph began building this site. Covering three acres, the grotto consists of more than 125 miniature, hand-carved and constructed reproductions of famous churches, shrines, and buildings.

Looney's Tavern and Amphitheater, 22400 Highway 278, Double Springs 35553; (800) LOONEYS; www.looneystavern.com. This site features the famous *Incident at Looney's Tavern* play and other major musical productions throughout the year. You'll also find miniature golf, a restaurant, and riverboat rides.

Semiannual Bluegrass Superjam, each April and November, 211 Second Avenue Northeast, Cullman 35056; (256) 739-4959. Featuring Grand Ole Opry–style music and pure family entertainment.

Indian Festival, second weekend of June, 211 Second Avenue Northeast, Cullman 35056; (256) 737-9163; www.geocities.com/echota_

Cherokee_powwow. This festival features Native American arts and crafts, food, dancing, and more.

Lodging

Moulton Motel, Moulton; (256) 974-0636.

Restaurants

Classical Fruit and Barbeque, 8831 Alabama Highway 157, Moulton 35650; (256) 974-8813.

Cardinal Drive-In, 15240 Court Street, Moulton 35650; (256) 974-9065.

John's Barbeque, 15165 Court Street, Moulton 35650; (256) 974-7721.

Nesmith's Hamburgers, 14396 Court Street, Moulton 35650; (256) 974-9806.

Little Kuntry Kitchen, 14258 Court Street, Moulton 35650; (256) 974-3380.

Organizations

Alabama Trails Association, P.O. Box 371162, Birmingham 35237; www.alabamatrailsasso.org.

Sierra Club North Alabama Chapter, Huntsville; www.alabama.sierraclub.org/na.html.

Other Resources

Alabama Environmental Council, 2431 Second Avenue North, Birmingham 35203-3809; (205) 322-3126; www.aecoline.ws/.

Alabama Wilderness Alliance, P.O. Box 223, Moulton 35650; (334) 265-6529.

Bama Environmental News, Montgomery; (205) 226-7739; www.bamanews.com.

Hikeweb: Sipsey Wilderness; www.montesano.com/hikeweb/sipsey.htm.

Wild Alabama, 11312 Alabama Highway 33, Moulton 35650; (256) 974-6166; www.wildalabama.com.

Wildflowers of Alabama; www.duc.auburn.edu/~deancar/index.html.

Wild Law, Montgomery; (334) 396-4729; www.wildlaw.org.

33 Trail 209 (Sipsey Fork Trail)

Trail 209 is the longest trail in the Sipsey Wilderness, following the flow of the Sipsey River through most of the canyon, with waterfalls and towering limestone cliffs lining the banks. Vegetation along the trail includes blackberry bushes and muscadine vines.

Start: From the Sipsey Wilderness Recreation Area.
Distance: 17.4-mile out-and-back.
Approximate hiking time: 12–14 hours.
Difficulty: Easy, over dirt paths; moderate to difficult at the fording of the Sipsey River near the end of the hike.
Trail surface: Dirt path.
Type of hike: Magnolia, hemlock, oak, and southern yellow pine; muscadine vines.
Land status: Wilderness area.
Nearest town: Double Springs.
Schedule: Open year-round.
Fees/Permits: There is a $3.00 day-use parking fee at the trailheads. Walk-ins are free.

Maps: USGS map: Bee Branch.
Brochures—Available at the ranger office or by writing the ranger office.
Trail contacts: USDA Forest Service William B. Bankhead District, 14396 Court Street, Moulton 35650; (205) 489-5111; www.southernregion.fs.fed.us/alabama/bankhead/default.htm; open Monday through Friday 7:30 A.M.–4:00 P.M.
Other trail users: None.
Canine compatibility: Dog friendly, with plenty of water available; no leash required.

Finding the trailhead: From Cullman take U.S. Highway 278 west for 44 miles to Alabama Highway 33 in Double Springs. Turn right and head 12 miles north on AL 33 to County Road 6. Take a left onto CR 6 and travel 3.8 miles to the Sipsey Recreational Area. The parking area is on the left and is well marked. *DeLorme: Alabama Atlas & Gazetteer:* Page 23, B10.

The Hike

Trail 209 (Sipsey Fork Trail) traces the flow of the Sipsey River for 8.7 miles through the 25,906-acre Sipsey Wilderness. Along the trail, the walls of the canyon rise high, dotted at their base with caves. You'll hear creeks as they cascade down the sandstone walls on their way to the river, and you'll see waterfalls high above the trail. The Sipsey River is an impressive sight to behold. The clear, cold waters run for 61 miles, forming the only nationally designated Wild and Scenic River in Alabama.

Near the end of Trail 209, you get a chance to test your river-fording skills. The crossing is made just before the trail intersects Trail 201. The current is usually not exceptionally strong, but you may want to wear boots or sandals because of the rocky bottom. During heavy rains, the river may be impossible to ford.

As you hike, be on the lookout for white-tailed deer, eastern wild turkeys, and foxes. If you're into fishing, largemouth bass and bluegill are the main catch—a state freshwater fishing license is required. The trail is lined with magnificent hemlocks,

Large boulders in the Sipsey River.

magnolias, and southern yellow pines. Wildflowers are too numerous to name, but the photographers who flock to the area in spring and summer will be more than happy to point them out.

The Forest Service encourages experienced hikers to leave the trail and explore the surrounding area. There is plenty to see and discover here. On one excursion I stumbled onto some beautiful waterfalls, with no one around but me and the sounds and sights of the wilderness. The key word here, though, is *experienced*. If you are not familiar with orienteering (using map and compass), the best thing is to stay on the trail. It's easy to get lost.

Most hikers make the Trail 209 hike into an overnight hike, instead of trying to tackle 17.4 miles in one day. Along the route are plenty of good campsites. To protect the river and the surrounding environment, the Forest Service asks that hikers camp away from rivers, streams, and the trail. Over the years, hikers have made camp at the edge of the river and, in some cases, directly on the trail. Rangers are okay with your using these established campsites, because the most damage to an area is when it is first camped on. Just make sure you don't expand the existing site.

Even though the Sipsey River is in a wilderness area, its water should still be treated before you drink it to kill disease organisms such as those that cause giardiasis, which results in severe diarrhea, nausea, fever, and other symptoms. Boil water for at least two minutes, treat it chemically, or use a filter.

Winter and spring are the best times to enjoy the wilderness. In winter, leaves are gone and there are better views of the canyon. In spring, the wildflowers add color, and the river is running swiftly after spring rain and winter thaw. Summer brings mosquitoes and bugs. The Forest Service allows hunting in the area generally between November 15 and January 31; contact the Forest Service for exact dates.

Miles and Directions

0.0 Start from the trailhead at the Sipsey Recreational Area into the woods. In 50 feet start heading downhill and pass under CR 60.

0.5 Come to a fork where Borden Creek branches off to the northeast from the river and go left. (Trail 200 continues to the right.) Ford the creek and pick up the trail on the opposite side.

0.8 Keep an eye out for small side trails that lead to the river and nice places to just relax.

1.5 The trail merges briefly with a dirt road known as the Cullman Motorway. Shortly it leaves the road and heads back to the woods to the west.

2.5 Pass a campsite next to the river.

4.5 Come to a wooden post with 202 on it, pointing across the river. This is Trail 202 (the Johnson Cemetery Trail). To get to Trail 202 you must ford the river. Continue straight and pass a campsite on the left.

5.3 Come to a fork and continue straight.

5.5 Pass a camp on the left.

5.6 A fork in the trail splits around a large uprooted tree and rejoins at the other side at a creek.

5.9 Come to a wooden post that points to Trail 204. Go straight to the west. In 50 feet pass another campsite. Just after, the trail splits again around some brush and rejoins at the other end.

Trail 209 (Sipsey Fork Trail)

SIPSEY WILDERNESS

WILLIAM BANKHEAD
NATIONAL FOREST

SIPSEY WILDERNESS

SIPSEY
WILDERNESS

Borden Creek

Fall Creek

FS 224

BUNYAN
HILL
ROAD

CULLMAN
MOTORWAY
(Abandoned)

P

Falls
Cave

BORDEN CREEK
TRAIL

TRAIL 200

Ford Stream

TRAIL 209

TRAIL 209

TRAIL 209

Sipsey River

(mile 4.5)

(mile 5.9)

TRAIL 201

BEE BRANCH
TRAIL

SIPSEY FORK
TRAIL

Ford Stream

TRAIL 209

TRAIL 205

TRAIL 206

Turnaround

TRAIL 201

(9)

JOHNSON
CEMETERY
TRAIL

TRAIL 202

Johnson
Cemetery

Wolfpen
Cemetery

CRANAL ROAD

CR 6

CR 60

Dedication
Marker

CRANAL ROAD

To
Cullman

SIPSEY
RIVER
RECREATIONAL
AREA

Sipsey River

START

N

1 Kilometer
0

1 Mile
0

Paved Road
Maintained Dirt
Unmaintained Dirt
Singletrack Trail
Selected Route

Intersection of Trails 209 and 202, where we cross the river.

6.1 Pass another camp on the right.

6.3 Pass a campsite on the left.

6.4 Come to a fork and go right. (The left fork heads to the river.)

6.5 Come to a fork and go left. (The right fork is the Bee Branch Trail and heads uphill following the feeder creek.) The left fork looks like a dead end that drops down to a creek, but you'll want to take this. Head down the short slope and cross the creek. There will be a campsite on the other side, next to the river.

7.5 Pass a campsite on the right, next to the river.

8.4 Come to a trail split. Turn left and cross the river. (A wooden post here indicates that Trail 206 goes right.) The river crossing is rocky, so you may want to wear boots or sandals. The current isn't exceptionally strong most days, but you can feel the push. During times of heavy rain, this crossing may be impassible. Climb the opposite bank and pick the trail up again. Several nice campsites can be found along the next 0.3 mile.

8.7 Reach another wooden post that marks Trails 201 and 209. This is the end of Trail 209. Turn around and retrace your tracks.

17.4 Arrive back at the Sipsey Recreational Area.

Hike Information

Local Information

North Alabama Tourism Association, 25062 North Street, Mooreseville 35649; (800) 648-5381; www.northalabama.org.

Lawrence County Chamber of Commerce, 14220 Court Street, Moulton 35650; (205) 974-1658; www.naiap.com.

Winston County Chamber of Commerce, 1200 Twenty-first Street, Hayleyville 35565; (205) 489-5447.

Cullman Area Chamber of Commerce, 211 Second Avenue Northeast, Cullman 35056; (800) 313-5114; www.cullmanchamber.org.

Local Events/Attractions

Ave Maria Grotto, 1600 Saint Bernard Avenue Southeast, Cullman 35055-3057; (256) 734-4110; www.avemariagrotto.com. In 1934 Brother Joseph began building this site. Covering three acres, the grotto consists of more than 125 miniature, hand-carved and constructed reproductions of famous churches, shrines, and buildings.

Looney's Tavern and Amphitheater, 22400 Highway 278, Double Springs 35553; (800) LOONEYS; www.looneystavern.com. This site features the famous *Incident at Looney's Tavern* play and other major musical productions throughout the year. You'll also find miniature golf, a restaurant, and riverboat rides.

Semiannual Bluegrass Superjam, each April and November, 211 Second Avenue Northeast, Cullman 35056; (256) 739-4959. Featuring Grand Ole Opry-style music and pure family entertainment.

Indian Festival, second weekend of June, 211 Second Avenue Northeast, Cullman 35056; (256) 737-9163; www.geocities.com/echota_ Cherokee_powwow. This festival features Native American arts and crafts, food, dancing, and more.

Lodging

Moulton Motel, Moulton; (256) 974-0636.

Restaurants

Classical Fruit and Barbeque, 8831 Alabama Highway 157, Moulton 35650; (256) 974-8813.

Cardinal Drive-In, 15240 Court Street, Moulton 35650; (256) 974-9065.

John's Barbeque, 15165 Court Street, Moulton 35650; (256) 974-7721.

Nesmith's Hamburgers, 14396 Court Street, Moulton 35650; (256) 974-9806.

Little Kuntry Kitchen, 14258 Court Street, Moulton 35650; (256) 974-3380.

Organizations

Alabama Trails Association, P.O. Box 371162, Birmingham 35237; www.alabamatrailsasso.org.

Sierra Club North Alabama Chapter, Huntsville; www.alabama.sierraclub.org/na.html.

Other Resources

Alabama Environmental Council, 2431 Second Avenue North, Birmingham 35203-3809; (205) 322-3126; www.aecoline.ws/.

Alabama Wilderness Alliance, P.O. Box 223, Moulton 35650; (334) 265-6529.

Bama Environmental News, Montgomery; (205) 226-7739; www.bamanews.com.

Hikeweb: Sipsey Wilderness; www.montesano.com/hikeweb/sipsey.htm.

Wild Alabama, 11312 Alabama Highway 33, Moulton 35650; (256) 974-6166; www.wildalabama.com.

Wildflowers of Alabama; www.duc.auburn.edu/ ~deancar/index.html.

Wild Law, Montgomery; (334) 396-4729; www.wildlaw.org.

34 Rainbow Mountain Loop Trail

An oasis amidst the subdivisions, the Rainbow Mountain Loop Trail follows a generally rocky path around the east face of the mountain and features unique rock formations such as Balance Rock, a cliffline with excellent views, fossils, Belly-Up and other caves, and a waterfall.

Start: From the water tower along Stoneridge Road.
Distance: 2.1-mile loop.
Approximate hiking time: 2 hours.
Difficulty: Easy, along rocky trail; moderate climb at the ravine.
Trail surface: Generally rocky, with small boulders and table rocks acting as pavers along the route.
Type of hike: Travels to unique geologic landscapes with a remarkable fossil record through redbud, dogwood, maple, and oak forest.

Land status: Huntsville Land Trust property.
Nearest town: Madison.
Schedule: Open year-round.
Fees/Permits: No fee to hike. Camping is not permitted.
Maps: USGS map: Madison.
Brochures—Available from Huntsville Land Trust free of charge.
Trail contacts: Huntsville Land Trust, 907 Franklin Street, Huntsville 35801; (205) 534-5263; www.landtrust-hsv.org.
Other trail users: None.
Canine compatibility: Must be on leash.

Finding the trailhead: From Madison take Interstate 565 exit 8. If heading west, make a right turn onto Wall-Triana Highway, otherwise make a left. (This highway changes names from Wall-Triana to Sullivan and back again.) Travel 4.2 miles and turn right onto Leathertree Lane. Continue 0.5 mile and turn right onto Hughes Road. Travel 0.1 mile and turn left onto Thomas Drive. In 0.3 mile turn left onto Concord Drive. Travel 0.1 mile and turn right onto Stoneridge. Follow it around 1.2 miles to the water tower on the left. You will pass a sign indicating the Rainbow Mountain Trail just before the parking lot. *Delorme: Alabama Atlas & Gazetteer:* Page 19, D6.

The Hike

The Rainbow Mountain Loop Trail is another excellent example of the hard work that the Huntsville Land Trust and North Alabama Sierra Club has put into saving what's left of the greenspace around the ever-expanding Huntsville-Madison city limits. Through their efforts, along with donations and acquisition of lands in the area, unique areas such as Rainbow Mountain and the Land Trust Trails on Monte Sano Mountain have survived the onslaught of urban sprawl.

As you drive to this hike, you will be traveling smack-dab in the middle of a very nice subdivision, complete with minivans. All the way up to the parking lot and the trailhead, you may think that you will be hiking the sidewalks instead of a dirt path. But the trailhead is where suburbia ends.

The trail is situated within a sixty-five-acre tract of land on the east side of the mountain, where the views of the surrounding valley, especially in fall and winter, are wonderful. As you walk, you will be traveling through forests thick with dogwood, maple, buckthorn, and oak trees. Wildflowers, especially in the area of Waterfall Spring and the Horacek Wildflower Glade, add vivid colors to the trip in spring and summer.

White-tailed deer, wild turkeys, horned owls, foxes, rabbits, and coyotes are just some of the wildlife that can still be found on the mountain. The sad fact, however, is that while the land trust and Sierra Club are doing their best to protect the land, encroachment from all sides threatens to cut off designated animal corridors, which would mean the end to the indigenous wildlife on the mountain.

The trail itself varies from leave-covered dirt paths to flat rock and is easily identifiable by the white-diamond RAINBOW MT. TRAIL markers located on trees along the route.

The highlight of the trip is the extraordinary geological features you will find here. The first portion of the hike takes you along the Cliffline, a rock ridge high on the hillside that offers wonderful views.

Pay close attention to the rocks through here. You will see wavy striations embedded in the rock, evidence of ocean activity in this area as far back as 225 million years ago. Because of this ocean, which was here during the Mississippian and Pennsylvanian periods, the fossil record on the mountain is rife with remnants of the distant past. You will easily spot crinoids, brachiopods, and rugosa coral fossils.

The action of the water and elements over the millennia has created an unusual structure that you will pass just after the start of the trip—Balance Rock. This rock stands about 50 to 75 feet tall and literally looks like a toy top balancing on its point.

If you are an *experienced* caver, you will find two favorites, including the 65-foot Rainbow Pit and the Belly-Up cave, if you travel down the Spring Head Trail. And speaking of the Spring Head Trail, in rainy months it is worth the short hike down the trail to view several nice cascades.

All in all, the trek is relatively easy; however, it does get strenuous over the last quarter of the hike as the trail weaves its way back up the side of a ravine from Waterfall Spring. And don't be surprised when the end of the hike takes you directly through a small children's playground just before returning to your vehicle at the water tower.

◀ *Hiking just below the Rainbow Mountain cliffline.*

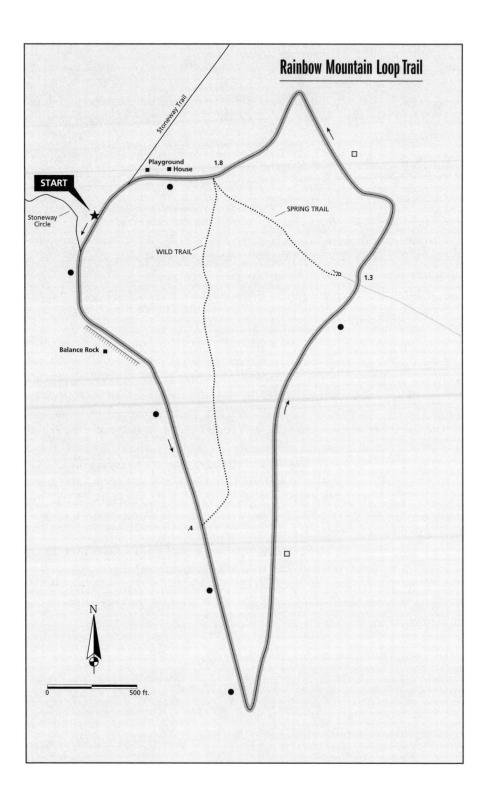

Rainbow Mountain Loop Trail

START

Stoneway Trail

Stoneway Circle

Playground
House

1.8

SPRING TRAIL

WILD TRAIL

.0

1.3

Balance Rock

.4

N

0   500 ft.

Balance Rock.

Miles and Directions

0.0 Start from the water tower and head south 50 feet on the gravel road. Cross over a log that marks the start of the trail. The trail is marked with white-diamond markers that read RAINBOW MT. TRAIL. The trail turns to the left.

0.1 The trail follows along the cliffline. In fall and winter, when the trees are bare, this area provides some nice views of the surrounding valley. Shortly you will come to Balance Rock. The trail is narrow as it travels between cuts in the cliff. The boulders in this area create small cavelike openings.

0.2 Pass several table rocks to the right, with some nice views of the valley.

0.4 Come to the intersection with the Wild Trail.

0.6 The trail Y's. Take the left fork. The trail is now along a 1- to 2-foot-wide flat rock path.

0.7 Come to a section that looks like a Y in the trail. Take the right side. The trail is narrowed by thick brush, and the rocks are heavy in moss. Markers disappear for a time through this section.

1.3 At the bottom of a ravine, come to a stream and a small cascade to the left. Cross the stream and begin to climb back up the ravine on the opposite side. The trail at this point weaves up the hillside.

1.8 Come to the intersection with Spring Trail. A short walk down this trail takes you to a very nice waterfall—when we're not in a drought period.

1.9 The trail levels out as it nears the top of the mountain. A house will be seen to the right, a playground straight ahead. At the playground, the trail jogs to the right and arrives at the road just down from the parking lot.

2.1 Turn left and travel a short distance back to your vehicle.

Hike Information

Local Information

Huntsville-Madison Chamber of Commerce, 225 Church Street, Huntsville 35804; (256) 535-8000.

Local Events/Attractions

Madison Street Festival, first Saturday in October, 225 Church Street, Huntsville 35804; (256) 535-8000. A day of food, parades, arts and crafts, and entertainment.

Historic Walking Tour of Madison, 700 Monroe Street, Huntsville 35801; (256) 772-5602. Tours are provided by the Madison Station Historic Society.

Lodging

Federal Square, 8781 Highway 20 West, Madison 35758; (256) 772-8470.

Heron's Nest, 176 Coffee Bluff Road, Madison 35801; (256) 885-4486.

Restaurants

Allen's Grill and Grog, 9076 Madison Boulevard, Madison 35758; (256) 772-8514.

Madison Coffee and Deli, 300 Hughes Road, Suite G, Madison 35758; (256) 772-2900.

Hike Tours

Huntsville Land Trust, 907 Franklin Street, Huntsville 35801; (205) 534-5263; www.landtrust-hsv.org. Check the Web site for a schedule of hikes.

Organizations

North Alabama Sierra Club, Huntsville; (256) 725-2168; alabama.sierraclub.org/na.html.

35 Plateau Loop Trail

The Plateau Loop Trail is actually a combination of two trails, the North and South Plateau Loop Trails. Together, they form a single loop around the summit of Monte Sano Mountain and offer two contrasting views of this unique state park—its geology and its history.

Start: From the hiker's parking lot next to the Monte Sano State Park office.
Distance: 4.8-mile loop.
Approximate hiking time: 1 hour.
Difficulty: Easy, over level footpaths.
Trail surface: Clay footpaths.
Type of hike: Waterfalls and bluffs overlooking the Huntsville Valley.
Land status: State park.
Nearest town: Huntsville.
Schedule: Open year-round.
Fees/Permits: No fee to hike. Camping fees are $14, base rate.

Maps: USGS maps: Huntsville; Meridianville. Park map—A brochure with trail map is available at the camp store for 50 cents.
Trail contacts: Monte Sano State Park, 5105 Nolen Avenue, Huntsville 35801; (256) 534-3757.
Other trail users: Cyclists.
Canine compatibility: Dog friendly over this easy path. Ample water available; leash recommended through picnic areas.

Finding the trailhead: From Huntsville take U.S. Highway 231 south from Interstate 565 (exit 19A) for 0.4 mile and merge onto U.S. Highway 431 south—stay in the center lane for this turn. Travel 4 miles up the side of Monte Sano Mountain and make a sharp left onto Monte Sano Boulevard. Head up the mountain 2.4 miles and make a right onto Nolen Avenue. Continue straight for 2 miles and Nolen Avenue forks. (To the right is the trailhead.) Take the left fork and travel 0.1 mile to the park office and camp store/campground. Park here. *DeLorme: Alabama Atlas & Gazetteer:* Page 19, D8.

The Hike

The phrase "monte sano" is Latin for *mountain of health*. In the early 1800s this mountain became a refuge for people with yellow fever, cholera, and malaria who sought out its cool air and clear waters. In 1827 Dr. Thomas Fearn established a colony here for people seeking relief from illness. He built an ornate home for himself and his family, complete with stables and a smokehouse. The colony flourished until Union soldiers destroyed it during the Civil War.

The area was rebuilt after the Civil War and flourished with income from tourists until the Great Depression. Members of the Civilian Conservation Corps arrived in 1935, and the rebuilding process began anew: cabins, picnic areas, horse barns, trails, roadways, and even a tavern were constructed. Monte Sano State Park was born in 1936.

A rest shelter along the Plateau Loop Trail on a foggy morning.

The southern portion of this trail, the South Plateau Loop, marked by white blazes, highlights the geologic processes that made the mountain and the stunning limestone formations of the area. Here the trail winds along high blufflines, favorites with cavers and rock climbers, and offers superb views of the surrounding mountains, including Round Top and McKay and Mills Hollows. Be sure to heed the warning signs that read DANGER: HIGH BLUFFS.

The trail will take us to the outcropping known as O'Shaughnessy Point. The point was named for Colonel James O'Shaughnessy from Dublin, Ireland, who came to the region to supervise construction of a trunk railroad line from Brunswick, Georgia, to St. Louis, Missouri, that would pass through Huntsville. O'Shaughnessy also helped supervise the building of the Monte Sano Hotel.

The north section of the trail will take you past beautiful waterfalls, the best being directly behind the picnic pavilion. Here 70-foot Blue Creek Falls cascades down the rocks. When we're not in a drought, it is well worth the short hike down the first few hundred feet of the McKay Hollow Trail to view the falls.

Traveling through a picnic area, the route reveals evidence of the CCC work in the Monte Sano Tavern—built in 1937 but destroyed by fire in 1947. This is one of the largest remains of CCC buildings in the state, and the site offers a fine look at the stone masonry skills of the Corps.

As the trail loops around the plateau, you'll enjoy views of the rocky outcroppings that mark the caverns known as the Sinks (where the Stone Cuts Trail travels) and of Mills Hollow.

The trail also leads to Von Braun Observatory. When Dr. Wernher von Braun came to Huntsville to work at the American space program facility, he and his colleagues helped guide the building of this planetarium and observatory, which opened in 1956. The facility is operated by the Von Braun Astronomical Society, which sponsors a public program on the first and second Saturdays of each month. The programs include lectures by astronomers and NASA scientists and, weather permitting, views through the telescopes.

Miles and Directions

0.0 Start from the east end of the hiker's parking lot following the blue blazes. Head straight across the paved road and pick up and follow a gravel walkway to the north. In about 100 feet, pass immediately next to the ranger station. Cross a parking lot, picking up the blazes on the other side.

0.1 Cross a paved road heading between sections of a split-rail fence and turn left (north).

0.2 Come to the overlooks, a paved cul-de-sac that affords the park's most spectacular view of the Huntsville Valley. Continuing straight, you will see that the road leading down the mountain is closed. To the left of this gate, pick up the blazes again into the woods. The trail travels to the left and just above this road for a time.

0.5 Pass behind the Von Braun Observatory.

0.6 Pass a campground to the left as the trail travels just below the ridge. In 200 feet come to a Y intersection. The red-blazed Fire Tower Trail branches to the right; take the left fork. Soon after, you will pass a large house to the right and cross over the Fire Tower Trail again.

0.8 Come to the picnic pavilion with a wonderful view of McKay Hollow. To the right of the structure is the McKay Hollow Trail. When there's plenty of water, take the short hike to the base of the cliff behind the pavilion for a spectacular view of the falls. Be careful! The McKay Hollow Trail is steep and dangerous when wet! The trail now passes through a picnic area over a gravel path.

1.1 Pass the ruins of the Monte Sano Tavern, built by the CCC in 1937. The tavern was destroyed by fire in 1947. Just past the ruins, cross a small stream and come to a Y. During wet seasons, take the right fork a short 50 feet to view a nice cascade; otherwise, continue straight.

1.2 Come to an intersection with the Fire Tower Road. Continuing straight on the blue-blazed North Loop Trail will take you back to the hiker's parking lot. Turn right, crossing a wooden bridge over a creek, and follow the red blazes. In a few yards reach the intersection with the South Plateau Loop. Turn right, following the white blazes to the south.

1.3 A sign on the left reads DANGER HIGH BLUFFS—and they aren't kidding. For the next 1.3 miles, although the views are very nice on the trail, the trail itself runs within 20 to 30 feet of some great cliffs that provide excellent views of the Huntsville Valley below. The

Plateau Loop Trail

Paved Road
Maintained Dirt
Unmaintained Dirt
Singletrack Trail
Selected Route

1. Logan Point Tr
2. Panther Knob Tr
3. Stone Cuts Trail
4. Mtn Mist Trail
5. Sinks Trail
6. Stone Cuts Bypass
7. Cold Springs Tr
8. N. Plateau Loop
9. Fire Tower Tr
10. S. Plateau Loop
11. Bog Trail
12. McKay Hollow Tr
13. Natural Well Tr
14. Warpath Ridge Tr

PANTHER KNOB

Stone Cuts

The Sinks

Von Braun Observatory

BANKHEAD PARKWAY

RV Parking

The Overlooks

Cold Springs

NOLEN AVENUE

MONTE SANO MOUNTAIN

MONTE SANO BLVD

Ruins

START

Blue Spring

Natural Well

MONTE SANO STATE PARK

Ruins

PANORAMA DRIVE

McKAY HOLLOW

N

0   1/2 Kilometer

0   1/2 Mile

O'Shaughnessy Point

To 431

first of several small side trails will be found here that leads to the bluffs; again, be careful! At this point, the trail narrows to 3 to 4 feet wide.

1.5 To the left, pass a small amphitheater used for nature lectures. In 200 feet the trail comes to a Y. This is a short connector trail to the opposite side of the loop. Take the right fork and continue to the southeast. Just past the Y cross a short 20-foot wooden footbridge over a nice creek. Travel another 100 feet and cross another 30-foot bridge over a creek with intermittent water. After crossing the bridge, the trail turns to the southwest.

1.6 Cross another 20-foot wooden footbridge over a small creek, and continue southwest.

1.8 The trail makes a turn to the southeast and widens to a good 5 to 6 feet; it's lined with heavy brush.

1.9 The orange-blazed Bog Trail joins the South Plateau Trail from the north. Continue heading to the southeast. In 100 feet the trail makes its closest approach to one of the bluffs on the right side. In another 200 feet, pass an old stone foundation on the left. Again, some nice bluffs and views will be seen on the right.

2.1 The trail crosses a creek and turns right to become a clay roadbed and travel uphill. In 50 feet the trail tops the hill and turns to the east. Here the red-blazed Fire Tower Trail merges briefly with this trail, and it once again turns into a 3-foot-wide dirt footpath.

2.2 The Fire Tower Trail branches off to the southeast. The South Plateau Trail continues to the left to the southwest. Another 100 feet ahead, the Bog Trail branches off to the left. The trail turns to the right and continues on to the southwest. After 200 feet, cross a series of 4 x 4 poles that aid in erosion prevention. Here the brush and trees open up to afford more views of the valley and surrounding mountains.

2.4 Pass a nice outcropping on the right. This is a great place to stop and take in the views. Another 200 feet ahead, pass the first trail shelter on the right. Fifty feet farther, the trail turns to the southeast and passes a sign reading MMT 6 (Mountain Mist Trail 6).

2.5 The South Plateau Trail merges with the yellow-blazed Mountain Mist Trail. The best view of the valley can be seen here. Travel 200 feet and pass the second, much better, trail shelter on the right.

2.7 The path now makes a "hairpin" turn as it begins its loop back to the parking area. A sign here reads WARPATH RIDGE and PARKING and points to the left. The Mountain Mist Trail continues straight. The Southern Plateau turns to the northeast and swings to the northwest. The trail here is 5 feet wide.

2.8 Pass a short connector trail to the Mountain Mist Trail on the right, with a sign pointing the direction to the trail. The MMT will be seen below the Southern Plateau Trail and runs parallel for a time.

3.1 Pass a third trail shelter on the right. The trail winds from here to the north-northwest. The best bluff on the trail is passed here. After 200 feet the trail merges with a gravel road. Continue straight on this road to the northwest.

3.2 Once again, the red-blazed Fire Tower Trail intersects the trail from the northeast. Continue straight to the north. The next 0.1 mile has considerable downed trees and limbs from winter winds and recent ice storms but are easily navigated.

3.4 Pass the fourth trail shelter.

3.5 Making a swing to the west, the trail runs into the orange-blazed Bog Trail again. The South Plateau makes a right turn and heads northeast. Travel 100 feet; the trail turns off the road and once again becomes a clay path about 4 to 5 feet wide, heading into the woods.

3.7 The Interpretive Geology Fossil Trail joins the South Plateau Trail. Along this section signs give hikers an idea of what to look for, including what scientists call today's "living fossils": willow, sassafras, and maple trees—all descendants of trees 63 to 150 million

years old. Head up the trail another 150 feet; it makes a jog to the northeast and then back to the north as it heads down and up a shallow ravine. Another series of bluffs and views are in store here. Pass the fifth trail shelter.

3.8 After crossing another ravine, pass several cabins to the left. Head north another 300 feet and pass radio towers on the left. Continue straight past two telephone poles sticking 4 feet out of the ground. They appear to have been used to hold an old gate at one time. Travel 30 feet farther and cross a gravel road. The trail makes a swing to the northwest and runs parallel to the park road as it travels over a series of rolling hills.

4.0 The trail now travels behind a cabin and an old cement water tower on the left.

4.1 The closest approach to the road is made by the trail as it turns left to the northwest. Cross a 10-foot bridge over a small creek. After crossing the bridge, the trail turns to the west. The parking area can be seen ahead to the right.

4.3 The trail intersects the first section of the trail as it comes out of the parking area after traveling through a small swamp. Turn right here and head 50 feet to the parking area.

4.8 End the trip at the parking area.

Hike Information

Local Information

Huntsville/Madison Chamber of Commerce, 225 Church Street, Huntsville 35801; (256) 535-2000; www.hsvchamber.org.

Huntsville/Madison County Convention and Visitors Bureau, 700 Monroe Street Northwest, Huntsville 35801; (256) 551-2230; www.Huntsville.org.

North Alabama Tourism Association, 25062 North Street, Mooreseville 35649; (800) 648-5381; www.northalabama.org.

Local Events/Festivals

Mountain Dulcimer Festival, third Sunday of September, 225 Church Street, Huntsville 35801; (256) 536-2882. Each September at the Burritt Museum on Monte Sano Mountain, the museum plays host to dozens of Mountain Dulcimer players from around the South. The sweet, chiming sounds of the dulcimer are created by using a small "mallet" to tap the strings of the instrument and are indigenous to the South and especially the Appalachians. Admission is free.

Big Spring Jam, 700 Monroe Street Southwest, Huntsville 35801; (256) 551-2359.

Polk Salad Festival, second Friday and Saturday in May, 225 Church Street, Huntsville 35801; (256) 535-2000. Polk salad is a purple, leafy, cabbagelike plant indigenous to the South that for two days becomes the centerpiece for this cooking contest and gathering.

Alabama Constitution Village, 109 Gates Avenue, Huntsville 35801; (800) 678-1819; www.earlyworks.com/village.html. A living history museum that features tour guides dressed in clothes of the period (1809–1819) who guide visitors through the site where the 1819 Constitutional Convention was held. Admission is charged. Call for dates and prices.

Early Works, 109 Gates Avenue, Huntsville 35801; (800) 678-1819; www.earlyworks.com. This is a hands-on science museum for kids and adults alike.

Huntsville-Madison County Botanical Garden, 4205 Schrimcher Road, Huntsville 35801; (256) 830-4447; www.hsvbg.org.

◀ *Blue Creek Falls.*

Huntsville Museum of Art, 4205 Schrimcher Road, Huntsville 35801; (800) 786-9095; www.hsvmuseum.org. Open Tuesday through Saturday 10:00 A.M.–5:00 P.M., Sunday 1:00–5:00 P.M.

North Alabama Railroad Museum, 694 Chase Road, Huntsville 35801; (256) 851-6276; www.suncompsvc.com/narm.

Sci-Quest (North Alabama Science Center), 102-D Wynn Drive Northwest, Huntsville 35801; (256) 837-0606; www.sci-quest.org.

U.S. Space and Rocket Center, 1 Tranquility Base, Huntsville 35801; (256) 827-3400; www.ussrc.com. A centerpiece of the U.S. space program, the Space and Rocket Center features a huge museum with the original Apollo 16 capsule, moon rocks from the mission, an IMAX theater. Tours of the complex take visitors to the booster testing facilities and to the actual assembly areas for Space Station *Freedom.*

Von Braun Astronomical Society, 5105 Noel Avenue Southeast, Huntsville 35801; (256) 539-0316; www.vbas.org. A wonderful attraction high atop Monte Sano Mountain is the Von Braun Astronomical Society and their observatory/planetarium. Twice a month, the club hosts a show for members and the public. A brief look at the sky in the planetarium is followed by a guest speaker and then, if the skies are clear, a spectacular look at the night sky through their telescopes. Check the Web site for dates and times of shows.

—

Lodging

Madison Inn, 4430 University Drive Northwest, Huntsville 35801; (256) 890-0700.

Southland Motel, 3808 Governors Drive Southwest, Huntsville 35805; (256) 539-9391.

Villager Lodge, 3100 University Drive, Huntsville 35801; (256) 533-0610.

Charles' Motel, 11603 Highway 231 North, Meridianville 35759; (256) 828-4801.

Restaurants

Fogcutter, 3805 University Drive Northwest, Huntsville 35801; (256) 883-0031.

Café Berlin, 505 Airport Road Southwest, Huntsville 35801; (256) 880-9920.

Clocktower, 7500 Memorial Parkway Southwest, Huntsville 35801; (256) 881-0904.

Eunice's Country Kitchen, 1006 Andrew Jackson Way North, Huntsville 35801; (256) 534-9550.

Mr. C's, 11247 Memorial Parkway Southwest, Huntsville 35801; (256) 882-1190.

Organizations

Sierra Club North Alabama (Huntsville) Chapter; alabama.sierraclub.org/na.html.

Other Resources

Tennessee Valley Trails; www.montesano.com/hikeweb.

36 McKay Hollow Trail

Plenty of people love to tackle the McKay Hollow Trail despite its difficulty. The trail drops steeply down the western ridge of Monte Sano Mountain, with great views of Blue Spring Falls, and heads down through imposing cliffs and boulders. O'Shaughnessy Point comes into view as the trail goes down and then up the hollow. The route also follows Blue Spring Creek along the bottom of the hollow.

Start: From the southern picnic area at Monte Sano State Park.
Distance: 5.0-mile out-and-back.
Approximate hiking time: 3–4 hours.
Difficulty: Difficult due to climbs down and then up the hollow, over rocky ledges and outcroppings.
Trail surface: Rock-covered trail on the sides of the hollow; dirt path along the creek.
Type of hike: Sassafras, maple, and white oak forest; wildflowers, including iris and larkspur.
Land status: State park.
Nearest town: Huntsville.

Schedule: Open year-round.
Fees/Permits: No fee to hike. Camping fees are $14, base rate.
Maps: USGS maps: Huntsville; Meridianville. Park map—A brochure with trail map is available at the camp store for 50 cents.
Trail contacts: Monte Sano State Park, 5105 Nolen Avenue, Huntsville 35801; (256) 534-3757.
Other trail users: None.
Canine compatibility: Not dog friendly due to steep, rocky terrain. If you do bring a dog, no leash required.

Finding the trailhead: From Huntsville take U.S. Highway 231 south from Interstate 565 (exit 19A) for 0.4 mile and merge onto U.S. Highway 431 south—stay in the center lane for this turn. Travel 4 miles up the side of Monte Sano Mountain and make a sharp left onto Monte Sano Boulevard. Head up the mountain 2.4 miles and make a right onto Nolen Avenue. Continue straight for 1.4 miles and the picnic area will be on the right. *DeLorme: Alabama Atlas & Gazetteer:* Page 19, D8.

The Hike

Hiking trails are only one of the lures of Monte Sano State Park. Visitors also can walk through one of several gardens on display at the park. The Japanese Garden, near the camp store, shows off delicate flowers, a rock garden, red bridges, and a teahouse.

The McKay Hollow Trail travels down and then back up the limestone cliffs and outcroppings that line each side of McKay Hollow. The trail connects the western ridge of Monte Sano Mountain to just north of O'Shaughnessy Point on the eastern side.

One of the high points of the trip, Blue Spring Waterfall, appears just after the trail begins at the southern picnic area. This 100-foot-high waterfall attracts visitors from all over, and it's not uncommon to find artists all season long sketching or

View of the Huntsville Valley.

painting the scene. A short side trail leads directly to the falls, where it's possible to duck into the small cave behind the falling water.

From here the path follows a narrow, rocky ledge down the side of an impressive limestone cliff. It may be tempting to explore the rock formations on the cliff sides, but it's best to heed the words of the park rangers and stay on the marked trail, safe from the loose rock of the cliff. Also be wary of where you rest. Snakes live in the rocks and might not enjoy the company—and could let you know about it.

On the way down, you can enjoy views of O'Shaughnessy Point and the mountains of Huntsville trailing off into the distance. Watch for the yellow blazes marking the trail as it weaves its way downward. In several areas, hikers have cut paths to shorten the trip, and many deer trails cross through here; it's only too easy to get off trail.

At the bottom of the cozy hollow, with its dense hardwood forest, the trail follows along the banks of Blue Spring Creek. Wildflowers bloom en masse in the brush. Lizards dart in and out along the path as it meanders along the creek. This is the easiest part of the trip, as the trail follows the tiny creek for about 0.6 mile before beginning to climb again.

The trail up the other side of the hollow provides a steep hike up limestone cliffs and around large boulders. The McKay Hollow Trail ends at its intersection with the southern loop of the Plateau Trail. If you don't relish the idea of retracing your tracks along the McKay Hollow Trail, then use the Plateau Loop Trail as an easy exit back to the parking area.

McKay Hollow Trail

Paved Road
Maintained Dirt
Unmaintained Dirt
Singletrack Trail
Selected Route

Von Braun
Observatory

BANKHEAD
PARKWAY

The
Overlooks

RV Parking

The Sinks

Cold
Springs

NOLEN AVENUE

MONTE SANO
MOUNTAIN

MONTE SANO BLVD

Ruins

START

Pedestal

1 Logan Point Tr
2 Panther Knob Tr
3 Stone Cuts Trail
4 Mtn Mist Trail
5 Sinks Trail
6 Stone Cuts Bypass
7 Cold Springs Tr
8 N. Plateau Loop
9 Fire Tower Tr
10 S. Plateau Loop
11 Bog Trail
12 McKay Hollow Tr
13 Natural Well Tr
14 Warpath Ridge Tr

Blue
Spring

Natural
Well

MONTE SANO
STATE PARK

Ruins

McKAY HOLLOW

PANORAMA
DRIVE

N

Turnaround

O'Shaughnessy
Point

0   1/2 Kilometer
0   1/2 Mile

To
431

To
The Burritt
Museum

Miles and Directions

0.0 Start from the southeast end of the picnic area parking. There is a chain blocking a gravel road to the south. The creosote-coated poles that hold the chain have yellow blazes on them. Cross the chain and head southwest on the gravel road. Yellow blazes are on the trees.

0.1 Cross the northern loop of the Plateau Loop Trail (blue blazes). Come to a shelter. **Side trip:** In a short while a side trail leads to 70-foot waterfall, which can be seen from the trail.

0.2 Come to a fork and go right.

0.3 As you walk below some tall bluffs to the right, the trail comes to what looks like a fork. (**FYI:** There are a series of these forks heading down the mountain. Some are deer trails, others are shortcuts created by hikers. The best bet is to stay on the main trail.) Take the right fork and head over large boulders. In 50 feet come to another fork and go right.

0.4 Come to another fork and go right. In 80 feet come to another fork and go right.

1.0 Come to a T intersection with a deer trail. Turn left. The trail will loop back to the southeast. It's very steep through here. Shortly, pass a small deer trail to the southeast and continue to the east.

1.1 The trail splits around some brush and rejoins in 30 feet.

1.2 Come to an intersection with the Natural Well Trail and go left. (**FYI:** The Natural Well Trail is an easy 2.5-mile path that will take you almost to the doorstep of the Burritt Museum.)

2.5 The trail makes a final steep grade and intersects the southern loop of the Plateau Loop Trail. Turn around here and retrace your tracks. **Option:** To form a loop and an easier exit, take a left on the southern loop of the Plateau Loop Trail and then a left on the northern loop and then a right on the McKay Hollow Trail and follow it back to your car.

5.0 Arrive back at the picnic area parking lot.

Hike Information

Local Information

Huntsville/Madison Chamber of Commerce, 225 Church Street, Huntsville 35801; (256) 535-2000; www.hsvchamber.org.

Huntsville/Madison County Convention and Visitors Bureau, 700 Monroe Street Northwest, Huntsville 35801; (256) 551-2230; www.Huntsville.org.

North Alabama Tourism Association, 25062 North Street, Mooreseville 35649; (800) 648-5381; www.northalabama.org.

Local Events/Festivals

Mountain Dulcimer Festival, third Sunday of September, 225 Church Street, Huntsville 35801; (256) 536-2882. Each September at the Burritt Museum on Monte Sano Mountain, the museum plays host to dozens of Mountain Dulcimer players from around the South. The

sweet, chiming sounds of the dulcimer are created by using a small "mallet" to tap the strings of the instrument and are indigenous to the South and especially the Appalachians. Admission is free.

Big Spring Jam, 700 Monroe Street Southwest, Huntsville 35801; (256) 551-2359.

Polk Salad Festival, second Friday and Saturday in May, 225 Church Street, Huntsville 35801; (256) 535-2000. Polk salad is a purple, leafy, cabbagelike plant indigenous to the South that for two days becomes the centerpiece for this cooking contest and gathering.

Alabama Constitution Village, 109 Gates Avenue, Huntsville 35801; (800) 678-1819; www.earlyworks.com/village.html. A living history museum that features tour guides dressed in clothes of the period (1809–1819) who guide visitors through the site where the

1819 Constitutional Convention was held. Admission is charged. Call for dates and prices.

Early Works, 109 Gates Avenue, Huntsville 35801; (800) 678-1819; www.earlyworks.com. This is a hands-on science museum for kids and adults alike.

Huntsville-Madison County Botanical Garden, 4205 Schrimcher Road, Huntsville 35801; (256) 830-4447; www.hsvbg.org.

Huntsville Museum of Art, 4205 Schrimcher Road, Huntsville 35801; (800) 786-9095; www.hsvmuseum.org. Open Tuesday through Saturday 10:00 A.M.–5:00 P.M., Sunday 1:00–5:00 P.M.

North Alabama Railroad Museum, 694 Chase Road, Huntsville 35801; (256) 851-6276; www.suncompsvc.com/narm.

Sci-Quest (North Alabama Science Center), 102-D Wynn Drive Northwest, Huntsville 35801; (256) 837-0606; www.sci-quest.org.

U.S. Space and Rocket Center, 1 Tranquility Base, Huntsville 35801; (256) 827-3400; www.ussrc.com. A centerpiece of the U.S. space program, the Space and Rocket Center features a huge museum with the original Apollo 16 capsule, moon rocks from the mission, an IMAX theater. Tours of the complex take visitors to the booster testing facilities and to the actual assembly areas for Space Station *Freedom.*

Von Braun Astronomical Society, 5105 Noel Avenue Southeast, Huntsville 35801; (256) 539-0316; www.vbas.org. A wonderful attraction high atop Monte Sano Mountain is the Von Braun Astronomical Society and their observatory/planetarium. Twice a month, the club hosts a show for members and the public. A brief look at the sky in the planetarium is followed by a guest speaker and then, if the skies are clear, a spectacular look at the night sky through their telescopes. Check the Web site for dates and times of shows.

Lodging

Madison Inn, 4430 University Drive Northwest, Huntsville 35801; (256) 890-0700.

Southland Motel, 3808 Governors Drive Southwest, Huntsville 35805; (256) 539-9391.

Villager Lodge, 3100 University Drive, Huntsville 35801; (256) 533-0610.

Charles' Motel, 11603 Highway 231 North, Meridianville 35759; (256) 828-4801.

Restaurants

Fogcutter, 3805 University Drive Northwest, Huntsville 35801; (256) 883-0031.

Café Berlin, 505 Airport Road Southwest, Huntsville 35801; (256) 880-9920.

Clocktower, 7500 Memorial Parkway Southwest, Huntsville 35801; (256) 881-0904.

Eunice's Country Kitchen, 1006 Andrew Jackson Way North, Huntsville 35801; (256) 534-9550.

Mr. C's, 11247 Memorial Parkway Southwest, Huntsville 35801; (256) 882-1190.

Organizations

Sierra Club North Alabama (Huntsville) Chapter; alabama.sierraclub.org/na.html.

Other Resources

Tennessee Valley Trails; www.montesano.com/hikeweb.

37 Stone Cuts Trail

The Stone Cuts, deep erosional clefts in a section of limestone, form the highlight of this hike. Stone Cuts Trail runs straight through the heart of these large, high-walled cuts. Kids will love climbing around in here. Mountain climbers love the high cliff walls, and small cavelike spaces in the rocks attract spelunkers.

Start: From the northeast end of the hiking trailhead at Monte Sano State Park.
Distance: 3.0-mile loop.
Approximate hiking time: 2½–3½ hours.
Difficulty: Moderate, over rocky terrain; some steep trail.
Trail surface: Dirt path studded with rocks and boulders.
Type of hike: Sassafras, maple, and white oak forest; iris and larkspur wildflowers; rock walls and tunnels.
Land status: State park.
Nearest town: Huntsville.
Schedule: Open year-round.

Fees/Permits: No fee to hike. Camping fees are $14, base rate.
Maps: USGS maps: Huntsville; Meridianville. Park map—A brochure with trail map is available at the camp store for 50 cents.
Trail contacts: Monte Sano State Park, 5105 Nolen Avenue, Huntsville 35801; (256) 534-3757.
Other trail users: Cyclists on the Mountain Mist section.
Canine compatibility: Dog friendly, but may be difficult for some dogs due to large boulders. Bring water; leash not required.

Finding the trailhead: From Huntsville take U.S. Highway 231 south from Interstate 565 (exit 19A) for 0.4 mile and merge onto U.S. Highway 431 South—stay in the center lane for this turn. Travel 4 miles up the side of Monte Sano Mountain and make a sharp left onto Monte Sano Boulevard. Head up the mountain 2.4 miles and make a right onto Nolen Avenue. Continue straight for 2 miles and Nolen Avenue forks. (To the right is the trailhead.) Take the left fork and travel 0.1 mile to the park office and camp store/campground. *DeLorme: Alabama Atlas & Gazetteer:* Page 19, D8.

The Hike

Monte Sano State Park's Stone Cuts Trail puts you in personal touch with the geological processes of the Highland Rim region as it passes through spectacular rock formations and tunnels, all of which was once covered with a shallow ocean. As the land began to emerge from the waters, shell banks and coral reefs were left high and dry. Their remains formed the limestone bedrock that makes up the mountains in this region. Throughout this hike, check the exposed rock and boulders for the fossils of ancient sea creatures.

Limestone is an extremely soft rock, and over time erosional forces have created numerous sinkholes, caverns, outcroppings, and cuts throughout the region. The Stone Cuts section is just one example of this process.

The Stone Cuts Trail travels through the narrow crevice of its namesake.

Stone Cuts Trail

Legend:
- Paved Road
- Maintained Dirt
- Unmaintained Dirt
- Singletrack Trail
- Selected Route

Trail List:
1. Logan Point Tr
2. Panther Knob Tr
3. Stone Cuts Trail
4. Mtn Mist Trail
5. Sinks Trail
6. Stone Cuts Bypass
7. Cold Springs Tr
8. N. Plateau Loop
9. Fire Tower Tr
10. S. Plateau Loop
11. Bog Trail
12. McKay Hollow Tr
13. Natural Well Tr
14. Warpath Ridge Tr

PANTHER KNOB

Von Braun Observatory

Stone Cuts

The Sinks

BANKHEAD PARKWAY

RV Parking

The Overlooks

Cold Springs

NOLEN AVENUE

MONTE SANO MOUNTAIN

Ruins

START

MONTE SANO BLVD

Blue Spring

Natural Well

MONTE SANO STATE PARK

Ruins

McKAY HOLLOW

PANORAMA DRIVE

N

O'Shaughnessy Point

To 431

0   1/2 Kilometer
0   1/2 Mile

The trail is only moderate in difficulty, but be aware that the return hike can be rather steep, especially for hikers not physically ready for it. To begin this trip, the trail travels through an area called the Overlooks—a parking area with a 180-degree view of Mills Hollow and Panther Knob. After following a closed park road, the trail heads back into the woods and heads steeply down Monte Sano Mountain to the bottom of Mills Hollow. Watch for the cyclists in the hollow, who use the yellow-blazed Mountain Mist Trail.

The Stone Cuts Trail then heads up the side of Panther Knob. At the top of the knob, you'll reach a group of rocks called the Sinks—a series of outcroppings exposed over the years to the elements. The path follows a route just to the right of the Sinks, but an easy hike on one of the tiny side trails takes you over to them. Huge boulders and crawl spaces invite exploration. But be careful. Water seeping through cracks in the rocks makes hiking slippery, and the bluffs here are both high and dangerous.

The trail then continues to the Stone Cuts and actually travels through the cuts. Rock walls tower 100 to 200 feet above trail. Rappellers and rock climbers appreciate this area for obvious reasons. And just as it seems the scenery can't get any better, turn a corner and it does.

In several areas, the trail travels into the rock through short, dark tunnels. Water trickles down into the cuts, letting us know that this is a work in progress. Again, footing can be tricky over the wet surfaces. Throughout the entire trip through the Stone Cuts, the white paint blazes are easy to find. Even through the tunnels there should be no problem navigating this unique trail.

Wildlife that may be found along the trail include bobcats, white-tailed deer, opossums, skunks, and woodchucks. The hardwoods of the hollow and mountainsides include silver and red maples, sassafras, and pin and live oaks. Wildflowers include larkspur (its blue-and-white flowers bloom in late spring), yellow lady's slipper, and purple dwarf iris.

Miles and Directions

0.0 Start from the northeast end of the hiker's parking area. Head across the park road. A blue-blazed gravel path is on the opposite side. This section of the loop follows the northern loop of the Plateau Loop Trail.

0.1 Come to the dead end of the park's cabin road. Cross the road and walk between the openings of a split-rail fence.

0.2 Come to the Overlooks. (**FYI:** This paved cul-de-sac offers up the most spectacular view of the Huntsville Valley in the park.) Cut across the paved parking area to a closed park road. The red blazes of the Sinks Trail begin here.

0.4 The trail makes a sharp turn into the woods. (**Note:** The trail is deep dirt and after a rain is very slick and muddy.)

0.6 Cross the yellow-blazed Mountain Mist Trail.

0.7 The trail merges with the orange-blazed Logan Point Trail. At the bottom of the hill, stay straight on the white-blazed Stone Cuts Trail. (The red Sinks Trail turns to the right.)

0.8 Come to a T intersection and turn right on the white-blazed Stone Cuts Trail. (The orange-blazed Logan Point Trail splits left.)

Entering the "Stone Cuts."

0.9 A double white blaze will be seen as the blue Panther Knob Trail branches off to the left. Continue on the Stone Cuts Trail to the right. (**FYI:** Behind you are the observatory and the cliffs of the Overlooks. Along this section, notice the layering of the rock formations from erosion.)

1.0 This area is known as the Sinks. There are some huge cliffs and boulders here to explore, but be very careful.

1.3 Reach the Stone Cuts.

1.4 From here the trail traverses the actual stone cuts, with 100-foot-high walls dripping with water and dark cavern passageways.

1.6 Come to a fork. The blue Stone Cuts Bypass Trail breaks right from the Stone Cuts Trail and will eventually rejoin. Go right.

1.7 The trail merges with the Sinks Trail. The blazes are now red.

1.8 Come to a fork, with a nature trail splitting off. Turn right.

2.0 The Sinks Trail intersects the yellow Mountain Mist Trail. Turn right and head north on the Mountain Mist Trail. (**Note:** Cyclists also use this trail so be on the lookout for them.)

2.4 Come to a T intersection with the Sinks Trail. Turn to the left onto the Sinks Trail. (The Mountain Mist Trail continues to the north.) Begin making a steep zigzag trip back up the hill, retracing the trip down. This is the most difficult stretch of the trail.

2.6 Reach the closed park road behind the observatory. Turn left onto the road. The Stone Cuts can be seen to the left.

2.7 Walk through the gate that closes the road to traffic. Head across the Overlooks and the blue blazes of the northern loop of the Plateau Loop Trail will be seen. Reenter the woods at this point.

2.8 Come to the park's cabin road and turn right. Pick up the trail again on the other side of the road as it dips back into the woods.

2.9 Cross the park road.

3.0 Arrive back at the hiker's parking area.

Hike Information

Local Information

Huntsville/Madison Chamber of Commerce, 225 Church Street, Huntsville 35801; (256) 535-2000; www.hsvchamber.org.

Huntsville/Madison County Convention and Visitors Bureau, 700 Monroe Street Northwest, Huntsville 35801; (256) 551-2230; www.Huntsville.org.

North Alabama Tourism Association, 25062 North Street, Mooreseville 35649; (800) 648-5381; www.northalabama.org.

Local Events/Festivals

Mountain Dulcimer Festival, third Sunday of September, 225 Church Street, Huntsville 35801; (256) 536-2882. Each September at the Burritt Museum on Monte Sano Mountain, the museum plays host to dozens of Mountain Dulcimer players from around the South. The sweet, chiming sounds of the dulcimer are created by using a small "mallet" to tap the strings of the instrument and are indigenous to the South and especially the Appalachians. Admission is free.

Big Spring Jam, 700 Monroe Street Southwest, Huntsville 35801; (256) 551-2359.

Polk Salad Festival, second Friday and Saturday in May, 225 Church Street, Huntsville 35801; (256) 535-2000. Polk salad is a purple, leafy, cabbagelike plant indigenous to the South that for two days becomes the centerpiece for this cooking contest and gathering.

Alabama Constitution Village, 109 Gates Avenue, Huntsville 35801; (800) 678-1819; www.earlyworks.com/village.html. A living history museum that features tour guides dressed in clothes of the period (1809-1819) who guide visitors through the site where the 1819 Constitutional Convention was held. Admission is charged. Call for dates and prices.

Early Works, 109 Gates Avenue, Huntsville 35801; (800) 678-1819; www.earlyworks.com. This is a hands-on science museum for kids and adults alike.

Huntsville-Madison County Botanical Garden, 4205 Schrimcher Road, Huntsville 35801; (256) 830-4447; www.hsvbg.org.

Huntsville Museum of Art, 4205 Schrimcher Road, Huntsville 35801; (800) 786-9095; www.hsvmuseum.org. Open Tuesday through Saturday 10:00 A.M.–5:00 P.M., Sunday 1:00–5:00 P.M.

North Alabama Railroad Museum, 694 Chase Road, Huntsville 35801; (256) 851-6276; www.suncompsvc.com/narm.

Sci-Quest (North Alabama Science Center), 102-D Wynn Drive Northwest, Huntsville 35801; (256) 837-0606; www.sci-quest.org.

U.S. Space and Rocket Center, 1 Tranquility Base, Huntsville 35801; (256) 827-3400; www.ussrc.com. A centerpiece of the U.S. space program, the Space and Rocket Center features a huge museum with the original Apollo 16 capsule, moon rocks from the mission, an IMAX theater. Tours of the complex take visitors to the booster testing facilities and to the actual assembly areas for Space Station *Freedom.*

Von Braun Astronomical Society, 5105 Noel Avenue Southeast, Huntsville 35801; (256) 539-0316; www.vbas.org. A wonderful attraction high atop Monte Sano Mountain is the Von Braun Astronomical Society and their observatory/planetarium. Twice a month, the club hosts a show for members and the public. A brief look at the sky in the planetarium is followed by a guest speaker and then, if the skies are clear, a spectacular look at the night sky through their telescopes. Check the Web site for dates and times of shows.

Lodging

Madison Inn, 4430 University Drive Northwest, Huntsville 35801; (256) 890-0700.

Southland Motel, 3808 Governors Drive Southwest, Huntsville 35805; (256) 539-9391.

Villager Lodge, 3100 University Drive, Huntsville 35801; (256) 533-0610.

Charles' Motel, 11603 Highway 231 North, Meridianville 35759; (256) 828-4801.

Restaurants

Fogcutter, 3805 University Drive Northwest, Huntsville 35801; (256) 883-0031.

Café Berlin, 505 Airport Road Southwest, Huntsville 35801; (256) 880-9920.

Clocktower, 7500 Memorial Parkway Southwest, Huntsville 35801; (256) 881-0904.

Eunice's Country Kitchen, 1006 Andrew Jackson Way North, Huntsville 35801; (256) 534-9550.

Mr. C's, 11247 Memorial Parkway Southwest, Huntsville 35801; (256) 882-1190.

Organizations

Sierra Club North Alabama (Huntsville) Chapter; alabama.sierraclub.org/na.html.

Other Resources

Tennessee Valley Trails; www.montesano.com/hikeweb.

38 Mountain Mist Trail

The Mountain Mist Trail gives you a good opportunity to explore the region known as the Highland Rim. The trail travels through the hollow just below the area known as the Overlooks. It's a pleasant walk through hardwood forest. This loop was created by combining the Plateau Loop Trail, the Stone Cuts Trail, and the Mountain Mist Trail.

Start: From the hiker's parking lot next to the Monte Sano State Park office.
Distance: 3.7-mile loop.
Approximate hiking time: 2–3 hours.
Difficulty: Easy hiking just below the plateau of Monte Sano Mountain; moderate climb up to intersection with the southern loop of the Plateau Loop Trail.
Trail surface: Dirt path.
Type of hike: Sassafras, maple, and white oak forest; wildflowers, including iris and larkspur.
Land status: State park.
Nearest town: Huntsville.

Schedule: Open year-round.
Fees/Permits: No fee to hike. Camping fees are $14, base rate.
Maps: USGS maps: Huntsville; Meridianville. Park map—A brochure with trail map is available at the camp store for 50 cents.
Trail contacts: Monte Sano State Park, 5105 Nolen Avenue, Huntsville 35801; (256) 534-3757.
Other trail users: Cyclists.
Canine compatibility: Dog friendly, with only a moderate rocky climb at the southern end. Bring water; leash recommended.

Finding the trailhead: From Huntsville take U.S. Highway 231 south from Interstate 565 (exit 19A) for 0.4 mile and merge onto U.S. Highway 431 south—stay in the center lane for this turn. Travel 4 miles up the side of Monte Sano Mountain and make a sharp left onto Monte Sano Boulevard. Head up the mountain 2.4 miles and make a right onto Nolen Avenue. Continue straight for 2 miles and Nolen Avenue forks. (To the right is the trailhead.) Take the left fork and travel 0.1 mile to the park office and camp store/campground. *DeLorme: Alabama Atlas & Gazetteer:* Page 19, D8.

The Hike

Monte Sano State Park's Mountain Mist Trail, when combined with the Stone Cuts Trail and the Plateau Loop Trail, makes for a great loop hike that just about everyone in the family can enjoy. The virtues of the loop are easier trailhead access and scenery that incorporates the beauty of the different trails.

The trail begins on the northern loop of the Plateau Trail by following a closed park road, quickly reaching the area called the Overlooks, a parking area with a 180-degree panorama of Mills Hollow and Panther Knob. The trail soon heads into the woods directly behind Von Braun Observatory and drops steeply down Monte Sano Mountain to near the bottom of Mills Hollow using the Stone Cuts Trail.

The descent down the Mountain Mist Trail is steep and enclosed. Watch for mountain bikes!

Mountain Mist Trail

▭	Paved Road
▭	Maintained Dirt
=·=·=	Unmaintained Dirt
- - -	Singletrack Trail
▭▭▭	Selected Route

Von Braun Observatory

RV Parking

The Overlooks

PANTHER KNOB

Stone Cuts

The Sinks

MILLS HOLLOW

Cold Springs

NOLEN AVENUE

MONTE SANO MOUNTAIN

MONTE SANO BLVD

Ruins

START

1 Bog Trail
2 Cold Springs Tr
3 Fire Tower Tr
4 Logan Point Tr
5 McKay Hollow Tr
6 Mtn Mist Trail
7 Natural Well Tr
8 N. Plateau Loop
9 Sinks Trail
10 Stone Cuts Trail
11 S. Plateau Loop
12 Warpath Ridge Tr
13 Panther Knob Tr
14 Bankhead Pkwy

Blue Spring

Natural Well

MONTE SANO STATE PARK

Ruins

PANORAMA DRIVE

McKAY HOLLOW

N

O'Shaughnessy Point

To Huntsville

0		1/2 Kilometer
0		1/2 Mile

Here the trail turns south and travels just below the Monte Sano Plateau over fairly level terrain. The peaceful walk through the hollow allows you to put a little distance between yourself and weekend visitors to the park.

Dense forest provides a cozy, enclosed feeling as the trail winds through silver and red maples, sassafras, and oaks. At creek crossings, wildflowers bloom. Larkspur, yellow lady's slipper, purple dwarf iris, and violets bloom from early spring to midsummer. Be aware that some sections of the trail can get pretty muddy after a good rain. Also, be conscious of the fact that cyclists share the Mountain Mist Trail with hikers.

The trail eventually makes a moderate climb up a rocky slope, the toughest of the trip, to its intersection with the southern loop of the Plateau Trail. This easy route follows the southern rim of the plateau at the top of Monte Sano Mountain.

The trail passes within 30 feet of high bluffs, from which you'll have great views of McKay and Mills Hollows, Round Top, and Monte Sano Mountain. Short side trails lead to overlooks, but be sure to heed the DANGER, HIGH BLUFFS signs.

The trail offers good opportunities for amateur geologists and their children. Fossils of sea life from ancient ocean reefs can be found almost anywhere along the way if you look closely.

Miles and Directions

0.0 Start from the northeast end of the hiker's parking area. Head across the park road. A blue-blazed gravel path is on the opposite side. This section of the loop follows the northern loop of the Plateau Loop Trail.

0.1 Come to the dead end of the park's cabin road. Cross the road and walk between the openings of a split-rail fence.

0.2 Come to the Overlooks. (This paved cul-de-sac offers up the most spectacular view of the Huntsville valley in the park.) Cut across the paved parking area to a closed park road. The red blazes of the Sinks Trail begin here.

0.4 The trail makes a sharp turn into the woods. (**Note:** The trail is deep dirt and after a rain is very slick and muddy.)

0.6 Come to the yellow-blazed Mountain Mist Trail and turn right. (**Note:** Cyclists also use this trail, so be on the lookout for them. The travel is very easy through here but can be very muddy during rainy weather.)

0.9 Pass the Sinks Trail spur.

2.2 The Mountain Mist Trail intersects the southern loop of the Plateau Trail. Turn right up the South Plateau Trail, following the white blazes.

2.3 Pass a short connector trail to the Mountain Mist Trail on the right, with a sign pointing the direction to the trail.

2.6 Pass a trail shelter on the right. Shortly the trail merges with a gravel road.

2.7 Pass the red-blazed Fire Tower Trail on the left. Continue straight.

2.9 Pass a second trail shelter.

3.0 The trail intersects the orange-blazed Bog Trail. Turn right and follow the South Plateau Trail. In 100 feet the trail turns off of the road and becomes a clay path heading into the woods.

Panther Knob.

3.1 The Interpretive Geology Fossil Trail joins the South Plateau Trail. (**FYI:** Along this section signs give hikers an idea of what to look for, including what scientists call today's "Living Fossils": willow, sassafras, and maple trees—all descendants of trees 63 to 150 million years old.) Pass the third trail shelter.

3.2 Cross a gravel road. The trail swings to the northwest and runs parallel to the park road as it travels over a series of rolling hills.

3.5 Cross a 10-foot bridge; the parking area can be seen ahead to the right.

3.7 The South Plateau Trail rejoins itself. Turn right and head 50 feet to the parking area to end the trip.

'BAMA FIRSTS

· The first ice-making machine was created in Mobile.

· The first national Veterans Day was celebrated in Birmingham in 1947.

· The gigantic meteor shower of 1833 was the basis for the title of Jimmy Buffett's song, "Stars Fell on Alabama."

· Orville and Wilbur Wright started the world's first flight school in 1910 in Montgomery.

· The world's first electric trolley system was introduced in Montgomery in 1886.

Hike Information

Local Information

Huntsville/Madison Chamber of Commerce, 225 Church Street, Huntsville 35801; (256) 535-2000; www.hsvchamber.org.

Huntsville/Madison County Convention and Visitors Bureau, 700 Monroe Street Northwest, Huntsville 35801; (256) 551-2230; www.Huntsville.org.

North Alabama Tourism Association, 25062 North Street, Mooreseville 35649; (800) 648-5381; www.northalabama.org.

Local Events/Festivals

Mountain Dulcimer Festival, third Sunday of September, 225 Church Street, Huntsville 35801; (256) 536-2882. Each September at the Burritt Museum on Monte Sano Mountain, the museum plays host to dozens of Mountain Dulcimer players from around the South. The sweet, chiming sounds of the dulcimer are created by using a small "mallet" to tap the strings of the instrument and are indigenous to the South and especially the Appalachians. Admission is free.

Big Spring Jam, 700 Monroe Street Southwest, Huntsville 35801; (256) 551-2359.

Polk Salad Festival, second Friday and Saturday in May, 225 Church Street, Huntsville 35801; (256) 535-2000. Polk salad is a purple, leafy, cabbagelike plant indigenous to the South that for two days becomes the centerpiece for this cooking contest and gathering.

Alabama Constitution Village, 109 Gates Avenue, Huntsville 35801; (800) 678-1819; www.earlyworks.com/village.html. A living history museum that features tour guides dressed in clothes of the period (1809-1819) who guide visitors through the site where the 1819 Constitutional Convention was held. Admission is charged. Call for dates and prices.

Early Works, 109 Gates Avenue, Huntsville 35801; (800) 678-1819; www.earlyworks.com. This is a hands-on science museum for kids and adults alike.

Huntsville-Madison County Botanical Garden, 4205 Schrimcher Road, Huntsville 35801; (256) 830-4447; www.hsvbg.org.

Huntsville Museum of Art, 4205 Schrimcher Road, Huntsville 35801; (800) 786-9095; www.hsvmuseum.org. Open Tuesday through Saturday 10:00 A.M.–5:00 P.M., Sunday 1:00-5:00 P.M.

North Alabama Railroad Museum, 694 Chase Road, Huntsville 35801; (256) 851-6276; www.suncompsvc.com/narm.

Sci-Quest (North Alabama Science Center), 102-D Wynn Drive Northwest, Huntsville 35801; (256) 837-0606; www.sci-quest.org.

U.S. Space and Rocket Center, 1 Tranquility Base, Huntsville 35801; (256) 827-3400; www.ussrc.com. A centerpiece of the U.S. space program, the Space and Rocket Center features a huge museum with the original Apollo 16 capsule, moon rocks from the mission, an IMAX theater. Tours of the complex take visitors to the booster testing facilities and to the actual assembly areas for Space Station *Freedom.*

Von Braun Astronomical Society, 5105 Noel Avenue Southeast, Huntsville 35801; (256) 539-0316; www.vbas.org. A wonderful attraction high atop Monte Sano Mountain is the Von Braun Astronomical Society and their observatory/planetarium. Twice a month, the club hosts a show for members and the public. A brief look at the sky in the planetarium is followed by a guest speaker and then, if the skies are clear, a spectacular look at the night sky through their telescopes. Check the Web site for dates and times of shows.

Lodging

Madison Inn, 4430 University Drive Northwest, Huntsville 35801; (256) 890-0700.

Southland Motel, 3808 Governors Drive Southwest, Huntsville 35805; (256) 539-9391.

Villager Lodge, 3100 University Drive, Huntsville 35801; (256) 533-0610.

Charles' Motel, 11603 Highway 231 North, Meridianville 35759; (256) 828-4801.

Restaurants

Fogcutter, 3805 University Drive Northwest, Huntsville 35801; (256) 883-0031.

Café Berlin, 505 Airport Road Southwest, Huntsville 35801; (256) 880-9920.

Clocktower, 7500 Memorial Parkway Southwest, Huntsville 35801; (256) 881-0904.

Eunice's Country Kitchen, 1006 Andrew Jackson Way North, Huntsville 35801; (256) 534-9550.

Mr. C's, 11247 Memorial Parkway Southwest, Huntsville 35801; (256) 882-1190.

Organizations

Sierra Club North Alabama (Huntsville) Chapter; alabama.sierraclub.org/na.html.

Other Resources

Tennessee Valley Trails;
www.montesano.com/hikeweb.

39 Land Trust Loop

The hike travels through a preserve created by volunteers and donors on the west side of Monte Sano Mountain in northern Alabama. The Land Trust Loop Trail is rugged and can be a challenge. Along the route are waterfalls and the huge Three Caves Quarry. Climbs down (or up) the upper Bluffline Trail and the Waterfall Trail are steep.

Start: From the southeast end of the Land Trust parking lot on Bankhead Parkway.
Distance: 4.7-mile loop.
Approximate hiking time: 2½–3½ hours.
Difficulty: Difficult hiking on a section of steep, rocky paths.
Trail surface: Part dirt path; part boulders and rocks.
Type of hike: Black walnut, hickory, and live oak trees; and muscadine vines; waterfalls and rock quarry.
Land status: State park.

Nearest town: Huntsville.
Schedule: Open year-round.
Fees/Permits: No fee to hike.
Maps: USGS maps: Madison; Meridianville.
Trail contacts: Land Trust Huntsville, 907 Franklin Street, Huntsville 35801; (256) 534-5263; www.landtrust-hsv.org.
Other trail users: Cyclists.
Canine compatibility: Dog friendly, though some areas may be difficult for some dogs. Ample water available; no leash required.

Finding the trailhead: From Huntsville take exit 19C off of Interstate 565. Turn left off the ramp onto Washington Street; at the first light, make a right onto Pratt Avenue. (Pratt Avenue eventually becomes Bankhead Parkway.) Go 2.6 miles; the next right is the Land Trust parking lot. *DeLorme: Alabama Atlas & Gazetteer:* Page 19, D8.

The Hike

Through the years, the mountain area around Huntsville has seen its share of business and residential development, posing a threat to forests along Round Top and Monte Sano Mountain. For a time, Monte Sano State Park was the only oasis of preservation. All that changed when a group of volunteers formed the Land Trust of Huntsville. Their objective: to "preserve nature in Madison County." Through contributions and land donations, several preserves were established, and more are on the way.

Among the nature sanctuaries created by the Land Trust are Wade Mountain Preserve and Rainbow Mountain. Wade Mountain Preserve features broad views along the ridge of the mountain. Rainbow Mountain offers a 2.5-mile trail to Balance Rock, a giant boulder that resembles a spinning top standing on its point.

The largest of the sanctuaries is Monte Sano Preserve, where we find this hike. With the acquisition of 567 acres, most of the forested hillside of Monte Sano Mountain received protection from further development. The Land Trust has done an excellent job of creating trails that show off the preserve's rugged beauty.

Huge, worn cliffs along the Waterline Trail. There are falls here in wet periods.

The Land Trust Loop traces the west side of Monte Sano Mountain. The area where the trail begins was once a Huntsville landfill, but the Land Trust has turned the property around. The first section of the route, known as the Bluffline Trail, travels just below massive limestone bluffs. The trail crosses several creeks, passes two waterfalls, and goes by a section where bluffs came crashing down in a 1998 landslide.

The path then turns down the Waterline Trail, where sections of a water main used during the 1950s are exposed. Suddenly the trail becomes steep and difficult, both up and down, along a streambed. A waterfall comes into view about halfway along this section, the rocks forming a huge horseshoe.

At the intersection of the Waterline and Alms House Trails is Three Caves Quarry. At the bottom of the quarry's tall walls are three caves cut into the mountainside. The trail comes up to the edge of the quarry, which is no longer in use. The quarry is a dangerous place. Landslides are possible, the drop is steep, and entry is allowed only by permission of the Trust.

The Alms House Trail levels things out for a bit through gently rolling hills and over several creeks. On the final stretch to the parking lot, however, you'll be hiking steeply uphill one last time.

Miles and Directions

0.0 Start from the southeast end of the Land Trust parking lot and head down the paved road. Pass the Alms House Trail on the right. (This is where the loop returns.) The pavement ends and turns to gravel. (**FYI:** Monte Sano Mountain can be seen ahead to the right.) Come to a T intersection with a wide gravel road. A sign here reads RAILROAD BED TRAIL/BLUFFLINE TRAIL. Turn right. The trail is marked with silver diamond blazes reading HLT–BLUFFLINE TRAIL. (**FYI:** Notice the glass on the road here. This short section was once a dumpsite for the city of Huntsville.)

0.1 Continue through an intersection. (A sign here reads RAILROAD BED and points to the south, BLUFFLINE, pointing northeast to southwest, and FAGAN SPRINGS, pointing to the south.)

0.2 Pass an unnamed trail to the right.

1.0 Reach the site of the 1998 landslide.

1.2 The Wagon Trail merges from the northwest (a sign here marks the intersection).

1.3 Come to a fork and go left onto Bluffline Trail, a sign marks the intersection.

1.9 The High Trail merges from the northeast (a sign indicates the trail). For the next 0.1 mile, there are two markers on the tree, one for the High Trail, the other for the Bluffline Trail.

2.0 Come to a fork and go right onto the Waterline Trail. (The Bluffline Trail continues to the left.) The trail is marked with diamond markers that read WATERLINE TRAIL.

2.2 The trail's namesake, the old waterline from the 1950s, is visible.

2.3 To the right is a huge seasonal waterfall. Even without water, the rock formation is spectacular, forming a 75-foot-tall cirque.

3.0 Come to a fork and go left. (The Alms House Trail turns to the right.) In another 10 feet come to another fork and stay left.

3.1 (**Note:** The trail leads to the edge of the Quarry. Be VERY careful here.) The trail rejoins the Waterline Trail. Turn right. In 150 feet come to the Alms House Trail intersection and turn left. (Not only are there diamond markers but also red paint blazes on the tree identifying the trail as it heads to the north/northeast.)

3.6 Pass the Wagon Trail (on the right). Continue on the Alms House Trail.

3.8 Comes to a very big hole, which marks a T intersection. Turn right. (An unmarked trail breaks left.)

4.0 Cross the Wagon Trail (a sign marks the path).

View of Three Caves Quarry.

4.4 Come to a fork and go right. (The left fork heads to a small area with log benches used for lectures.)

4.5 Pass the Fagan Springs Trail, which intersects to the right. (**FYI:** The Fagan Springs Trail is a short 0.6-mile path that leads to a nice spring.) Continue on until you come to a fork. Go right, staying on the Alms House Trail. (The Railroad Bed Trail takes the left fork.)

4.7 The trail finally starts to level off and turns to gravel. In 50 feet it emerges out of the woods and back to the beginning of the trail at the parking lot.

Hike Information

Local Information

Huntsville/Madison Chamber of Commerce, 225 Church Street, Huntsville 35801; (256) 535-2000; www.hsvchamber.org.

Huntsville/Madison County Convention and Visitors Bureau, 700 Monroe Street Northwest, Huntsville 35801; (256) 551-2230; www.Huntsville.org.

North Alabama Tourism Association, 25062 North Street, Mooreseville 35649; (800) 648-5381; www.northalabama.org.

Local Events/Festivals

Mountain Dulcimer Festival, third Sunday of September, 225 Church Street, Huntsville 35801; (256) 536-2882. Each September at the Burritt Museum on Monte Sano Mountain, the museum plays host to dozens of Mountain Dulcimer players from around the South. The sweet, chiming sounds of the dulcimer are created by using a small "mallet" to tap the strings of the instrument and are indigenous to the South and especially the Appalachians. Admission is free.

Big Spring Jam, 700 Monroe Street Southwest, Huntsville 35801; (256) 551-2359.

Polk Salad Festival, second Friday and Saturday in May, 225 Church Street, Huntsville 35801; (256) 535-2000. Polk salad is a purple, leafy, cabbagelike plant indigenous to the South that for two days becomes the centerpiece for this cooking contest and gathering.

Alabama Constitution Village, 109 Gates Avenue, Huntsville 35801; (800) 678-1819; www.earlyworks.com/village.html. A living history museum that features tour guides dressed in clothes of the period (1809-1819) who guide visitors through the site where the 1819 Constitutional Convention was held. Admission is charged. Call for dates and prices.

Early Works, 109 Gates Avenue, Huntsville 35801; (800) 678-1819; www.earlyworks.com. This is a hands-on science museum for kids and adults alike.

Huntsville-Madison County Botanical Garden, 4205 Schrimcher Road, Huntsville 35801; (256) 830-4447; www.hsvbg.org.

Huntsville Museum of Art, 4205 Schrimcher Road, Huntsville 35801; (800) 786-9095; www.hsvmuseum.org. Open Tuesday through Saturday 10:00 A.M.-5:00 P.M., Sunday 1:00-5:00 P.M.

North Alabama Railroad Museum, 694 Chase Road, Huntsville 35801; (256) 851-6276; www.suncompsvc.com/narm.

Sci-Quest (North Alabama Science Center), 102-D Wynn Drive Northwest, Huntsville 35801; (256) 837-0606; www.sci-quest.org.

U.S. Space and Rocket Center, 1 Tranquility Base, Huntsville 35801; (256) 827-3400; www.ussrc.com. A centerpiece of the U.S. space program, the Space and Rocket Center features a huge museum with the original

Apollo 16 capsule, moon rocks from the mission, an IMAX theater. Tours of the complex take visitors to the booster testing facilities and to the actual assembly areas for Space Station *Freedom.*

Von Braun Astronomical Society, 5105 Noel Avenue Southeast, Huntsville 35801; (256) 539-0316; www.vbas.org. A wonderful attraction high atop Monte Sano Mountain is the Von Braun Astronomical Society and their observatory/planetarium. Twice a month, the club hosts a show for members and the public. A brief look at the sky in the planetarium is followed by a guest speaker and then, if the skies are clear, a spectacular look at the night sky through their telescopes. Check the Web site for dates and times of shows.

Lodging

Madison Inn, 4430 University Drive Northwest, Huntsville 35801; (256) 890-0700.

Southland Motel, 3808 Governors Drive Southwest, Huntsville 35805; (256) 539-9391.

Villager Lodge, 3100 University Drive, Huntsville 35801; (256) 533-0610.

Charles' Motel, 11603 Highway 231 North, Meridianville 35759; (256) 828-4801.

Restaurants

Fogcutter, 3805 University Drive Northwest, Huntsville 35801; (256) 883-0031.

Café Berlin, 505 Airport Road Southwest, Huntsville 35801; (256) 880-9920.

Clocktower, 7500 Memorial Parkway Southwest, Huntsville 35801; (256) 881-0904.

Eunice's Country Kitchen, 1006 Andrew Jackson Way North, Huntsville 35801; (256) 534-9550.

Mr. C's, 11247 Memorial Parkway Southwest, Huntsville 35801; (256) 882-1190.

Organizations

Sierra Club North Alabama (Huntsville) Chapter; alabama.sierraclub.org/na.html.

Other Resources

Tennessee Valley Trails; www.montesano.com/hikeweb.

40 Lickskillet Trail

A pleasant walk through the woods and some of the best views of Town Creek and Lake Guntersville are in store along this trail. The route provides a moderate hike for the first half of the trip over a long and often rocky climb up Bailey Ridge. Then the trail joins the easier Seales and Meredith Trails to complete the loop.

Start: From the camp store on Audrey J. Carr Road.
Distance: 5.0-mile loop.
Approximate hiking time: 2½–3½ hours.
Difficulty: Easy to moderate over wide, leaf- and needle-covered paths, with some rocky portions and steep drop-offs.
Trail surface: Dirt path.
Type of hike: Mixed forest, with hickory, maple, chestnut, upland willow oak, and pine.
Land status: State park.
Nearest town: Guntersville.
Schedule: Open year-round.

Fees/Permits: No fee charged for hiking. Camping is $15, per night, base rate.
Maps: USGS map: Columbus City. Brochures—Trail and park brochures and trail maps are available free of charge at the park office.
Trail contacts: Lake Guntersville State Park, 7966 Alabama Highway 227, Guntersville 35976; (256) 571-5444 or (800) LGVILLE.
Other trail users: None.
Canine compatibility: Dog friendly over dirt footpaths. Bring water; leash required.

Finding the trailhead: From Guntersville take Alabama Highway 227 north to the park office. From the park office, continue on AL 227 for 2 miles. Turn left onto a short connecting road and travel 0.2 mile. Come to a T intersection and make a left turn. Travel 1 mile. Make a left turn onto Audrey J. Carr Road. The camp store and parking area will be on the left. *DeLorme: Alabama Atlas & Gazetteer:* Page 26, A2.

The Hike

Lake Guntersville State Park is a favorite with tourists and residents year-round, and this is not surprising. Water-related activities on the 66,470-acre lake are almost endless: swimming, boating, water-skiing, and, of course, great fishing. The park also has an eighteen-hole golf course and pro shop, tennis courts, picnic areas, and campgrounds.

The park has 31 miles of trails around the peaks, lake, and rivers. Among the trails is a half-mile nature walk, behind the park lodge, which serves up an overview of the local geology and natural life. Trails within the park are well maintained and clear of downed trees, limbs, and brush. Hikes are easy to moderate in difficulty.

The Lickskillet Trail, combined with the Seales and Meredith Trails, makes for a nice hike around Bailey Ridge and the banks of Town Creek. Much of the trail travels through tall members of the beech family, including chestnuts and upland willow oaks. The chestnuts provide food for squirrels, woodchucks, and other animals.

As the trip follows the Meredith Trail, we get a glimpse of Town Creek and Stubblefield Mountain.

Keep your eyes open, as it's not uncommon to see groups of deer wandering through these woods, unfazed by the intrusion of hikers.

Wildflowers often line the path. The lavender-leafed liatris blooms in early fall. The smooth foxglove grows on the side of willow oak trees, bearing yellow flowers from June through October. Also showing off seasonally is the purple penstemon, with leafy clusters of fifty or so lavender flowers.

The orange-blazed Lickskillet Trail heads uphill from its start at the camp store to just below the summit of Bailey Ridge. The moderate hiking eases in a hollow of Bailey Ridge as the Lickskillet reaches its junction with the red-blazed Meredith Trail. The Meredith offers an easy, rolling trip around one of the points of the ridge. As it moves to the northeast, views open up of Stubblefield Mountain and of Hurricane Branch, a feeder stream of Town Creek.

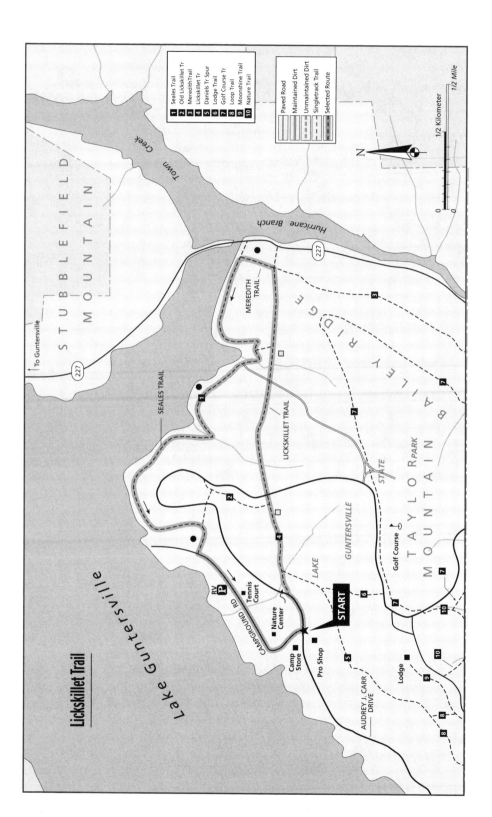

Lickskillet Trail

Lake Guntersville

STUBBLEFIELD MOUNTAIN

Town Creek

To Guntersville

227

SEALES TRAIL

Hurricane Branch

227

MEREDITH TRAIL

BAILEY RIDGE

LICKSKILLET TRAIL

STATE

TAYLOR PARK MOUNTAIN

Golf Course

GUNTERSVILLE LAKE

CAMPGROUND RD

RV P

Tennis Court

Nature Center

Camp Store

Pro Shop

START

AUDREY J. CARR DRIVE

Lodge

1	Seales Trail
2	Old Lickskillet Tr
3	Meredith Trail
4	Lickskillet Tr
5	Daniels Tr Spur
6	Lodge Trail
7	Golf Course Tr
8	Loop Trail
9	Moonshine Trail
10	Nature Trail

Paved Road
Maintained Dirt
Unmaintained Dirt
Singletrack Trail
Selected Route

N

0   1/2 Kilometer
     1/2 Mile

Soon the trail runs headlong into the banks of Town Creek at the Seales Trail. This trail, with its blue blazes, was named for Rick and Ruth Seale, who led the building of the park's 31 miles of trail. They continue to be active in maintaining the trails, and it is only fitting that the prettiest trail in the park bears their name. Maple, hickory, oak, and other trees along the trail provide spectacular colors in the fall, as well as a thick, leafy path to walk on.

The most striking views on the trail are of Town Creek and Lake Guntersville. The trail mostly follows a narrow ledge along the banks of the creek and lake, with a sharp drop-off of about 50 feet. A cable is strung in some sections between trees for use as a handrail.

Just before the meandering trail returns to the campground, it opens up into a stand of pines. A small, grassy finger of land juts out into the lake, making a great place to just sit and relax.

Miles and Directions

0.0 Start from the parking lot of the camp store. Follow the Audrey J. Carr Drive to the east 500 feet. The trailhead with a wooden sign reading LICKSKILLET TRAIL will be seen across the road. Enter the woods here. The trail is well marked with orange paint blazes.

0.2 Pass a short connector that branches off to the right and heads up the hill to the Lake Guntersville Lodge. Continue straight. (**FYI:** On park maps, connecting trails are marked with black dots. In reality, the trails have white blazes.)

0.6 Cross a paved park road.

1.2 Cross a gravel power line road.

1.7 A white-blazed connector trail crosses the path here. Continue straight.

2.0 Intersect the red-blazed Meredith Trail and turn left. (Lickskillet continues straight.)

2.3 At the bottom of the hill, 20 feet of the banks of Town Creek, the Meredith Trail comes to a T intersection with the Seales Trail. Turn to the left onto the blue-blazed Seales Trail.

2.9 Come to a fork and go right. (To the left are blue blazes with a sign reading HIGH WATER BRIDGES.) Don't be confused by the two different blazes, just take the right fork.

3.0 Cross the gravel power line road and reenter the woods.

3.3 The trail opens up to nice views of Stubblefield Mountain to the right.

A rock outcropping along the banks of Town Creek.

4.3 Pass a white-blazed connector trail on the left.

4.4 Come to the gravel Campground Road and turn left. The road becomes paved road and heads through the campground.

4.6 Pass the park's tennis court on the left.

4.7 Pass a road that leads to the park's nature center on the left.

5.0 Arrive back at the camp store parking area.

Hike Information

Local Information
Lake Guntersville Chamber, 200 Gunter Avenue, Guntersville 35976; (800) 869–LAKE; www.lakeguntersville.org.

Local Events/Attractions
Eagle Awareness, weekends in January, 7966 Alabama Highway 227, Guntersville 35976; (256) 571–5440. American bald eagles have made a huge comeback in Alabama, and each January hundreds of visitors come to Guntersville State Park to view the birds. There is a special 5:00 A.M. watch as the eagles leave their nests and a 4:00 P.M. return-to-roost watch.

Summerfest, second weekend of August, Guntersville; (256) 582–3612. A weekend filled with music, arts and crafts, and food, held at the Civitan Park.

The Whole Backstage Theatre, 1120 Rayburn Avenue, Guntersville 35976; (256) 582–SHOW; www.wholebackstage.com. Marshall County's well-known community theater, which features four shows every season, including a summer musical in July.

Noccalula Falls Park, 1500 Noccalula Road, Gadsden 35904; (256) 549-4663. A 90-foot waterfall and canyon. Legend has it that an Indian princess, faced with the choice of being married to someone she didn't love, jumped to her death at these falls, and so they were named for her. On a happier note, the beautiful park has nature trails, a botanical garden with more than 25,000 azaleas, pioneer village, war memorial, gift shop, children's playground, and campground.

Lodging

Lakeview Inn, Highway 431 South, Guntersville 35976; (256) 582-3104.

Overlook Mountain Inn, 13045 U.S. Highway 431, Guntersville 35976; (256) 582-3256.

Covenant Cove, 7001 Val Monte Drive, Guntersville 35976; (256) 582-1000.

Lake Guntersville State Park Lodge, 7966 Alabama Highway 227, Guntersville 35976; (800) 548-4553.

Restaurants

Bruce's Restaurant, 21235 Highway 431, Guntersville 35976; (256) 582-8261.

State Lodge Restaurant, 7966 Alabama Highway 227, Guntersville 35976; (256) 582-3666.

Other Resources

Alabama Mountain Lakes (North Alabama information), Mooresville; (800) 648-5381; www.almtlakes.org.

Bama Environmental News, (205) 226-7739; www.bamanews.com.

Wildflowers of Alabama; www.duc.auburn.edu/ ~deancar/index.html.

41 Cascade Loop Trail

During times of decent rainfall, the Cascade Loop is an especially wonderful hike. You'll pass numerous creeks and cascades as the trail leads to a 200-foot-high rock wall. Here the trail travels a narrow ledge around the cliff and past a shallow cave. As it loops around and returns, the trail passes the remains of an old moonshine still.

Start: At the Terrell Trail trailhead on Audrey J. Carr Drive.
Distance: 2.3-mile loop.
Approximate hiking time: 2–3 hours.
Difficulty: Moderate, with some steep sections up a rock wall and along a rocky creek.
Trail surface: Rocky at the start; then dirt.
Type of hike: A mixture of oak, hickory, maple, and pine trees; lichen-covered boulders and fern-lined pathways; 200-foot cliffs.
Land status: State park.
Nearest town: Guntersville.
Schedule: Open year-round.
Fees/Permits: No fee charged for hiking. Camping is $15, base rate.

Maps: USGS map: Columbus City. Brochures—Trail and park brochures and trail maps are available free of charge at the park office.
Trail contacts: Lake Guntersville State Park, 7966 Alabama Highway 227, Guntersville 35976; (256) 571-5444 or (800) LGVILLE.
Other trail users: None.
Canine compatibility: Dog friendly, with ample water available. Leash recommended near the halfway point due to the number of people on the intersecting nature trail.

Finding the trailhead: From Guntersville take Alabama Highway 227 north. Make a left turn into the park across from the Pure gas station. Head up this short entrance road 0.1 mile and make a right onto Audrey J. Carr Drive. Travel 0.6 mile. The Terrell Trail parking area, a grassy shoulder with a TERRELL TRAIL sign, will be on the left. *DeLorme: Alabama Atlas & Gazetteer:* Page 26, A1.

The Hike

The Cascade Loop Trail at Lake Guntersville State Park is just a fun trail—plain and simple. After a brief start along the Terrell Trail, the loop trail starts a moderate climb over large rocks along a stream. The stream is seasonal, but after some rain views of the cascade make the hike even better.

The hike gets even more interesting as it approaches tall rock walls. The trail makes an abrupt turn and heads up the cliff to a point about 50 feet above its base and then travels around the cliff on a 2-foot-wide rock ledge. In the middle of this "mountaineering," you'll pass a 60-foot-deep cave to the left that was carved into the rocks by wind and weather over the years.

At the top of the cliff, the trail briefly joins the nature trail that visitors to Lake Guntersville Lodge use for morning exercise. It then turns south onto the Waterfall

During wet times, the trail's namesake is a beautiful cascade over this rocky bluff.

Trail. The trail follows another streambed downhill. Once again, the stream is seasonal, but after a good rain you'll discover a waterfall here.

Just before you reach the intersection with the Cascade Trail that completes the loop for the return trip, the trail goes east to reach the site of an old moonshine still. Here is a collection of parts and equipment used to make moonshine liquor during Prohibition. Take a walk around the site and note the deep ax cuts in the metal parts. It may not have been Elliot Ness, but the revenuers made an appearance here and shut this operation down with axes.

As with all paths at the park, these hiking trails are in excellent condition. All are well maintained and virtually clear of downed trees, limbs, and brush. Trail markers consist of paint blazes on the trees. On this hike, the colors include orange for the first 0.1 mile, where the Terrell Trail begins the trip; white for the connecting trail that links the Terrell Trail with the Cascade Trail; blue on the Cascade Trail; orange again on the Waterfall Trail; and finally red on the part of the route to the old still.

Cascade Loop Trail

The trail travels through mixed forest that includes tall members of the beech tree family, like chestnut and upland willow oaks. Squirrels and woodchucks are abundant here, feeding off the chestnuts. White-tailed deer are seen here in large numbers, and ring-necked pheasants may surprise you from the brush as you round the mountainside.

From early spring through fall, wildflowers line the trail. These include the lavender-leafed liatris, which blooms in early fall. You'll also find penstemon, with leafy clusters of fifty or so lavender flowers. The smooth foxglove grows on the side of white oak trees, bearing yellow flowers from June through October.

If it's a hot day, complete the Cascade Loop and then head in the car up Audrey J. Carr Drive for about another mile. On the left is a day-use area with a great beach for swimming in Lake Guntersville. There is also a picnic area and a nice little country store for snacks and some of the extra supplies you may need.

Miles and Directions

0.0 Start from the Terrell Trail parking area off Audrey J. Carr Drive. Cross the road to the north and pick up the yellow-blazed Terrell Trail as it enters the woods.

0.1 Come to a T intersection and turn right, following white blazes. A sign here says CASCADE TRAIL and points to the east and WATERFALL TRAIL and points to the west. White blazes now line the trail. This is a connector between the Terrell and Cascade Trails. The trail runs parallel to the road.

0.3 The path comes within 50 feet of Audrey J. Carr Drive. Next to the road, a sign marking the Cascade Trail will be seen. Turn left here, away from the road, to the northeast. This is now the Cascade Trail, with blue blazes.

0.7 Come to a fork and go right. (The left fork, marked by a sign, is the Old Still Path Trail that we'll use on the return trip.)

0.8 Pass a 60- to 70-foot-deep cave in the cliff to the left.

0.9 Come to a fork and go left. (A sign indicates that Town Creek and Meredith Trail go right. The other sign here says CASCADE/LODGE and point to the northwest.) Shortly pass the white connector trail.

1.0 An unmarked white connector trail heads off to the north. Continue straight.

The remains of a moonshine still.

1.1 Turn left onto the yellow-blazed Waterfall Trail. (A nature trail travels down to this intersection from the lodge and continues straight ahead to the west.)

1.3 Pass the white connector trail that leads back to the Cascade Trail to the left.

1.5 The Old Still Path intersects the Waterfall Trail from the southeast. Turn left here and head on the orange-blazed trail to the southeast.

1.6 Arrive at the Old Still Site. This was a moonshine still used in the '20s and was destroyed by the Feds. Notice the ax marks in the metal.

1.8 Come to a T intersection with the Cascade Trail and turn right, following the blue blazes back downhill, retracing the previous path.

2.0 Come to the edge of Audrey J. Carr Drive and make a sharp right turn. Follow the white-blazed connector trail back toward the Terrell Trail.

2.2 Return to the intersection of the Terrell Trail with the white connector trail. Turn left here and follow the Terrell back to the parking area.

2.3 Arrive at the Terrell Trail parking area.

Hike Information

Local Information

Lake Guntersville Chamber, 200 Gunter Avenue, Guntersville 35976; (800) 869–LAKE; www.lakeguntersville.org.

Local Events/Attractions

Eagle Awareness, weekends in January, 7966 Alabama Highway 227, Guntersville 35976; (256) 571-5440. American bald eagles have made a huge comeback in Alabama, and each January hundreds of visitors come to Guntersville State Park to view the birds. There is a special 5:00 A.M. watch as the eagles leave their nests and a 4:00 P.M. return-to-roost watch.

Summerfest, second weekend of August, Guntersville; (256) 582-3612. A weekend filled with music, arts and crafts, and food, held at the Civitan Park.

The Whole Backstage Theatre, 1120 Rayburn Avenue, Guntersville 35976; (256) 582-SHOW; www.wholebackstage.com. Marshall County's well-known community theater, which features four shows every season, including a summer musical in July.

Noccalula Falls Park, 1500 Noccalula Road, Gadsden 35904; (256) 549-4663. A 90-foot waterfall and canyon. Legend has it that an Indian princess, faced with the choice of being married to someone she didn't love, jumped to her death at these falls, and so they were named for her. On a happier note, the beautiful park has nature trails, a botanical garden with more than 25,000 azaleas, pioneer village, war memorial, gift shop, children's playground, and campground.

Lodging

Lakeview Inn, Highway 431 South, Guntersville 35976; (256) 582-3104.

Overlook Mountain Inn, 13045 U.S. Highway 431, Guntersville 35976; (256) 582-3256.

Covenant Cove, 7001 Val Monte Drive, Guntersville 35976; (256) 582-1000.

Lake Guntersville State Park Lodge, 7966 Alabama Highway 227, Guntersville 35976; (800) 548-4553.

Restaurants

Bruce's Restaurant, 21235 Highway 431, Guntersville 35976; (256) 582-8261.

State Lodge Restaurant, 7966 Alabama Highway 227, Guntersville 35976; (256) 582-3666.

Other Resources

Alabama Mountain Lakes (North Alabama information), Mooresville; (800) 648-5381; www.almtlakes.org.

Bama Environmental News, (205) 226-7739; www.bamanews.com.

Wildflowers of Alabama; www.duc.auburn.edu/~deancar/index.html.

42 Tom Bevill Interpretive Trail

The Tom Bevill Interpretive Trail circles around the summit of Ellenburg Mountain. The hike is highlighted by numbered stops that provide a look at the geology and plant life of the mountain. You'll spot old farmhouse ruins along the way.

Start: From the parking lot at the Lake Guntersville State Park office.

Distance: 3.8-mile loop.

Approximate hiking time: 2–3 hours.

Difficulty: Easy walking on dirt footpaths, except for a moderate 0.1-mile rocky section at the start.

Trail surface: Dirt path; short rocky stretch.

Type of hike: Mixture of oak, hickory, maple, and pine trees; lichen-covered boulders and fern-lined pathways.

Land status: State park.

Nearest town: Guntersville.

Schedule: Open year-round.

Fees/Permits: No fee charged for hiking. Camping is $15 per night, base rate.

Maps: USGS map: Columbus City. Brochures—Trail and park brochures and trail maps are available free of charge at the park office.

Trail contacts: Lake Guntersville State Park, 7966 Alabama Highway 227, Guntersville 35976; (256) 571-5444 or (800) LGVILLE.

Other trail users: None.

Canine compatibility: Dog friendly over easy trail. Bring water; no leash required.

Finding the trailhead: From Guntersville take Alabama Highway 227 north to the park office. The trailhead is directly across AL 227 from the park office. *DeLorme: Alabama Atlas & Gazetteer:* Page 26, A2.

The Hike

This path is a nature trail, pure and simple, but the high route around Ellenburg Mountain and the variety of wildlife and vegetation that can be seen make it a special hike for people of all ages.

To hike the trail most enjoyably, pick up a copy of the brochure *A 3 Mile Walk With Nature,* available free at the Lake Guntersville State Park office across from the trailhead. Throughout the hike, numbered markers on trees point out historical and natural sites that correspond with a description in the brochure. (The office is open Monday through Friday from 7:30 A.M. to 5:00 P.M. and on Saturday and Sunday from 8:00 A.M. to 5:00 P.M.)

Up until 1980, the trail was a simple footpath around Ellenburg Mountain. In that year, members of the Youth Conservation Corps of the Tennessee Valley Authority took it upon themselves to make the trail something more. The Youth Conservation Corps is a nationwide group of teenagers who earn school credit and learn about the environment while working to protect and enhance it.

Lake Guntersville.

In a short time, the youngsters cleared and improved the trail and rerouted it to highlight unique features of the mountain. They also prepared the brochure and marked the corresponding sites along the route.

The trail takes you through a variety of plant life. Hardwoods such as sweet gum, yellow poplar, white oak, and maple line the trail. Of course, no walk in the Southern woods would be complete without pine trees. Along the Tom Bevill Trail, named for a U.S. congressman from Alabama, you'll find loblolly, Virginia, and shortleaf pines. Flowers to be seen include pink azaleas, which serve up a deep fragrance as they bloom in spring, and oak leaf hydrangea, which blooms in late June.

On the west side of Ellenburg Mountain, watch for royal ferns. On the east side, look for Christmas ferns. On the northwest side, muscadine vines grow entangled in the trees. The grapelike fruit of the muscadine has been used for jelly, and muscadine wine has been called the original American wine. Muscadine is also a source of food for wildlife.

With patience and quiet walking, you can see the wildlife of the Tom Bevill Trail. From the rocky top of the mountain, the screeching of red-tailed hawks may be heard. On the ground, raccoons, foxes, wild turkeys, and white-tailed deer are the most common animals.

The area has a fare share of human history. Families such as the Kings, the Terrells, and the Newmans—you'll encounter their names on various landmarks—moved to this region to farm. The ruins of a large farmhouse with its root cellar sits near the trail, along with a one-room cabin that was used for cooking. Note how the settlers fashioned sandstone into bricks and made them fit together to build these structures.

A few nice views grace the trail. Near the start of the hike, to the left, the waters of Lake Guntersville glint through the trees. As the trail swings around to the northeast, views open up to Graveyard Hill, where many of the early settlers to the area are buried. A short side trail leads to the cemetery.

The Tom Bevill Interpretive Trail offers an opportunity to learn more about the environment and how humans interact with it. It's an excellent hike for children, providing a way to get outdoors and involved in something educational—probably without their even knowing it. If you're with young children, give them a helping hand during the first 0.1 mile, where the trail is moderately steep.

Miles and Directions

0.0   Start from the park office and cross AL 227. A trail sign marks the entrance. Head into the woods along the orange-blazed trail.

0.1   Come to a T intersection with the Tom Bevill Trail and take a left. (This is where the trail loops back onto itself for the return trip.)

0.4   Pass Marker #4 and the "Decomposer" tree.

0.8   Pass Marker #5 and the Century Tree.

1.9   Come to Marker #9 and the intersection of the Cave Trail (to the left). Turn right onto the Spring Trail. (Straight will take the Tom Bevill Trail, which merges with the Cave Trail here, and blue and orange blazes will be seen. The Cave Trail heads to Cemetery Hill and to the King's Chapel Cemetery, where many of the early settlers who lived here are buried.)

2.2   Come to a deep ravine. The blaze on the tree here is blue-orange-blue-orange. At the bottom, the Tom Bevill splits from the Cave Trail. Turn to the south. It will only be orange blazes from here.

2.3   To the right is an old stone chimney and a stone foundation. At one time this was a one-room cabin that was used for cooking by area settlers. Heading straight 100 feet, the trail runs into an old sandstone foundation. This was an old farmhouse and root cellar.

2.7   Come to a nice view of Graveyard Hill and King Hollow to the left.

3.0   Pass Marker #14.

3.6   Turn left onto the side trail to the park office. (A sign marks the turn.)

3.8   Arrive at the parking lot.

Ruins of an old farmhouse.

Hike Information

Local Information

Lake Guntersville Chamber, 200 Gunter Avenue, Guntersville 35976; (800) 869-LAKE; www.lakeguntersville.org.

Local Events/Attractions

Eagle Awareness, weekends in January, 7966 Alabama Highway 227, Guntersville 35976; (256) 571-5440. American bald eagles have made a huge comeback in Alabama, and each January hundreds of visitors come to Guntersville State Park to view the birds. There is a special 5:00 A.M. watch as the eagles leave their nests and a 4:00 P.M. return-to-roost watch.

Summerfest, second weekend of August, Guntersville; (256) 582-3612. A weekend filled with music, arts and crafts, and food, held at the Civitan Park.

The Whole Backstage Theatre, 1120 Rayburn Avenue, Guntersville 35976; (256) 582-SHOW; www.wholebackstage.com. Marshall County's well-known community theater, which features four shows every season, including a summer musical in July.

Noccalula Falls Park, 1500 Noccalula Road, Gadsden 35904; (256) 549-4663. A 90-foot waterfall and canyon. Legend has it that an Indian princess, faced with the choice of being married to someone she didn't love, jumped to her death at these falls, and so they were named for her. On a happier note, the beautiful park has nature trails, a botanical garden with more than 25,000 azaleas, pioneer village, war memorial, gift shop, children's playground, and campground.

Lodging

Lakeview Inn, Highway 431 South, Guntersville 35976; (256) 582-3104.

Overlook Mountain Inn, 13045 U.S. Highway 431, Guntersville 35976; (256) 582-3256.

Covenant Cove, 7001 Val Monte Drive, Guntersville 35976; (256) 582-1000.

Lake Guntersville State Park Lodge, 7966 Alabama Highway 227, Guntersville 35976; (800) 548-4553.

Restaurants

Bruce's Restaurant, 21235 Highway 431, Guntersville 35976; (256) 582-8261.

State Lodge Restaurant, 7966 Alabama Highway 227, Guntersville 35976; (256) 582-3666.

Other Resources

Alabama Mountain Lakes (North Alabama information), Mooresville; (800) 648-5381; www.almtlakes.org.

Bama Environmental News, (205) 226-7739; www.bamanews.com.

Wildflowers of Alabama; www.duc.auburn.edu/~deancar/index.html.

In Addition

A State of Perpetual Motion

The hiking trails of Alabama provide a variety of challenges and scenery for everyone. But there are plenty of other outdoor activities in the state to keep people on the move outdoors.

Probably the fastest growing outdoor activity is mountain biking. Trails are popping up all over. And, of course, hikers and cyclists are battling it out in many areas over the question of how to coexist and protect the environment at the same time.

The State of Alabama is going out of its way to provide areas for both in some of the prettiest of places. The Red Trail (a.k.a. the Bump Trail) at Oak Mountain State Park is a world-class track that has served as a training course for Olympic mountain bikers. The park also boasts a huge bicycle motocross facility. Cheaha State Park offers a bike trail that takes cyclists around Cheaha Mountain, the highest point in the state. The Mountain Mist Trail at Monte Sano State Park is the site of regular competitions. Even the smaller city parks are joining in. Near Mobile, Chickasabogue Park has the multi-use Cemetery Trail, which has cyclists traveling in one direction and hikers in the opposite direction.

The waters of Alabama provide a lot of rafting, canoeing, and kayaking options. On the Gulf of Mexico, sea kayaking is popular at places like Orange Beach, Gulf Shores, and Dauphin Island. In Northeast Alabama, the rapids of the Little River were used for training by Olympic kayakers. In the Sipsey Wilderness, canoeists float down the Sipsey River through some of the most pristine forests and canyons in the country.

For those who love horses, equestrian trails are scattered throughout the state. Most state parks have trails set aside just for horseback riding. Many parks are near stables where horses can be rented. And some parks, like Oak Mountain State Park, have stables right on site and offer guided rides.

People in Alabama also find adventure on the rocks. Little River Canyon National Preserve, Point Rock at Buck's Pocket State Park, and the Rock Garden at Cheaha State Park are favorite sites for rock climbers.

43 Cutchenmine Trail

The Cutchenmine Trail, once a mining road, follows the banks of Lake Guntersville, going through a dense forest of hickory, maple, and beech trees. The highlight of this trip in Lake Guntersville State Park is the wildlife, including herons and ducks. The trail is a prime location for spotting eagles.

Start: From the Cutchenmine trailhead on Alabama Highway 227.
Distance: 4.2-mile out-and-back.
Approximate hiking time: 2-3 hours.
Difficulty: Easy walk around the base of Berry Point and along the banks of Lake Guntersville.
Trail surface: Dirt footpath.
Type of hike: Mixture of hickory, maple, and large beech trees, with some loblolly pines.
Land status: State park.
Nearest town: Guntersville.
Schedule: Open year-round.
Fees/Permits: No fee charged for hiking. Camping is $15 per night, base rate.

Maps: USGS maps: Columbus City; Albertville. Brochures—Trail and park brochures and trail maps are available free of charge at the park office.
Trail contacts: Lake Guntersville State Park, 7966 Alabama Highway 227, Guntersville, AL; (256) 571-5444 or (800) LGVILLE.
Other trail users: None.
Canine compatibility: Dog friendly along a level dirt footpath. Bring water; leash not required.

Finding the trailhead: From Guntersville take AL 227 north to the park office. Continue past the office a short 0.6 mile. The trailhead parking area is a shoulder along the right side of the highway. A sign marks the location. *DeLorme: Alabama Atlas & Gazetteer:* Page 26, A2.

The Hike

Mining in Alabama goes back to the mid 1800s, when large deposits of coal and iron were discovered throughout what became known as the state's "black belt." A miner by the name of Cutchen, looking to transport his loads of coal to buyers, built the original roadway along Berry Point and the banks of Lake Guntersville. Today that roadway is the scenic Cutchenmine Trail.

The real beauty of this trip is not so much the history of the area as it is the wildlife to be seen, especially birds. Large blue herons soar off the pond and marsh area at the beginning of the walk. Mallards and wood ducks float along the shores of the lake as red-tailed hawks circle overhead.

The big excitement at the lake comes each January for a winter round of eagle watching. Each weekend throughout the month, crowds of birdwatchers descend on the area bearing binoculars, cameras, lots of snacks, and hot chocolate. In the cold, crisp air just before dawn, the raptor watchers plod the trail and get a vantage point to watch bald eagles take to the skies.

Lake Guntersville.

After catching the morning show, the watchers return to the lodge at the park to hear speakers lecture on the subject of eagles. This month of activity, known as Eagle Awareness, has become the most popular and anticipated birding event in the state.

Once at serious risk, the bald eagle has made a remarkable comeback and now makes Lake Guntersville one of its nesting areas. The eagle population in the state had dropped to just a few during the 1960s and 1970s, but a program established in the mid 1980s began to bring them back. Although January has been set aside for the Eagle Awareness program, bald eagles can be seen just about any time of the year at the lake.

The Cutchenmine Trail is a level dirt route that winds around the base of Berry Point just east of a finger of Lake Guntersville. The lake is in sight through most of the trip, just 50 to 60 feet from the trail. Be prepared for a bit of disappointment if you decide to walk down to the lake itself. Debris such as milk cartons and soda bottles often washes up here. During late spring and summer when the heat starts to rise, so do the number of mosquitoes, so bring bug spray.

The trail goes to the southern end of Lake Guntersville State Park, where it ends at the CCC Trail, a trail built by the Depression-era Civilian Conservation Corps. This is a short, white-blazed connector trail that leads to the westernmost boundary of the park.

Cutchenmine Trail

Miles and Directions

0.0 Start from the orange-blazed Cutchenmine trailhead on AL 227.

0.1 Ellenburg Mountain, the home of the Tom Bevill Trail, can be seen to the right.

0.5 On the right is the lake and ahead to the northwest is a nice view of Bald Knob across the lake.

2.1 The trail reaches a creekbed and the trail dead-ends into the white-blazed CCC Trail. Turn around here and retrace the path back to the parking area.

4.2 Arrive back at the parking area.

Hike Information

Local Information

Lake Guntersville Chamber, 200 Gunter Avenue, Guntersville 35976; (800) 869–LAKE; www.lakeguntersville.org.

Local Events/Attractions

Eagle Awareness, weekends in January, 7966 Alabama Highway 227, Guntersville 35976; (256) 571–5440. American bald eagles have made a huge comeback in Alabama, and each January hundreds of visitors come to Guntersville State Park to view the birds. There is a special 5:00 A.M. watch as the eagles leave their nests and a 4:00 P.M. return-to-roost watch.

Summerfest, second weekend of August, Guntersville; (256) 582–3612. A weekend filled with music, arts and crafts, and food, held at the Civitan Park.

The Whole Backstage Theatre, 1120 Rayburn Avenue, Guntersville 35976; (256) 582–SHOW; www.wholebackstage.com. Marshall County's well-known community theater, which features four shows every season, including a summer musical in July.

Noccalula Falls Park, 1500 Noccalula Road, Gadsden 35904; (256) 549–4663. A 90-foot waterfall and canyon. Legend has it that an Indian princess, faced with the choice of being married to someone she didn't love, jumped to her death at these falls, and so they were named for her. On a happier note, the beautiful park has nature trails, a botanical garden with more than 25,000 azaleas, pioneer village, war memorial, gift shop, children's playground, and campground.

Lodging

Lakeview Inn, Highway 431 South, Guntersville 35976; (256) 582–3104.

Overlook Mountain Inn, 13045 U.S. Highway 431, Guntersville 35976; (256) 582–3256.

Covenant Cove, 7001 Val Monte Drive, Guntersville 35976; (256) 582–1000.

Lake Guntersville State Park Lodge, 7966 Alabama Highway 227, Guntersville 35976; (800) 548-4553.

Restaurants

Bruce's Restaurant, 21235 Highway 431, Guntersville 35976; (256) 582-8261.

State Lodge Restaurant, 7966 Alabama Highway 227, Guntersville 35976; (256) 582-3666.

Other Resources

Alabama Mountain Lakes (North Alabama information), Mooresville; (800) 648-5381; www.almtlakes.org.

Bama Environmental News, (205) 226-7739; www.bamanews.com.

Wildflowers of Alabama; www.duc.auburn.edu/~deancar/index.html.

44 Camp Road

The Camp Road Trail at Buck's Pocket State Park is an easy hike along the dirt camp road that follows the flow of South Sauty Creek. The Sauty is lined with sandstone boulders that create active rapids. During periods of low rainfall, you can hike along the banks of the river, which runs parallel to the trail—though you may find some of the boulders difficult to get around. The views of the sandstone cliffs along Hilley Point are quite beautiful.

Start: From the parking area of the Buck's Pocket State Park office.
Distance: 2.6-mile out-and-back.
Approximate hiking time: 1½–2½ hours.
Difficulty: Easy, over dirt road and footpath.
Trail surface: Dirt road.
Type of hike: Sandstone cliffs; blue beech and white walnut trees.
Land status: State park.
Nearest town: Guntersville.
Schedule: Open year-round.
Fees/Permits: No fee for hiking. Camping is $12 per night, base rate.

Maps: USGS map: Grove Oak.
Brochures—Available free of charge at the park office.
Trail contacts: Buck's Pocket State Park, 393 County Road 174, Grove Oak 35975; (256) 659-2000—The park office is open 7:30 A.M.–5:00 P.M. Monday through Friday, 8:00 A.M.–5:00 P.M. Saturday and Sunday.
Other trail users: None.
Canine compatibility: Dog friendly, level dirt roads, ample water; no leash required.

Finding the trailhead: From Guntersville follow Alabama Highway 227 north through Guntersville State Park. Just after crossing the bridge over Town Creek and Lake Guntersville, come to an intersection. AL 227 turns right here. Continue 2.8 miles and make a left onto County Road 19. In 1.6 miles CR 19 becomes County Road 152. In 0.6 mile, the road comes to a fork. Take the right fork (this is the park road) and travel 0.3 mile to the parking lot on the left side of the road next to the park office. *DeLorme: Alabama Atlas & Gazetteer:* Page 20, H3.

The Hike

Located just a few miles from Guntersville, Buck's Pocket State Park is another jewel in the Alabama park system, offering waterways, sandstone bluffs, rare plants, and high overlooks for taking it all in. The 2,000-acre park cradles the ruggedly beautiful South Sauty Creek, which is responsible for the park's stunning canyon scenery.

The Camp Road Trail follows the flow of South Sauty Creek to just above Morgan's Cove. The trail has no markers but is easy to follow. The walk travels along the banks of the creek for a short distance until huge boulders force the route onto the campground road. It's possible to hike the entire trail along the riverbank, but this can be difficult; some of the boulders make formidable obstacles—some boulders are more than 20 feet high. And in spring after heavy rains or snowmelt, the area is

South Sauty Creek.

prone to flooding and the stream runs fast and dangerous. The beautiful blue-green creek averages 30 to 50 feet in width as it tumbles over the rocks.

The route affords not only great views of the creek and its rapids but also of Hilley Point to the northwest, with its high bluffs, cliffs, and overlooks. Keep an eye on the cliffs for the rock climbers who congregate here. Hilley Point was formed at a time in the geological past when a vast ocean covered the region. Eventually the area was thrust upward and the sea receded, leaving the action of the stream to shape the canyon.

The route displays some interesting plant life as it runs along the base of Sand Mountain. A rare species of trillium, the wake robin trillium, with its elliptical cluster of flowers, blooms here in May and June. This species is found in Buck's Pocket and nowhere else in the world. The white yellow-centered flowers of the bloodroot also bloom along the trail. The flower got its name from the red fluid inside the plant, which was used by Native Americans for paint.

Rhododendrons, with their broad, waxy leaves and lavender or white flowers, favor this area. You may also see foamflowers—wildflowers with leaves that resemble those of the maple. The flowers, white with a touch of orange, cluster on the stem. Along the route are several varieties of fern, including Christmas, broad beech, and rattlesnake ferns.

You'll also be walking in the company of such trees as white walnut, blackjack oak, and smooth-barked blue beech. Also seen are painted buckeyes, small trees that display yellow-green leaves and are usually found as underbrush. Sassafras, whose bark can be used to brew sassafras tea, also grow here, but since all vegetation in Alabama state parks is protected, you can't remove the bark.

To add a bit more distance, continue down the trail on the dirt road another mile to Morgan's Cove. The route makes a turn south and ascends steeply one-third of the way up Bethune Point before heading down to the cove, which is on 66,470-acre Lake Guntersville. The cove offers picnic areas, swimming, and fishing; an Alabama freshwater fishing license is required.

If you've brought the kids along and are looking for an easy stroll, follow the white-blazed South Sauty Creek Trail, which you'll use at times on this route. The South Sauty Trail crosses the creek at the dam and leads to fine views of the river and its many rapids.

It is possible to hike the riverbank when the water is low—but did I mention it's a bit rocky?

Miles and Directions

0.0   Start from the parking lot at the park office. Walk behind the park office and come to the banks of South Sauty Creek. (The water will be to the right throughout the entire hike.) At the creek, turn left and walk along the bank. (**Note:** There are no markings for this hike.)

0.6   Intersect a road that runs over the top of the dam. Cross the road and continue following the creek. In 200 yards the trail scrambles over some boulders. But wait! After 100 feet the boulders are HUGE! It is advised to take the short 50-foot side trail uphill to the left and take the dirt camp road for the next 0.2 mile.

1.4   The road comes to a feeder stream flowing down from the mountain. Turn around here and follow the road all the way back to the park office. **Option:** If the water level permits, you can hike back to the office along the creek.

1.8   The road splits around some brush and a few trees and then reconnects in 30 feet. Continue 100 feet and come to a locked gate. Walk around the gate and continue on the road.

2.1   Come to a closed metal gate. Walk around the gate; the road is now paved. Follow the road until it comes to a fork and go right. (To the left is the dam road under which the South Sauty flows.)

2.2 Come to a fork and go left. A sign here reads OFFICE/CAMPING. Point Rock can be seen ahead to the right through the trees.

2.6 Arrive back at the parking lot.

Hike Information

Local Information

Marshall County Tourism Commission, 200 Gunter Avenue, Guntersville 35976; (800) 582-6282.

Lake Guntersville Chamber, 200 Gunter Avenue, Guntersville 35976; (800) 869-LAKE; www.lakeguntersville.org.

Local Events/Attractions

Guntersville Museum and Cultural Center, 2132 Debow Street, Guntersville 35976; (256) 571-7597; www.alabamamuseums. org/g-gmcc.htm. In addition to displays of Native American artifacts, a steamboat exhibit, and a local art collection, this museum has special exhibits throughout the year. Admission is free. Closed on Monday.

Pre-Civil War Cemetery, West Main Street, Albertville; (800) 878-3821. Stroll through this cemetery where the inscriptions on the stones tell unique and fascinating stories of the region. Admission is free.

Unclaimed Baggage Center, 509 West Willow Street, Scotsboro 35768; (256) 259-1525; www.unclaimedbaggage.com. Oprah Winfrey called this the best-kept shopping secret. The center is the largest purchaser of lost and unclaimed luggage in the country and in turn, "sells them direct to you!" Closed on Sunday.

Lodging

Covenant Cove, 7001 Val Monte Drive, Guntersville 35976; (256) 582-1000.

Lake Guntersville Bed and Breakfast, 2204 Scott Street, Guntersville 35976; (256) 505-0133.

Lakeview Inn, Highway 431 South, Guntersville 35976; (256) 582-3104.

Overlook Mountain Inn, 13045 U.S. Highway 431, Guntersville 35976; (256) 582-3256.

Restaurants

Bruce's Restaurant, 21235 Highway 431, Guntersville 35976; (256) 582-8261.

State Lodge Restaurant, 7966 Alabama Highway 227, Guntersville 35976; (256) 582-3666.

Other Resources

North Alabama Tourism Association, Mooresville; (800) 648-5381; www.northalabama.org.

Bama Environmental News; (205) 226-7739; www.bamanews.com.

Wildflowers of Alabama; www.duc.auburn.edu/ ~deancar/index.html.

45 Point Rock Trail

The high point of Buck's Pocket State Park is this hike to Point Rock. The trail starts out around a boulder-strewn runoff area that during periods of rainfall can have a wild tropical look to it, with heavy moss. Before the trail ascends to Point Rock, a 70-foot waterfall pops out of the boulders and drops into the underground caverns known as the Big Sink. From the top of the point are expansive views of the sandstone cliffs lining surrounding mountains.

Start: From the parking area of the Buck's Pocket State Park office.

Distance: 3.5-mile out-and-back.

Approximate hiking time: 2–3 hours.

Difficulty: Moderate, due to large boulders and ascent to Point Rock.

Trail surface: Dirt path; some rocky trail.

Type of hike: Butternut and blue beech trees; wildflowers, including Jack-in-the-pulpit and trout lily.

Land status: State park.

Nearest town: Guntersville.

Schedule: Open year-round.

Fees/Permits: No fee for hiking. Camping is $12 per night, base rate.

Maps: USGS map: Grove Oak.

Brochures—Available free of charge at the park office.

Trail contacts: Buck's Pocket State Park, 393 County Road 174, Grove Oak 35975; (256) 659-2000—The park office is open 7:30 A.M.–5:00 P.M. Monday through Friday, 8:00 A.M.–5:00 P.M. Saturday and Sunday.

Other trail users: None.

Canine compatibility: Not dog friendly due to large boulders; no leash required.

Finding the trailhead: From Guntersville follow Alabama Highway 227 through Guntersville State Park. Just after crossing the bridge over Town Creek and Lake Guntersville, come to an intersection. AL 227 turns right here. Continue 2.8 miles and make a left onto County Road 19. In 1.6 miles CR 19 becomes County Road 152. In 0.6 mile, the road comes to a fork. Take the right fork (this is the park road) and travel 0.3 mile to the parking lot on the left side of the road next to the park office. *DeLorme: Alabama Atlas & Gazetteer:* Page 20, H3.

The Hike

Situated within a deep canyon, Buck's Pocket State Park encompasses more than 2,000 acres of forest and canyon. The canyon was formed by erosion from the turbulent action of South Sauty Creek. The result is a park with such features as Point Rock, standing 900 feet above sea level, and the boulder-strewn Big Sink ravine.

The first inhabitants of the area were Native Americans, mainly Cherokee, who used the canyon overhangs as protection from the weather. The park derives its name from a story about a Native American hunter who cornered a buck atop one of the high bluffs above the creek. Rather than be taken, the buck decided to jump to its death in the "pocket" of the canyon.

A view across the canyon from the summit of Point Rock.

The blue-green waters of South Sauty Creek cascade over the boulders of the canyon floor, putting on a splashy show as the creek heads to Morgan's Cove and into Lake Guntersville. The best times to see the creek are in winter and spring, when rain is more frequent. The creek often dries up in summer.

The Point Rock Trail begins at the park office and heads into the woods at the bottom of a ravine, where it climbs over huge boulders. Just before the trail turns to ascend the mountain, a 70-foot waterfall on Little Sauty Creek pops out from deep within the rocks and then drops back underground as it travels to meet South Sauty Creek.

The trail makes its way to the top of Point Rock, a 285-foot-tall sandstone bluff whose top is at an elevation of just over 900 feet. An outcropping popular with rock climbers drops off steeply here. The trail makes its way to the very edge of Point Rock, offering panoramic views of the canyon and its sandstone walls.

▶ **A sign next to the park office reads** A HAVEN FOR DEFEATED POLITICIANS. **The park got this nickname when former governor "Big" Jim Folsom, conceding defeat in an election bid for the U.S. Senate, said he was going to Buck's Pocket to gather his thoughts and lick his wounds.**

From February until late June, wildflowers bloom by the trail. Among them are jack-in-the-pulpit (also known as Indian turnip) and bright yellow-flowered trout lilies. Among the trees along the Point Rock Trail is blue beech, an extremely hard wood—also known as ironwood—that was once used to make tool handles. Also on the trail are butternut, or white walnut, trees with an ash-gray trunk. The walnuts are good to eat, but tough to crack.

Point Rock Trail

The park has an ample supply of tent campsites, both primitive and with drinking water. The best part about camping at Buck's Pocket is the natural air-conditioning: A cool breeze blows through the canyon most of the year, even in the dead of summer when the rest of the state is sweltering.

Miles and Directions

0.0 Start from the park office, head down the paved park road. South Sauty Creek runs parallel to the right.

0.2 Come to a sign that reads HIKING TRAIL TO POINT ROCK. Turn left here and onto the trail into the woods. Shortly you'll begin to see red blazes.

0.8 Point Rock can be seen through the trees to the left.

1.0 A stream will be seen to the right tumbling through the rocks of the ravine and disappearing underground. This is an area known as the Big Sink.

1.1 **Side trip:** Come to a short 30-foot side trail that leads to the falls seen to the right. There you'll find nice spots to sit and lunch.

1.6 Cross the paved overlook road and come to the edge of the cliffs. (**FYI:** This is a popular area for rock climbers and repelers.) At the edge a sign reads LYNN OVERLOOK AREA. Turn left and head down a gravel footpath. The trail turns into a wooden footbridge that travels over Point Rock. Continue on the footbridge as it circles the outcropping. The bridge ends and turns into another gravel footpath.

1.7 A short 50-foot-long footbridge heads to an overlook. Turn to the left and come to the main bluff. This is the end of the hike. Retrace the trail back down to the parking area. (**Note:** The blazes are less noticeable on the downhill trip, so keep an eye out for them.)

3.5 Arrive back at the parking lot.

Hike Information

Local Information

Lake Guntersville Chamber, 200 Gunter Avenue, Guntersville 35976; (800) 869–LAKE; www.lakeguntersville.org.

Local Events/Attractions

Eagle Awareness, weekends in January, 7966 Alabama Highway 227, Guntersville 35976; (256) 571-5440. American bald eagles have made a huge comeback in Alabama, and each January hundreds of visitors come to Guntersville State Park to view the birds. There is a special 5:00 A.M. watch as the eagles leave their nests and a 4:00 P.M. return-to-roost watch.

Summerfest, second weekend of August, Guntersville; (256) 582-3612. A weekend filled with music, arts and crafts, and food, held at the Civitan Park.

The Whole Backstage Theatre, 1120 Rayburn Avenue, Guntersville; (256) 582-SHOW; www.wholebackstage.com. Marshall County's well-known community theater, which features four shows every season, including a summer musical in July.

Noccalula Falls Park, 1500 Noccalula Road, Gadsden 35904; (256) 549-4663. A 90-foot waterfall and canyon. Legend has it that an Indian princess, faced with the choice of being married to someone she didn't love, jumped to her death at these falls, and so they were named for her. On a happier note, the beautiful park has nature trails, a botanical garden with more than 25,000 azaleas, pioneer village, war memorial, gift shop, children's playground, and campground.

Lodging

Lakeview Inn, Highway 431 South, Guntersville 35976; (256) 582-3104.

Overlook Mountain Inn, 13045 U.S. Highway 431, Guntersville 35976; (256) 582-3256.

Covenant Cove, 7001 Val Monte Drive, Guntersville 35976; (256) 582-1000.

Lake Guntersville State Park Lodge, 7966 Alabama Highway 227, Guntersville 35976; (800) 548-4553.

Restaurants

Bruce's Restaurant, 21235 Highway 431, Guntersville 35976; (256) 582-8261.

State Lodge Restaurant, 7966 Alabama Highway 227, Guntersville 35976; (256) 582-3666.

Other Resources

Alabama Mountain Lakes (North Alabama information), Mooresville; (800) 648-5381; www.almtlakes.org.

Bama Environmental News, (205) 226-7739; www.bamanews.com.

Wildflowers of Alabama; www.duc.auburn.edu/~deancar/index.html.

46 Eberhart Trail

Here's a fine hike to the bottom of a major canyon. It's a steep climb down a wide, nicely graded and grass-covered path to the rocky banks of Little River. The canyon walls rise high above as you trek down toward the blue-green waters of the river, all as waterfalls continue to work their magic shaping the soft sandstone.

Start: From the Eberhart Point parking area on Alabama Highway 176.
Distance: 1.8-mile out-and-back.
Approximate hiking time: 1½–2½ hours.
Difficulty: Difficult due to steep hiking into and out of Little River Canyon.
Trail surface: Grass path on the way down; rocky along the river.
Type of hike: Sandstone cliffs; thick rhododendron.
Land status: National preserve.
Nearest town: Fort Payne.
Schedule: Open year-round.

Fees/Permits: No fee charged for hiking. Hunting is allowed in the preserve at specified times of the year. Contact the National Park Service for dates.
Maps: USGS map: Little River. Brochures—Available free of charge by writing the preserve.
Trail contacts: Little River Canyon National Preserve, 2141 Gault Avenue North, Fort Payne 35967-3533; (256) 845-9605; www.nps.gov/liri.
Other trail users: None.
Canine compatibility: Not dog friendly due to steep incline; no leash required.

Finding the trailhead: From Fort Payne take Alabama Highway 35 east and make a right turn onto Alabama Highway 176 west. (A sign clearly marks LITTLE RIVER CANYON.) Drive 11.4 miles to a sign that reads CANYON MOUTH PARK. The parking area and trailhead are to the right. *DeLorme: Alabama Atlas & Gazetteer:* Page 27, A7.

The Hike

Little River gets its start high atop Lookout Mountain in Georgia and flows along the mountain into Alabama through Alabama's DeSoto State Park and the adjacent Little River Canyon National Preserve—a preserve of more than 14,000 acres that was added to the national park system in 1992. The canyon through which it courses was formed by the action of the river on the soft sandstone over thousands of years, creating the deepest and largest canyon east of the Mississippi. The National Park Service considers the river to be one of the cleanest in the South and one of the wildest—thanks to prohibitions on dam construction and other development.

Eberhart Trail is a short out-and-back route that makes for a tough hike, but it's worth the effort. Although the trail is wide—about 10 to 15 feet—it winds sharply down the canyon wall to the river. A saving grace is that the path is sod-covered, making it comfortable for walking. Benches are strategically placed for resting.

Little River and a view of the canyon walls to the south.

Views on the way down are obscured a bit by the trees. Watch for the overlook halfway down the trail, behind one of the benches. Thick rhododendron lines the path. The real payoff is at the bottom. The first thing you see is a 600-foot sandstone wall across the river, towering above the rocky beach. Turning to the left and heading upriver, the trail becomes rough, with rocks 6 to 12 inches wide covering the route. Here the river races through narrow, boulder-strewn channels.

Keep safety in mind during this hike. While Eberhart Trail is a hike and not a rock climb, several places—including the overlook along the way—hang out over the canyon. Don't bushwhack off the paths. There could be hidden drop-offs.

The trip can be extended by hiking along the river bank either to the north or south. Just keep in mind that long, steep trip you just made down the canyon wall. You will need to allow plenty of time to get back up to the top.

The auto route at the preserve, Canyon Rim Parkway, offers views as spectacular as those on Eberhart Trail. Along the drive down the canyon, several overlooks afford an opportunity to park and take in the vistas. At the Hawk's Glide Overlook, you may see rock climbers at play. Grace Falls Overlook shows off the pencil-thin,

Eberhart Trail

	Paved Road
	Maintained Dirt
	Unmaintained Dirt
	Singletrack Trail
	Selected Route

To 35

CANYON RIM
PARKWAY

Bear

176   LITTLE RIVER CANYON   176

NATIONAL PRESERVE

CANYON RIM
PARKWAY

CROW
POINT

START

EBERHART
POINT

Creek

Little

River

Turnaround

176

275

N

0   1/4 Kilometer
0   1/4 Mile

600-foot waterfall plunging down the canyon wall. Also along the way is Needle Rock, where the forces of wind and water have created crawl spaces and overhangs that the kids, and adults, love. At the bottom of Canyon Rim Parkway is Canyon Mouth Park, a day-use facility with a nature trail and picnic area.

Miles and Directions

0.0 Start from the Canyonland parking lot and cross Canyon Rim Parkway to an information board on the other side. Head into the woods beyond the sign. Come to a T intersection and turn left.

0.3 Behind the bench here is a short 20-foot side trail that comes out on top of a ledge that overhangs the canyon wall. (**Note:** Be VERY careful here.)

Don't let this picture fool you. The grade is extremely steep.

0.6 The trail turns into solid rocks as it comes out at the banks of Little River. Straight ahead across the river is an impressive 600-foot canyon wall. From here you can meander quite a distance north and south along the river bank—just remember that you have a steep walk back up. (**Note:** The path is very rocky, so watch your footing. Remember the currents in the river are swift, so be careful along the rapids as well.)

0.9 Turn around and retrace your tracks back to the parking area.

1.8 Arrive back at the parking area.

AND THE WINNER IS . . . It's official. Add to the list of state birds, songs, trees, and whatever else, Alabama's official amphibian.

In April 2000 students from Fairhope Elementary School presented a bill to the state legislature to make the red hill salamander the official state amphibian. The debate on the floor was intense. One House member was upset because his earlier effort in favor of the dusky gopher frog had failed. Another member wondered whether the red hill salamander would make good fishing bait.

When the dust cleared, the salamander was voted in, 95–0.

Hike Information

Local Information

North Alabama Tourism Association, 25062 North Street, Mooresville 35649; (800) 648-5381; www.northalabama.org.

DeKalb County Tourist Association, 1503 Glenn Boulevard Southwest, Fort Payne 35968-3530; (256) 845-3957; www.tourdekalb.com.

Fort Payne; at www.fortpayne.net/ Default.htm. Includes information on DeSoto State Park, Little River Canyon, and Lookout Mountain.

Local Events/Attractions

Rhododendron Festival, third weekend in May, Mentone; (888) 805-4740.

DeSoto Caverns Park, Childersburg; (800) 933-2283; www.cavern.com/desoto/ index.html. Large cathedral-type caves featuring the Great Onyx Cathedral and a laser light show.

DeSoto Falls, 1503 Glenn Boulevard Southwest, Fort Payne 35968; (256) 845-5380; www.mentone.com. DeSoto Falls plunges 104 feet from the end of DeSoto Lake as the waters form the raging Little River. The area is touted as having the largest variety of wildflowers in the world outside China.

Shady Grove Dude Ranch/Cloudmont Ski & Golf Resort, 721 County Road 614, Mentone 35984; (256) 634-4344. Bringing "Montana to Mentone," this resort features snow skiing in winter and a "dude" ranch with trail rides through the mountains to DeSoto and Veil Falls—and, of course, golf! Open year-round.

Sequoyah Caverns, 1438 County Road 731, Fort Payne 35967; (256) 635-0024; www.bham.net/sequoyah/caverns.html. Sequoyah Cavern is a quarter-mile-deep cave in the side of Sand Mountain. Inside, there are a series of rooms with pools of mineral water, 120-foot-high ceilings, and Native American artifacts. The cavern is so named because Cherokee Chief Sequoyah and his tribe used the cave for shelter. A column in the cave has etched in it the words 1830–SAM HOUSTON. Houston married Sequoyah's daughter.

Lodging

DeSoto State Park Lodge, 13883 County Road 89, Fort Payne 35968; (800) 568-8840.

Mentone Inn, Mentone; (800) 455-7470.

Mountain View Motel, 2302 Gault Avenue South, Fort Payne 35967; (256) 845-2303.

Shady Grove Dude Ranch/Cloudmont Ski & Golf Resort, 721 County Road 614, Mentone 35984; (256) 634-4344.

Restaurants

Blue Moon Café, Fort Payne; (256) 997-9908.

DeSoto State Park Lodge, 13883 County Road 89, Fort Payne 35968; (800) 568-8840.

Jack's Char-Coal Broiled Hamburgers, 1401 Gault Avenue North, Fort Payne 35967-3235; (256) 845-3565.

Other Resources

Tennessee Valley Trails; www.montesano.com/hikeweb.

47 Rhododendron Trail

The Rhododendron Trail provides an easy-to-moderate walk through DeSoto State Park. The western section follows gentle rolling hills; the eastern section has the added challenge of large rocks and possibly downed trees. The trail is lined with rhododendron bushes that bloom in late spring. The path takes you past Indian and Lodge Falls.

Start: From the country store parking lot.
Distance: 1.3-mile loop.
Approximate hiking time: 2 hours.
Difficulty: Easy, over gently rolling hills; moderate, over rocks and some downed trees.
Trail surface: Primarily dirt path.
Type of hike: Rhododendron bushes, plus live oak and longleaf pine forest.
Land status: State park.
Nearest town: Fort Payne.
Schedule: Open year-round.
Fees/Permits: No fee charged for hiking.

Maps: USGS maps: Valley Head; Jamestown. Brochures—Available free of charge at the camp store.
Trail contacts: DeSoto State Park, 13883 County Road 89, Fort Payne 35968; (256) 845-0051; www.desotostatepark.com.
Other trail users: Cyclists along sections near the campgrounds.
Canine compatibility: Dog friendly on the western part of the trail, which has ample water and easy terrain; not dog friendly along the eastern section due to large rocks along the river; leash is recommended.

Finding the trailhead: From Fort Payne go east on Alabama Highway 35 for about a mile, and turn left onto DeSoto Parkway. Travel 5.1 miles (DeSoto Parkway turns into County Road 89) to the park entrance. Continue straight for 2.1 miles and park at the country store on the left. *DeLorme: Alabama Atlas & Gazetteer: Page 21, G7.*

The Hike

Situated at an elevation of about 1,750 feet on top of Lookout Mountain, DeSoto State Park includes the beginnings of Little River Canyon. The park is near Fort Payne, home of superstar country group Alabama. Walking the trails here and seeing the river and canyon, you can picture Alabama singing a line from one of their songs: "From high on Lookout Mountain I look down with pride and say that my home's in Alabama."

The Rhododendron Trail gets its name, quite obviously, from the dense collection of rhododendron bushes that line the way, particularly along the banks of the west fork of the Little River. The off-white blossoms and their sweet fragrance fill the air in late spring, usually peaking by the third week of May.

The most beautiful part of this trail is the section between DeSoto State Park Lodge and the river. The trail winds around the canyon wall as it travels to the river. Along the way you'll pass Lodge Falls, just below the lodge, and Indian Falls, where

Another view of the Little River.

a new park recreation building was constructed above the head of the falls. And, of course, there is the Little River itself, its blue-green waters rushing through narrow sections of rapids and around huge boulders.

Along the river and canyon, the trail can be a bit difficult. The hike up and down the canyon wall is moderately steep in some areas. And along the river where the trail joins and follows the DeSoto Scout Trail, you'll have to climb over large boulders from time to time.

The runoff from rainfall has gouged out routes that look in some places like trails. Many hikers end up on these runoff paths and soon find themselves bush-whacking as they look for the main trail. Keep in mind that hiking to the top of the canyon should lead you to the lodge or cabin area, while hiking down to the river

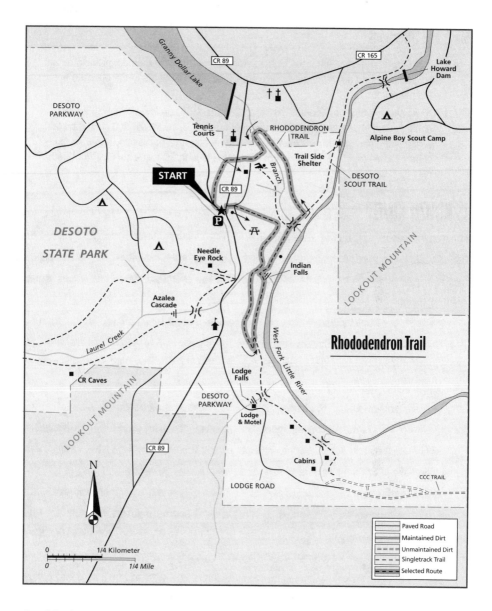

should take you to the section where the Rhododendron and DeSoto Scout Trails join along the riverbank.

As you hike the Rhododendron Trail, don't be surprised if you have to scramble around some downed trees. A severe ice storm in 1999 dropped many trees, and park managers expect cleanup to be a long-term job.

The full Rhododendron Trail extends farther to the western section of DeSoto State Park, near the wilderness campground, but the greatest beauty of the hike lies along the 1.3-mile loop described here.

Miles and Directions

0.0   Start from the parking lot at the country store. Cross CR 89 to the park picnic area and fee station. Head down the paved picnic area road and continue to the opposite end of the parking lot.

0.1   Head past a picnic pavilion built by the CCC in the 1930s. A short pole with a hiker emblem on it will be seen here. Although not marked, the worn dirt trail should be fairly easily seen heading down an easy hill. In 100 feet the trail ducks into the woods and shortly comes to a T intersection. Turn right. (**Side trip:** In 20 feet a short 30-foot path

IS KUDZU KING?
When kudzu was introduced to Americans at the 1876 Centennial Exposition in Philadelphia, it was to a warm reception. The Japanese government had honored the United States' one-hundredth birthday by constructing a garden exhibit of their native plants. American gardeners were quick to fall in love with the oversized leaves and sweet, grape-smelling blooms.

It wasn't until the 1920s that the soon-to-be-a-pest plant found a more legitimate function. Those looking to point fingers should look to Chipley, Florida, where Charles and Lillie Pleas made the unfortunate discovery that livestock took a shine to the tasty foliage. In no time, kudzu plants were flying out their door and through the mail.

To make matters worse, the Depression-era Soil Conservation Service found another use for the plant, as a ground-stabilizing agent. The government's army of out-of-work bachelors, the Civilian Conservation Corps, were enlisted to spread the plant. By the 1940s farmers were being paid upward of $8.00 an acre to further distribute this "miracle vine."

In the South kudzu had found its perfect host. Not only was the weather ideal but Southerners seemed to encourage its spread. In short order it had worn out its welcome. By 1953 the government ceased promoting the plant. And in 1973 the USDA delivered the heaviest blow. The former darling of the Centennial Exposition was officially a "weed."

Why all the fuss? Well, in the summer months kudzu can grow as much as a foot a day—60 feet a year under optimum conditions. And as it blankets all that doesn't move, it robs precious sunlight from competing vegetation, effectively suffocating most everything beneath it. Today kudzu covers more than seven million acres of the Deep South and reaches as far north as Pennsylvania.

Though many consider it a scourge on the South, kudzu does, in all fairness, have its well-wishers. Not only are resourceful Southerners coming up with recipes for kudzu jelly and soup, but some are erecting Web sites in homage to the adopted creeper.

Love it or hate it, kudzu may be here awhile. Might as well learn to make tea with it.

Indian Falls.

leads to an overlook to the left for a good view of Indian Falls.) Continue to a wooden bridge that spans Indian Falls. (An area of downed trees at the far end of the bridge requires that you get off the bridge into the shallow creek and bushwhack around the debris.) After the bridge, come to a fork and go right. Follow the white blazes of the Rhododendron Trail.

0.2 Lodge Falls can be seen through the trees.

0.3 The Rhododendron Trail merges with the DeSoto Scout Trail as it heads along the banks of the Little River. (The blazes are now the yellow markers of the DeSoto Scout Trail.)

0.5 Come to a T intersection and turn right on the hard dirt path. (To the left, an unmarked trail leads uphill to the park's swimming pool.)

0.6 The white-blazed Rhododendron Trail returns and makes a sharp turn to the left (the DeSoto Scout Trail continues straight). Follow the Rhododendron Trail.

0.8 Through the trees to the left, the DeSoto State Park swimming pool building can be seen.

0.9 Come to a fork and go left.

1.0 Exit the woods, pass the tennis courts, and come to CR 89. Cross the highway and head back into the woods.

1.1 A short, unmarked trail merges into the Rhododendron Trail from the southeast. Make a sharp left turn and head down this trail to the southeast.

1.3 Come to the campground road and turn left. Follow the road to the parking lot at the country store.

Hike Information

Local Information

North Alabama Tourism Association, 25062 North Street, Mooresville 35649; (800) 648-5381; www.northalabama.org.

DeKalb County Tourist Association, 1503 Glenn Boulevard Southwest, Fort Payne 35968-3530; (256) 845-3957; www.tourdekalb.com.

Fort Payne; at www.fortpayne.net/Default.htm. Includes information on DeSoto State Park, Little River Canyon, and Lookout Mountain.

Local Events/Attractions

Rhododendron Festival, third weekend in May, Mentone; (888) 805-4740.

DeSoto Caverns Park, Childersburg; (800) 933-2283; www.cavern.com/desoto/index.html. Large cathedral-type caves featuring the Great Onyx Cathedral and a laser light show.

DeSoto Falls, 1503 Glenn Boulevard Southwest, Fort Payne 35968; (256) 845-5380; www.mentone.com. DeSoto Falls plunges 104 feet from the end of DeSoto Lake as the waters form the raging Little River. The area is touted as having the largest variety of wildflowers in the world outside China.

Shady Grove Dude Ranch/Cloudmont Ski & Golf Resort, 721 County Road 614, Mentone 35984; (256) 634-4344. Bringing "Montana to Mentone," this resort features snow skiing in winter and a "dude" ranch with trail rides through the mountains to DeSoto and Veil Falls—and, of course, golf! Open year-round.

Sequoyah Caverns, 1438 County Road 731, Fort Payne 35967; (256) 635-0024; www.bham.net/sequoyah/caverns.html. Sequoyah Cavern is a quarter-mile-deep cave in the side of Sand Mountain. Inside, there are a series of rooms with pools of mineral water, 120-foot-high ceilings, and Native American artifacts. The cavern is so named because Cherokee Chief Sequoyah and his tribe used the cave for shelter. A column in the cave has etched in it the words 1830–SAM HOUSTON. Houston married Sequoyah's daughter.

Lodging

DeSoto State Park Lodge, 13883 County Road 89, Fort Payne 35968; (800) 568-8840.

Mentone Inn, Mentone; (800) 455-7470.

Mountain View Motel, 2302 Gault Avenue South, Fort Payne 35967; (256) 845-2303.

Shady Grove Dude Ranch/Cloudmont Ski & Golf Resort, 721 County Road 614, Mentone 35984; (256) 634-4344.

Restaurants

Blue Moon Café, Fort Payne; (256) 997-9908.

DeSoto State Park Lodge, 13883 County Road 89, Fort Payne 35968; (800) 568-8840.

Jack's Char-Coal Broiled Hamburgers, 1401 Gault Avenue North, Fort Payne 35967-3235; (256) 845-3565.

Other Resources

Tennessee Valley Trails; www.montesano.com/hikeweb.

48 DeSoto Scout Trail

The DeSoto Scout Trail follows the rapids of the west fork of Little River as the stream twists its way through the mountains. Overall, the narrow trail is relatively easy, but the necessity of clambering over large boulders and the occasional downed tree makes the trip moderately difficult.

Start: From the south trailhead at the end of the road that leads to the DeSoto State Park lodge and cabins.
Distance: 4.6-mile out-and-back.
Approximate hiking time: 4–6 hours.
Difficulty: Moderate, due to rocky areas; may be some downed trees on the trail.
Trail surface: Rocky footpath.
Type of hike: Thick rhododendron and pine.
Land status: State park.
Nearest town: Fort Payne.
Schedule: Open year-round.

Fees/Permits: No fee charged for hiking. Camping is $13 per night, base rate.
Maps: USGS maps: Valley Head; Jamestown. Brochures—Available free of charge at the camp store.
Trail contacts: DeSoto State Park, 13883 County Road 89, Fort Payne 35968; (256) 845-5380; www.desotostatepark.com.
Other trail users: None.
Canine compatibility: Not dog friendly because of the rocky path and possible downed trees; leash is recommended.

Finding the trailhead: From Fort Payne go east on Alabama Highway 35 for about a mile and turn left onto DeSoto Parkway. Travel 5.1 miles (DeSoto Parkway turns into County Road 89) to the park entrance. Continue straight 2.1 miles to the intersection of Lodge Road (located at the park office) and make a right turn. Travel 0.9 mile. A sign reads TRAILHEAD PARKING. Make a left turn here and, in 100 feet, an immediate right into a grassy parking area. *DeLorme: Alabama Atlas & Gazetteer:* Page 21, G7.

The Hike

Over time, the Little River of Northern Alabama has cut through soft sandstone to form the deepest and largest canyon east of the Mississippi—23 miles long, with an average depth of 600 feet. The region is wild and beautiful, but fragile. Recognizing this, the state of Alabama and the federal government teamed up to help protect the region.

In the mid 1930s the Civilian Conservation Corps, under guidance of the National Park Service, created DeSoto State Park, which encompasses the northern portion of the river, including the west fork that flows into Little River Canyon. The National Park Service then established Little River Canyon National Preserve, a narrow stretch of land that protects the canyon itself, from where it begins at Little River Falls.

The DeSoto Scout Trail offers great vantage points for viewing the river. The full trail begins farther north, at the Comer Boy Scout Reservation, but the section described here falls within the boundaries of DeSoto State Park.

Overlooking Little River from the trail shelter.

This route begins on top of the ridge that runs high above the river. Descending at an ever-increasing grade from the park's cabins, the trail eventually reaches the west fork of Little River. As the trail travels along the cold, blue-green waters of the river, you'll see pools and eddies that harbor bass and trout. Large, flat boulders in the river provide popular spots for sunbathers.

Moving away from the river, the trail heads up a short hill to the north and soon reveals spectacular views of the cliffs overlooking the river. Some of the best views are from a trail shelter along this part of the hike.

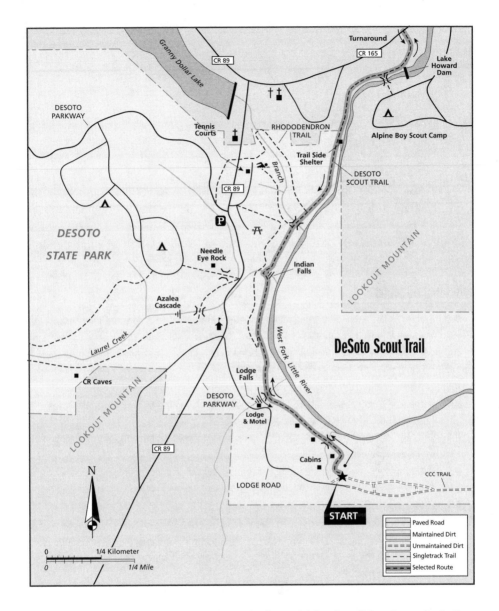

Much of this hike is over a rocky path along the banks of the river—including some clambering over large boulders. You may also encounter downed trees on the trail, victims of storms. An especially severe ice storm in 1999 left the trail littered with trees and handed park managers a huge cleanup job.

The trail is much easier toward its northern end, where it travels over large, smooth rocks. The trail ends at its intersection with County Road 165.

The main wildlife to look for on this trip are the hawks that soar above the canyon and the fish in the river. Lizards dart in and out of the rocks, which also are inhabited by some snakes, including the northern black racer, northern cottonmouth, and timber rattlesnake. Along the trail are dense clusters of rhododendron bushes, plus longleaf pines.

Miles and Directions

0.0 Start from the trailhead parking lot and head into the woods. Come to a T intersection and turn left. (A bike trail goes right.) Follow the white paint blazes.

0.2 Come to a fork and go right. (The left fork leads to a cabin.) Pass another cabin on the left, with a trail that branches off to that cabin.

0.3 Come to a fork in the trail and go right. (The white-blazed trail goes left.)

0.4 Come to a T intersection with the DeSoto Scout Trail along the banks of the Little River. Turn left and follow the flow of the river.

0.7 Pass an unmarked trail to the left. (This path leads straight up the hillside to the lodge.) Continue along the river.

0.8 **Note:** This is a very heavy area of downed trees and will require some bushwhacking. Just remember to keep heading along the riverbank and you'll come out of it.

0.9 Pass a side trail on the left. (A yellow sign reads D.S.T.)

1.1 Cross a 10-foot wooden bridge over Lodge Falls Creek.

1.2 Come to a fork. The white-blazed Rhododendron Trail turns uphill and heads to the lodge; continue straight ahead to the northeast. The trail will once again reach the banks of the river in just a few feet.

1.4 Come to a T intersection and turn right. (An unmarked trail goes left and leads uphill to the park's swimming pool.)

1.5 The white-blazed Rhododendron Trail turns back to the northwest. The DeSoto Scout Trail levels off.

1.8 Come to a fork and go left. (The right fork is a short trail to the edge of the bluffs and is very dangerous! Be careful if you go there.) In 100 feet the two forks rejoin.

2.3 Pass a short bridge to the right, which leads over the river to the Alpine Boy Scout Camp. Continue straight. The trail ends at CR 165. Turn around here and retrace your route back to the parking area.

4.6 Arrive back at the parking area.

The west fork of Little River, as seen from the trail shelter on the DeSoto Scout Trail.

Hike Information

Local Information

North Alabama Tourism Association, 25062 North Street, Mooresville 35649; (800) 648-5381; www.northalabama.org.

DeKalb County Tourist Association, 1503 Glenn Boulevard Southwest, Fort Payne 35968-3530; (256) 845-3957; www.tourdekalb.com.

Fort Payne; at www.fortpayne.net/Default.htm. Includes information on DeSoto State Park, Little River Canyon, and Lookout Mountain.

Local Events/Attractions

Rhododendron Festival, third weekend in May, Mentone; (888) 805-4740.

DeSoto Caverns Park, Childersburg; (800) 933-2283; www.cavern.com/desoto/index.html. Large cathedral-type caves featuring the Great Onyx Cathedral and a laser light show.

DeSoto Falls, 1503 Glenn Boulevard Southwest, Fort Payne 35968; (256) 845-5380; www.mentone.com. DeSoto Falls plunges 104 feet from the end of DeSoto Lake as the waters form the raging Little River. The area is touted as having the largest variety of wildflowers in the world outside China.

Shady Grove Dude Ranch/Cloudmont Ski & Golf Resort, 721 County Road 614, Mentone 35984; (256) 634-4344. Bringing "Montana to Mentone," this resort features snow skiing in winter and a "dude" ranch with trail rides through the mountains to DeSoto and Veil Falls—and, of course, golf! Open year-round.

Sequoyah Caverns, 1438 County Road 731, Fort Payne 35967; (256) 635-0024; www.bham.net/sequoyah/caverns.html. Sequoyah Cavern is a quarter-mile-deep cave in the side of Sand Mountain. Inside, there are a series of rooms with pools of mineral water, 120-foot-high ceilings, and Native American artifacts. The cavern is so named because Cherokee Chief Sequoyah and his tribe used the cave for shelter. A column in the cave has etched in it the words 1830–SAM HOUSTON. Houston married Sequoyah's daughter.

Lodging

DeSoto State Park Lodge, 13883 County Road 89, Fort Payne 35968; (800) 568-8840.

Mentone Inn, Mentone; (800) 455-7470.

Mountain View Motel, 2302 Gault Avenue South, Fort Payne 35967; (256) 845-2303.

Shady Grove Dude Ranch/Cloudmont Ski & Golf Resort, 721 County Road 614, Mentone 35984; (256) 634-4344.

Restaurants

Blue Moon Cafe, Fort Payne; (256) 997-9908.

DeSoto State Park Lodge, 13883 County Road 89, Fort Payne 35968; (800) 568-8840.

Jack's Char-Coal Broiled Hamburgers, 1401 Gault Avenue North, Fort Payne 35967-3235; (256) 845-3565.

Other Resources

Tennessee Valley Trails; www.montesano.com/hikeweb.

49 Lost Falls Trail

The Lost Falls Trail takes you to Laurel Falls, Lost Falls, and Azalea Cascade. Geological highlights include Needle Eye Rock, a boulder that has split in half, leaving an "eye." The trail also travels by the CR Caves, small cavelike overhangs cut away over the millennia by Laurel Creek.

Start: From the hiker's parking lot 2.1 miles past the entrance to DeSoto State Park.
Distance: 3.2-mile loop.
Approximate hiking time: 2½–3½ hours.
Difficulty: Mostly easy, with some moderate sections due to downed trees and limbs.
Trail surface: Dirt path; some rocky slopes.
Type of hike: Azaleas and mountain laurel; waterfalls; unusual rock formations.
Land status: State park.
Nearest town: Fort Payne.
Schedule: Open year-round.

Fees/Permits: No fee for hiking. Camping is $8.00 for primitive tent sites, $14.00 for improved with water.
Maps: USGS maps: Valley Head; Jamestown. Brochures—Available free of charge at the camp store.
Trail contacts: DeSoto State Park, 13883 County Road 89, Fort Wayne 35968; (256) 845-0051; www.desotostatepark.com.
Other trail users: None.
Canine compatibility: Dog friendly along this dirt footpath, with ample water; leash required.

Finding the trailhead: From Fort Payne go east on Alabama Highway 35 for about a mile and turn left onto DeSoto Parkway. Travel 5.1 miles (DeSoto Parkway turns into County Road 89) to the park entrance. Continue straight for 1.6 miles. The trailhead is on the right. Go another 0.5 mile to the park headquarters and camp store. *DeLorme: Alabama Atlas & Gazetteer:* Page 21, G7.

The Hike

Water is everywhere at DeSoto State Park, with waterfalls scattered throughout the park and the Little River churning white within Little River Gorge. You'll also find lush forests and colorful wildflowers. It's no wonder the park is sometimes called the home of Mother Nature.

The park straddles the river and covers more than 5,000 acres within Little River Canyon National Preserve. While the park's DeSoto Scout and Rhododendron Trails focus more on Little River, the Lost Falls Trail turns its focus on the other wonders of the park.

Lost Falls Trail is actually a combination of several different trails, each marked in its own color. It is, however, possible to get off track by mistakenly following deer trails or short, unmarked connector trails. It's generally not difficult to get back to the main path, but it's a nuisance to have to backtrack.

The gravel parking area that serves as the starting point for Lost Falls Trail is rather small, so get there early to find a spot. The trail begins on a long wooden foot-

Lost Falls Trail

bridge across a marshy area. Picnic areas and gazebos along the bridge provide opportunities to sit and view the marsh.

After the bridge, the trail heads uphill rather steeply and passes through the eye of Needle Eye Rock. The trail then weaves its way up the hillside until it tops a ridge and heads into a ravine. This portion of the trail brings you to the two largest waterfalls, Laurel Falls and Lost Falls.

The worst winter storm in decades struck this area in 1999, and this means some bushwhacking for hikers. Downed trees across the trail can be difficult to get around, and park officials say it could be some time before all the debris is cleaned up. Just keep an eye out in the general direction of travel over these areas, and look for trail markers around the debris.

Laurel Falls is aptly named, set in a landscape filled with mountain laurel that usually blooms in mid May. A 200-foot side trail—marked by a small stone engraved with the name of the falls—takes you to the waterfall. The view is nice from the side trail, but an even better approach is to endure a little bushwhacking and hike right to the base of the falls. Layered rock forms a jagged frame around the 60-foot cascade. The area by the pool at the bottom of the falls makes a lovely spot for lunch.

Back on the main trail, another mile takes you to a second engraved stone, this one reading LOST FALLS. A short side trail goes to the 50-foot-high falls. The main trail then crosses over the head of the falls to the other side of Laurel Creek.

On the way down the trail, you'll arrive at the area known as the CR Caves, where the creek has slowly eroded the rock walls. The result is a series of rock overhangs, almost like caves, approximately 50 feet deep and 4 feet high.

Azalea Cascade is reached just before the trail returns to the parking lot. Surrounded by azaleas, the 30-foot-high Azalea Cascade is the smallest of the three falls along the trail. A wooden footbridge leads across the pool at the base of the falls.

Miles and Directions

0.0 Start from the gravel parking lot along CR 89. Head west from the parking lot across a wooden footbridge over a marsh. To the right, steps head off into the woods. Head down the stairs, following the red paint blazes.

0.1 The Red Trail intersects another red-marked trail. Continue straight. In 100 feet reach Needle Eye Rock.

0.2 The trail appears to fork but it doesn't. This is a deer trail. Take the left fork and continue uphill.

0.3 Come up behind the RV campground and to the paved Campground Road. Turn to the left onto the road.

0.4 A sign shows the direction of the trail back into the woods. The blazes are now orange.

0.8 Come to a fork and go left. You're going to travel about 200 feet to a nice view of the falls and then return. A little bushwhacking will lead to the base of the falls. Be careful, though. It is extremely slippery in this area. Return to the fork by retracing your steps.

0.9 Back at the fork, take the right fork on the orange-blazed trail.

1.9 Come to a fork and take the left fork. In about 100 feet you'll reach the 50-foot Lost Falls. Cross the creek at the top of the falls. Once across, the blue paint blazes of the CR Caves Trail appear. Follow the blue blazes.

2.5 The CR Caves Trail merges with the Yellow Trail. (Yellow and blue markers are now on the trees.)

2.8 Pass the CR Caves.

3.1 Come to the top of a hill. See the park business offices through the trees. In 200 feet the trail intersects and crosses a connector trail. Turn left and take the connector downhill. Travel over stairs formed by 4 x 4 timbers. The stairs end at a creek and a wooden footbridge. Cross the bridge. (To the left is the 30-foot-tall Azalea Cascades.)

3.2 The bridge returns you to the parking lot.

Hike Information

Local Information

North Alabama Tourism Association, 25062 North Street, Mooresville 35649; (800) 648-5381; www.northalabama.org.

DeKalb County Tourist Association, 1503 Glenn Boulevard Southwest, Fort Payne 35968-3530; (256) 845-3957; www.tourdekalb.com.

Fort Payne; at www.fortpayne.net/Default.htm. Includes information on DeSoto State Park, Little River Canyon, and Lookout Mountain.

Local Events/Attractions

Rhododendron Festival, third weekend in May, Mentone; (888) 805-4740.

DeSoto Caverns Park, Childersburg; (800) 933-2283; www.cavern.com/desoto/index.html. Large cathedral-type caves featuring the Great Onyx Cathedral and a laser light show.

DeSoto Falls, 1503 Glenn Boulevard Southwest, Fort Payne 35968; (256) 845-5380; www.mentone.com. DeSoto Falls plunges 104 feet from the end of DeSoto Lake as the waters form the raging Little River. The area is touted as having the largest variety of wildflowers in the world outside China.

Shady Grove Dude Ranch/Cloudmont Ski & Golf Resort, 721 County Road 614, Mentone 35984; (256) 634-4344. Bringing "Montana to Mentone," this resort features snow skiing in winter and a "dude" ranch with trail rides through the mountains to DeSoto and Veil Falls—and, of course, golf! Open year-round.

Sequoyah Caverns, 1438 County Road 731, Fort Payne 35967; (256) 635-0024; www.bham.net/sequoyah/caverns.html. Sequoyah Cavern is a quarter-mile-deep cave in the side of Sand Mountain. Inside, there are a series of rooms with pools of mineral water, 120-foot-high ceilings, and Native American artifacts. The cavern is so named because Cherokee Chief Sequoyah and his tribe used the cave for shelter. A column in the cave has etched in it the words 1830–SAM HOUSTON. Houston married Sequoyah's daughter.

Lodging

DeSoto State Park Lodge, 13883 County Road 89, Fort Payne 35968; (800) 568-8840.

Mentone Inn, Mentone; (800) 455-7470.

Mountain View Motel, 2302 Gault Avenue South, Fort Payne 35967; (256) 845-2303.

Shady Grove Dude Ranch/Cloudmont Ski & Golf Resort, 721 County Road 614, Mentone 35984; (256) 634-4344.

Restaurants

Blue Moon Cafe, Fort Payne; (256) 997-9908.

DeSoto State Park Lodge, 13883 County Road 89, Fort Payne 35968; (800) 568-8840.

Jack's Char-Coal Broiled Hamburgers, 1401 Gault Avenue North, Fort Payne 35967-3235; (256) 845-3565.

Other Resources

Tennessee Valley Trails; www.montesano.com/hikeweb.

50 Russell Cave Trail

The Russell Cave Trail provides a nice hike through forest and wildflowers in extreme northeast Alabama. The trail first heads up the side of Montague Mountain, then winds downhill. At the foot of the mountain, the trail becomes a wooden boardwalk into Russell Cave, a large limestone cave that has sheltered humans for more than 9,000 years.

Start: From the back of the visitor center at Russell Cave National Monument.
Distance: 2.0-mile loop.
Approximate hiking time: 1½–2 hours.
Difficulty: Moderate due to steepness on the path up Montague Mountain; easy over the wooden boardwalk to Russell Cave.
Trail surface: Asphalt footpath; wooden boardwalk.
Type of hike: Hickory and chestnut forest; wildflowers; boulder-strewn landscape.
Land status: National monument.
Nearest town: Bridgeport.
Schedule: The cave is open April to October 8:00 A.M.–5:00 P.M. and November to March

from 8:00 A.M.–4:30 P.M.
Fees/Permits: No fee to hike the trail or for admission into Russell Cave National Monument. Donations are requested to help maintain the park.
Maps: USGS map: Doran Cove.
Brochures—Available free of charge at the visitor center.
Trail contacts: National Park Service/Russell Cave National Monument, 3729 County Road 98, Bridgeport 35740-6825; (256) 495-2672; www.nps.gov/ruca.
Other trail users: None.
Canine compatibility: Dog friendly. Water available; leash required.

Finding the trailhead: From Bridgeport take County Road 75 west. Travel 0.5 mile from U.S. Highway 72 to the intersection of CR 75 and County Road 98. Go straight onto CR 98 and travel 8 miles. The entrance to Russell Cave is on the left and is marked with a large NATIONAL MONUMENT sign. Turn left and drive to the visitor center. Park here. *DeLorme: Alabama Atlas & Gazetteer: Page 20, A5.*

The Hike

Situated near the borders of Alabama, Tennessee, and Georgia, Russell Cave National Monument has been operated by the National Park Service since 1962. The cave and surrounding landscape are said to hold the oldest and most complete archaeological records of human existence in the eastern United States.

The Russell Cave Trail includes a 2-foot-wide asphalt path up the side of Montague Mountain, to an elevation of about 1,300 feet. The steep trail weaves through stands of chinquapin, hickory, and chestnut. Deep-green moss clings to rocks along

A view of the sinkhole at the start of the hike.

the trail. Wildflowers such as bluets and white rue anemones line the path. White-tailed deer are often seen darting in and out of the brush.

Because the trail is so narrow, you can't avoid coming in contact with brush. Watch out for poison ivy. Another bit of caution: The Park Service says the area is pockmarked with hidden sinkholes and drop-offs and asks hikers to stay on the trail.

Dotted along the path are split-log benches, strategically placed after steeper sections of the climb. Along the trail and through the trees are views of farm pastures in the valley below and of the Bullhead, Little, and Summerhouse Mountains that border the Tennessee River.

After looping the top of a ridge and returning to the base of the mountain, the trail turns onto a wooden boardwalk that takes you to Russell Cave. A park ranger will walk you down to the mouth of the cave and along the way tell the story of the cave and its former inhabitants.

The limestone cave was formed when the ancient inland sea that covered this region receded. Water found its way into fissures in the limestone and began carv-

Entrance to Russell Cave.

ing out the cave. The cavern roof collapsed about 11,000 years ago, creating an opening to the outside world, now the entrance to Russell Cave.

Humans first inhabited the cave about 7000 B.C., at the end of the Ice Age. The cave was used as a hunting camp, and carved weapons found within are on display at the monument's visitor center. Rangers give demonstrations on the construction and use of these weapons.

The public trail goes a short distance into the main chamber of the cave. Chambers and passageways farther inside the cave can be explored only after securing written permission from the park superintendent. The creek that flows into the cave is prone to flash flooding, so keep an eye on the weather when visiting.

Miles and Directions

0.0 Start from the inside of the visitor center at the very back of the building. A sign here points to the left and reads CAVE TRAIL. Head out the door and turn right onto a 3-foot-wide asphalt footpath. In 150 feet a short 10-foot wooden bridge turns off the boardwalk to the right. Turn right and head over the bridge. A short 50-foot side trail leads to a railing. From here, the Sinkhole can be seen. Backtrack to the asphalt footpath and continue on.

0.1 Little Mountain and Summerhouse Mountain can be seen through the trees to the right. Come to a fork and continue on the asphalt path.

1.2 Pass Slant Rock.

The trail passes Slant Rock.

WATCH YOUR STEP
Hiking in the South isn't all smiles. We do have our own set of annoyances to deal with—and one that affects many hikers may be right under your feet.

Picture this: You are standing in a meadow, taking in the scenery, when something starts crawling up your leg. By the time you get around to swatting at it, you feel a burning sensation—then another. You find yourself standing in a fire ant hill.

Fire ants are ferocious little boogers that think that anything within 2 feet of their mound is an enemy, and they'll attack to defend their home. Their name is well deserved. The bite is painful and, for people allergic to it, can sometimes be fatal.

It's believed that fire ants first came to the United States on a ship from South America that docked at Mobile, Alabama, in the 1920s. Fire ants also like to use man-made roads for their travels. Road construction loosens soils, and loose soil provides an excellent base for fire ant travel. In the rapidly developing South, finding new roads is no problem. So far, the fire ant has spread to 13 southeastern states.

1.4 Come to a fork and go right. (The left fork is the dirt footpath passed earlier for the short nature trail.)

1.7 Pass the side trail on the right to the Sinkhole. Continue straight. The trail crosses a short bridge and rejoins the main boardwalk.

1.8 The boardwalk continues to the entrance of the cave. A park ranger will greet you and escort you to the cave. The boardwalk enters the cave for about 100 feet, where it turns around and follows the same boardwalk for the return trip.

1.9 On the left, pass the hiking trail traveled earlier and continue straight.

2.0 Arrive at the visitor center.

Hike Information

Local Information

North Alabama Tourism Association, 25062 North Street, Mooresville 35649; (800) 648-5381; www.northalabama.org.

Local Events/Attractions

Stevenson Railroad Depot/Museum, Highway 117, Stevenson 35772; (256) 437-3012. Admission is free to this museum of railroad and Native American artifacts. Open December to April, Monday through Friday 9:00 A.M.–5:00 P.M., April to November Monday through Saturday 9:00 A.M.–5:00 P.M.

Lodging

Hess Motor Inn, 50621 Alabama Highway 277, Bridgeport 35740-6523; (256) 495-2600.

Honorable Mentions

Northern Alabama

Northern Alabama gives you diverse hiking adventures, from panoramic views to breathtaking waterfalls at the geologic fall line. The following trails didn't make the top of our list, but while in the area, you may want to check them out. These hikes still provide interesting scenery and challenges. Let us know what you think about the selection. Maybe one should be upgraded to the A-list, or maybe you know of a hidden gem that would make a good honorable mention.

L Dismals Canyon

The Dismals Canyon in northwest Alabama has been described as "one of the finest examples of ecological and geological features composing our Nation's Natural History." The area was declared a National Natural Landmark in 1975—one of 697 in the country.

The property is privately owned, with no developed camping areas in the canyon proper to keep the land pristine. The upper part of the canyon has campsites available. At the bottom of the canyon are several hiking trails that take you past a wide variety of wildflowers, as well as past waterfalls, moss-covered canyon walls, and towering boulders. This region was also a hiding spot for outlaw Jesse James and was a secret ritual area for the Chickasaw Indians.

If you'd like to canoe, you can take a lazy float trip through the canyon down the lower Bear Creek or try your luck at the class I–IV rapids at upper Bear Creek.

The main attraction at the Dismals is the nightly summertime light show put on by the dismalites. Scientifically known as *Arachnocampa luminosa,* these "glowworms" are found in New Zealand and a handful of other locations on earth, the Dismals being one. It is said that at night on the canyon floor, if you were to look up, it is hard to tell where these tiny little creatures end and the stars begin. The light is used to attract food.

To get to the Dismals, go south on U.S. Highway 43 from Russellville, and turn right on County Road 8. The park will be on your left. The Dismals are open 10:00 A.M.–6:00 P.M. Sunday through Thursday and Friday and Saturday 10:00 A.M.–10:00 P.M. Special tours are held Friday and Saturday at 8:30 P.M. For more information call (205) 993–4559 or visit www.dismalscanyon.com. *DeLorme: Alabama Atlas & Gazetteer:* Page 23, B6.

Pencil-thin Grace Falls cascades down the walls of Little River Canyon.

M Black Warrior Horse Trails–Bankhead National Forest

Located within the confines of the William B. Bankhead National Forest in northern Alabama, home of the Sipsey Wilderness, the Black Warrior Horse Trails—30 miles worth—travel through some of the most beautiful canyons and rivers in the South, passing waterfalls, fast-moving rivers, towering cliffs, and deep gorges. These trails are primarily equestrian trails but are also open to hikers. If you plan a trip, just be cautious and courteous with the equestrians and their mounts. Startling horses in any way can be dangerous to everyone around!

The forest is located about 21 miles west of the town of Cullman off U.S. Highway 278. For more information contact the Bankhead National Forest ranger station Monday through Friday 7:30 A.M.–5:00 P.M. at (205) 489–5111, or visit www.southernregion.fs.fed.us/alabama/bankhead/default.htm. *DeLorme: Alabama Atlas & Gazetteer:* Page 24, B1.

N Wheeler National Wildlife Refuge

Covering more than 34,000 acres, the Wheeler National Wildlife Refuge is yet another great spot for hikers to view many rare and endangered species. The refuge was established in 1938 as a "wintering ground for migratory waterfowl." Today, thanks to a series of five nature trails traveling through several "satellite" refuges, hikers can see endangered gray and Indiana bats, watercress darters, and Alabama cavefish, not to mention the hundreds of birds that call the refuge home.

There is plenty to take in at the refuge, including the wildlife observation building and interpretive exhibits. The refuge is located just outside Decatur on Alabama Highway 67 (exit 334 off Interstate 65). For more information call the refuge office weekdays 7:00 A.M.–5:00 P.M. at (256) 353–7243, or visit wheeler.flos.gov. *DeLorme: Alabama Atlas & Gazetteer:* Page 18, G4

○ Old Railroad Bed Trail–Land Trust of Huntsville

Monte Sano Mountain stands like an island amidst a rapidly developing landscape. The city and suburbs of Huntsville are continually expanding and threatening the mountain landscape. The Land Trust of Huntsville is working hard to protect our remaining treasures.

Their efforts have given us the Land Trust Loop (see Hike 39). Another interesting hike at the Monte Sano Preserve is the Old Railroad Bed Trail. The trail follows the path of an old narrow gauge railroad used early in Huntsville's history and features many of the original trestles.

A brochure on the Old Railroad Bed Trail can be picked up free of charge at any Alabama Welcome Center along the interstates. Trail information can also be found on-line at www.landtrust-hsv.org. Call the Trust at (256) 534–5263 for more information. There is no charge to hike these trails. (See Hike 39 for park directions and additional information.) *DeLorme: Alabama Atlas & Gazetteer:* Page 19, D8.

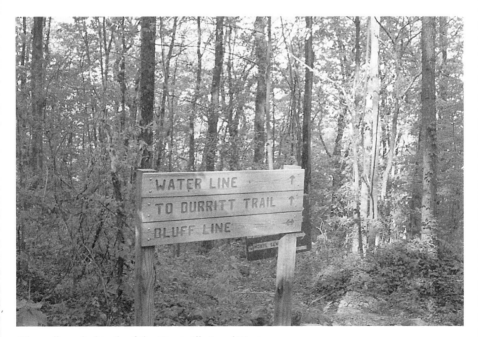

The well-marked trails of the Huntsville Land Trust.

P The Chief Ladiga Rail-Trail

The Chief Ladiga Trail is Alabama's first major rails-to-trails project and is the creation of Jacksonville State University. The trail meanders approximately 33 miles through Calhoun and Cleburne Counties between Piedmont and Anniston.

The trail—designed for hikers, bikers, and equestrians—provides beautiful glimpses of the Alabama countryside, including wetlands, streams, forests, farmland, and, of course, the surrounding mountains.

For more information visit the JSU Web site at www.jsu.edu/depart/epic/Rail-Trail.htm or call (256) 782–5681. *DeLorme: Alabama Atlas & Gazetteer:* Page 27, G8.

Q Ruffner Mountain Nature Center

Ruffner Mountain Nature Center is a secret hideaway nestled within a bustling city: Located just outside of Birmingham, it is a treasure trove of hiking trials. The park has 11 miles of beautifully maintained trails—the degree of difficulty ranges from easy to moderate. From Hawk's View Overlook and Cambrian Overlook, hikers will find stunning views of the quarry that's located on the mountain. The quarry gives hikers a glimpse into the area's geologic past and reveals a marvelous fossil record.

A spectacular view of the quarry from the Cambrian Overlook at the Ruffner Mountain Nature Center.

Wildflower and plant lovers will enjoy the trails, which are often lined with bright, colorful blooms. Events are held at the center almost year-round, and there's something for every interest. The nature center also offers an extraordinary array of K–12 educational programs. Contact the Ruffner Mountain Nature Center for more information at (205) 833-8264, or visit their Web site at www.bham.net/ruffner/index.html. Trail maps can also be downloaded from this site. The center is located at 1214 81st Street.

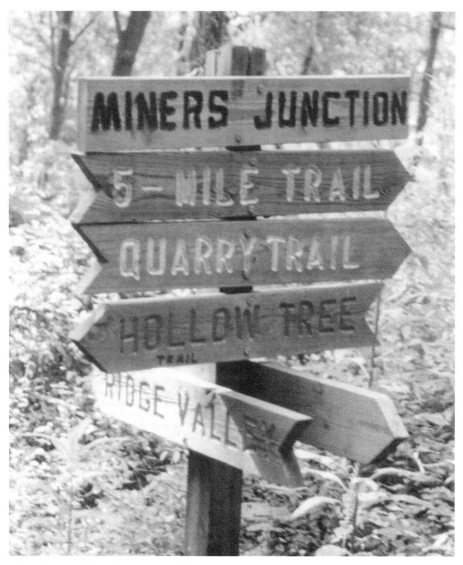

All trails are well marked at the Ruffner Mountain Nature Center.

The Art of Hiking

When standing nose to nose with a mountain lion, you're probably not too concerned with the issue of ethical behavior in the wild. No doubt you're just terrified. But let's be honest. How often are you nose to nose with a mountain lion? For most of us, a hike into the "wild" means loading up the SUV with expensive gear and driving to a toileted trailhead. Sure, you can mourn how civilized we've become—how GPS units have replaced natural instinct and Gore-Tex, true-grit—but the silly gadgets of civilization aside, we have plenty of reason to take pride in how we've matured. With survival now on the back burner, we've begun to reason—and it's about time—that we have a responsibility to protect, no longer just conquer, our wild places: that they, not we, are at risk. So please, do what you can. The following section will help you understand better what it means to "do what you can" while still making the most of your hiking experience. Anyone can take a hike, but hiking safely and well is an art requiring preparation and proper equipment.

Trail Etiquette

Zero impact. Always leave an area just like you found it—if not better than you found it. Avoid camping in fragile, alpine meadows and along the banks of streams and lakes. Use a camp stove versus building a wood fire. Pack up all of your trash and extra food. Bury human waste at least 100 feet from water sources under 6 to 8 inches of topsoil. Don't bathe with soap in a lake or stream—use prepackaged moistened towels to wipe off sweat and dirt, or bathe in the water without soap.

Stay on the trail. It's true, a path anywhere leads nowhere new, but purists will just have to get over it. Paths serve an important purpose; they limit impact on natural areas. Straying from a designated trail may seem innocent but it can cause damage to sensitive areas—damage that may take years to recover, if it can recover at all. Even simple shortcuts can be destructive. So, please, stay on the trail.

Leave no weeds. Noxious weeds tend to overtake other plants, which in turn affects animals and birds that depend on them for food. To minimize the spread of noxious weeds, hikers should regularly clean their boots, tents, packs, and hiking poles of mud and seeds. Also brush your dog to remove any weed seeds before heading off into a new area.

Keep your dog under control. You can buy a flexi-lead that allows your dog to go exploring along the trail, while allowing you the ability to reel him in should another hiker approach or should he decide to chase a rabbit. Always obey leash laws and be sure to bury your dog's waste or pack it in resealable plastic bags.

Respect other trail users. Often you're not the only one on the trail. With the rise in popularity of multiuse trails, you'll have to learn a new kind of respect, beyond the nod and "hello" approach you may be used to. First investigate whether you're on a multiuse trail, and assume the appropriate precautions. When you encounter motorized vehicles (ATVs, motorcycles, and 4WDs), be alert. Though they should always yield to the hiker, often they're going too fast or are too lost in the buzz of their engine to react to your presence. If you hear activity ahead, step off the trail just to be safe. Note that you're not likely to hear a mountain biker coming, so be prepared and know ahead of time whether you share the trail with them. Cyclists should always yield to hikers, but that's little comfort to the hiker. Be aware. When you approach horses or pack animals on the trail, always step quietly off the trail, preferably on the downhill side, and let them pass. If you're wearing a large backpack, it's often a good idea to sit down. To some animals, a hiker wearing a large backpack might appear threatening. Many national forests allow domesticated grazing, usually for sheep and cattle. Make sure your dog doesn't harass these animals, and respect ranchers' rights while you're enjoying yours.

Getting into Shape

Unless you want to be sore—and possibly have to shorten your trip or vacation—be sure to get in shape before a big hike. If you're terribly out of shape, start a walking program early, preferably eight weeks in advance. Start with a fifteen-minute walk during your lunch hour or after work and gradually increase your walking time to an hour. You should also increase your elevation gain. Walking briskly up hills really strengthens your leg muscles and gets your heart rate up. If you work in a storied office building, take the stairs instead of the elevator. If you prefer going to a gym, walk the treadmill or use a stair machine. You can further increase your strength and endurance by walking with a loaded backpack. Stationary exercises you might consider are squats, leg lifts, sit-ups, and push-ups. Other good ways to get in shape include biking, running, aerobics, and, of course, short hikes. Stretching before and after a hike keeps muscles flexible and helps avoid injuries.

Preparedness

It's been said that failing to plan means planning to fail. So do take the necessary time to plan your trip. Whether going on a short day hike or an extended backpack trip, always prepare for the worst. Simply remembering to pack a copy of the U.S. Army Survival Manual is not preparedness. Although it's not a bad idea if you plan on entering truly wild places, it's merely the tourniquet answer to a problem. You need to do your best to prevent the problem from arising in the first place. In order to survive—and to stay reasonably comfortable—you need to concern yourself with the basics: water, food, and shelter. Don't go on a hike without having these bases covered. And don't go on a hike expecting to find these items in the woods.

Water. Even in frigid conditions, you need at least two quarts of water a day to function efficiently. Add heat and taxing terrain and you can bump that figure up to one gallon. That's simply a base to work from—your metabolism and your level of conditioning can raise or lower that amount. Unless you know your level, assume that you need one gallon of water a day. Now, where do you plan on getting the water?

Preferably not from natural water sources. These sources can be loaded with intestinal disturbers, such as bacteria, viruses, and fertilizers. *Giardia lamblia,* the most common of these disturbers, is a protozoan parasite that lives part of its life cycle as a cyst in water sources. The parasite spreads when mammals defecate in water sources. Once ingested, Giardia can induce cramping, diarrhea, vomiting, and fatigue within two days to two weeks after ingestion. Giardiasis is treatable with prescription drugs. If you believe you've contracted giardiasis, see a doctor immediately.

Treating water. The best and easiest solution to avoid polluted water is to carry your water with you. Yet, depending on the nature of your hike and the duration, this may not be an option—one gallon of water weighs eight-and-a-half pounds. In that case, you'll need to look into treating water. Regardless of which method you choose, you should always carry some water with you in case of an emergency. Save this reserve until you absolutely need it.

There are three methods of treating water: boiling, chemical treatment, and filtering. If you boil water, it's recommended that you do so for ten to fifteen minutes. This is often impractical because you're forced to exhaust a great deal of your fuel supply. You can opt for chemical treatment, which will kill Giardia but will not take care of other chemical pollutants. Another drawback to chemical treatments is the unpleasant taste of the water after it's treated. You can remedy this by adding powdered drink mix to the water. Filters are the preferred method for treating water. Many filters remove Giardia, organic and inorganic contaminants, and don't leave an aftertaste. Water filters are far from perfect as they can easily become clogged or leak if a gasket wears out. It's always a good idea to carry a backup supply of chemical treatment tablets in case your filter decides to quit on you.

Food. If we're talking about survival, you can go days without food, as long as you have water. But we're also talking about comfort. Try to avoid foods that are high in sugar and fat like candy bars and potato chips. These food types are harder to digest and are low in nutritional value. Instead, bring along foods that are easy to pack, nutritious, and high in energy (e.g., bagels, nutrition bars, dehydrated fruit, gorp, and jerky). If you are on an overnight trip, easy-to-fix dinners include rice mixes with dehydrated potatoes, corn, pasta with cheese sauce, and soup mixes. For a tasty breakfast, you can fix hot oatmeal with brown sugar and reconstituted milk powder topped off with banana chips. If you like a hot drink in the morning, bring along herbal tea bags or hot chocolate. If you are a coffee junkie, you can purchase coffee that is packaged like tea bags. You can prepackage all of your meals in heavy-duty resealable plastic bags to keep food from spilling in your pack. These bags can be reused to pack out trash.

Shelter. The type of shelter you choose depends less on the conditions than on your tolerance for discomfort. Shelter comes in many forms—tent, tarp, lean-to, bivy sack, cabin, cave, etc. If you're camping in the desert, a bivy sack may suffice, but if you're above the treeline and a storm is approaching, a better choice is a three- or four-season tent. Tents are the logical and most popular choice for most backpackers as they're lightweight and packable—and you can rest assured that you always have shelter from the elements. Before you leave on your trip, anticipate what the weather and terrain will be like and plan for the type of shelter that will work best for your comfort level (see Equipment later in this section).

Finding a campsite. If there are established campsites, stick to those. If not, start looking for a campsite early—around 3:30 or 4:00 P.M. Stop at the first decent site you see. Depending on the area, it could be a long time before you find another suitable location. Pitch your camp in an area that's level. Make sure the area is at least 200 feet from fragile areas like lakeshores, meadows, and stream banks. And try to avoid areas thick in underbrush, as they can harbor insects and provide cover for approaching animals.

If you are camping in stormy, rainy weather, look for a rock outcrop or a shelter in the trees to keep the wind from blowing your tent all night. Be sure that you don't camp under trees with dead limbs that might break off on top of you. Also, try to find an area that has an absorbent surface, such as sandy soil or forest duff. This, in addition to camping on a surface with a slight angle, will provide better drainage. By all means, don't dig trenches to provide drainage around your tent—remember you're practicing zero-impact camping.

If you're in bear country, steer clear of creekbeds or animal paths. If you see any signs of a bear's presence (i.e., scat, footprints), relocate. You'll need to find a campsite near a tall tree where you can hang your food and other items that may attract bears such as deodorant, toothpaste, or soap. Carry a lightweight nylon rope with which to hang your food. As a rule, you should hang your food at least 20 feet from the ground and 5 feet away from the tree trunk. You can put food and other items in a waterproof stuff sack and tie one end of the rope to the stuff sack. To get the other end of the rope over the tree branch, tie a good size rock to it, and gently toss the rock over the tree branch. Pull the stuff sack up until it reaches the top of the branch and tie it off securely. Don't hang your food near your tent! If possible, hang your food at least 100 feet away from your campsite. Alternatives to hanging your food are bear-proof plastic tubes and metal bear boxes.

Lastly, think of comfort. Lie down on the ground where you intend to sleep and see if it's a good fit. For morning warmth (and a nice view to wake up to), have your tent face east.

First Aid

I know you're tough, but get 10 miles into the woods and develop a blister and you'll wish you had carried that first-aid kit. Face it, it's just plain good sense. Many companies produce lightweight, compact first-aid kits. Just make sure yours contains at least the following:

- Band-Aids
- mole skin
- various sterile gauze and dressings
- white surgical tape
- an Ace bandage
- an antihistamine
- aspirin
- Betadine solution
- a first-aid book
- Tums

- tweezers
- scissors
- antibacterial wipes
- triple-antibiotic ointment
- plastic gloves
- sterile cotton tip applicators
- syrup of ipecac (to induce vomiting)
- thermometer
- wire splint

Here are a few tips for dealing with and hopefully preventing certain ailments.

Sunburn. Take along sunscreen or sun block, protective clothing, and a wide-brimmed hat. If you do get a sunburn, treat the area with aloe vera gel, and protect the area from further sun exposure. At higher elevations, the sun's radiation can be particularly damaging to skin. Remember that your eyes are vulnerable to this radiation as well. Sunglasses can be a good way to prevent headaches and permanent eye damage from the sun, especially in places where light-colored rock or patches of snow reflect light up in your face.

Blisters. Be prepared to take care of these hike-spoilers by carrying moleskin (a lightly padded adhesive), gauze and tape, or adhesive bandages. An effective way to apply moleskin is to cut out a circle of moleskin and remove the center—like a doughnut—and place it over the blistered area. Cutting the center out will reduce the pressure applied to the sensitive skin. Other products can help you combat blisters. Some are applied to suspicious hot spots before a blister forms to help decrease friction to that area, while others are applied to the blister after it has popped to help prevent further irritation.

Insect bites and stings. You can treat most insect bites and stings by applying hydrocortisone 1% cream topically and taking a pain medication such as ibuprofen or acetaminophen to reduce swelling. If you forgot to pack these items, a cold compress or a paste of mud and ashes can sometimes assuage the itching and discomfort. Remove any stingers by using tweezers or scraping the area with your fingernail or a knife blade. Don't pinch the area as you'll only spread the venom.

Some hikers are highly sensitive to bites and stings and may have a serious allergic reaction that can be life threatening. Symptoms of a serious allergic reaction can include wheezing, an asthmatic attack, and shock. The treatment for this severe type of reaction is epinephrine. If you know that you are sensitive to bites and stings, carry a pre-packaged kit of epinephrine, which can be obtained only by prescription from your doctor.

Ticks. Ticks can carry diseases such as Rocky Mountain spotted fever and Lyme disease. The best defense is, of course, prevention. If you know you're going to be hiking through an area littered with ticks, wear long pants and a long sleeved shirt. You can apply a permethrin repellent to your clothing and a Deet repellent to exposed skin. At the end of your hike, do a spot check for ticks (and insects in general). If you do find a tick, coat the insect with petroleum jelly or tree sap to cut off its air supply. The tick should release its hold, but if it doesn't, grab the head of the tick firmly—with a pair of tweezers if you have them—and gently pull it away from the skin with a twisting motion. Sometimes the mouth parts linger, embedded in your skin. If this happens, try to remove them with a disinfected needle. Clean the affected area with an antibacterial cleanser and then apply triple antibiotic ointment. Monitor the area for a few days. If irritation persists or a white spot develops, see a doctor for possible infection.

Poison ivy, oak, and sumac. These skin irritants can be found most anywhere in North America and come in the form of a bush or a vine, having leaflets in groups of three, five, seven, or nine. Learn how to spot the plants. The oil they secrete can cause an allergic reaction in the form of blisters, usually about twelve hours after exposure. The itchy rash can last from ten days to several weeks. The best defense against these irritants is to wear clothing that covers the arms, legs and torso. For summer, zip-off cargo pants come in handy. There are also nonprescription lotions you can apply to exposed skin that guard against the effects of poison ivy/oak/sumac and can be washed off with soap and water. If you think you were in contact with the plants, after hiking (or even on the trail during longer hikes) wash with soap and water. Taking a hot shower with soap after you return home from your hike will also help to remove any lingering oil from your skin. Should you contract a rash from any of these plants, use an antihistamine to reduce the itching. If the rash is localized, create a light bleach/water wash to dry up the area. If the rash has spread, either tough it out or see your doctor about getting a dose of cortisone (available both orally and by injection).

Snakebites. Snakebites are rare in North America. Unless startled or provoked, the majority of snakes will not bite. If you are wise to their habitats and keep a careful eye on the trail, you should be just fine. When stepping over logs, first step on the log, making sure you can see what's on the other side before stepping down. Though your chances of being struck are slim, it's wise to know what to do in the event you are.

If a *nonpoisonous* snake bites you, allow the wound to bleed a small amount and then cleanse the wounded area with a Betadine solution (10% povidone iodine). Rinse the wound with clean water (preferably) or fresh urine (it might sound ugly, but it's sterile). Once the area is clean, cover it with triple antibiotic ointment and a clean bandage. Remember, most residual damage from snakebites, poisonous or otherwise, comes from infection, not the snake's venom. Keep the area as clean as possible and get medical attention immediately.

If you are bitten by a poisonous snake, remove the toxin with a suctioning device, found in a snakebite kit. If you do not have such a device, squeeze the wound—DO NOT use your mouth for suction, as the venom will enter your bloodstream through the vessels under the tongue and head straight for your heart. Then, clean the wound just as you would a nonpoisonous bite. Tie a clean band of cloth snuggly around the afflicted appendage, about an inch or so above the bite (or the rim of the swelling). This is NOT a tourniquet—you want to simply slow the blood flow, not cut it off. Loosen the band if numbness ensues. Remove the band for a minute and reapply a little higher every ten minutes.

If it is your friend who's been bitten, treat him or her for shock—make the person comfortable, have him or her lie down, elevate the legs, and keep him or her warm. Avoid applying anything cold to the bite wound. Immobilize the affected area and remove any constricting items such as rings, watches, or restrictive clothing— swelling may occur. Once your friend is stable and relatively calm, hike out to get help. The victim should get treatment within twelve hours, ideally, which usually consists of a tetanus shot, antivenin, and antibiotics.

If you are alone and struck by a poisonous snake, stay calm. Hysteria will only quicken the venom's spread. Follow the procedure above, and do your best to reach help. When hiking out, don't run—you'll only increase the flow of blood throughout your system. Instead, walk calmly.

Dehydration. Have you ever hiked in hot weather and had a roaring headache and felt fatigued after only a few miles? More than likely you were dehydrated. Symptoms of dehydration include fatigue, headache, and decreased coordination and judgment. When you are hiking, your body's rate of fluid loss depends on the outside temperature, humidity, altitude, and your activity level. On average, a hiker walking in warm weather will lose four liters of fluid a day. That fluid loss is easily replaced by normal consumption of liquids and food. However, if a hiker is walking briskly in hot, dry weather and hauling a heavy pack, he or she can lose one to three liters of water an hour. It's important to always carry plenty of water and to stop often and drink fluids regularly, even if you aren't thirsty.

Heat exhaustion is the result of a loss of large amounts of electrolytes and often occurs if a hiker is dehydrated and has been under heavy exertion. Common symptoms of heat exhaustion include cramping, exhaustion, fatigue, lightheadedness, and nausea. You can treat heat exhaustion by getting out of the sun and drinking an electrolyte solution made up of one teaspoon of salt and one tablespoon of sugar dissolved in a liter of water. Drink this solution slowly over a period of one hour. Drinking plenty of fluids (preferably an electrolyte solution/sports drink) can prevent heat exhaustion. Avoid hiking during the hottest parts of the day, and wear breathable clothing, a wide-brimmed hat, and sunglasses.

Hypothermia is one of the biggest dangers in the backcountry, especially for day hikers in the summertime. That may sound strange, but imagine starting out on a hike in midsummer when it's sunny and 80 degrees out. You're clad in nylon shorts and a cotton T-shirt. About halfway through your hike, the sky begins to cloud up, and in the next hour a light drizzle begins to fall and the wind starts to pick up. Before you know it, you are soaking wet and shivering—the perfect recipe for hypothermia. More advanced signs include decreased coordination, slurred speech, and blurred vision. When a victim's temperature falls below 92 degrees, the blood pressure and pulse plummet, possibly leading to coma and death.

To avoid hypothermia, always bring a windproof/rainproof shell, a fleece jacket, tights made of a breathable, synthetic fiber, gloves, and hat when you are hiking in the mountains. Learn to adjust your clothing layers based on the temperature. If you are climbing uphill at a moderate pace you will stay warm, but when you stop for a break you'll become cold quickly, unless you add more layers of clothing.

If a hiker is showing advanced signs of hypothermia, dress him or her in dry clothes and make sure he or she is wearing a hat and gloves. Place the person in a sleeping bag in a tent or shelter that will protect him or her from the wind and other elements. Give the person warm fluids to drink and keep him awake.

Frostbite. When the mercury dips below 32 degrees, your extremities begin to chill. If a persistent chill attacks a localized area, say, your hands or your toes, the circulatory system reacts by cutting off blood flow to the affected area—the idea being to protect and preserve the body's overall temperature. And so it's death by attrition for the affected area. Ice crystals start to form from the water in the cells of the neglected tissue. Deprived of heat, nourishment, and now water, the tissue literally starves. This is frostbite.

Prevention is your best defense against this situation. Most prone to frostbite are your face, hands, and feet, so protect these areas well. Wool is the material of choice because it provides ample air space for insulation and draws moisture away from the skin. Synthetic fabrics, however, have recently made great strides in the cold weather clothing market. Do your research. A pair of light silk liners under your regular gloves is a good trick for keeping warm. They afford some additional warmth, but more importantly they'll allow you to remove your mitts for tedious work without exposing the skin.

If your feet or hands start to feel cold or numb due to the elements, warm them as quickly as possible. Place cold hands under your armpits or bury them in your crotch. If your feet are cold, change your socks. If there's plenty of room in your boots, add another pair of socks. Do remember, though, that constricting your feet in tight boots can restrict blood flow and actually make your feet colder more quickly. Your socks need to have breathing room if they're going to be effective. Dead air provides insulation. If your face is cold, place your warm hands over your face, or simply wear a head stocking.

Should your skin go numb and start to appear white and waxy, chances are you've got or are developing frostbite. Don't try to thaw the area unless you can maintain the warmth. In other words, don't stop to warm up your frostbitten feet only to head back on the trail. You'll do more damage than good. Tests have shown that hikers who walked on thawed feet did more harm, and endured more pain, than hikers who left the affected areas alone. Do your best to get out of the cold entirely and seek medical attention—which usually consists of performing a rapid rewarming in water for twenty to thirty minutes.

The overall objective in preventing both hypothermia and frostbite is to keep the body's core warm. Protect key areas where heat escapes, like the top of the head, and maintain the proper nutrition level. Foods that are high in calories aid the body in producing heat. Never smoke or drink when you're in situations where the cold is threatening. By affecting blood flow, these activities ultimately cool the body's core temperature.

Altitude sickness (AMS). High lofty peaks, clear alpine lakes, and vast mountain views beckon hikers to the high country. But those who like to venture high may become victims of altitude sickness (also known as Acute Mountain Sickness—AMS). Altitude sickness is your body's reaction to insufficient oxygen in the blood due to decreased barometric pressure. While some hikers may feel lightheaded, nauseous, and experience shortness of breath at 7,000 feet, others may not experience these symptoms until they reach 10,000 feet or higher.

Slowing your ascent to high places and giving your body a chance to acclimatize to the higher elevations can prevent altitude sickness. For example, if you live at sea level and are planning a weeklong backpacking trip to elevations between 7,000 and 12,000 feet, start by staying below 7,000 feet for one night, then move to between 7,000 and 10,000 feet for another night or two. Avoid strenuous exertion and alcohol to give your body a chance to adjust to the new altitude. It's also important to eat light food and drink plenty of nonalcoholic fluids, preferably water. Loss of appetite at altitude is common, but you must eat!

Most hikers who experience mild to moderate AMS develop a headache and/or nausea, grow lethargic, and have problems sleeping. The treatment for AMS is simple: stop heading uphill. Keep eating and drinking water and take meds for the headache. You actually need to take more breaths at altitude than at sea level, so breathe a little faster without hyperventilating. If symptoms don't improve over twenty-four to forty-eight hours, descend. Once a victim descends about 2,000 to 3,000 feet, his signs will usually begin to diminish.

Severe AMS comes in two forms: High Altitude Pulmonary Edema (HAPE) and High Altitude Cerebral Edema (HACE). HAPE, an accumulation of fluid in the lungs, can occur above 8,000 feet. Symptoms include rapid heart rate, shortness of breath at rest, AMS symptoms, dry cough developing into a wet cough, gurgling sounds, flu-like or bronchitis symptoms, and lack of muscle coordination. HAPE is life threatening so descend immediately, at least 2,000 to 4,000 feet. HACE usually occurs above 12,000 feet but sometimes occurs above 10,000 feet. Symptoms are similar to HAPE but also include seizures, hallucinations, paralysis, and vision disturbances. Descend immediately—HACE is also life threatening.

Hantavirus Pulmonary Syndrome (HPS). Deer mice spread the virus that causes HPS, and humans contract it from breathing it in, usually when they've disturbed an area with dust and mice feces from nests or surfaces with mice droppings or urine. Exposure to large numbers of rodents and their feces or urine presents the greatest risk. As hikers, we sometimes enter old buildings, and often deer mice live in these places. We may not be around long enough to be exposed, but do be aware of this disease. About half the people who develop HPS die. Symptoms are flu-like and appear about two to three weeks after exposure. After initial symptoms, a dry cough and shortness of breath follow. Breathing is difficult. If you even think you might have HPS, see a doctor immediately!

Natural Hazards

Besides tripping over a rock or tree root on the trail, there are some real hazards to be aware of while hiking. Even if where you're hiking doesn't have the plethora of poisonous snakes and plants, insects, and grizzly bears found in other parts of the United States, there are a few weather conditions and predators you may need to take into account.

Lightning. Thunderstorms build over the mountains almost every day during the summer. Lightning is generated by thunderheads and can strike without warning, even several miles away from the nearest overhead cloud. The best rule of thumb is to start leaving exposed peaks, ridges, and canyon rims by about noon. This time can vary a little depending on storm buildup. Keep an eye on cloud formation and don't underestimate how fast a storm can build. The bigger they get, the more likely a thunderstorm will happen. Lightning takes the path of least resistance, so if you're the high point, it might choose you. Ducking under a rock overhang is dangerous as you form the shortest path between the rock and ground. If you dash below tree-line, avoid standing under the only or the tallest tree. If you are caught above tree-line, stay away from anything metal you might be carrying, Move down off the ridge slightly to a low, treeless point and squat until the storm passes. If you have an insulating pad, squat on it. Avoid having both your hands and feet touching the ground at once and never lay flat. If you hear a buzzing sound or feel your hair standing on end, move quickly as an electrical charge is building up.

Flash floods. On July 31, 1976, a torrential downpour unleashed by a thunderstorm dumped tons of water into the Big Thompson watershed near Estes Park. Within hours, a wall of water moved down the narrow canyon killing 139 people and causing more than $30 million in property damage. The spooky thing about flash floods, especially in western canyons, is that they can appear out of nowhere from a storm many miles away. While hiking or driving in canyons, keep an eye on the weather. Always climb to safety if danger threatens. Flash floods usually subside quickly, so be patient and don't cross a swollen stream.

Bears. Most of the United States (outside of the Pacific Northwest and parts of the Northern Rockies) does not have a grizzly bear population, although some rumors exist about sightings where there should be none. Black bears are plentiful, however. Here are some tips in case you and a bear scare each other. Most of all, avoid scaring a bear. Watch for bear tracks (five toes) and droppings (sizable with leaves, partly digested berries, seeds, and/or animal fur). Talk or sing where visibility or hearing are limited. Keep a clean camp, hang food, and don't sleep in the clothes you wore while cooking. Be especially careful in spring to avoid getting between a mother and her cubs. In late summer and fall bears are busy eating berries and acorns to fatten up for winter, so be extra careful around berry bushes and oakbrush. If you do encounter a bear, move away slowly while facing the bear, talk softly, and avoid direct eye contact. Give the bear room to escape. Since bears are very curious, it might stand upright to get a better whiff of you, and it may even charge you to try to intimidate you. Try to stay calm. If a bear does attack you, fight back with anything you have handy. Unleashed dogs have been known to come running back to their owners with a bear close behind. Keep your dog on a leash or leave it at home.

Mountain lions. Mountain lions appear to be getting more comfortable around humans as long as deer (their favorite prey) are in an area with adequate cover. Usually elusive and quiet, lions rarely attack people. If you meet a lion, give it a chance to escape. Stay calm and talk firmly to it. Back away slowly while facing the lion. If you run, you'll only encourage the curious cat to chase you. Make yourself look large by opening a jacket, if you have one, or waving your hiking poles. If the lion behaves aggressively throw stones, sticks, or whatever you can while remaining tall. If a lion does attack, fight for your life with anything you can grab.

Moose. Because moose have very few natural predators, they don't fear humans like other animals. You might find moose in sagebrush and wetter areas of willow, aspen, and pine, or in beaver habitats. Mothers with calves, as well as bulls during mating season, can be particularly aggressive. If a moose threatens you, back away slowly and talk calmly to it. Keep your pets away from moose.

Other considerations. Hunting is a popular sport in the United States, especially during rifle season in October and November. Hiking is still enjoyable in those months in many areas, so just take a few precautions. First, learn when the different hunting seasons start and end in the area in which you'll be hiking. During this time frame, be sure to wear at least a blaze orange hat, and possibly put an orange vest over your pack. Don't be surprised to see hunters in camo outfits carrying bows or muzzleloading rifles around during their season. If you would feel more comfortable without hunters around, hike in national parks and monuments or state and local parks where hunting is not allowed.

Navigation

Whether you are going on a short hike in a familiar area or planning a weeklong backpack trip, you should always be equipped with the proper navigational equipment—at the very least a detailed map and a sturdy compass.

Maps. There are many different types of maps available to help you find your way on the trail. Easiest to find are Forest Service maps and BLM (Bureau of Land Management) maps. These maps tend to cover large areas, so be sure they are detailed enough for your particular trip. You can also obtain National Park maps as well as high quality maps from private companies and trail groups. These maps can be obtained either from outdoor stores or ranger stations.

U.S. Geological Survey topographic maps are particularly popular with hikers—especially serious backcountry hikers. These maps contain the standard map symbols such as roads, lakes, and rivers, as well as contour lines that show the details of the trail terrain like ridges, valleys, passes, and mountain peaks. The 7.5-minute series (1 inch on the map equals approximately ⅔ mile on the ground) provides the closest inspection available. USGS maps are available by mail (U.S. Geological Survey, Map Distribution Branch, P.O. Box 25286, Denver, CO 80225), or at mapping.usgs.gov/esic/to_order.html.

If you want to check out the high-tech world of maps, you can purchase topographic maps on CD-ROM. These software-mapping programs let you select a route on your computer, print it out, then take it with you on the trail. Some software mapping programs let you insert symbols and labels, download waypoints from a GPS unit, and export the maps to other software programs.

The art of map reading is a skill that you can develop by first practicing in an area you are familiar with. To begin, orient the map so the map is lined up in the correct direction (i.e. north on the map is lined up with true north). Next, familiarize yourself with the map symbols and try and match them up with terrain features around you such as a high ridge, mountain peak, river, or lake. If you are practicing with a USGS map, notice the contour lines. On gentler terrain these contour lines are spaced further apart, and on steeper terrain they are closer together. Pick a short loop trail, and stop frequently to check your position on the map. As you practice map reading, you'll learn how to anticipate a steep section on the trail or a good place to take a rest break, and so on.

Compasses. First off, the sun is not a substitute for a compass. So, what kind of compass should you have? Here are some characteristics you should look for: a rectangular base with detailed scales, a liquid-filled housing, protective housing, a sighting line on the mirror, luminous alignment and back-bearing arrows, a luminous north-seeking arrow, and a well-defined bezel ring.

You can learn compass basics by reading the detailed instructions included with your compass. If you want to fine-tune your compass skills, sign up for an orienteering class or purchase a book on compass reading. Once you've learned the basic skills of using a compass, remember to practice these skills before you head into the backcountry.

If you are a klutz at using a compass, you may be interested in checking out the technical wizardry of the GPS (Global Positioning System) device. The GPS was developed by the Pentagon and works off twenty-four NAVSTAR satellites, which were designed to guide missiles to their targets. A GPS device is a handheld unit that calculates your latitude and longitude with the easy press of a button. The Department of Defense used to scramble the satellite signals a bit to prevent civilians (and spies!) from getting extremely accurate readings, but that practice was discontinued in May 2000, and GPS units now provide nearly pinpoint accuracy (within 30 to 60 feet).

There are many different types of GPS units available and they range in price from $100 to $400. In general, all GPS units have a display screen and keypad where you input information. In addition to acting as a compass, the unit allows you to plot your route, easily retrace your path, track your travelling speed, find the mileage between waypoints, and calculate the total mileage of your route.

Before you purchase a GPS unit, keep in mind that these devices don't pick up signals indoors, in heavily wooded areas, on mountain peaks, or in deep valleys.

Pedometers. A pedometer is a small, clip-on unit with a digital display that calculates your hiking distance in miles or kilometers based on your walking stride. Some units also calculate the calories you burn and your total hiking time. Pedometers are available at most large outdoor stores and range in price from $20 to $40.

Trip Planning

Planning your hiking adventure begins with letting a friend or relative know your trip itinerary so they can call for help if you don't return at your scheduled time. Your next task is to make sure you are outfitted to experience the risks and rewards of the trail. This section highlights gear and clothing you may want to take with you to get the most out of your hike.

Day Hikes
- camera/film
- compass/GPS unit
- pedometer
- daypack
- first-aid kit
- food
- guidebook
- headlamp/flashlight with extra batteries and bulbs
- hat
- insect repellant
- knife/multipurpose tool
- map
- matches in waterproof container and fire starter
- Polar Fleece jacket
- raingear
- space blanket
- sunglasses
- sunscreen
- swimsuit
- watch
- water
- water bottles/water hydration system

Overnight Trip

- backpack and waterproof rain cover
- backpacker's trowel
- bandanna
- bear repellant spray
- bear bell
- biodegradable soap
- pot scrubber
- collapsible water container (2–3 gallon capacity)
- clothing—extra wool socks, shirt and shorts
- cook set/utensils
- ditty bags to store gear
- extra plastic resealable bags
- gaiters
- garbage bag
- ground cloth
- journal/pen
- nylon rope to hang food
- long underwear
- permit (if required)
- rain jacket and pants
- sandals to wear around camp and to ford streams
- sleeping bag
- waterproof stuff sack
- sleeping pad
- small bath towel
- stove and fuel
- tent
- toiletry items
- water filter
- whistle

Equipment

With the outdoor market currently flooded with products, many of which are pure gimmickry, it seems impossible to both differentiate and choose. Do I really need a tropical-fish-lined collapsible shower? (No, you don't.) The only defense against the maddening quantity of items thrust in your face is to think practically—and to do so before you go shopping. The worst buys are impulsive buys. Since most name brands will differ only slightly in quality, it's best to know what you're looking for in terms of function. Buy only what you need. You will, don't forget, be carrying what you've bought on your back. Here are some things to keep in mind before you go shopping.

Clothes. Clothing is your armor against Mother Nature's little surprises. Hikers should be prepared for any possibility, especially when hiking in mountainous areas. Adequate rain protection and extra layers of clothing are a good idea. In summer, a wide-brimmed hat can help keep the sun at bay. In the winter months the first layer you'll want to wear is a "wicking" layer of long underwear that keeps perspiration away from your skin. Wear long underwear made from synthetic fibers that wick moisture away from the skin and draw it toward the next layer of clothing, where it then evaporates. Avoid wearing long underwear made of cotton as it is slow to dry and keeps moisture next to your skin.

The second layer you'll wear is the "insulating" layer. Aside from keeping you warm, this layer needs to "breathe" so you stay dry while hiking. A fabric that provides insulation and dries quickly is fleece. It's interesting to note that this one-of-a-kind fabric is made out of recycled plastic. Purchasing a zip-up jacket made of this material is highly recommended.

The last line of layering defense is the "shell" layer. You'll need some type of waterproof, windproof, breathable jacket that will fit over all of your other layers. It should have a large hood that fits over a hat. You'll also need a good pair of rain pants made from a similar waterproof, breathable fabric. Some Gore-Tex jackets cost as much as $500, but you should know that there are more affordable fabrics out there that work just as well.

Now that you've learned the basics of layering, you can't forget to protect your hands and face. In cold, windy, or rainy weather you'll need a hat made of wool or fleece and insulated, waterproof gloves that will keep your hands warm and toasty. As mentioned earlier, buying an additional pair of light silk liners to wear under your regular gloves is a good idea.

Footwear. If you have any extra money to spend on your trip, put that money into boots or trail shoes. Poor shoes will bring a hike to a halt faster than anything else. To avoid this annoyance, buy shoes that provide support and are lightweight and flexible. A lightweight hiking boot is better than a heavy, leather mountaineering boot for most day hikes and backpacking. Trail running shoes provide a little extra cushion and are made in a high-top style that many people wear for hiking. These running shoes are lighter, more flexible, and more breathable than hiking boots. If you know you'll be hiking in wet weather often, purchase boots or shoes with a Gore-Tex liner, which will help keep your feet dry.

When buying your boots, be sure to wear the same type of socks you'll be wearing on the trail. If the boots you're buying are for cold weather hiking, try the boots on while wearing two pairs of socks. Speaking of socks, a good cold weather sock combination is to wear a thinner sock made of wool or polypropylene covered by a heavier outer sock made of wool. The inner sock protects the foot from the rubbing effects of the outer sock and prevents blisters. Many outdoor stores have some type of ramp to simulate hiking uphill and downhill. Be sure to take advantage of this test, as toe-jamming boot fronts can be very painful and debilitating on the downhill trek.

Once you've purchased your footwear, be sure to break them in before you hit the trail. New footwear is often stiff and needs to be stretched and molded to your foot.

Hiking poles. Hiking poles help with balance, and more importantly take pressure off your knees. The ones with shock absorbers are easier on your elbows and knees. Some poles even come with a camera attachment to be used as a monopod. And heaven forbid you meet a mountain lion, bear, or unfriendly dog, the poles can make you look a lot bigger.

Backpacks. No matter what type of hiking you do you'll need a pack of some sort to carry the basic trail essentials. There are a variety of backpacks on the market, but let's first discuss what you intend to use it for. Day hikes or overnight trips?

If you plan on doing a day hike, a daypack should have some of the following characteristics: a padded hip belt that's at least 2 inches in diameter (avoid packs with only a small nylon piece of webbing for a hip belt); a chest strap (the chest strap helps stabilize the pack against your body); external pockets to carry water and other items that you want easy access to; an internal pocket to hold keys, a knife, a wallet, and other miscellaneous items; an external lashing system to hold a jacket; and a hydration pocket for carrying a hydration system (which consists of a water bladder with an attachable drinking hose).

For short hikes, some hikers like to use a fanny pack to store just a camera, food, a compass, a map, and other trail essentials. Most fanny packs have pockets for two water bottles and a padded hip belt.

If you intend to do an extended, overnight trip, there are multiple considerations. First off, you need to decide what kind of framed pack you want. There are two backpack types for backpacking: the internal frame and the external frame. An internal frame pack rests closer to your body, making it more stable and easier to balance when hiking over rough terrain. An external frame pack is just that, an aluminum frame attached to the exterior of the pack. An external frame pack is better for long backpack trips because it distributes the pack weight better and you can carry heavier loads. It's easier to pack, and your gear is more accessible. It also offers better back ventilation in hot weather.

The most critical measurement for fitting a pack is torso length. The pack needs to rest evenly on your hips without sagging. A good pack will come in two or three sizes and have straps and hip belts that are adjustable according to your body size and characteristics.

When you purchase a backpack, go to an outdoor store with salespeople who are knowledgeable in how to properly fit a pack. Once the pack is fitted for you, load the pack with the amount of weight you plan on taking on the trail. The weight of the pack should be distributed evenly and you should be able to swing your arms and walk briskly without feeling out of balance. Another good technique for evaluating a pack is to walk up and down stairs and make quick turns to the right and to the left to be sure the pack doesn't feel out of balance. Other features that are nice to have on a backpack include a removable day pack or fanny pack, external pockets for extra water, and extra lash points to attach a jacket or other items.

Sleeping bags and pads. Sleeping bags are rated by temperature. You can purchase a bag made of synthetic fiber, or you can buy a goose down bag. Goose down bags are more expensive, but they have a higher insulating capacity by weight and will keep their loft longer. You'll want to purchase a bag with a temperature rating that fits the time of year and conditions you are most likely to camp in. One caveat: The techno-standard for temperature ratings is far from perfect. Ratings vary from manufacturer to manufacturer, so to protect yourself you should purchase a bag rated 10 to 15 degrees below the temperature you expect to be camping in. Synthetic bags are more resistant to water than down bags, but many down bags are now made with a Gore-Tex shell that helps to repel water. Down bags are also more compressible than synthetic bags and take up less room in your pack, which is an important consideration if you are planning a multiday backpack trip. Features to look for in a sleeping bag include a mummy style bag, a hood you can cinch down around your head in cold weather, and draft tubes along the zippers that help keep heat in and drafts out.

You'll also want a sleeping pad to provide insulation and padding from the cold ground. There are different types of sleeping pads available, from the more expensive self-inflating air mattresses to the less expensive closed-cell foam pads. Self-inflating air mattresses are usually heavier than closed-cell foam mattresses and are prone to punctures.

Tents. The tent is your home away from home while on the trail. It provides protection from wind, snow, rain, and insects. A three-season tent is a good choice for backpacking and can range in price from $100 to $500. These lightweight and versatile tents provide protection in all types of weather, except heavy snowstorms or high winds, and range in weight from four to eight pounds. Look for a tent that's easy to set up and will easily fit two people with gear. Dome type tents usually offer more headroom and places to store gear. Other tent designs include a vestibule where you can store wet boots and backpacks. Some nice-to-have items in a tent include interior pockets to store small items and lashing points to hang a clothesline. Most three-season tents also come with stakes so you can secure the tent in high winds. Before you purchase a tent, set it up and take it down a few times to be sure it is easy to handle. Also, sit inside the tent and make sure it has enough room for you and your gear.

Cell phones. Many hikers are carrying their cell phones into the backcountry these days in case of emergency. That's fine and good, but please know that cell phone coverage is often poor to nonexistent in valleys, canyons, and thick forest. More importantly people have started to call for help because they're tired or lost. Let's go back to being prepared. You are responsible for yourself in the backcountry. Use your brain to avoid problems, and if you do encounter one, first use your brain to try to correct the situation. Only use your cell phone, if it works, in true emergencies.

Hiking with Children

Hiking with children isn't a matter of how many miles you can cover or how much elevation gain you make in a day; it's about seeing and experiencing nature through their eyes.

Kids like to explore and have fun. They like to stop and point out bugs and plants, look under rocks, jump in puddles, and throw sticks. If you're taking a toddler or young child on a hike, start with a trail that you're familiar with. Trails that have interesting things for kids, like piles of leaves to play in or a small stream to wade through during the summer, will make the hike much more enjoyable for them and will keep them from getting bored.

You can keep your child's attention if you have a strategy before starting on the trail. Using games is not only an effective way to keep a child's attention, it's also a great way to teach him or her about nature. Play hide and seek, where your child is the mouse and you are the hawk. Quiz children on the names of plants and animals. If your children are old enough, let them carry their own daypack filled with snacks and water. So that you are sure to go at their pace and not yours, let them lead the way. Playing follow the leader works particularly well when you have a group of children. Have each child take a turn at being the leader.

With children, a lot of clothing is key. The only thing predictable about weather is that it will change. Especially in mountainous areas, weather can change dramatically in a very short time. Always bring extra clothing for children, regardless of the season. In the winter, have your children wear wool socks, and warm layers such as long underwear, a fleece jacket and hat, wool mittens, and good rain gear. It's not a bad idea to have these along in late fall and early spring as well. Good footwear is also important. A sturdy pair of high top tennis shoes or lightweight hiking boots are the best bet for little ones. If you're hiking in the summer near a lake or stream, bring along a pair of old sneakers that your child can put on when he wants to go exploring in the water. Remember when you're near any type of water, always watch your child at all times. Also, keep a close eye on teething toddlers who may decide a rock or leaf of poison oak is an interesting item to put in their mouth.

From spring through fall, you'll want your kids to wear a wide-brimmed hat to keep their face, head, and ears protected from the hot sun. Also, make sure your children wear sunscreen at all times. Choose a brand without Paba—children have sensitive skin and may have an allergic reaction to sunscreen that contains Paba. If you are hiking with a child younger than six months, don't use sunscreen or insect repellent. Instead, be sure that their head, face, neck, and ears are protected from the sun with a wide-brimmed hat, and that all other skin exposed to the sun is protected with the appropriate clothing.

Remember that food is fun. Kids like snacks so it's important to bring a lot of munchies for the trail. Stopping often for snack breaks is a fun way to keep the trail interesting. Raisins, apples, granola bars, crackers and cheese, cereal, and trail mix all make great snacks. If your child is old enough to carry her own backpack, fill it with treats before you leave. If your kids don't like drinking water, you can bring boxes of fruit juice.

Avoid poorly designed child-carrying packs—you don't want to break your back carrying your child. Most child-carrying backpacks designed to hold a forty-pound child will contain a large carrying pocket to hold diapers and other items. Some have an optional rain/sun hood.

Hiking with Your Dog

Bringing your furry friend with you is always more fun than leaving him behind. Our canine pals make great trail buddies because they never complain and always make good company. Hiking with your dog can be a rewarding experience, especially if you plan ahead.

Getting your dog in shape. Before you plan outdoor adventures with your dog, make sure he's in shape for the trail. Getting your dog into shape takes the same discipline as getting yourself into shape, but luckily, your dog can get in shape with you. Take your dog with you on your daily runs or walks. If there is a park near your house, hit a tennis ball or play Frisbee with your dog.

Swimming is also an excellent way to get your dog into shape. If there is a lake or river near where you live and your dog likes the water, have him retrieve a tennis ball or stick. Gradually build your dog's stamina up over a two- to three-month period. A good rule of thumb is to assume that your dog will travel twice as far as you will on the trail. If you plan on doing a 5-mile hike, be sure your dog is in shape for a 10-mile hike.

Training your dog for the trail. Before you go on your first hiking adventure with your dog, be sure he has a firm grasp on the basics of canine etiquette and behavior. Make sure he can sit, lie down, stay, and come. One of the most important commands you can teach your canine pal is to "come" under any situation. It's easy for your friend's nose to lead him astray or possibly get lost. Another helpful command is the "get behind" command. When you're on a hiking trail that's narrow, you can have your dog follow behind you when other trail users approach. Nothing is more bothersome than an enthusiastic dog that runs back and forth on the trail and disrupts the peace of the trail for others. When you see other trail users approaching you on the trail, give them the right of way by quietly stepping off the trail and making your dog lie down and stay until they pass.

Equipment. The most critical pieces of equipment you can invest in for your dog are proper identification and a sturdy leash. Flexi-leads work well for hiking because they give your dog more freedom to explore but still leave you in control. Make sure your dog has identification that includes your name and address and a number for your veterinarian. Other forms of identification for your dog include a tattoo or a microchip. You should consult your veterinarian for more information on these last two options.

The next piece of equipment you'll want to consider is a pack for your dog. By no means should you hold all of your dog's essentials in your pack—let him carry his own gear! Dogs that are in good shape can carry 30 to 40 percent of their own weight.

Most packs are fitted by a dog's weight and girth measurement. Companies that make dog packs generally include guidelines to help you pick out the size that's right for your dog. Some characteristics to look for when purchasing a pack for your dog include a harness that contains two padded girth straps, a padded chest strap, leash attachments, removable saddle bags, internal water bladders, and external gear cords.

You can introduce your dog to the pack by first placing the empty pack on his back and letting him wear it around the yard. Keep an eye on him during this first introduction. He may decide to chew through the straps if you aren't watching him closely. Once he learns to treat the pack as an object of fun and not a foreign enemy, fill the pack evenly on both sides with a few ounces of dog food in resealable plastic bags. Have your dog wear his pack on your daily walks for a period of two to three weeks. Each week add a little more weight to the pack until your dog will accept carrying the maximum amount of weight he can carry.

You can also purchase collapsible water and dog food bowls for your dog. These bowls are lightweight and can easily be stashed into your pack or your dog's. If you are hiking on rocky terrain or in the snow, you can purchase footwear for your dog that will protect his feet from cuts and bruises.

Always carry plastic bags to remove feces from the trail. It is a courtesy to other trail users and helps protect local wildlife.

The following is a list of items to bring when you take your dog hiking: collapsible water bowls, a comb, a collar and a leash, dog food, plastic bags for feces, a dog pack, flea/tick powder, paw protection, water, and a first-aid kit that contains eye ointment, tweezers, scissors, stretchy foot wrap, gauze, antibacterial wash, sterile cotton tip applicators, antibiotic ointment, and cotton wrap.

First aid for your dog. Your dog is just as prone—if not more prone—to getting in trouble on the trail as you are, so be prepared. Here's a rundown of the more likely misfortunes that might befall your little friend.

Bees and wasps. If a bee or wasp stings your dog, remove the stinger with a pair of tweezers and place a mudpack or a cloth dipped in cold water over the affected area.

Porcupines. One good reason to keep your dog on a leash is to prevent it from getting a nose full of porcupine quills. You may be able to remove the quills with pliers, but a veterinarian is the best person to do this nasty job because most dogs need to be sedated.

Heat stroke. Avoid hiking with your dog in really hot weather. Dogs with heat stroke will pant excessively, lie down and refuse to get up, and become lethargic and disoriented. If your dog shows any of these signs on the trail, have him lie down in the shade. If you are near a stream, pour cool water over your dog's entire body to help bring his body temperature back to normal.

Heartworm. Dogs get heartworms from mosquitoes which carry the disease in the prime mosquito months of July and August. Giving your dog a monthly pill prescribed by your veterinarian easily prevents this condition.

Plant pitfalls. One of the biggest plant hazards for dogs on the trail are foxtails. Foxtails are pointed grass seed heads that bury themselves in your friend's fur, between his toes, and even get in his ear canal. If left unattended, these nasty seeds can work their way under the skin and cause abscesses and other problems. If you have a long-haired dog, consider trimming the hair between his toes and giving him a summer haircut to help prevent foxtails from attaching to his fur. After every hike, always look over your dog for these seeds—especially between his toes and his ears.

Other plant hazards include burrs, thorns, thistles, and poison oak. If you find any burrs or thistles on your dog, remove them as soon as possible before they become an unmanageable mat. Thorns can pierce a dog's foot and cause a great deal of pain. If you see that your dog is lame, stop and check his feet for thorns. Dogs are immune to poison oak but they can pick up the sticky, oily substance from the plant and transfer it to you.

Protect those paws. Be sure to keep your dog's nails trimmed so he avoids getting soft tissue or joint injuries. If your dog slows and refuses to go on, check to see that his paws aren't torn or worn. You can protect your dog's paws from trail hazards such as sharp gravel, foxtails, lava scree, and thorns by purchasing dog boots.

Sunburn. If your dog has light skin he is an easy target for sunburn on his nose and other exposed skin areas. You can apply a nontoxic sunscreen to exposed skin areas that will help protect him from overexposure to the sun.

Ticks and fleas. Ticks can easily give your dog Lyme disease, as well as other diseases. Before you hit the trail, treat your dog with a flea and tick spray or powder. You can also ask your veterinarian about a once-a-month pour-on treatment that repels fleas and ticks.

Mosquitoes and deer flies. These little flying machines can do a job on your dog's snout and ears. Best bet is to spray your dog with fly repellent for horses to discourage both pests.

Giardia. Dogs can get giardia, which results in diarrhea. It is usually not debilitating, but it's definitely messy. A vaccine against giardia is available.

Mushrooms. Make sure your dog doesn't sample mushrooms along the trail. They could be poisonous to him, but he doesn't know that.

When you are finally ready to hit the trail with your dog, keep in mind that national parks and many wilderness areas do not allow dogs on trails. Your best bet is to hike in national forests, BLM lands, and state parks. Always call ahead to see what the restrictions are.

Contact Info

General State Information

Alabama Bureau of Tourism – www.touralabama.org
532A Perry Street, Montgomery 36104; (800) ALABAMA
Alabama Live (Webpage of Alabama's major newspapers) – www.alabamalive.com
Birmingham Chamber of Commerce – www.birminghamchamber.com/home/home.htm
Twenty-eighth Street North, Birmingham 35203; (205) 324–2100
Calhoun County Chamber of Commerce – www.calhounchamber.org
P.O. Box 1087, Anniston 36202; (256) 237–3536
City of Mobile Department of Tourism – www.mobile.org
1 South Water Street, Mobile 36602; (800) 5–MOBILE
Dothan Convention & Visitors Bureau – www.dothanalcvb.com
P.O. Box 8765, Dothan 36304; (334) 794–6622
Eastern Shore Chamber of Commerce – www.siteone.com/towns/chamber
29750 Larry Dawyer Drive, P.O. Box 310, Daphne 36526; (251) 621–8222
Eufaula-Barbour County Chamber of Commerce – www.eufaula-barbour chamber.com
P.O. Box 697, Eufaula 36072–0697; (800) 524–7529
Fort Payne (Including information on DeSoto State Park, Little River Canyon, and Lookout Mountain) – www.fortpayne.net/Default.htm
Gulf Shores Area Chamber of Commerce – www.alagulfcoastchamber.com
3150 Gulf Shores Parkway, Gulf Shores 36542; (251) 968–6904
Huntsville Convention and Visitors Bureau – www.huntsville.org
700 Monroe Street, Huntsville 35801; (800) SPACE–4U or (256) 551–2230
Lawrence County Chamber (Including information on the Sipsey and Bankhead National Forests) – home.hiway.net/~lcc; 14220 West Court Street, P.O. Box 325, Moulton 35650; (256) 974–1658
Mobile Chamber of Commerce – www.mobcham.org
451 Government Street, Mobile 36652; (251) 433–6951
Montgomery Chamber of Commerce – www.montgomerychamber.org
41 Commerce Street, P.O. Box 79, Montgomery 36101; (334) 834–5200
Saraland Area Chamber of Commerce – www.saralandcoc.com
939 Highway 43 South, Saraland 36571; (251) 675–4444

State Government Organizations

Alabama Department of Environmental Management – www.dcnr.state.al.us
P.O. Box 301463, Montgomery 36130-1463; (334) 271–7710

Alabama Environmental Council – www.aeonline.ws
2717 Seventh Avenue South, Suite 207, Birmingham 35233; (205) 322–3126
Alabama Forestry Commission – www.forestry.state.al.us
P.O. Box 302550, Montgomery 36130-2550; (334) 240–9300
Alabama Recreation – www.bama.ua.edu/~foley001
Alabama State Parks – www.dcnr.state.al.us/parks/state_parks_index_1a.html
c/o Alabama Department of Conservation and Natural Resources –
64 North Union Street, Montgomery, (800) ALAPARK
North Alabama Tourism Association – www.northalabama.org
25062 North Street, P.O. Box 1075, Mooresville 35649; (800) 648–5381

State Hiking and Outdoor Clubs and Organizations

Alabama Camping – (scouts) www.yustaga385.com/campbook/alabama.htm
Alabama Natural Heritage Program – www.natureserve.org/nhp/uslae
Huntingdon College Massey Hall, 1500 East Fairview Avenue, Montgomery 36106-2148; (334) 834–4519
Alabama Trail Guides by M. Lee van Horn – www.alabamatrail.org/hikingAL/htm
Alabama Trails – www.alabamatrailsasso.org
P.O. Box 371162, Birmingham 35237-1162
Alabama Wilderness Alliance – www.wildlaw.org/awa-wild.htm
P.O. Box 223, Mouton 35650; (334) 265–6529
Alabama Wildlife Rehabilitation Center – www.alawildliferehab.org
c/o Oak Mt. State park, 100 Terrace Drive, Pelham 35124; (256) 663–7930
Anniston Outdoor Association – www.ag.auburn.edu/grassroots/aoa/
P.O. Box 2168, Anniston 36202; (256) 231–7675
Appalachian Trail Club of Alabama – sport.al.com/sport/atca
P.O. Box 381842, Birmingham 35238–1842; (205) 991–0534
Atmore Chamber of Commerce – www.frontiernet.net/~atmoreal
501 South Pensacola Avenue, Atmore 36502; (251) 368–3305
Bama Environmental News – www.bamanews.com
(205) 226–7739
Birmingham Audubon Society – www.birminghamaudubon.org
P.O. Box 314, Birmingham 35201
Bon Secour National Wildlife Refuge – bonsecour.fws.gov
12295 State Highway 180, Gulf Shores 36542; (251) 540–7720
Chickasabogue Park – www.mobilecounty.org/recreation-chickasabogue.htm
760 Adlock Road, Eight Mile 36613; (334) 452–8496
Claude D. Kelley State Park – www.dcnr.stateal.us/parks/state-parks-index.1a.html
(334) 862–2511

Covington County/South Alabama Birding Association – www.alaweb.com~kenwood/saba/
(800) 382–2696

DeSoto State Park – www.destostatepark.com
13883 County Road 89, Ft. Payne 35967

Eufaula National Wildlife Refuge – eufaula.fws.gov
509 Old Highway 165, Eufaula 36027; (334) 687–4065

Fort Conde, Mobile – www.mobile.org/html/conde/index.php
150 South Royal Street, Mobile 36602; (251) 208–7509

Georgia Pinhoti Trail Association – www.georgiapinhoti.org
(770) 414–0211

Gulf State Park –
20115 State Highway 135, Gulf Shores 36542; (251) 948–7275

Historic Blakeley State Park – www.siteone.com/tourist/blakeley
P.O. Box 7279, Spanish Fort 35677; (251) 626–0798

Longleaf Alliance – www.longleafalliance.org

Sierra Club Cahaba (Birmingham) – sierraclub.org/chapters/al/cahaba.html

Sierra Club Coastal Chapter – .sierraclub.org/chapters/al/coastal.html
(251) 540–2121

Sierra Club East Alabama Chapter –
129 Carter Street, Auburn 36830-6230; (334) 821–9817

Sierra Club Mobile Chapter – sierraclub.org/mobile.html
(251) 621–8767

Sierra Club Montgomery Chapter – alabama.sierraclub.org/montgomery.htm

Sierra Club North Alabama (Huntsville) Chapter – alabama.sierraclub.org/na.html

Sierra Club Tennessee River (Decatur) Chapter –
(205) 685–9416

Sierra Club West Alabama Chapter – alabama.sierraclub.org/west-al.html

Tennessee Valley Audubon Society – fly.hiwaay.net/~pgibson/tvas/

Tennessee Valley Trails – www.montesano.com/hikeweb/

Trail of Tears – rosecity.net/tears/

U.S.S. Alabama Historical Trail, Inc, Mobile; (334) 675–7037

Vulcan Trail Association – www.mindspring.com/~vulcan_trail
P.O. Box 19116, Birmingham, 35219-9166; (205) 982–4022

Walking and Volkssports Events – www.ava.org/walk/alyre.htm

AVA National Headquarters
1001 Pat Booker Road, Suite 101, Universal City, TX 78148-4147

Wild Alabama – www.wildalabama.com
P.O. Box 117, Moulton 35650; (256) 974–6166

Wildflowers of Alabama – www.auburn.edu/~deancar/

National Hiking and Outdoor Organizations

American Hiking Society – www.americanhiking.org
1422 Fenwick Lane, Silver Spring, MD 20910
Ducks Unlimited – www.ducks.org
1 Waterfowl Way, Memphis, TN 38120; (800) 45–DUCKS
Native Forest Network – www.nativeforest.org
P.O. Box 57, Burlington, VT 05402; (802) 863–0571
National Park Service – www.nps.gov/parks/html
USDA Forest Service – www.fs.fed.us
Sydney R. Yates Federal Building, 201 Fourteenth Street SW at Independence Avenue SW, Washington, DC 20074

Southern Region Office (Including Alabama)
1720 Peachtree Road NW, Atlanta, GA 30309; (404) 347–4177
Forest Supervisor National Forests in Alabama
1765 Highland Avenue, Montgomery 36107; (334) 832–4470
Talladega National Forest
District Ranger, USDA Forest Service, 1001 North Street,
Highway 21 North, Talladega 35150; (256) 362–2909
District Ranger, USDA Forest Service, 450 Highway 46,
Heflin 36264; (256) 463–2272; www.r8web.com/alabama/bankhead/default.html
Bankhead National Forest
District Ranger, USDA Forest Service, P.O. Box 278, South Main Street,
Double Springs 35553; (256) 489–5111; www.r8web.com/alabama/talledega/
default.html
Conecuh National Forest
District Ranger, USDA Forest Service, P.O. Box 310,
1100 South Three Notch Street, Andalusia 36420;
(334) 222–2555
Tuskegee National Forest
District Ranger, USDA Forest Service, Route 1, Box 204AA,
Tuskegee 36083; (334) 727–2652

Wild Law – www.wildlaw.org
300B Water Street, Suite 214, Montgomery 36104; (334) 265–6529
E-mail: wildlaw@aol.com
Wilderness Society – www.wilderness.org
900 Seventh Street NW, Washington, DC 20006-2506; (800) THE–WILD

About the Author

Joe Cuhaj is an Alabama transplant, having grown up in Mahwah, New Jersey, near the Harriman/Bear Mountain State Parks, where his love of hiking and the outdoors began.

Joe, his wife Maggie, daughter Kellie, three dogs, and two horses live in Daphne, Alabama, just east of Mobile, on the Gulf Coast.

Joe is a full-time software programmer for a local company and a dreamer—having applied three times without success to be on the television series *Survivor*. While he waits for his big chance on a deserted island, he finds frequent visits to area wildlife refuges, wetlands, and the state's northern mountains solace from the keyboard.

Joe also enjoys canoeing the many rivers of the state, having coauthored the book *Paddling Alabama* with former friend Curt Burdick. (Hey, you can only flip a canoe over so many times before you lose a friend!) He is also co-author (with Tamra Carraway-Hinckle) of *The History of Mobile Baseball*.